INSIGHT GUIDES

Created and Directed by Hans Höfer

LOIRE VALLEY

Edited by Rosemary Bailey
Photography by Lyle Lawson

Editorial Director: Brian Bell

Houghton Mifflin

APA PUBLICATIONS

Höfer

Bailey

The Loire Valley offers a rich diet of Renaissance art, peerless architecture and endless beautiful landscapes, not to mention the more familiar French diet of excellent food and wine.

A romantic region of France once known as the valley of the kings, the Loire Valley lends itself perfectly to the *Insight Guides* approach, combining as it does fine writing, objective journalism and outstanding photography to produce a guide giving travellers an insight into a destination's history and culture. The 200-title award-winning *Insight Guides* series was created in 1970 by **Hans Höfer**, founder of Apa Publications.

The prospect of compiling a book on the Loire Valley, a travel cliché come to life, presented a familiar challenge to the project editor **Rosemary Bailey**; she was just recovering from the challenging task of editing the *Insight Guide: Tuscany.*

Bailey is that increasingly familiar phenomenon, an English francophile who spends as much time as she can in what she considers "the most civilised country on earth". Based in London, she contributes articles regularly to the *Sunday Times*, *The Guardian*, *Elle* magazine and many other British and foreign publications. She has also edited guides to New York. In this book, she writes about Joan of Arc (a childhood heroine) and explores the regions of Anjou and Touraine. "What was so curious about the area," she says, "was discovering a whole English heritage of history and architecture entwined with the French."

Like all *Insight Guides*, this book owes much to the superb photography.

On this occasion, it is the work of inveterate world traveller **Lyle Lawson**. An American who lives in England, she was editor and photographer of Apa's *Waterways of Europe*, and has contributed to many Insight Guides, including those on Malta, Brittany, India, Pakistan, Yemen, Turkey and Korea, Jordan, Baltic States, Sicily and the Old South. Here, she takes an evocative look at both historical and contemporary Loire, and has been an enthusiastic and invaluable collaborator in the final picture editing process.

"Discussions with Rosemary Bailey gave me an understanding of the 'feel' she wanted for the book," says Lawson, "and I went off armed with a shot list as long as my arm. Three trips, numerous phone calls and endless rolls of film later, this book is the result."

Lawson

Ardagh

The talented writing team is no less expert. **John Ardagh** will be a familiar name to francophiles, as the author of many illuminating books on the country, including the enduringly popular *France Today*. His chapter on Loire literature has been adapted from his book *Writers' France*, and in it he captures not only the writers themselves, from Rabelais to Alain-Fournier and Genevoix, but also the inspiration they have drawn from the region.

Peter Graham is another French stalwart, living in a small village in the Auvergne. He is a regular contributor of articles on food and wine to *The Guardian*, *The Times* and the *Sunday Times Magazine*, has translated several books and co-written a number of guidebooks. His most recent book is *Classic Cheese Cookery*, winner of the André Simon Memorial Prize. After moving to France from Britain in 1962, he lived in the Sologne and here he gives an insider's views of its secrets, and in particular the wealth of wildlife to be found. He also regales us with

Gerard-Sharp

the pleasures of food and wine – a favourite subject, and according to his friends, the main reason he moved to France in the first place.

Writer and broadcaster **Lisa Gerard-Sharp**, a frequent contributor to *Insight Guides*, brings to the book a wealth of experience of living and working in Europe. When she lived in Paris, trips to the Loire provided escapism; this time, it was more like hard work. She has contributed thought-provoking chapters on Renaissance history, for which she has a passion, and a fascinating account of village life, as well as a guide to Touraine, Berry, and the Blésois region. Most of all, she says, she enjoyed "Blois and Tours out of season, the lesser known châteaux such as Talcy, Gué-Péan or Beauregard, encounters with peasants in Berry and the Beauce, following the literary trail from Ronsard to Zola, and swimming in moats when no-one was watching."

Ward Rutherford, who grew up in Jersey, is what the French call an "Anglo-Normande". He is a broadcaster and author of numerous books of history, including a popular account of Celtic mythology. "I was particularly interested in the Celtic influence in the Loire Valley," he says. "The *omphalos* or navel of a locality had great significance for the Celts and they believed this was the true centre of France. Even today, Orléans is still regarded as the heart of the country." As well as his analyses of early Loire history, he explores the delights of Orléans and its surrounding countryside.

Rutherford

Martha Rose Shulman is a food and travel writer, an American who has lived in Paris since 1981. She is the author of 12 cookery books, and contributor to numerous international magazines. In Paris she runs a private "supper club" for friends and new acquaintances. Here she writes about

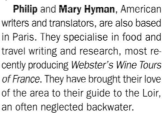

mushroom growing in Saumur and interviews a master *vigneron* about his style of wine-growing. She has also compiled an excellent guide to the Loire Valley's best hotels and restaurants – of which there are a reassuringly large number.

Bill Grantham has contributed chapters on recent history and current affairs, as well as interviewing a modern *châtelain* about *la vie en château* as it is experienced by today's aristocracy. Grantham is a British magazine publisher and journalist based in Paris, and his frequent visits to the Loire Valley are, he says, "always in search of food, wine, history – and peace and quiet."

Grantham

Philip and **Mary Hyman**, American writers and translators, are also based in Paris. They specialise in food and travel writing and research, most recently producing *Webster's Wine Tours of France*. They have brought their love of the area to their guide to the Loir, an often neglected backwater.

Jill Adam produced a thorough and comprehensive Travel Tips section, providing essential back-up information and also keeps it up to date. She has plenty of experience in marshalling facts into a digestible form, having compiled Travel Tips for *Insight Guide: Brittany* and edited for some years the *French Farm and Village Holiday Guide*. Another francophile with a house in southwest France, she welcomes any opportunity to spend more time there with her family.

Adam

For the original edition of the book **Jill Anderson** guided the text skilfully through a variety of Macintosh computers; proof-reading and indexing were expertly handled by **Kate Owen**.

CONTENTS

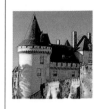

TRAVEL TIPS

A BOURGEOIS PARADISE

The Loire Valley is the quintessence of romantic France; it is the France of the tapestries, the hunt of the Sun King, the magnificent royal châteaux, the France of Rabelais and gargantuan feasts. It is the France of the poets like du Bellay and Ronsard and their nostalgic longing for *"la douceur vie"*. This is the region where the inhabitants still claim to speak the purest French.

It is also, of course, the France of wine. The region may not yet have the reputation of Burgundy or Bordeaux, but for the people of the Loire Valley wine is as much a way of life – a matter of consuming interest both as business and as bibulous pleasure.

What was once a valley of kings has given way to a more bourgeois paradise that can be enjoyed by all. Indeed, for the diligent tourist, it is rather like having every great castle and country house in England crammed into an area the size of the Cotswolds. We can stroll inquisitively round the castles and mansions, examining the bed hangings and kitchen arrangements. There is food and wine of a quality and sophistication to delight the palate of the most jaded gourmet. And for the more energetically inclined there is a wide range of activities from water sports to hunting, bird-watching to ballooning.

Lashing violence: The river itself is a constant pleasure, its moods varying from languid gentleness to lashing violence. The seasons offer different perspectives: the golden poplars and woody smells of autumn, the bright freshness of spring fragrant with lilac, wisteria and roses, the high sun and luminosity of summer and the quiet contemplation of winter landscapes.

In a single day the Loire can change its appearance completely; its melancholic misty sadness, what the French call *grisaille* (a grey drizzle which sounds so much more poetic in French), can suddenly lift to reveal a glorious sunset—not the full-blooded sunset of the South but something more subtle, of tender pastels, mauves and lavender hues.

deepening as the sun slips below the horizon.

Perhaps one of the greatest joys is simply to sit on the river bank and watch the *"avenue qui marche"* flow slowly by on its inexorable journey to the sea. Take time just to lean over a bridge and contemplate its passing; stop the car and breathe the country air; or follow the many detours suggested in this book to explore the smaller tributaries: the Vienne, the Cher, the Indre, the Mayenne, the Sarthe, or the confusingly named little cousin, le Loir. Or consider venturing further

afield into the rustic backwaters of Berry or the forests of Sologne.

The bucolic charms of the region are easily matched by the sophistication of its cities, which provide a wealth of magnificent architecture, fine museum collections, superb restaurants and elegant shopping. Don't miss the old quarter of Blois, the excellent museums of Tours, the narrow streets of Chinon or the grand parks of Orléans.

If you stick too closely to the well-trodden châteaux route, compelling though it is, you may never discover the true *pays de Loire* of tiny hamlets, quiet country lanes, hidden streams and woodland full of wildlife and

Preceding pages: Fleur de Lys, Loches; detail, Maison de Adam; ballooning at Chaumont; Chenonceau Château; Blois; Mayenne river; Anjou cows. Left, Chez Mick Jagger. Above, Orléans bourgeoisie.

birdsong. You need only stray a little to make chance discoveries, without a tourist coach sniffing at your heels. You would be well advised to do so; now that the Loire Valley is no longer the playground of the few, the many have a tendency to descend, especially in the summer months.

It is an area so rich in history and architecture that it is easy to get confused and overwhelmed; think of it as a series of sedimentary layers and enjoy its complexity. It is not an area to approach without preconceptions; even Apollonius sang the praises of Loire wine and the first guide books to include the area were written by monks on the pilgrimage to Santiago de Compostella.

people of the Loire and their history is through the architecture, from the most grand châteaux or abbey churches to humble peasant dwellings and tiny troglodyte chapels. Succeeding generations have added layer upon layer, using different construction materials or building for purposes from defensive to decorative.

The layers go back to Foulques Nerra and his original strongholds. Most were built of wood and only a few stone keeps have survived, but in many cases they have provided the base for subsequent developments. Church architecture thrived from the 11th century onwards and there are many fine examples of Romanesque and Gothic ab-

Don't fight the spirit of Rabelais, who is constantly evoked, and enjoy the prospect of excess – or at least plenty. Literary references reverberate; if you read Henry James's descriptions of his travels, you will also find genuflections to Balzac, who still captures better than any other writer the bitter-sweet, nostalgic quality of the landscape.

For centuries the Loire has provided inspiration for poets and artists. Now it also inspires filmmakers; Jean Renoir made one of his greatest films here, *Le Règle du Jeu*, which poignantly captures the misty magic of the Sologne.

Perhaps the best way to understand the

beys and churches; in particular, the fine Angevin or Plantagenet style of vaulting is characteristic of the region.

Jewels of the Renaissance: But it is the châteaux for which the Loire is justifiably famous, beginning with fierce defensive castles like Chinon, and gradually evolving into the more domesticated jewels of the Renaissance such as Azay-le-Rideau and Chenonceau. Their development reflects the complex history of the region, its long period of English rule and its central role in the French struggle for power, providing both a rural retreat and occasional refuge for the French Crown and Court. For a period it was the epicentre of the Renaissance in France; architecture blossomed into the glories of Blois and Chambord, and even Leonardo da Vinci came to stay (and die) at Amboise.

There is, too, another human history: that of the vast majority of peasants, farmers and sailors living off the land and the river. The exigencies of their lives, the constant battle against failed harvests and famine, are here described with more realism than the often sentimentalised accounts by aristocratic novelists – lives that were certainly more Zola than George Sand.

The Loire itself is, of course, the main character in the book. It is the longest river in France, at 627 miles (1,012 km), and has

described by French writer Jules Renard as "*un fleuve de sable où coule un peu d'eau*".

From Orléans, the Loire flows sedately in a westerly direction towards the sea, neatly dividing France into north and south, and enjoying the benefits of both. The climate is gentle and warm, any extremes cooled by Atlantic breezes.

The region remains a conservative one, and a remarkable number of the French aristocracy have hung on to their land and their titles. During the Bicentennial celebrations, a Dutch TV team seeking a château owner who was against the Revolution received the reply: "All will be pleased to welcome you." There has, however, also been an influx of a

played a crucial role in the development of modern France, transporting goods, people and ideas along its length. It rises in the Ardèche and carves its way through steep gorges until it reaches the gentler pastures of the Vallée itself, where its rich alluvial deposits make for prosperous farmland.

Today the Loire itself is barely navigable, and its commercial role has been superseded by its attractions as a tourist haven. Windsurfers have replaced the transport barges of old. During the summer months in particular, the river is more sandbank than river,

more meritocratic élite. Actors and pop stars have replaced monarchs and courtiers in many of the châteaux; Gerard Dépardieu reigns in Anjou, and Mick Jagger and Jerry Hall entertain the local *gendarmerie* at their château near Amboise.

Where once the beauties of nature inspired the poets, now the wine and *beurre blanc* inspire foodies to ecstasy. But none of the traditional ingredients has gone away and a rich *mélange* of pleasures remains, making the Loire Valley a rewarding experience, whether you diligently investigate châteaux and history or sit indolently with a glass of Chinon and watch the river flow by.

Left, château life. **Above**, a stroll *en famille*.

Marie Joneau
1787

France's rivers, which have served it like arteries, have carried the lifeblood not only of its commerce but also its history. The Seine, the Marne, the Oise, the Garonne, the Rhône, the Saône and the Loire have all witnessed events which in many cases represented turning points in French, European and, indeed, in human history.

Coasts and rivers have always attracted habitation—the latter because they provided natural highways, which is one reason why river banks are such fruitful places for archaeological investigation. The Loire is no exception and worked flints and tools from deer and reindeer horn, from Palaeolithic times, are to be seen in local museums.

But one aspect of the Loire's prehistory is on open display. Like Brittany, the area is studded with dolmens and menhirs, built by a people who, from about 3000 BC, migrated to both areas, probably from the Near East. There are examples of their workmanship near Baugé, at Baignon between Bonneval and Chateaudun, and at Connerré.

Amazing accuracy· At Bagneux is one of the biggest monuments, a gallery grave, its thirteen 9-ft (3-metre) high stone uprights supporting a roof of four massive stone slabs. The 36-ft (11-metre) long, so-called "fairy grotto" dolmen at Mettray, though smaller than Bagneux, demonstrates the skill of these prehistoric stone masons. Twelve 12-ft (4-metre) high stones have been hewn to an amazing degree of accuracy.

The end of the second millennium BC saw the arrival of newcomers, the Celts, from whom France acquired its original name of Gaul. Among tribes who settled in the Loire area were the Bituriges and Carnutes, the latter establishing their capital, Cenabum, on the site of the modern Orléans.

Julius Caesar, to whom we are indebted for much of our knowledge of Celtic life, tells us that religion was governed by the druids and mentions an annual convention which took place "in the country of the Carnutes, which is supposed to be the centre

of Gaul". Though there is doubt about this statement, the area actually is the geographical centre of France. As the *omphalos* or navel of a locality, as the human navel is the median point of the body, the centre had great significance for the Celts. The French Celticist Jean Markale draws a parallel between the Bituriges, whose name means "kings of the world", and the Irish Celtic high king whose seat was at Tara in Co. Meath, a name which means "the centre".

Though never able to weld themselves into a nation, the Celts, inventive and artistic, established a society ruled by its own system of law and custom, much of it far in advance of its time. However, these qualities were accompanied by an insatiable appetite for war. Their sacking of Rome in 387 BC led to a series of campaigns against them and, by 50 BC, their conquest.

The occupied territory was divided into four administrative provinces, with that from the Channel coast to the Loire, and including most of the river, becoming Lugdunensis. It was here, in AD 68, that the Roman governor, Gaius Julius Vindex, launched the rebellion which led to the overthrow of the tyrannical emperor Nero.

The region still abounds in traces of its Gallo-Roman past. It is recalled in Celtic place names such as Lanthenay (*lan* = a sacred place), Vienne (*Ven* = white), Trélazé, Trèves and Triou (*trebo* = a town). The place name Loudun is derived from the Celtic solar deity, Lugh, combined with the suffix -*dunum*, a fortress, also found in names like Dundee.

The Musée Historique at Orléans houses statuettes and representations of wild boar taken from a temple at Neuvy-en-Sullias, as well as Celtic statuary. There are Gallo-Roman remains at Marboué between Bonneval and Châteaudun and in Le Mans Old Town, while part of the city wall at Tours is a reminder that, as Caesarodunum, it was a thriving Roman city.

Christianity was adopted as the state religion during the latter years of Roman occupation. It was introduced into the Loire region by St Gatien in the 2nd century, but it was not until the 4th century that the former Roman

Preceding pages: plate in Saumur Museum: the Loire at Nevers. Left, Charles II, son of Charlemagne, on the banks of the Loire.

DECISIVE DATES

5000–2000 BC: Neolithic peoples (from Near East?) build first megalithic monuments.
1000–600 BC: Celtic tribes arrive in Gaul.
109–105 BC: Germanic Teutones and Cimbri reach Aquitania, south of the Loire.
59–51 BC: Julius Caesar conquers Gaul. Loire absorbed into province of Lugdunensis.
AD 68: Revolt of Vindex, governor of Lugdunensis, leads to fall of the emperor Nero.
circa 250: St Gatien introduces Christianity.
circa 397: St Martin, Bishop of the Gauls, dies at Candes.
From 4th century: Loire region invaded by Franks, Visigoths, Huns. St Aignan and citizen army thwart Attila's attack on Orléans.

481: The Merovingian Frankish chieftain Clovis conquers Gaul.
732: Charles Martel defeats the Saracens.
796: St Alcuin abbot at Tours.
843: Viking raiders sack Nantes and Tours.
862: Robert the Strong sent to the Loire to end Viking incursions.
987: Hugues Capet founds Capet dynasty.
1104: First Council of Beaugency excommunicates Philippe I.
1152: Second Council of Beaugency annuls marriage of Louis VII. Henry Plantagenet marries Eleanor of Aquitaine.
1189: Henry II dies at Chinon.
1199: Richard Lionheart dies at Chinon.
1258: The Treaty of Paris reduces English possessions to Guyenne.
1305: First university of Orléans founded.
1328: Charles IV of France dies without heir. The claim by England's Edward III to the throne of France is dismissed.
1337: French king's attempted confiscation of Guyenne leads Edward to declare himself heir to French throne.
1340: Hundred Years' War, starts with English victories at Crécy (1346) and Calais (1347).
1355: Black Prince marches on Loire.
1415: French chivalry routed at Agincourt.
1417: Henry V continues advance. The Dauphin, Charles, withdraws to Berry, then Bourges.

1420: Treaty of Troyes makes Henry V of England also king of France.
1422: Charles VI of France dies.
1427: English invade Loire. Charles moves from Bourges to Chinon.
1428: In October, Orléans besieged by Anglo-Burgundian army.
1429: 24 Feb, Joan of Arc at Chinon; 27 April, Joan reaches Orléans; 8 May, siege of Orléans raised; 17 July, Dauphin is crowned Charles VII.
1430: Joan captured at Compiègne in May.
1431: Joan burnt at the stake on 30 May.
13 April 1432: Treaty of Arras ends civil war between France and Burgundy,
1475: Treaty of Picquiny formally ends Hundred Years' War.
1491: Charles VIII marries Anne, Duchess of Brittany, at Langeais.
1496: First manifestations of Italian Renaissance influence are seen on local architecture at Amboise.
1519: Beginning of the French Renaissance. Death of Leonardo da Vinci at Clos-Lucé.
1560: The Amboise Plot by French Protestants. Death of François II at Orléans. Beginning of Religious Wars.
1562: St Benoît sacked by Huguenots and battles at Ponts-de-Cé, Beaugency and Sancerre.
1719: Voltaire at Sully.
1756: Royal College of Surgeons founded at Tours.
1789: Beginning of the French Revolution. The University of Orléans is destroyed.
1793: Battles between revolutionaries and Vendéens. In October, Vendéens defeated at Le Mans. In December, Vendéens amnestied.
1832: First steamboat on Loire.
1870: Franco-Prussian War and defence of Châteaudun.
1923: First 24-hour race at Le Mans.
1939: World War II begins.
1969: New university opens at Orléans-la-Source. Nuclear power station at Avoine-Chinon comes on stream.
1970: Founding of University of Tours.
1974: Nuclear power station at St-Laurent-des-Eaux comes on stream. A10 motorway links Tours and Paris.
1989: Opening of the TGV Atlantique. Plans for controversial dam project rejected.

legionary St Martin made it a popular creed, at the same time founding monastic communities at Ligugé and, after his translation to Bishop of Tours in 371, at Marmoutier.

St Martin lived through the period of Roman retrenchment which left their former provinces prey to external marauders. Attila's Huns, failing to take Paris, turned on Orléans where they were held by a determined citizen-army mustered by its bishop, St Aignan.

Then, 70 years after St Martin's death, an astonishing 20-year-old burst on the scene. He was the Frankish king Clovis who, setting out from his Belgian capital on a campaign of conquest, by his death at the age of

three centuries as a rich landowner might dispose of his assets—by sharing them among his sons. Thus the area on either side of the Loire became the Kingdom of Orléans, one of four such realms ruled by each of Clovis's sons. A fresh share-out as each brother died brought temporary unity until the last survivor too died and it was partitioned afresh.

The instabilities inherent in such a system were intensified by the Franks' practice of appointing a major domus to administer their households. The office of palace mayor, as it was called, became the hereditary office of a single family, the Pepins, who, partly because several kings acceded as minors,

45, was master of almost the whole of Gaul.

Among his last acts was the summoning of the council of bishops at Orléans responsible for the promulgation of the Lex Salica. This was the principal Frankish legal code, and its clause that daughters could not inherit land was to be repeatedly invoked in subsequent history in attempts to disbar heirs in the female line from the French throne.

Another clause led to the disposing of country and people over most of the next

Left, Carolingian illuminated manuscript with early text. **Above**, Saumur tapestry of Saracens in battle.

partly because of a growing indolence, became extremely powerful.

By the early 8th century when Charles Pepin, nicknamed Martel (the Hammer), succeeded, even command of the army had been delegated to them. His immediate concern was the threat from the Muslim Saracens who had conquered most of Spain. In 732, hearing that a large force had sacked Bordeaux and was advancing towards the Loire, he defeated it at Poitiers.

The practice of partitioning the kingdom among sons, maintained by Charles and his heirs, was discarded only in 771 by another Charles who, as Charlemagne, consolidated the authority of what was to be known, on account of the prevalence of Charles as a first name, as the Carolingian dynasty.

Where his predecessors had been totally absorbed in military affairs, Charlemagne, crowned Holy Roman Emperor on Christmas Day 800, was determined to make his court an intellectual and cultural centre. Among those he employed was the English humanist scholar St Alcuin who became abbot of the monastery of St-Martin at Tours. Like other monasteries, its activities included the copying and illuminating of manuscripts and Alcuin encouraged the development of the Carolingian script, still the basis of modern typefaces. A surviving

example of a scriptorium can be seen at Notre Dame de l'Epau Abbey at Connerré near Le Mans. Turmoil followed Charlemagne's death. In 843 raiders from the north sacked Nantes in the Loire estuary, killing its bishop. A few years later they sailed down the Loire to Alcuin's city of Tours, setting its basilica and 26 of its churches ablaze.

In 862, Robert the Strong, one of the kingdom's ablest soldiers, was sent to try to check them. He had only temporary success and, in desperation, Charles III, the Simple, was driven to try appeasement. He gave the Norman invaders the tract of land on either side of the Seine north of Paris which was to

become known as Normandy (Land of the Northmen).

Charles III's magnates were so angered by this act that they deposed him in favour of Robert the Strong's son, who, in 987, was succeeded by Hugues, great-grandson of Robert the Strong. He was a former lay-abbot of the monastery of St-Martin at Tours and took the surname Capet from its most precious relic, the saint's cape, founding a line which was to rule France until the 14th century.

But power was actually shifting away from the Frankish kingdom and towards Normandy. Legally this was a fief and its ruler a vassal, but by his conquest of England in 1066, its reigning duke, William, had become a king in his own right. With the resources of his new realm to draw on, he was now an equal and hence a threat.

The period was one which saw the building of many of the great cathedrals and basilicas in the Loire. They were a reflection of the power of the Church. That this extended to secular matters was demonstrated by its unyielding attitude to William of Normandy's French contemporary, Philippe I. While negotiating the acquisition of the Gâtinais, he fell in love with its owner's wife, whom he abducted with her apparent complicity. He sought from the Church what it had granted before and was to grant again: annulment of their respective marriages.

Unfortunately for Philippe, he had fallen out with the Pope in a dispute over who should control ecclesiastical appointments. The bench of bishops, who met at Beaugency to try the question of the king's annulment, instead excommunicated him and continued to do so until 1104 when the quarrel was made up. It was not to be the only time the bishops met at Beaugency and deliberated on a royal marriage; in 1152 Louis VII, Philippe I's grandson, sought the annulment of his marriage to the brilliant and beautiful Eleanor of Aquitaine on the grounds of her misconduct.

It was readily granted, but by so doing the bishops had inadvertently given a twist to the fortunes of France, and especially the Loire region, which was to have enduring and far-reaching consequences.

Above, marriage of Eleanor of Aquitaine and Louis VII. **Right**, knight's armour at Chaumont.

Within eight weeks of Louis's annulment of their marriage Eleanor of Aquitaine remarried. By her new marriage she brought about a compounding of the destinies of France and England lasting over two centuries, most of it scarred by long and savage conflict. Eleanor's new husband was the 19-year-old Duke of Normandy, Henry Plantagenet. Henry came from a hugely powerful Le Mans family, the Plantagenets, who, besides Normandy, were lords of Anjou, Maine and Touraine. By his marriage, he added not only Aquitaine, but Gascony, Poitou and the Auvergne to his estates.

With these acquisitions the Plantagenets (the name reputedly derives from the sprig of broom (*genet*) the first Plantagenet wore in his hat) were masters of a greater area of France than the king himself. This was ominous enough, but there was a further cause for anxiety. Henry's mother, Matilda, was the daughter of Henry I of England, making him heir to the English throne. In 1154 he acceded as Henry II, founding the Angevin line (after his title of Count of Anjou). What seemed like an opportunity to reduce Plantagenet power occurred when Henry's five sons by Eleanor rebelled against him with their mother's backing. Louis VII gave his support but, thanks to Henry's ruthless energy, the revolt failed and the queen was imprisoned in England.

Race for the throne: Only two of Henry's sons survived him and in 1189, the elder, Richard Lionheart succeeded as Richard I. He had named a nephew, Arthur, as his heir, but when he died in 1199, the other surviving brother, John, surnamed Lackland, seized both throne and his other possessions.

To the alarm of Eleanor, now almost 80, Louis VII's son, Philip Augustus, backed Arthur. In an attempt to end the rivalry of the Plantagenet and French royal houses, she raced off across the Pyrenees to collect her granddaughter, Blanche of Castile, whom she married off to Philip's son.

Left, illustration for month of May from 15th-century illuminated manuscript, *Les Très Riches Heures du Duc de Berry*. **Above**, effigy of Eleanor of Aquitaine at Fontevraud.

The dynastic truce she had secured ended abruptly when Arthur died, supposedly at John's hand. The Plantagenets held their French estates as fiefdoms and Philip, as John's liege-lord, summoned him to account for the murder. When he failed to appear Normandy was seized. It was the first in a sequence of forfeitures which, by the reign of Philip's successor, had deprived the Plantagenets of all their domains in France except Guyenne, an area comprising Gascony and part of Aquitaine. As events were to show, the loss was not one that the English kings bore with resignation.

In 1328 Charles IV of France died without heir. One of the two claimants who presented themselves was Edward III, son of Charles's sister, Isabella. Debarred by invocation of the Lex Salica, when the successful claimant, Philippe de Valois, threatened to forfeit Guyenne, Edward renewed his own title to the throne by force of arms. The Hundred Years' War had begun.

The crushing French defeat at Crécy in 1346, and the loss of Calais in 1347, was followed by a truce and this pattern of sporadic fighting and truce was to be characteristic, imposing long periods of inactivity particularly on the English troops far from home. Across the Loire from Beaugency is the village of Dry, the name acquired because the troops were chagrined to be stationed in one of the few places in the Loire where the wine-grape was not cultivated. They solved the problem by trading with the enemy. In 1355 the truce was ended by Edward III's eldest son, Edward the Black Prince, who, after he had sacked the Languedoc, turned towards the Loire. The French king, Jean II, attempting to stop him, was defeated and captured. His parliament balked at an English offer to trade him for the old Angevin lands and Edward ravaged the

shown much enthusiasm for their English lands. Henry II, for instance, spent a mere 14 years of his 34-year reign in England; his son Richard Lionheart even less.

The longest consecutive period Eleanor of Aquitaine spent there was 15 years as her husband's prisoner. She died at Fontevraud Abbey, where she lies near her husband and son and not far from the hearts of King John and Henry III.

Revolts against his usurpation prevented Henry IV from active participation in the French war. But when the Duke of Burgundy's murder of the Duke of Orléans, younger son of the king, plunged France into civil war, his son, Henry V, seized the oppor-

Artois, Champagne and the Beauce, the fertile plain north of Orléans, forcing them to give in, though much of the territory gained was lost in a series of English defeats.

England's *coup d'état*: There was a growing desire for peace in both countries and this might have come about in England but for the palace revolution which dethroned the English king, Richard II, in favour of Henry Bolingbroke, leader of a group of knights who had profited from the war.

With Bolingbroke's accession as Henry IV, the line which had linked France and England was ended. It had lasted 245 years, though the Angevin monarchs had never

tunity, taking Harfleur by storm and routing the French at Agincourt. The revolt forced the Dauphin, Charles, to flee from Paris to Berry, then to Bourges. Then the Duke of Burgundy was himself murdered. Charles was held responsible and the new duke made an alliance with the English.

Faced with such formidable forces, the ageing French king accepted terms by which England and France would become a dual-monarchy through the marriage of his daughter Catherine to Henry V.

As this eliminated the Dauphin himself from the succession, he denounced the agreement and, on his father's death, declared himself Charles VII. Jokers dubbed him "King of Bourges" (by contrast, Henry was "King of Paris"), but he was the effective ruler of central and much of southern France, though his sovereignty would be unassailable only when he had been anointed at Reims according to tradition.

In fact, this possibility looked remote, especially in 1427 when English and Burgundian forces invaded the Loire Valley and, in the autumn of 1428, moved on Orléans, threatening Charles's remaining territories. Hasty defensive measures were taken and a force, which included a 5,000-strong citizens' levée, scratched together.

Having taken the fort of Les Tourelles at tumn gave way to winter. By February the English garrison was reduced to a few thousand by desertions and calls elsewhere; but the defenders were running short of essentials. And it was as surrender looked imminent that a 16-year-old Domrémy shepherdess came on the scene. Convinced she was the divinely chosen instrument of France's deliverance, she persuaded a reluctant Dauphin, now at Chinon, to grant her an audience and told him she could defeat his enemies and have him anointed king at Reims.

Silencing opposition by force of personality, her sincerity and by a series of predictions which were proved true, on 27 April 1429 she slipped through the Orléans block-

the head of a bridge, the attackers found themselves unable to advance further. The only artillery of the time was the wood and iron bombard, capable of throwing a stone ball of up to 200 lb (90 kg) a little less than a mile. But batteries of them had been emplaced on the ramparts and every attempt on the walls brought the attackers under their fire. With insufficient men to ring the city, the English commander, the Earl of Salisbury, was forced to adopt siegecraft. Autumn

Left, Hundred Years' War illumination from 15th-century chronicle of Jean Froissant. Above, Joan of Arc meets the Dauphin.

ade at the head of a small force. Such was the effect of her presence that when she entered the fray a week later the previously faltering defenders stormed and captured an English fort. Two days later, she crossed the Loire and advanced on another. Though the English withdrew to stronger positions, she maintained the impetus of her attack and took them. Early the next day the fort of Les Tourelles, scene of the first English victory, fell. Though wounded, she pressed forward and, by next morning, 8 May, the English were seen to be in retreat. Pursuit forbidden, on the grounds that it was Sunday, the day was instead given over to a solemn celebration commemorated every year since. Two days later she was at Tours, urging the Dauphin to go to Reims for his coronation. While he procrastinated she cleared the enemy from a wider area. Alençon fell, then Beaugency. On 18 June, at Patay, she promised the Dauphin a greater victory than any so far and, by the end of the day, the once invincible English were routed. Again Joan pressed the Dauphin, now at Sully, to go to Reims. This time he agreed and, on 25 June, an army was assembled at Gien. When it reached Reims on 16 July the city threw open its gates and the coronation took place next day. More vacillation followed. Instead of making for Paris at once as Joan wanted,

year after her death when the Treaty of Arras ended the Franco-Burgundian civil war. On 13 April Charles entered his capital.

Peace agreement: Over the next 20 years the English were forced out of their possessions. By 1453 even their hold on Aquitaine was finally and irrevocably broken. All that remained were Calais and Guînes. In August 1475, Edward IV of England and Louis XI met at Picquiny where they agreed that future differences would be settled by negotiation rather than by recourse to arms.

Before the turn of the century, the Loire was to witness two more great events in French history. At Langeais in 1491 Charles VIII of France married Anne of Brittany, a

Charles returned to the Loire. She accompanied him to Bourges where her kindness to the needy remained a legend for generations.

Early in 1430 she hurried to Compiègne, threatened by the Burgundians and, during a tactical retreat, fell into their hands. Sold to the English, she was arraigned as a witch before a French ecclesiastical court and, on 30 May 1431, burnt at Rouen.

Throughout Charles remained inert, but 20 years later, when he entered Rouen, he ordered an inquiry into the trial which rehabilitated her. In 1920 she was canonised.

If she had turned the tide of war, the change was made irreversible less than a

union which led to the duchy's annexation.

It was in Charles's time that the other event took place. In 1494 he embarked on a campaign to claim the kingdom of Naples. It was a failure, but he returned fired with enthusiasm for Italian art and architecture and bringing with him a team of architects, designers and gardeners to whom he delegated the task of rebuilding his Amboise château in the Italianate style, a foretaste of the Renaissance soon to spread through the whole of Europe.

Above, Louis XI. **Right**, Joan of Arc, portrait in Maison Jeanne d'Arc, Orléans.

THE MYSTIQUE OF JOAN OF ARC

Joan of Arc is a heroine who has captured the popular imagination for centuries with her bravery and sincerity. The familiar tale of her fight for France and her tragic martyrdom at the age of 19 has inspired countless versions of her story, from children's books of heroism to paintings, plays and many films. The image of the young shepherdess with her cropped hair, armour and flying pennant is as well known as Florence Nightingale or Robin Hood.

She appeared on the scene of history in 1429 during the bitter conflict of the Hundred Years' War between England and France. In 1422 the English, allied with the Burgundians, had captured Paris and ruled all of northern France. The French king, Charles VII, known as the Dauphin because he had yet to be crowned, took refuge in the royal châteaux of the Loire. It was here, at Chinon, that Joan, a young peasant girl from the village of Domrémy in Lorraine, confronted him. She claimed to have been inspired by heavenly voices and instructed to help save her king.

Although the Dauphin disguised himself amongst his courtiers, Joan identified him immediately and sank to her knees at his feet. She was interrogated, her virginity verified, and equipped with a suit of armour. She

set out for Blois and the French army encampment, and although she had been given no official position she rallied the troops sufficiently to relieve the siege of Orléans, where she was received with great rejoicing, thus reversing the fortunes of the French. The English forces were driven from the Loire Valley, as Joan led her devoted troops triumphantly on to recapture Jargeau, Meung, Beaugency and Patay. Both sides in the war were convinced of her divine authority; although her military skills were rudimentary, all believed her presence was crucial. She insisted that the Dauphin must go to Reims to be crowned—the objective of her divine mission. She led him through the hostile territory of Burgundy for the official consecration, where the

ceremony took place on 17 July 1429. Once it was completed the king was determined to withdraw to safer country, and to Joan's frustration he began to retreat. Funds were low so he disbanded the army and signed a truce with the Duke of Burgundy. Joan, however, ignored the treaty, and attacked Paris, but, for the first time, she failed and was seriously wounded in the battle; her brief period of glory was almost over.

The once loyal troops rapidly lost faith in the Maid, and a series of failed attacks resulted in her capture at Compiègne, by the Burgundian army. She was handed over to the English, who put her on trial as a witch. From the transcripts of the trial comes much of the information available about Joan, who impressed her judges with her honour and purity despite their determination to discredit her and her claim to be a divine messenger.

She was charged with heresy by the Inquisition. Her own side saw her as an inspired and holy virgin; her enemies were convinced she was a sorceress. After many months in prison, she was burned at the stake on 30 May 1431.

Joan became a potent political symbol, but was not canonised as a saint until 1920. Almost immediately after her death, questions were raised about the validity of the trial, and a further hearing held to rehabilitate her; the guilty verdict was reversed in 1455. She rapidly entered the realm of myth, a knight in shining armour, an Amazon in men's dress, a holy saint and an inspiring, independent woman.

Her image is enshrined in statues at Chinon and Orléans, stained glass in Orléans Cathedral, frescoes at Domrémy, and Ingre's painting in the Louvre. She has also inspired many literary interpretations, including works by Robert Southey, Schiller, Jules Michelet, Charles Péguy, Paul Claudel, André Malraux and George Bernard Shaw. The cinema also took up her story: Cecil B. De Mille in 1917 with his silent spectacular *Joan the Woman*; Ingrid Bergman in Roberto Rossellini's *Jeanne au Bûcher*, and productions by Otto Preminger and Robert Bresson. Recently, Marina Warner's book *Joan of Arc: The Image of Female Heroism* looked at the myth of the Maid of Orléans and its enduring power.

The 15th century closed with the sun setting on the western châteaux and rising again in the east, on Amboise, Blois and Chambord. The faded charms of Chinon, Loches and Plessis symbolised the age, a draughty, medieval kingdom riven by religious wars, enfeebled royal leadership and intellectual uncertainty. Superficially, the 16th century looked little better, opening with plagues, poor harvests, inflation, peasant revolts and precarious royal finances.

However, the privileged nobility was sheltered from the worst buffets, cushioned by patronage and a burgeoning royal administration. This account follows in the steps of the history-makers, a trail of kings, courts and châteaux. Although the influence of the common people during the Wars of Religion was significant, it is not until the Revolution that the *petites gens* really begin to shape the history of the region.

Courtly life: In Renaissance times, the king was encircled by a moveable royal court of 12,000 people, an extraordinary number given that only 25 towns in the kingdom had over 10,000 inhabitants. François I's military household comprised French, Scots and Swiss guards, as well as a *corps d'élite*. This rotating group of 200 gentlemen served four months at court and lived on their estates the rest of the year.

There were separate royal households for each member of the royal family, including children. The king's royal household might include 1,000 court officials in addition to contingents of surgeons and confessors, valets and barbers, cooks and *maîtres d'hôtel*, poets, musicians and fools, and separate hunting and falconry sections.

The royal court cultivated a hot-house atmosphere in which enlightened ideas and liberated manners flourished. By the turn of the 16th century, Louis XII, the reigning monarch, had given the Third Estate a voice for the first time and admitted members of the emerging *haute bourgeoisie* to his circle of advisers. In addition, the presence of his

wife, Anne de Bretagne, encouraged a new piety at court, coupled with a civilising feminine influence and a receptiveness to new Italian ideas.

From Amboise, the Renaissance spread to the rest of the Val de Loire and heralded a period of sustained châteaux building. The king led the way at Amboise and Blois, adding new wings and Renaissance gardens. The ornamental gardens at Amboise were designed by Pacello, the knowledgeable landscape gardener who introduced rare

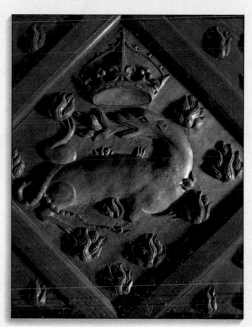

herbs and orange trees to France.

Inside the château were further signs of Renaissance learning, including a library containing 87,000 books. All were written in the languages considered civilised by the French court: Latin, French, Italian, Hebrew and Greek. The lighter side of Renaissance learning is represented by the discoveries of Luca Vigeno, an Italian engineer credited with inventing the first contraption for keeping battery hens.

While based at Amboise, the court witnessed extravagant festivities but the strangest was the visit of Archduke Maximilian of Austria and his wife in 1501. No banquet was

Preceding pages: Chaumont. **Left,** building in progress, Chaumont stained glass. **Above,** salamander emblem of François I.

permissible on the Virgin's birthday yet Louis XII and Anne de Bretagne needed to honour their guests. The archduke and his retinue fasted but a compromise was reached as far as his wife was concerned.

After the archduchess had gone hungry to bed, a torchlit procession of six noblewomen and six pages brought her the greatest delicacy in the château: jam. Twelve gold boxes, covered with crimson velvet, the mark of royalty, concealed an assortment of the finest jams, eaten straight from the pots. The archduchess was later brought a silver mirror, brushes, hair pins, hand and foot towels, all presumably to repair the damage wrought by gorging on sticky jams.

Towards the end of Louis XII's reign, Blois became the French administrative centre, a tradition continued until Henri IV's time. Until Queen Anne died in 1514, shortly followed by her husband, the court at Blois represented a society in transition. It strove to reward virtue and piety with material riches yet was aware that the new spirit of the age favoured merit, enterprise and prodigality. François I embodied this new spirit and his reign coincided with the apogée of the French Renaissance and the most glorious period in the Val de Loire. The Renaissance is reflected in the king's airy wing at Blois, its tiers of Italianate loggias exposed to fresh material and intellectual currents. Both the king and his wife, Claude de France, were brought up in the Loire Valley and ensured that the region retained its royal supremacy.

François had spent a sunny, intellectual childhood at Clos-Lucé, the manor house adjoining Amboise. One of his first acts upon accession was to exempt both estates from all taxes, including the obligation to provide the Crown with one-eighth of the estate's produce and wine. As Louis XII's daughter, Claude was brought up at Blois and, until the end of her short life, loved the château above all others. Upon her marriage, she presented her husband with a dowry including the Duchy of Milan and countless French estates; Blois was the only château she retained for herself.

The king's Italian campaigns, designed to protect French interests in Italy, brought the unexpected pleasures of Renaissance art, architecture and craftsmanship, new perspectives François quickly brought back to the Val de Loire. When François chose Lorenzo de' Medici to become godfather to his son, Lorenzo repaid the honour with a gift of two Raphaels, *The Holy Family* and *Saint Michael*, now in the Louvre.

Close political contact with the Florentine Medici also ensured a flow of artists, craftsmen and landscape gardeners, including the arrival of Leonardo da Vinci. The presence of the Italians ensured that Chambord and Chenonceau became the first great châteaux in France to cast Renaissance ideas in bricks and mortar.

At Blois, Claude de France employed Italian and French gardeners to create magnificent terraces. Pierre Belon, her chief landscape gardener, brought back horticultural ideas and exotic plants from Egypt and Palestine. He also planted the famous plums that still bear the Claude name today. The queen brought up her six children on the first floor of the Renaissance wing while François lived on the floor above, reached by means of lavish reception rooms and a series of secret staircases. The king's imperious mother, Louise de Savoie, was relegated to the uncomfortable Louis XII wing, along with senior courtiers.

François himself is linked more closely to Chambord, the château conceivably designed by Leonardo da Vinci, François' permanent guest at Clos-Lucé. Begun in 1518,

Chambord took until the end of the reign to finish and exhausted the depleted royal finances. François was foiled in his grand scheme to divert the Loire via Chambord and settled for the waters of the humble River Cosson instead. This, however, was the only compromise in his grandiose attempt to write his name in stone.

In 1524, after Claude's death and the king's humiliating defeat at Pavia, François was imprisoned for five years by Charles V in Spain and released only after his two sons had been offered as hostages. A ransom of two million gold ecus was eventually paid but during the king's absence, most royal châteaux building came to a halt.

For nine days afterwards, the two monarchs indulged in an orgy of hunting over the Chambord estates; Charles V was also impressed by the French king's 300 sparrow hawks and falcons, presented for his inspection. The hectic entertainment ended with jousting followed by a simulated siege: a mock fortress was built on the estate and two armies battled for control. However, the presence of open coffins at the joust failed to act as a deterrent and the mock battle ended with a number of real deaths.

During François' long imprisonment in Spain, his courtiers' passion for châteaux building continued unabated. Between the reigns of Louis XI and François I, the *haute*

In 1539 the king staged a conciliatory banquet at Amboise for his rival, Charles V. After a blazing torch set fire to a tapestry, Charles feared a French plot against his life, but he was placated by a grand banquet at Chambord. The château was scented with incense, flowers and herbs while the emperor's apartments were decorated entirely in black, his favourite colour. Black tapestries were hung above chests covered in black taffeta and damask; only the golden eagle emblem relieved the sombre scene.

Left, François I. **Above**, January illustration from
Les Très Riches Heures du Duc de Berry.

bourgeoisie had profited from the silk trade, banking and enlightened royal administration and invested their profits in châteaux, *hôtels particuliers* and manor houses. Azay-le-Rideau, Chenonceau, Clos-Lucé, Langeais, Valençay, Villandry and Ville-savin were built by this new class.

After making their fortunes in business, members consolidated their prestige and power by pledging their fortunes to the Crown. As royal financiers or senior court officials, they not only bankrolled the Crown but brought a fresh entrepreneurial spirit to the dilettante upper classes. The effect filtered downwards to the bourgeoisie: in

Angers, Orléans and Tours, merchants, lawyers and town magistrates built sophisticated town houses. One effect of such property speculation was the reclaiming of medieval town centres, deserted by the upper classes since the Hundred Years' War. In Tours, this new appetite for town architecture is seen in Hôtel Gouin, a peak in Renaissance architecture. Almost as impressive is the Hôtel Babou, built by Philibert Babou, both François' financier and husband of la belle Babou, the king's fun-loving mistress.

Despite their great contribution to royal revenues, the financiers were wrongly blamed for royal profligacy. Many were bankrupted, like the Bohier family, original

owners of Chenonceau, or executed, as was Jacques de Beaune, owner of Beaune Semblançay in Tours. The court's financial problems ran deep: most nobles were heavily in debt as a result of their gilded lifestyles and slavishness to court fashions.

During the reigns of François I and his son, Henri II, few of the 12,000 courtiers could afford the lavish court dress, yet debt was preferable to an admission of poverty. Most courtiers possessed at least 100 pairs of gloves, often dipped in sheep's fat or whale's sperm to make the leather more supple. To curb costly fashions, François I forbade courtiers to wear gold embroidery, crushed velvet, crimson silk or fabrics woven with pure gold or silver thread.

But even fines of 1,000 gold ecus had little effect and the strictures were reinforced by Henri II. Only princes were allowed to wear crimson silk while knights were permitted only one piece of precious fabric and only bishops could wear velvet. Although "no artisans, peasants or labourers should wear precious silk" was a redundant piece of advice, the barring of courtiers from wearing "silk on silk" provoked a storm of protest and the measure was withdrawn.

The accession of Henri II in 1547 marked a continuation of Renaissance excess, from château building to hunting, banqueting and fashion. Court dress provides a parallel to court mentality. Although Henri always wore black and white, it was an echo of Diane de Poitiers' colours, rather than a concession to simplicity. If Henri's wife, Catherine de Médicis, always wore black, it was rumoured to be a symbol of the king's rejection of his plain young wife in favour of his lifelong relationship with the peerless Diane. As the uncrowned queen, Diane was renowned for her charm, cunning and beauty. As the quintessential court beauty, Diane was praised for "possessing three of everything". She boasted three white features (skin, teeth, hands); three black (eyes, lashes, eyebrows); three red (lips, cheeks, nails); three long (body, hands, hair); three short (teeth, ears, feet); three small (breasts, nose, head); three narrow (mouth, waist, ankles); and three plump ones (arms, calves, thighs). No one was under any illusions about Henri's preference in bed, except perhaps his wife, who regularly spied on the couple. Catherine had clearly not studied Baldassar Castiglione's *The Perfect Courtier*, a manual of love and manners in vogue at the royal court. Modesty and discretion are the highest values in any model courtier, but a female courtier should also "be never envious, spiteful, jealous or vain".

However, Henri and Diane also failed to live up to the courtly ideal. "If, in the course of her duties, a woman falls in love, she must never betray her feelings in public". She and her lover must act respectably so "the eyes are faithful messengers of the heart". Castiglione's manual also failed to advise courtiers on the correct etiquette to follow when the king, in a fit of passion, made love to Diane, oblivious to the presence of courtiers playing cards in the royal bedchamber.

While the court was officially based at Blois, Henri spent much of his time at Chenonceau, a gift to "*sa parfaite amie*". Under Diane's shrewd influence, Chenonceau was transformed into the most romantic of châteaux and a profitable estate, typical of many in the Val de Loire. The grounds, like those at Villandry, were planted with fruit trees, herb and vegetable gardens but equal attention was paid to the economic viability of the estate. From the *chatellenie* of mills, meadows, vineyards, farms and dovecotes, Diane received produce at Easter and on the feasts of Toussaint (All Saints') and St

became available, as did Rabelais' earthy and satirical works.

With the death of Henri II in a jousting accident, foreseen by Nostradamus, the court astrologer, the regency fell to Catherine de Médicis in 1559. As regent, Catherine reasserted herself and helped navigate the kingdom through a stormy period. The following 30 years were dominated by the Wars of Religion and weak leadership provided by her three sons, the last kings of the Valois dynasty. After years of extravagance, the royal coffers were empty so Catherine sold jewels and confiscated all private gifts made by François I and Henri II. However, her decision to exchange her château at

Martin and had sufficient to supply the royal château at Blois in addition to her own needs.

Earthy and satirical: During the reigns of François I and Henri II, intellectual life was at a premium. Angers was known as "the Athens of the west", a home to humanists and poets. Most courtiers were familiar with humanist works, Arthurian legends, the chivalric *Roman de la Rose* and more modern encyclopaedia of courtly manners. As the Renaissance unfolded, the poetry of Ronsard and Joachim du Bellay gradually

Left, Henri II. <u>**Above**</u>, rivals for his love, Catherine de Médicis and Diane de Poitiers.

Chaumont for Diane's at Chenonceau must have afforded the regent more than a little personal satisfaction.

Until 1559, the Val de Loire was at the grim centre of French history, a period of bloody massacres, brief truces and permanent conspiracies. The marriage of Catherine's 17-year-old son, François II, to Mary Stuart brought the court under the excessive influence of the young queen's plotting uncles, the Duc de Guise and the Cardinal de Lorraine. This Catholic faction, known as the League, originally had the upper hand over the Calvinists, who were led by Admiral Coligny and the Prince de Condé. However, the Crown was still powerless to prevent the ensuing civil war.

Angers, Châteaudun, Orléans, Nantes, Saumur and Tours were Protestant strongholds, largely supported by the rural nobility, minor clergy, artisans, weavers and the working classes. The itinerant royal court was resolutely Catholic, backed by the aristocracy, senior clerics and the *haute bourgeoisie*. Persecution of Protestants had been rife since the 1540s, especially in Anjou, but the first sign of a Calvinist backlash came in 1560, when a plot to kidnap François II was foiled. The Protestant conspiracy, known as the *conjuration d'Amboise*, was nipped in the bud when the forewarned Guise faction

the leading conspirators were beheaded for *lèse-majesté* and their bodies hung over the château balconies. The Duc de Guise ordered the executions to take place after dinner "to amuse the ladies who were in danger of getting bored".

At Catherine's invitation, the court immediately withdrew to Chenonceau to celebrate the Catholic victory. Despite many more years of civil war, the court turned in on itself and, moving from one Loire château to another, indulged in balls, masquerades and jousts with renewed enthusiasm.

In 1577, the regent held a transvestite ball at Chenonceau in honour of her libidinous daughter, Marguerite de Navarre, and her

moved the royal court from Blois to Amboise, a much easier château to defend.

After the expected date for the conspiracy passed, the court relaxed, the king went hunting and the two queens went to Chenonceau with most of the court. However, a Catholic reconnaissance party found the Protestant army was already halfway between Tours and Amboise. The Catholic Duc de Nemours gathered a makeshift army from Amboise and captured Le Renaudie, the Protestant general, and other leaders.

Bloody vengeance for the conspiracy was later extracted at Amboise: Protestant soldiers were drowned in sacks in the Loire while

favourite son, Henri III, an effeminate dandy rarely seen without his coterie of devoted fops, known as *mignons*. After the ball degenerated into an orgy, scandalised participants later denounced the affair in a pamphlet as "a monstrous banquet overflowing with pagan licentiousness" and attended by "an island of hermaphrodites".

The ball was also attended by Catherine's beautiful "flying squad" of bare-breasted women, ineffectually masquerading as men. This *escadron volant*, loosely referred to as "ladies of honour", were there to further the regent's political ends. Catherine's first act as regent was to increase the squad from 24 to 200 and to instruct members on duty to be "decked out as duchesses but welcoming as women". Her unorthodox methods bore fruit during her secret negotiations with the Protestant leaders, Henri de Condé and Henri de Navarre. Both men were presented with the women of their choice as a reward for signing a peace treaty favourable to the Crown.

Such interludes were sorely needed in 1572 when the horrific Saint Bartholomew's Day Massacre in Paris had reverberations all over the Val de Loire, not least in Angers. The marriage of the Protestant Henri de Navarre and the Catholic Marguerite de Valois was designed to reconcile both sides but merely unleashed more violence. For the

In 1588, the Estates General again met at Blois amid rumours of assassination plots on all sides. Even a Venetian troupe of actors due to perform at Blois was kidnapped en route by a band of Protestants and the king was forced to pay a considerable ransom merely to assure the court's evening entertainment. Henri III was desperate, aware that the Estates General would refuse to approve either his budget or policies favouring rapprochement with the Protestants. By contrast, the Guise faction pressed for sanctions to eliminate the Protestant opposition.

In his address to the clergy, nobles and Third Estate who constituted the assembly, Henri made an impassioned speech de-

next three years, the court abandoned the Loire châteaux for the relative safety of Fontainbleau and Saint Germain.

In 1576, however, the court moved back to Blois to coincide with the meeting of the Estates General, a parliament dominated by supporters of the Leaguers, the Guise faction. Known as the Roi de Paris, the Duc de Guise was by then too powerful to be trusted by Catherine and was plotting to depose the king, her son. Henri failed to sway the Estates General and the civil war continued.

Left, Chambord's famous staircase. <u>Above</u>, the Great Hall at Blois.

nouncing the "plotting, leaguers and crimes of *lèse-majesté*", a clear challenge to Guise and the Catholic League. The plea failed to move the assembly and Henri resolved to murder the Duc de Guise, and thus decapitate the intransigent Catholic faction. The path would then be clear for a reconciliation with the Protestants, led by his brother-in-law, Henri de Navarre.

Catherine de Médicis acquiesced to the plot, as did Henri's secret war cabinet of 45 trusted supporters. While the court was distracted by the marriage of Catherine's favourite granddaughter, Christine de Lorraine, to Ferdinando de' Medici, Henri III feigned joviality with de Guise while, "in a black bile of a mood", plotting his rival's death.

The plan was to plant trusted assassins in hidden monks' cells in the king's apartments; in order not to arouse suspicion, the assassins would descend to the royal bedchamber while the council was in session and await the arrival of the duke, summoned on a pretext. All went according to plan and de Guise, rejecting all warnings, attempted to cross the king's bedchamber in the direction of the royal study. The château and all rooms had been sealed off in readiness and the duke, tired and hungry after an exhausting night with a member of the "flying squad", was caught unawares by eight assassins in the royal bedchamber.

The king hid behind a tapestry and overheard the duke's last words. Asked to beg forgiveness of God and the king, de Guise managed to say "Misere Deus" but put his fist in his mouth so that he did not have to utter his royal enemy's name. Prominent Leaguers were immediately arrested and de Guise's brother hanged. Both bodies were burnt to avoid a cult of martyrdom being attached to a particular site.

In 1589, a triumphant Henri III left for Plessis-les-Tours and, amidst cries of "*Vivent les rois*", staged a reconciliation with Henri de Navarre. Their joint armies confronted the remaining Leaguers at Tours but victory was by no means assured because the Leaguers, led by the Duc de Mayenne, outnumbered the joint force. However, the women of Tours accidentally saved the day. According to chronicles, the Catholic troops were inflamed by the beauty of the *belles* Tourangelles and "abandoned Mars for Venus". After scenes of rape and pillage, the Leaguers were eventually crushed and royal authority reasserted itself from the Val de Loire to the rest of the kingdom.

Early deaths: Catherine died of pleurisy shortly after the assassination of the Duc de Guise. When Henri informed his mother of the successful outcome, she reputedly said, "God grant that you have not become king of nothing at all". Her prescience was perhaps linked to the warnings of her sons' early deaths predicted by Ruggieri, her astrologer at Chaumont. Less than a year later, Henri, the last of the Valois, was murdered by a Catholic fanatic in Paris and his brother-in-law became King Henri IV.

During Henri III's reign, artistic life flourished, not merely because of the king's predilection for participating in ballets, dressed as an exotic bird or humble shepherdess. Although increasingly decadent, the court attended Venetian ballets, lute concerts, impromptu plays and Spanish pastorals as well as transvestite balls.

Pointless duels: Intellectual life had declined since its peak during Henri II's reign. Likewise, courtiers had little time for the ideals of courtly love, preached but rarely practised during earlier reigns. Henri III's beautiful *mignons* were regularly killed in pointless duels, including St-Sulpice, his favourite, named Colette for his fashionable high collars in dramatic colours. There was drama enough in political events to propel courtiers towards refuge in safe, hedonistic pursuits. The court fulfilled Ronsard's dictum: "*Cueillez aujourd'hui les roses de la vie*" for tomorrow you may be dead.

As far as the Val de Loire was concerned, Henri IV's reign was an anti-climax. From then onwards, the door closed on the Loire's centre-stage role: the region shrank to a mere window on the antics of *les grands* in Paris.

Henri IV's reign was spent pacifying the kingdom and routing intransigent Catholics, including François de Lorraine, the League's last hope. Following this success, the king promulgated the Edict of Nantes, guaranteeing freedom of worship to all Protestants, a liberty later revoked by Louis XIV.

After Henri IV's assassination by a fanatic in 1610, Marie de Médicis acted as regent until her son came of age in 1617 and promptly exiled his mother to Blois. After she escaped by dressing as a laundry woman and climbing down the side of the château, the ever-fearful Louis XIII then exiled his brother, Gaston d'Orléans, to the same château. There, Gaston contentedly amused himself by building a classical wing and made no attempt to escape from his perfect new residence. Given the proximity of undesirable relatives, Louis avoided Blois but often visited Chambord. In the somewhat dilapidated château he indulged his passions for hunting and solitude.

Queen Anne of Austria, wife of Louis XIII, gave lavish balls at Chambord but left politics to her controversial minister, Mazarin. In the middle of the 16th century, the Frondeurs, protesters against Mazarin's extortionate taxes, orchestrated uprisings all over France. After an unsuccessful rebellion in Angers, the region's resistance crumbled and even heavier taxes were imposed. Under both Louis XIII and Louis XIV, burdensome taxes ruined many landowners, particularly in Touraine and Sologne.

With Mazarin's death, the reign of Louis XIV brought little sun to the Loire, merely reflected glory. Molière performed his plays for the king at Chambord but even the Val de Loire's most magnificent château only encouraged Louis to dream of a still grander Versailles. In keeping with the fashion of the times, Chambord's ceilings were lowered, alcoves were created for beds, ornate mirrors

Chanteloup, a once great estate near Amboise, was created by the exiled Duc de Choiseuil, Louis XV's disgraced minister. Walpole announced that the Cour de Chanteloup was more impressive than Versailles. Apart from elegant soirées, the "court" indulged in the noble sports of billiards, darts, dominoes, pheasant hunting and kite-flying. All that remains of Choiseuil's legendary château is a Chinese pagoda, erected to "*Amitié Eternelle*", a tribute to the friends who did not leave him to swim alone in the Loire backwaters.

But great château building did not end with the Renaissance, as shown by Chanteloup, Beauregard, Cheverny, Ménars and the

installed and new stables built. Even so, Colbert, Louis XIV's minister, complained that the château was "in a pitiful state with window panes broken and rain pouring in".

Until Revolutionary times, the Val de Loire provided royalty with light-hearted diversions and a refuge from real life. For exiled nobles, it represented refuge and real life. In the 18th century, there were still sparks of the old escapist magic, as when a Montgolfier balloon rose over the blue-grey domes of Cheverny.

Above, porcupine emblem of Louis XII over a fireplace at Blois.

classical wing at Blois. However, from the 17th century onwards, the architectural emphasis shifts away from sprawling châteaux to elegant urban development. Blois, Orleans, Saumur and Tours were all embellished with broad avenues, bridges and stately 18th-century town houses.

Until the Revolution, the Val de Loire was no longer a history-maker but a quiet backwater in the shadow of the Ile-de-France. Sterner critics might say that, since the Renaissance, the region has gone to sleep as deeply as *la belle au bois dormante*, the Sleeping Beauty celebrated in the fairytale Château d'Ussy.

A DAY IN THE LIFE
OF A CHATEAU

François I awoke, usually alone, in his red damask bed on the first floor. Given the itinerant nature of French Renaissance courts, the royal levée was equally at home in Amboise, Blois or Chambord. Although the backdrop varied, the ritual and decor remained the same. The stage furniture, including tapestries, chests and a portable library, was as mobile as the court itself. The royal apartments were soon full of privileged courtiers, there to chat, listen to the king's engagements or the astrologer's daily forecast. Following aristocratic custom, the king breakfasted lightly on boiled milk mixed with raw egg, fruit and honey.

After consultation with advisers or ambassadors, François, the royal family and senior courtiers attended mass, held in the new château chapel. Renaissance chapels had just been added to Amboise, Blois, Chaumont and Chenonceau, popular royal haunts. The presence of Scots guards was essential in an environment where "Sicilian vespers" or quiet assassinations could lurk around the corner. After chapel, the morning was devoted to sport, whether romantic assignations or games of *pail-mail*, a version of croquet played along straight avenues in the grounds. Lunch, usually eaten before midday, was a relatively restrained

affair: four courses, including soup, pâtés, fish, roast meats and fruit. Royalty usually ate at a separate table but ambassadors, artists or advisers were occasionally invited: the business lunch was not a modern invention.

Shortly afterwards, the king discussed household affairs with his mother, Louise de Savoie, or met his wife, Claude de France, perhaps their only chance to get together that day. The afternoon was devoted entirely to leisure, whether *jeu de paume*, hunting or falconry. *Jeu de paume*, a forerunner to tennis and squash, was played on partially enclosed courts and watched by courtiers in the gallery. Both François and Henri were fanatical about the sport and built several courts at each royal château.

Innocent pleasures were not without an undercurrent of violence or wanton cruelty. The royal pages regularly nailed the fool's ears to a post and dared Caillette, the victim, to remain silent. In the first year of his reign, François sent his courtiers into the forest in search of a wild boar. The king had just been persuaded not to risk himself in single combat when "the boar ran to attack, aiming for the king's thighs to give him a mortal wound". The king ran a dagger through the beast's heart and celebrated by staging a fight between three lions and three mastiffs.

To celebrate the *jour des rois* at Amboise in 1521, François challenged courtiers to bombard him with snowballs, apples and eggs for being an unsatisfactory king. However, an over-excited courtier threw a blazing log out of a window: the log hit François in the face, so doctors had to shave his head; the king grew his beard long to hide the scar. The result was a court fashion for short hair and long beards until the end of his reign.

Amboise represented 5,000 acres (2,000 hectares) of woodland with just one tenant, ideal hunting territory. Accompanied by 200 noblemen and archers as well as Pierrot, master of the hunt, the king hunted until nightfall or hunger intervened. Fortunately, the entourage was accompanied by provisions: 50 carts, each pulled by six horses, were laden with tents, animal traps and enough provisions for impromptu picnics in the woods or full-scale banquets at a neighbouring château.

Unusual hunting companions were the *filles de joie*, the official court prostitutes, only phased out by Catherine de Médicis whose own ladies of honour had a very thin veneer of intellectual sophistication. During hunts at Chambord, female courtiers watched from the rooftop galleries, while at Blois, the women made their own amusement by playing cards, chess or tric-trac. To while away the time before the return of the hunt, pious ladies in waiting worked for Claude's charities while more worldly gentlewomen read Castiglione's *The Perfect Courtier* or idly snipped manuscripts into miniature designs, the latest court fashion.

Dinner usually took place before seven o'clock

and was accompanied by Italian music, reading aloud from humanist texts, and by the antics of the king's fools, Triboulet and Caillette.

A typical dinner is described by Mathurin Cordier, a contemporary writer. Salted ham, smoked eel and tongue promoted a thirst and were accompanied by salads, veal pâté, game fricassé, egg and saffron soups as well as boiled chicken, veal and pork. Roast meats always followed boiled meats and included pork, chicken, rabbit, lamb and woodcock. The château's vegetable garden provided artichokes, asparagus and chick peas to accompany the fish course. The trout, salmon and shrimps were doused in rich sauces made from lemons, olives and gooseberries. The meal ended with fresh fruit, perhaps figs, dates or the court's favourite, melons.

rooftops or in the rose gardens. During the dancing of the daring gaillard, women were constrained to wear belts to keep their dresses under a semblance of control: in case of indecent exposure, long drawers protected the *pudeur* of the female wearer. Costumes were lavish concoctions of layered damask, satin, velvet or silk.

The rooftop galleries or shadowy gardens provided ample scope for romantic assignations, often led by the king as master of ceremonies. At Chambord, François pursued Marie Babou, the mistress known as "the royal mattress". When not with the king, la belle Babou boasted of bedding Charles V and Pope Clement VI. A more permanent fixture was Françoise de la Foix, who strayed as often as her royal lover. On one occasion, Françoise was in bed with Guillaume Gouf-

Unsurprisingly, the king and courtiers favoured a summer stroll after dinner, taking in an inspection of the herb gardens, moats or royal menagerie. The king often returned to his library or listened to music, conserving his strength for the twice-weekly balls. On other evenings, there were masquerades, lute concerts or games of *flux*, an addictive card game played with tarot cards.

On Thursday and Sunday, the grounds of Chambord were illuminated with blazing torches and fireworks. Dancing began in the ballroom but the excitement of the pavane, cotillon and gaillard drove courtiers to cooler retreats on the

Left, court of François I. **Above**, Renaissance bathtime.

frier, the Admiral of France, when the terrified couple heard the king approaching. The admiral hid behind foliage in the fireplace but had to remain silent until the king had both exhausted Françoise and then relieved himself over the unseen admiral.

As the torches were dimmed, six servants unpacked the camp beds at the foot of the king's four-poster. Foolhardy courtiers played games of snuffing out torches with their noses. In *Gargantua*, Rabelais writes of the Abbaye Thélème, parodying a thinly disguised Chambord. The abbey's motto, "*Fais ce que voudras*" (Do as you wish), could easily apply to Chambord under François I's liberated reign. Living in a Renaissance film set meant rarely going to bed alone.

In December 1793, Joseph Bara, aged 14, from Palaiseau, near Paris, found himself part of the Republican army near the town of Cholet, about 40 miles (60 km) south-southeast of the crossing of the Loire at Saumur. It was the time of the most serious counter-revolution against the still young French republican movement (King Louis XVI had been executed only in January).

France was at war with most of Europe, and in March 1793, when the revolutionary government attempted to introduce conscription, the Vendée had risen, forming at Saumur an army which described itself as "Catholic and royal". By July, the Vendéens controlled a large portion of western France and were besieging Nantes. The ruling Convention voted itself money that did not exist to wage war; as a result, inflation raged and food riots broke out. Although, by the end of the year, the Vendéens had been checked in their attempts to reach the Cherbourg peninsula and link up with the British fleet, the bloody conflict, marked by a series of vicious reprisals and massacres, was to drag on for seven years. Maximilien Robespierre, by that time a leading member of the Committee of Public Safety and at the height of his political and rhetorical powers, was to use Joseph Bara as a heart-rending example of the heroism of the republicans and the viciousness of the counter-revolutionaries.

In Robespierre's elaborated, exaggerated version, produced in a speech demanding Bara's reburial in the Pantheon (the former Parisian church of St-Geneviève, transformed by the revolutionaries into a mausoleum for the great figures of their struggle), Joseph Bara had found himself surrounded by Vendéen troops in a skirmish near Cholet. Exhorted by the Vendéens to shout *"Vive le Roi!"*, he shouted instead, *"Vive la République!"* The Vendéens shot him dead.

The painter Jacques-Louis David started a strangely erotic representation of the naked, dying Bara, but did not finish it, finding the kind of declamatory propaganda demanded by his revolutionary patrons not to his taste.

Ninety years later, 500,000 photographic prints of another painting, Jean-Joseph Weerts' *The Death Of Bara*, were distributed in French schools and later reproduced regularly in textbooks. Weerts received the Légion d'Honneur from the French Republic. A street was named after Joseph Bara in Angers and, in 1907, another in Paris.

If the mythification of a hero of modern France's creation preoccupied the national

memory, in the Loire and the Vendée a different memory remained—that of defeat, repression, persecution and even ambivalence towards the state created out of the Revolution. This was reflected in the region's snubbing of the 1989 celebrations of the bicentenary of the Revolution.

In 1984, when Pope John Paul II visited Angers, it was not to honour the memory of Joseph Bara, but to hold a service of beatification for 89 Vendéen martyrs, such as the carter and pedlar Jacques Cathelineau, elected leader of the rebel army. Wounded at the siege of Nantes, he died at Saint-Florent-le-Vieil, four years to the day after the storm-

Preceding pages: St-Julien Cathedral, Le Mans. Left, traditional Touraine costume – *Portrait de Madame Neveu*, by Jean Pierre Vallet. **Above**, Robespierre.

ing of the Bastille. Eighty-nine martyrs of the "Catholic and royal" army pledged to roll back the Revolution and overthrow the secular state. Further east, in the Orléanais, the Revolution had, at least at the outset, been better received, with the nobility joining the other classes in what was principally a revolt against the onerous tax system imposed by the monarchy. Even much of the clergy was pro-revolutionary, and accepted both the nationalisation of Church lands and the imposition, in 1790, of the Civil Constitution which dissolved those religious orders not involved in teaching and charity work, and imposed the free election of bishops and curés. Whereas nationally, only seven bis-

first meeting of the Convention, he demanded the abolition of the monarchy, saying: "Kings are to the moral order what monsters are to the physical order; courts are the workshop of crime, the home of corruption: the history of kings is the martyrology of nations." He remained a revolutionary to his death, at the age of 81; but his career effectively ended in 1801, when he was one of three senators who refused to elect Napoleon Bonaparte emperor, turning down in passing the title of count for himself.

After the initial enthusiasm for the Revolution across all classes, however, the abolition of the monarchy in 1792 and the onset of the Terror dissolved many of the bonds of

hops out of 160 and perhaps one-third of the lower clergy took the loyalty oath imposed by the Constitution, some 70 percent of the clergy in the Eure-et-Loir *département*, 90 percent in the Loiret (including the bishop of Jarente), with a similar proportion in Loir-et-Cher, took the revolutionary oath.

Kings and masters: Most prominent of the new breed of revolutionary clergy (apart from those, such as the Blois Jacobin Rochejean, who broke entirely with the Church), was the Abbé Gregoire, the elected bishop of Blois, who rose also to be president of the Loir-et-Cher *département*, a deputy in the Convention and finally a senator. At the

unanimity. Even so, few in the Orléanais took up arms against the Revolution, and relatively few aristocrats (by comparison with the rest of France) emigrated. Of the 17,000 people executed during the Terror, just 30 died in the three *départements* of the Orléanais. The district leant towards tolerance and supported the Chartres-born Brissot who represented Eure-et-Loir in the Convention, and whose moderate faction was skilfully routed by Robespierre. Brissot went to the guillotine in October 1793.

What politicised the people of the eastern Loire most effectively was food. In July 1788, one year before the Revolution, bread in Orléans cost 3 sols 10 deniers. (Up to 1801, the French currency was denominated in the same way as the pre-metric British pounds, shillings and pence—12 deniers to the sol, 20 sols to the livre.) The average worker earned between 2 sols 10 deniers and 4 sols per day.

On 4 July, 300 rioters pillaged an Orléans flour merchant's home, accusing him of monopolising the market. In April 1789, troops fired on a food demonstration in Orléans, killing 10. Between August 1789, the month after the Revolution, and April 1791, the price of corn in Orléans fell 43 percent, but by May 1793, prices had risen to beyond the pre-Revolution level. The result

December. These popular uprisings made their point: in the month of June 1793 alone, the price of bread fell 16 percent in Orléans.

The bigger political impact of the Revolution was the redistribution of land. Surprisingly, perhaps, the nobility's losses, though substantial, were not crippling—largely because the number of aristocrats abandoning their lands for exile was relatively small. It was the Church which suffered near-complete confiscation of its property, while the chief beneficiary of redistribution was the peasantry. In 1790, 14 percent of the land in Ver-les-Chartres was held by peasants: in 1828, the figure had risen to 44 percent. The clergy, on the other hand, had lost all of the

J'arrive à TOURS et vous envoie le Bonjour   LL.

was huge popular unrest, with crowds of up to 10,000 gathering in Blois, Tours, Sologne, Amboise, Beaugency and Chartres, intercepting grain shipments and sometimes killing merchants.

The appearance of such a crowd in Vendôme in November 1792 had the immediate effect of halving the price of wheat. Six thousand men then left the town and by 29 November had passed through Blois and Amboise and arrived at Tours, with another crowd reaching Sologne at the beginning of

Left, calming unrest in 1790. **Above**, the railway comes to Tours.

25 percent it had held in 1790, and the nobility just under half of its 27 percent.

And it was the rural dimension which became dominant in the Loire in the 19th century. Despite the proximity of the region to Paris and the centre of political and economic developments, its towns tended to stagnate while the countryside prospered. In 1818, up to 16 percent of the populations of major towns such as Chartres and Blois worked in agriculture.

Among the smaller towns, this phenomenon was even more marked: in 1851, over 40 percent of the populations of Vendôme and Romarantin were agricultural workers.

One reason was the growing success of agriculture. By the mid-19th century, the number of sheep raised in the Chartres district had doubled in 40 years, while, thanks to the use of manure, wheat yields in the Eure-et-Loir rose one-third in the three decades to 1850. By 1885, wheat production in the Beauce was 285 percent higher than in 1816. Early mechanisation of agricultural production combined with the arrival of the steam railway (the Orléans–Tours line was constructed in 1843–45) to make the Loire Valley into the nation's granary.

The agricultural boom was largely carried out by smallholders. In 1884, over 90 percent of the farmers in the Eure-et-Loir, Loiret and

river traffic plummeted: between 1855 and 1859, the weight of goods transported from Blois by boat halved. By 1892, the figure was down to just 2.5 percent of the amount 37 years earlier.

After the Concordat between Napoleon Bonaparte and Pope Pius VII in 1802, the Church began to regain its strength—and shed the radicalism it had known in the region during the Revolution. To the conservatism of the agricultural class was added the historic associations of the Orléanais with the monarchy and the aristocratic connections of many of the post-Concordat bishops. The Joan of Arc commemoration marches were resumed, and church attendance and

GUERRE EUROPÉENNE 1914

Environs de TOURS — JOUÉ (Parc de la Frazelière) - Réunion de Blessés de différentes armes
Zouave, Turco et Fantassins, atteints dans les premiers combats - N. P.

Loir-et-Cher *départements* were peasants working holdings of less than 12 acres (5 hectares). Only 1 percent of farmers held more than 120 acres (50 hectares).

Severe damage: The arrival of the railway had a major influence on the towns, too. These had already been suffering decline: in Orléans in 1831, some 11,500 people relied on public assistance. The railway inflicted severe damage on the commercial viability of the River Loire for transporting goods and people. The arrival of the Paris line in Orléans in 1846 cut travelling time to the capital from 10 hours to four. Despite the advent of steam-powered boats on the Loire,

enrollment at Church schools rose. By 1897, the number of priests in the Orléans diocese passed the 1791 level for the first time.

This conservative Church, living uneasily and forceably separated from the state, nevertheless did its best to exert an influence on public affairs: the bishop of Orléans, Dupanloup, famous for having converted the statesman Talleyrand on his death-bed, saw his book *Atheism and the Social Peril* translated into nine languages and detected the work of Satan in the Paris Commune.

But this resurgence had reached a plateau. By the end of the 19th century, candidature for the priesthood had begun to fall once more, and the traditional divergence between the lay and religious elements of French culture became sharper again. Thus, the religious, patriotic right wing succeeded in the beatification of Joan of Arc in 1909 (she was canonised in 1920): on the other hand, Orléans (following a 1905 law enshrining the separation of Church and State) decided in 1907 to secularise the annual Joan of Arc procession. Politically, at least until the outbreak of World War II, the people of the Loire tended towards radicalism, rather than the more left-wing currents of socialism and communism.

The end of the 19th century saw the Loire slip into decline. Competition from America

krieg had succeeded in obtaining all the French soil it had failed to gain by the attrition of trench warfare in the 1914–18 war. By mid-June, the government had abandoned Paris, which had been declared an "open city", and established itself at various châteaux near Tours. It has been estimated that, between 15 and 20 June 1940, between 6 and 8 million French abandoned their homes and headed either for the sea—or for the Loire, considered to be a strategic barrier to the advancing German army.

But by 17 June the last bridge at Gien was blown up (killing many refugees who ignored soldiers' warnings), and the Loire was impassable from Tours to Nevers. Despite a

brought about a sharp slide in wheat prices. The people who felt the squeeze most were the smallholders, who could not afford the investment needed for further mechanisation. The result, compounded by the 1914–18 war and high unemployment and business failure caused by the international economic crisis of the 1930s, was the concentration of land in a smaller number of hands. Population slowly declined.

The Loire at war: By 15 May 1940, after five days of fighting, the German army's blitz-

broadcast by Marshal Pétain that day, calling for surrender, fighting continued. The officers and cadets of the cavalry school at Saumur resisted the German advance heroically (more than 2,000 shells fell on the town). The prefect of Eure-et-Loir, Jean Moulin, cut his throat following severe torture rather than sign a declaration that would blame colonial troops from Senegal for "Judaeo-Negro" barbarism: the slaughtered in question had died from German aerial bombardments. By October 1940, the French government (now established at Vichy) was ready to sign an armistice with the Germans. The President, Marshal Philippe Pétain, made a direct appeal to Hitler, declaring his readiness to provide "collaboration in every domain". After a preliminary meeting in Spain between Hitler and the prime minister, Pierre Laval, Pétain shook hands with the Führer on 24 October 1940 in a railway carriage at Montoire. Less than a week later, Pétain announced he was in favour of all-out political collaboration and a "compensation agreement" was signed with Germany.

At the fall of France, the Loire river formed part of the border between the occupied zone and the Vichy-controlled part of the country. In the tangled, controversial history of resistance and collaboration which wracked France even before the Liberation, and has never fully been addressed since, it seems clear from the statistical record that the balance in the region was tilted towards defiance of the enemy.

At the end of the war, 3,281 inhabitants of the three *départements* under the jurisdiction of the Orléans court were found guilty of collaboration—of whom 2,239 received the lightest form of punishment and 177 were sentenced to death: this in a region that included recruitment centres for both a Nazi volunteer company and the Waffen SS. By contrast, it has been estimated that 2,386 people served in the Resistance in just one of these *départements*, the Loiret—of whom 353 were deported and 176 shot.

In the neighbouring Selles-et-Cher *département*, the inhabitants were fined one million francs by the Germans for establishing an escape network across the demarcation line between the occupied and Vichy zones.

In the summer of 1944, as Allied troops swept through France, the retreating German army took a heavy toll. On 25 August, in the village of Maillé, near Sainte-Maure, 124 inhabitants were shot in cold blood. In the Loiret *département*, 82 died in fighting—while 305 perished in front of firing squads and 732 were deported, of whom only 327 returned home after the war.

Through the month of August, Patton's Third US Army progressively liberated Le Mans, Angers, Châteaudun, Chartres and Orléans as it advanced on Paris, reversing, 250 years later, Joseph Bara's journey in another war of liberation.

Loire railway and industry today.

Sailors Of The Loire

Broad-brimmed hat set jauntily on his head, dressed in jacket and breeches of rough brown cloth, coloured handkerchief twisted round neck, blue stomacher round waist and always with an earthenware pitcher of wine at hand, the Loire sailor was once as familiar a sight in the streets of the riverside towns as the ships he manned were upon its waters. His race became extinct in the late 19th century and, with his passing, the Loire's function as a line of communication and a trade route ended too.

It had started before the dawn of history, as the remains of dugout canoes found on or near its banks prove. It was continued by the Celts, who used it to import goods from the classical world, and by the Romans to carry the oysters to which they were so partial from their Atlantic beds.

By the 14th century its traffic had become so important that the Loire mariners formed themselves into a guild with two objectives. The first was mutual protection against the duties imposed by local authorities and the exactions of local seigneurs, who, as riparian proprietors, could turn a nice profit selling licences to ply the river or operate ferries.

The second was to make sure the river was kept navigable and that its facilities were maintained and, as commerce grew, extended. The 17th century saw the beginning of a major project with the building of the canal network which, by its completion 200 years later, linked the Loire with other major French rivers.

The work included such engineering achievements as the 2,000-ft (610-metre) iron Pont Canal at Briare, built in 1896, and the system of locks at Rogny les Sept Écluses, built in 1642, which could raise a vessel over 100 ft (30 metres) and which continued in service until 1887.

Though the guild's membership included a handful of fleet owners with large vessels, the overwhelming majority owned a single small boat. Many were local tradesmen, who left the care of the shop to their wives when they travelled, and used their stockrooms as warehouses for the goods they carried. Some of these Aladdin's caves of luxuries from all over France and even abroad would be open to the local buying public—prototypes for the supermarkets of a later epoch.

In good times profits could be substantial, but, especially for the ordinary sailor, it was a life of constant uncertainty. There were times when work and money were plentiful, though much of the latter was squandered on drinking bouts, often culminating in brawls.

On the other hand, summer drought could reduce the river to an indolent stream too shallow for even the flat-bottomed Loire vessels. Such periods were a chance to carry out maintenance work on the river and its banks and there was the unceasing need to renew buoys and other aids to navigation. This might provide work for some.

Others might volunteer for the navy and indeed the Loire taverns were a fruitful recruiting ground, though the transfer to the high seas was not always easy for those brought up to fresh-water seamanship. The fact remained that many, unable to find the rent for the tiny, low-ceilinged one-room cottages in which they and their families lived, were reduced to taking to the roads as beggars.

And on this most capricious of rivers the work itself was often dangerous. Always a place of unpredictable currents, vortexes and shifting shoals, in winter its waters could freeze with a suddenness that locked everything on it in a steely embrace, as happened in 1788.

At other times it could be swollen to a roaring torrent, at its most violent overflowing banks and bursting dykes to flood fields and villages, leaving a trail of havoc and death, as it did in 1846, 1856, 1866 and 1910.

To assist helmsmen struggling in such conditions, ships were fitted with enormous rudders known as *plaustres* or *piautres*. This purely local word is an example of the Loire sailor's argot in which his stomacher was a *cadis*, the stern of his vessel its *coue*, his oar a *gache*, the blanket in which he rolled himself to sleep his *garriot*, and the leader in a train of barges the *mère* (mother).

The design of the vessels he sailed was essentially dictated by the river's character and a shipbuilding industry grew up to meet it. From its stocks came the most typical craft: the *gabarres*, up to about 90 ft (28 metres) in length and usually powered by a single sail, and the *toues*, lighters from 30 to 70 ft (9 to 21 metres), which they towed behind them.

Sail was not the only form of motive power, for many vessels were hauled along towpaths, some of which can still be found, by horses, teams of oxen or sheer human effort. Examples of the harnesses of leather or webbing which were attached to tow-ropes for the purpose can still be seen in local museums.

The variety of goods carried was enormous. Timber and coal from Forez, pottery from Nevers, cereals from the Beauce, fruit and vegetables from the Orléans region, wines from Anjou and Touraine. Fish was transported from the coast in vessels called *bascules* equipped with tanks, known as *huchets*, so that the cargo could be kept alive through the journey.

The availability of the river as a means of transport had led to the establishment of many local industries, as, for example, the forging of guns and anchors for the French navy at Cosne-sur-Loire. These were often conveyed by another unique Loire vessel, the *sapine*, little more than a raft of fir planks put together for a single voyage and dismantled at the end of it.

Even more rudimentary means were employed for transporting timber from the local forests. It reached its downstream destinations by the expedient of floating it on the current.

Shipbuilding gave rise to a whole range of ancillary activities: sail-lofts, ropewalks, chandleries supplying balers, oars and boathooks, often made on the premises, down to cottage industries turning out such things as nails. One important item was the *bâton*, in effect a punt-pole for pushing a vessel off a sandbank and in some circumstances even for propulsion.

It was not only goods that travelled by river. There was also its human freight and, from time to time, it would be enlivened by the tapestry-hung barges of a royal or an aristocratic progress.

Left, sailors with a cargo of salt. **Above**, sailors depicted in Cheverny tapestry.

It was thus that the dying Cardinal Richelieu was conveyed, lying on a litter, under a red damask tent. In 1481, when the inhabitants of Arras were expelled by Louis XI for rising against him, a train of barges carried the men, women and children sent by royal decree to repeople it.

From the late 17th century, regular "water coach" services provided an alternative form of public transport to the horse-drawn "mail coaches" on the roads. The vessels involved were, in practice, simply freight-barges with an improvised superstructure, called a *cabane* (literally, a hut), as shelter for the passengers.

To reach Nantes from Orléans could take about six days with a favourable wind, the return anything up to three weeks. It was, in any case, a hazardous journey, for the river could become unnavigable at any point along the route. The traveller would then have to reach his destination by road, a considerable inconvenience if he was encumbered with heavy baggage. There were, besides, a number of recorded accidents, some of them fatal.

However, it was the 1830s that saw what was perhaps the greatest revolution on the river: the coming of steamboats. The journey now took just two days, but a series of boiler explosions led to a loss of confidence not restored until the *Inexplosibles* were introduced in 1843.

Though more than 100,000 passengers were carried on the paddle-steamers which ran from Nantes to Moulins, they were to prove a passing phenomenon before a new threat: the railway. When the last Loire steamboat company closed down in 1862 it was part of a general decline of river transportation.

The arduous and costly labour of keeping the Loire clear for navigation ceased to be economic and was gradually abandoned. Depression settled on the once thriving port towns and was relieved only as new industrial developments helped to revive the region.

From time to time, some scheme to revive the Loire as a commercial highway is canvassed. None has so far gone beyond the discussion stage and, as the passage of each year makes the task of restoring it more difficult, it seems unlikely that any ever will.

65

"If the peasants could read and write, what would become of us?" exclaims a minor aristocrat in Balzac's *Les Paysans*. Such fears of peasant literacy were unfounded: in the 1850s, peasants were too busy battling with failed harvests, famine and bread riots to learn to read Balzac. Yet on the eve of World War I, literacy was still the preserve of the upper classes and the social order remained intact. Not far from the *Loire royale* and its noble châteaux lay an equally conservative landscape, one governed by the old agricultural calendar, community spirit and thriving rural crafts.

Balzac's bourgeois novel portrays the peasants as sullen, thrusting and brutish or, at best, purveyors of cheap charm "concealing an incredible vanity". Paradoxically, the poet Alfred de Musset described the same peasants as "simple as their life, gentle as the air that they breathe, strong as the hardy soil that they fertilise". Most 19th-century accounts of peasant life, written by the uncomprehending upper classes, tend to be equally pejorative or idealised.

Outside the pages of romantic fiction, the "simple life" was rarely sentimental or simple. Aristocratic George Sand, steeped in the folklore of her beloved Berry, portrays the peasants as sensitive, dignified and uncorrupted, a brave miss. However, it is not until Zola's naturalistic fiction that a realistic view of village life takes root. More recently, the chronicles of Bernard Briais and Gérard Boutet offer a fresh view of village life straight from the peasant's mouth.

This account is largely based on three ordinary villages from the turn of the century to the present day, individual yet representative voices. Pontlevoy, a large village north of Montrichard, has benefited from its proximity to a rich wine and grain growing region near the River Cher. By contrast, Josnes, situated on the bleak Beauce plains, has been in decline since 1918. Most young people have left the hamlet for the comforts of nearby Beaugency. Chédigny, a small village on a lush stretch of the River Indrois, is ploughing a lonely furrow, revitalising dying local crafts. However, the encouraging result is a resurgence of community spirit and the beginnings of low-key tourism.

At the turn of the century, villages such as Chédigny were lit by gas lamps. Communal fountains, pumps and wells were widespread until mains drainage, sanitation and electricity finally reached the countryside in the 1950s. Jean-Marie Rougé describes his farm in the early 1900s as "low, squat, squashed

under a roof of old tiles; a stable to the left; a sheep pen to the right; in front, a sloping farmyard leads to a pond where horses and cows come to drink".

In the farmhouses, *paysans* made do with oil lamps or even candles. Inside the whitewashed living room were stone or wooden benches, a walnut table and a few wicker chairs. Cooking was done over the fireplace, hung with heavy copper pots. The master bedroom contained a rustic wardrobe, a dressing table or chest and, by the bed, a chamber pot and perhaps a crucifix blessed on Palm Sunday. So far, so typical.

At the turn of the century, market day

Preceding pages: village festival portrayed in Ussé tapestry. **Left**, Loire Valley farmer. **Above**, Bourgeuil pig market.

presented a clear dress rehearsal of the rural social order. The village notables, including the schoolmaster and local gentry, wore *tenue de ville*, or town clothes, completed by a black top hat for men and an equally grand hat for women. Millers and farmers wore felt hats, blue cotton shirts, a kerchief, trousers and clogs. Craftsmen and farmers with pretensions favoured waistcoats and suits fastened with copper buttons.

Matrons wore black capes, shawls and long, dark skirts. Elderly women, out of respect for the dead, were always dressed in mourning. All but the youngest women wore embroidered cotton bonnets, especially in Sologne and Berry. Easter and All Saints'

deals were struck with great politeness, often with an agreement to pay half then and half at the next market or fair. After the *dernier prix* was agreed, the deal was sealed with a glass of wine."

Before World War I, Josnes had 40 farms, 19 family businesses, seven cafés and six grocers. Apart from the market gardener and greengrocer, the artisans ranged from barrelmakers, masons and cabinet makers to seamstresses, laundresses and weavers. In addition, there was a rabbit-skinner, a woodcutter, a herring seller and a woman whose sole function was to repair umbrellas.

Apart from the resident craftsmen and agricultural workers, the villagers were visi-

Day marked the seasonal change of wardrobe: for the preceding weeks, women sewed frantically to replace woollen corsets with light cotton ones.

After the 1950s, clogs were replaced by shoes, at least on market day, and jackets, corduroys and caps were worn by most agricultural workers. However, there have always been regional variants in costume. André Renard, a retired farmer, remembers market day at Loches: "Butchers and tradesmen dressed in black shirts, peasants in blue and smartly dressed farmers jogged from one beast to another. Despite the apparent confusion, everyone knew his place and

ted by a procession of supplicants. Pilgrims en route to Santiago de Compostella required board and lodging, whilst gypsies sold lace and read fortunes. Travelling salesmen tempted housewives with buttons, threads and, more originally, *noisettes*, condoms beautifully packaged in boxes decorated with holy images. In the autumn, little chimneysweeps from Savoy were given stale bread, cheese rind and a few sous for cleaning the chimneys. As a child, Pierre Couratier remembers giving sweets to one of these 10-year-old acrobats: sweets and payment were promptly pocketed by the accompanying taskmaster.

However, as Gérard Boutet says: "Before vehicles-without-horses paraded round the village, it was the arrival of the mail coach that caused the greatest commotion in the village." Until 1910, letters, parcels and occasionally animals were dumped unceremoniously in the middle of the village square in Josnes.

Variety of crafts: But these old crafts and trades were by no means exclusive to Josnes. Most Loire villages had a tradition of self-sufficiency until World War I and were therefore well provided with cabinet and clock makers, masons and millers, locksmiths and blacksmiths, barrel-makers and potters, basket weavers and waggoners.

humbler clogs. He measured everything by "a thumb's length" and, until the invention of rubber soles made his trade obsolete, he would sit outside his workshop shaping and preparing the wood while nibbling on chestnuts and galettes.

Although most Val de Loire clogs are now museum pieces adorning second homes, several other old crafts survive, passed on from father to son. Monsieur Raboulet in Meung-sur-Loire represents the fifth generation of cabinet makers. His heavy, old-fashioned furniture is finely carved in rustic style. In the 1950s, poverty caused the peasant to use such 18th-century sideboards as rabbit cages. More recently, however, tradi-

Monsieur Roux, the last waggoner in Sologne, died only recently. Basket weaving, described by Balzac in *Le Lys dans la Vallée*, is still carried out in Villaines-les-Rochers, near Amboise. There, a hundred craftsmen sort, strip and soak the wood in scenes unchanged since the 19th century.

Henri Dedun, son of the last clog maker in Sologne, remembers how his father used to polish clogs with bees' wax, attach leather uppers to the more stylish clogs and, in later years, used bits of old tyres as soles on

Left, doing the laundry at the well. **Above**, woodcut of family quarrel.

tional rustic furniture has been sacrificed in the name of modernity.

Most peasants have sold their family heirlooms to local junk shops in exchange for quick cash, glass cabinets, melamine tables and fitted kitchens. As a result, exposed beams, Louis Philippe chairs, walnut tables, Louis XV dressers, bread ovens and dough chests are now more common in bourgeois conversions.

Unlike the sentimental upper classes, the peasants have been only too eager to rid their homes of domestic clutter. In peasant philosophy, convenience outweighs good taste. Likewise consigned to memory are the dank workshops, filled with the faint odours of spilt paraffin, mouldy apples or left-over sour herring.

Although the old crafts and trades were important spokes on the wheel, the hub was agriculture. While the Loire is traditionally associated with magnificent châteaux and royal estates, the grand lifestyle was subsidised by revenues from rich agricultural land. The economy was also fuelled by the efforts of the *petits gens*, commonly known as peasants.

However, the term *paysans* fails to do justice to the range of complex tasks performed. While unskilled labourers were imported from Belgium, Poitou or Brittany

to handle the harvests, most native labour was highly skilled, if poorly paid, until the 1960s.

The rivalry between *vignerons* (wine-growers on the slopes) and *varenniers* (agricultural workers in the valleys) did not die out with the new century. The valley-dwellers were bitter that land planted with vines was worth twice as much as arable land.

The wine-growers resented their restricted access to communal land by the rivers and demanded the right to cut down the rushes needed for making wine paniers. Partly as a result of this simmering feud, the two sides went their separate ways long

before mechanisation in the 1940s redressed the balance in favour of arable farming. The wine-growers had a reputation for being less religious and more sophisticated than the average valley-dwellers. Moreover, from the Revolution to modern times, they have been protected by favourable laws and strong *confraternités*, or wine guilds. The wine-growing calendar has changed little since medieval times and is traditionally linked to saints' days. At the feast of St Vincent, the wine presses are prepared; at St-Hubert, the vats, barrels and baskets are prepared; and at Toussaint (All Saints'), the harvest usually begins.

Until 1918, only the finest wines were bottled and so the role of the barrel-maker was paramount while, as late as the 1950s, families on horses and carts trundled out to the vineyards to collect the grapes piled high in wicker baskets. Even now, wine-making is often a family business and helpful neighbours are still rewarded with sweet wine and grilled chestnuts. Whereas additional grape-pickers used to be housed uncomfortably in troglodyte caves, most are now accommodated on local farms. A successful harvest is still as much a relief as it was when Rabelais cried: "*Adieu paniers, vendages sont faites.*"

Fog and frost: Early this century, farming adhered to the agricultural calendar. Passed from generation to generation, it is a mixture of common sense and experience, shot through with superstition. Faded frescoes in the church at Lignières depict the seasonal occupations which prevailed until recently. January and February were spent hunting wild fowl and collecting firewood. March meant the sowing of sugar beet, alfalfa, barley, hay and wheat, in that order. April entailed the planting of young *cèpes*; all with due regard to local lore: for example, "Thunder in March means frost in April", while "Fog in April means frost in May".

May and June were spent watching over the crops and tending the sheep. Haymaking and sheep-shearing took place just before the feast of John the Baptist in late June. July and August were devoted to binding and cutting vines and harvesting the crops. Bad weather caused confusion: to some, "a thundery July means a tough winter" while to others "*Juillet sans orage, famine au village*" (July without storms means famine in the village).

Both the wine harvest and nutting took

place in October and November but there was gloom if the chestnuts and walnuts ripened early: "*Septembre de noix, hiver froid*". November was a favourable time to plant saplings because "*A la sainte Catherine, tout arbre prend racine*". December brought early spring cleaning and pig-killing, thus providing the household with a year's supply of tasty *rillons*.

In Pontlevoy, farm animals were a major concern. The pigs, however, were little trouble—although, as the locals said, "Pigs are like poets—you only appreciate them after their death". Death came at the beginning and end of winter and provided posthumous pleasure and amusement: the head was

stopped at all the bistros and later took their inebriated owners the long way home.

The feudal share-cropping system (*métayage*) died out early this century but while it lasted, tenant farmers had to sacrifice 50 percent of their crops to the landowner. The farmer's wife also had to supply the landowner with his daily needs and offer his family wine, milk or rabbit stew whenever they called. Mechanisation and the ending of the *métayage* transformed the rural picture. However, as late as the 1950s, photographs show harvesting carried out by hand: in one, like a scene painted by Millet, a peasant in clogs stands, head bowed, amidst a field of harvested hay. Before World War I, saffron,

the greatest possible delicacy while the corkscrew tail was used as a child's toy before ending its days greasing peasants' scythes.

The sheep lived outdoors for only four months of the year, protected by a shepherd "poor in money but rich in spirit". The shepherd, supplied with a flask of brandy to keep out the cold, slept on a bale of straw or in a tiny rolling cabin. He kept an eye out for sheep rustlers rather than the proverbial wolf. Well-trained horses, affectionately named Bijou, Mouton or Ami, automatically

Left, sowing seeds today. **Above**, 14th-century illuminated manuscript of the peasant's year.

linen and flax were grown as well as cereals. The chronicler Prevost describes a dreamy saffron harvest at the turn of the century: children and adults danced around a glowing hill of flowers and at midnight toasted "*ces automnes-là*". In the 1920s, dairies were formed and the striking Charollais and Nevers cows were gradually replaced with higher milk-yielding varieties, first Normans and then Frisians. At the same time, the creation of an artificial insemination plant at Joué-les-Tours did away with the jollity surrounding the siring ritual.

Further mechanisation, in the form of primitive combine harvesters, finally arrived in the 1930s, bringing to a close methods of harvesting little changed since medieval times. In the 1950s, government subsidies, fixed prices for crops and the use of chemicals made farming less labour-intensive. The peasants' life was also transformed by the arrival of running water and electricity: candles, oil lamps and wells gradually became an image of harder times.

Before mechanisation took hold, haymaking and harvesting were highly skilled crafts, involving experienced cutters, gatherers, binders, threshers and haystack-makers. Scything was a male art and experienced workers could cut half a hectare before the church bells chimed the angelus, a signal for

The day often ended with a competition to see who could hold aloft the greatest number of sheaves on the end of a pitchfork.

At harvest time, the *curé* was given the last sheaf of corn, left at the church door. Inside, a harvest supper took place, an unusual event in France but still carried on in the Beauce region. The yearly harvest celebration was the closest most peasants got to summer leisure. After feasting on stew, rabbit casserole, goat's cheese and plum tarts, the energetic youngsters amused themselves by running barefoot on the rough sheaves while their elders played cards, sang, told stories and drank *marc*, pure white spirit. The exhausted and inebriated collapsed in the sheep

lunch. Near Josnes, hay-makers were in the fields before 4 a.m. and had nothing but their *fromagée*, usually a few *rillettes*, until midday. The arrival of potato cakes and a litre of wine per worker made the afternoon pass more quickly but men were only allowed to stop every 500 metres to sharpen their blades. The gatherers were usually seamstresses and laundry women who closed their workshops in summer to help with the harvest. Haystack making, often performed by local builders, was a skilled task: the builder masterminded the construction of a vast mushroom shape which was then bound with a metal ring and weighted with stones.

sheds, then full of wheat. Camille Aubard recalls harvest time at La Chatre in 1911. On that day, Halley's Comet was supposed to presage the end of the world. In the fields, all talk was of *le dernier jour*, apparently foreshadowed by a sky full of dark clouds. To keep their spirits high, harvesters were singing rousing renditions of *Le Moulin de Monsieur Jean* when a huge noise made everyone believe the end was nigh. "But instead of God's band of angels coming to judge the villagers of Neuvy-St-Sulpice, it was only a riotous boar hunt."

Nonetheless, lively harvests are still within living memory: any country person over the age of 30 remembers the noise and mystique of the Merlin, the new-fangled mechanical threshing machine, powered by a traction engine. Jeanine Berducet remembers the colourful harvests in the Berry of 40 years ago: after dancing to the sound of violins and bagpipes, the peasants ate fruit galettes and drank plum *eau de vie* until work began again at 5 a.m. But more than 80 years separate us from a classic harvest photo in the Pontlevoy photographic exhibition: the humble thresher carrying a wooden flail could not be further removed from today's EC-subsidised farmer, in a black moleskin jacket, posed against his landrover.

Except at harvest time, women rarely

lit with pine kernels and thistles, was filled with loaves, galettes, terrines, pâtés, peas drenched in wine, and even potatoes, known as "poor man's bread". Pears, plums and apples were dried in the oven, then flattened and hung along the sloping roof and porches. Known as "cat's ears", the fruit was later soaked and cooked in winter, if passing children hadn't stolen the tastiest portions first.

Dirty washing: By contrast with such self-sufficiency, laundry days required joint action. In Josnes, the monthly laundry was in the farm's steam boiler while the twice-yearly heavy wash was a communal task. The infrequency of washing meant that most trousseaux consisted almost exclusively of

worked in the fields: they had to be self-sufficient, organising the laundry, bread and butter-making and fruit preservation.

Until 1920, home baking in Chédigny took place every eight days but never between Christmas and St Sylvestre, thought to be unlucky. At dawn, the yeast, in reality just a ball of old dough, was fetched from the bottom steps of the cellar. After mixing it with fresh flour and honey, the dough was made into shapes and put under a warm eiderdown to make it rise quickly. The oven,

Left, traditional haymaking. **Above**, grape harvest in Touraine.

sheets while drawers and chests remained full of dirty washing for months.

At Easter and in the autumn, the women heaped all their washing together and gathered with washing soda and three months' supply of cinders. The sacks of cinders were put in the bottom of a vast copper cauldron and the clothes were continually passed between the cauldron and a steam boiler. At the end of the day, the washing was rinsed in the village pond or wash house and spread on the grass to dry.

While scrubbing and beating the washing, the women often sang. One favourite concerned a shepherdess and her would-be swain. After pestering her with such questions as "Whose are the sheep?" and "Is the pond deep?", he says "Aren't you afraid of the wolf?" and is answered sharply, "Less than I am of you". In another song, a girl falls into a fountain and is accosted by three passing lads who ask, "What will you give us, beauty, if we save you?" "Just pull me out, sirs, and you'll find out" is her cunning reply. She rejects their amorous advances on the grounds that she is promised to a broth-drinking boy from Chinon, "*un garçon de Chinon qui boit bien le bouillon*".

After the washing was taken in, it was time to prepare food, a subject never far from the women's minds. The Val de Loire was un-

Special occasions had their own rituals and foods: Mardi Gras was celebrated with crêpes in Anjou and Touraine while Sologne and Berry, following southern custom, preferred doughnuts. The end of harvest was feted with the traditional *beurlot*, a feast of goose followed by a barn dance. The eleventh of November was given over to wine-tasting: "*A la St Martin, on goute le vin*". Fairs were dedicated to the local crop, from saffron to wine or melons. Several such fairs still exist, including the Foire aux Prunes at Preuilly and the celebration of garlic and basil at the Foire a l'Ail et au Basilic in Tours. Less formal food rituals include the insulting of "immoral" girls by placing a

usual in favouring four meals a day in summer. Breakfast was usually a milky meat broth, supplemented at harvest by hearty helpings of stew. Lunch, brought out to the fields by the farmer's daughter, consisted of *rillons*, potato cakes, cheese and a litre of wine per person. Before a storm, peasants in the fields would fortify themselves with *miot*, pieces of bread soaked in wine. *Collation*, or tea, was bread and cheese eaten on the hoof. Supper was usually a vegetable stew or, in poorer households, cabbage or bread soup. Dried plums, jams and cakes were delicacies reserved for special occasions such as weddings.

crate of leeks by their front door. Food and country lore make for a rich mixed stew. According to popular belief, drinking milk in May made one wealthy while a flea bite in June promised good wine. The pear and apple harvests signalled the season of serious drinking: "*Après la poire, il faut boire*" and "*Après la pomme, vide ton verre, bonhomme.*"

Life on the farm was never too fraught to exclude courtesy. Until the late 1950s, even slight acquaintances were invited to "come and have a bite to eat with us" (*V'allez bien manger un morceau avec nous*). The farmer's wife, addressed as *la maîtresse*, would offer a plate of bread to the guest while *le maître*, her husband, fetched a *pichet* of wine. The toast "*A vot' bonne santé*" is a reminder that the countryside used a version of old French unchanged since Rabelais' time.

But behind the festive bonhomie lay a complex pattern of social rituals and relationships bound by conventions. Courtship, marriage or pregnancy were frowned upon during the busiest times in the agricultural calendar. Courtship, in particular, was generally restricted to March, May and September, relatively quiet months. However, if March coincided with Lent, relationships could be fraught because "When you make

tation and provided material ripe for cautionary tales. While an attractive girl was called *chouette*, unattractive ones were likened to *bringues*, castrated bulls.

Marriage was only sanctioned if neither libidinous pleasures nor pregnancy disrupted the 50-day season of haymaking and harvest. Gentle match-making often took place amongst relatives to ensure material advantages to both parties, the arrangement Briais calls "the marriage of so many acres to so many acres". In St-Maure, marriageable girls were taken to an auspicious menhir to place a bunch of lucky flowers and to swear to marry the family's choice, provided the groom was "neither hunchback nor lame".

love in Lent, there's nothing left for Easter". There was considerable social pressure on girls to marry young and to marry quickly but never during May, out of respect to the Virgin's birth.

Girls of easy virtue were held up to ridicule in Chédigny, with the placing of a bale of straw by their front door. In Josnes, flirtatious girls were warned that they would end up as hostesses in the infamous Moulin Rouge club in Beaugency. In Pontlevoy, shepherdesses had a particularly loose repu-

Left, a farm kitchen at St Fargeau. **Above**, traditional *sabots*.

Wedding breakfast: At the turn of the century, wedding rituals included the decoration of the bride's door with pine branches and a procession to the church door, the bride on a white horse led by the miller. Guests usually danced to accordion music but violins and bagpipes gradually became more popular. The wedding breakfast tradition is unique to this region: close relatives brought the newly weds a fricassée, a nourishing broth enriched with red wine.

Before 1918, guests still brought flour and butter as their contribution to the wedding feast. Symbolically, knives were never given as gifts in case the fragile bond between the couple was broken. This remains a custom today, as does the placing of a garter on the bride's leg, delivered with the words "*Honi soit qui mal y pense*".

Once a child was born, if the mother had no milk, she appealed to St Agatha, patron saint of wetnurses. Until World War I, rural schools were shut in key seasons so that children could help in the fields. Although the school-leaving age was 13, many young girls had already gone into service by then, just as boys had left to become junior cowhands, often hired at the spring fairs.

Health was a major preoccupation, often linked to herbal remedies and superstitions. In Sologne, hawthorn is still placed on farm

compost heaps to scare away both vipers and bad luck. Crushed buttercups were thought to heal cuts, while wounds licked by a goat reputedly healed better. Rye bread was eaten to relieve constipation; tired feet were soothed in mustard oil; and ears were pierced to protect against eye-strain. As an alternative to the proverbial knitting needle horror stories, abortions were performed with long stalks of parsley. The success rate is not recorded. When cures were unknown, the peasants found comfort in illness: stings from white nettles were said to improve the circulation while rheumatism was a sign of longevity. If all else failed, there was always

a proverb at hand, such as "*Araignée du matin, chagrin, araignée du soir, espoir*" (A spider in the morning means sorrow while a spider at night means hope).

Death was quickly communicated by the church bells which chimed different times according to the sex and age of the deceased. A married man was buried in his wedding jacket while a wife was buried in her wedding garland of faded orange blossom.

Drink and dancing: In a rural society unused to leisure, festivals provided light relief. January celebrated St Vincent, patron saint of *vignerons*, with a procession of the wine *confraternities* to cellars full of wine. In June, St Jean is still celebrated with cider and dances around the fire, especially in Sologne and Berry. At New Year, children in the Beauce were given doughnuts and sugared almonds and wished kind adults "Happy New Year, good health and paradise at the end of your days". Ungenerous adults were wished "a bullet in the neck, an arrow in the stomach and strangulation by the Devil".

Leisure, as such, was rarely unadulterated pleasure but linked to hunting, fishing and handicrafts. The old *veillées*, or gatherings, had virtually died out by the turn of the century. Then the peasants met, often in troglodyte caves, to play cards, gossip, eat roasted chestnuts and drink *bernache*, bitter new wine. Women brought along braziers and concealed them under their long skirts, often to choruses of suggestive comments. In summer, peasants were too tired to do much except sleep and occasionally read the provincial newspaper, *Conseillier des Campagnes*, shared amongst several households.

For males, leisure was generally linked to hunting and fishing. Salmon, bream and pike were fished in the Loire; carp and tench in lakes; roach in the Indre; and shrimps in brooks. Although most peasants owned guns, few could afford cartridges or shooting permits, so hunting was generally restricted to birds, snails and mushroom foraging. In the autumn, mild, dry weather brought out partridges, woodcock, field ducks and quails, all fair game for the cunning peasants.

But the most accessible sport was illegal lark hunting: marauding boys used torches, mirrors, decoys and nets to catch the gullible larks. If caught themselves by mounted police, the culprits were fined or sentenced to eight days in prison. But the deterrent only sharpened the appetite for the chase. The birds were later eaten with lard or in a sugar beet and turnip stew. Few boys came back empty-handed: even a handful of thrushes or crows made a tolerable broth.

For both men and women, social life centred on the market. Elderly residents in Pontlevoy can still recall the traditional Wednesday markets of their youth. The more astute villagers bought their produce from the cheaper market at Contres and then resold it here. At the foot of the old Charles VII tower, black-clad matrons arranged slabs of butter on large cabbage leaves and, as the sun changed position, the complaining women moved to a different spot with their

live rabbits and the rabbit skinner, an odd character who always arrived with a small cart pulled by a large dog.

Madame Maillard, her hand-cart laden with mushrooms from neighbouring Montrichard, often made the return journey with a cart full of goods intended for resale in Bourré. The load included asparagus, apples, pears, dead chickens and over-excited rabbits.

On the surface, Pontlevoy is still a prosperous community today but lacks colour and sociability. However, these erstwhile peasants, in conjunction with their friends in Montrichard, are as gregarious a community as any in the Val de Loire. Apart from clubs

melting butter. Labourers drank *chopines* in the Café du Commerce and laughed at Madame Gaillard from St-Aignan, pulled along by her lolloping pig. Processions of bleating goats were led along Rue de la Sibérie to the market while goat's cheese was sold in plantain leaves in Rue de Chevrière.

Live rabbits often arrived in high-tiered baskets while others were towed several kilometres on long pieces of string. There was little love lost between the owners of

Left, ducklings for sale in Loudon. **Above**, farm life today.

for *boules*, tarot, dog-hunting and fishing, there is the *Association du Twirling Danse* and the *Amitié-loisirs Troisième Age* for the elderly. Controversy is also just under the surface as the *Secours Catholique* and the secular *Foyer Laique Populaire* fight for the elusive Pontlevoy soul.

By contrast, Josnes today is a shrinking hamlet with a dozen farms, numerous neglected holiday homes, two grocers and one café. Gérard Boutet berates his place of birth as "a characterless, straggling village, its shutters closed as a mark of mourning for a dying way of life". Boutet, from peasant stock himself, complains that villagers have sealed up bread ovens and even sold their homes to Parisians in search of a weekend cottage. Boutet's family naturally cherished its *patrimoine* of Second Empire clocks and walnut wood cabinets. His books are an elegy to a dying way of life in rural France.

Between the two extremes lies Chédigny, a thriving village that preserves its heritage in an experimental way. Pierre Louault, the youngish mayor, claims that his first priority is to "present a common front and to stop the flight from the land". He took over a *Clochemerle* situation with a village "divided between elderly church-goers and young radicals" and has united the warring factions by reviving traditional craft indus-

tries, promoting modern agricultural methods and fostering local pride.

The mayor rightly says that Chédigny is an ordinary village, not a prettified adjunct to a major château. It is symptomatic of this frank attitude that Chédigny's spectacular *son et lumière* aims to portray the life of the peasants during the Revolution, incorporating the whole village as actors. Community spirit is also noticeable in protective attitudes to local buildings. The Moulin des Foulons, an old water mill, still keeps turning, for no better reason than as a reminder of its once pivotal role in village life. As the name suggests, the mill was once used in the

weaving process. The villagers know that if the wheel is allowed to dry up, it quickly disintegrates. This sums up their attitude to community spirit, too.

What the Val de Loire villages have in common is a divide between the "authentic" breed of peasants and their more prosperous successors. The new breed of peasant runs a fully mechanised farm and uses European Community grants to produce pâté de foie gras and *biologique* bread and wine. Several farms in Vendôme even go so far as to invite tourists to sample a sanitised version of village life. By contrast, the dying breed of peasant is typically anti-waste and never "burns" a light unnecessarily.

Civic duties: Elderly Berrichons, Marie and Serge, still live without a television set, cooker, fridge or central heating. The only sign of progress is a rusty scooter Serge uses to "go and buy tobacco, drink a glass of wine in the village, attend friends' funerals, or to vote". A good peasant is conscious of his civic duties. If you compliment Serge on his tomatoes, he is modestly dismissive, *"Rien de tout ça"* (nothing to it). On summer evenings, the couple sit on their porch and watch the glow worms for entertainment.

Armand Girard, a witty 74-year-old Solognot, presents the reverse side of this glowing portrait of the simple life. An agricultural labourer and wood-cutter all his life, Armand regrets never having married, "but I could never get a girl to live in this wilderness with me". He would like to have had a successor but believes that "a peasant in Sologne lives on thorns—a young person has to borrow too much to start up".

"The rabbit that runs fast loses its memory," claims an old Tourangeau expression. Fortunately, the inhabitants of the Val de Loire are in no danger of forgetting, particularly as so many village traditions are still rooted in the soil. The French are fanatical about their roots and the rediscovery of their rural past, often within living memory. There is inverse snobbery at work in the tracing of a great-grandfather who was a miller, clog maker or rabbit skinner, or of a grandmother who did the washing in the communal wash house and who made traps to catch larks.

Left, ploughing a new furrow. **Above**, displaying a good catch.

Long before the railway had reached the Loire Valley, Count Pierre Bruno Daru, a writer and henchman of Napoleon, declared: "Orléans is becoming a suburb of Paris!" In the autumn of 1989, the TGV-Atlantique— a 180-mph rail express headed for Brest, Quimper, Le Croisic, La Rochelle, Dax, Tarbes and Toulouse—began its first services from Paris, radically cutting journey times to the Loire region and bringing the area even closer to the metropolis.

Le Mans can now be reached from Paris in 54 minutes, Angers in 90. The opening of the second stage in late 1990 placed Vendôme just an hour away from the capital city, with Tours and Poitiers under 90 minutes. France's first TGV line, from Paris to Lyons, has boosted property prices in all the regions it serves, as metropolitans have raced to buy *residences secondaires* (for weekends and vacations), which suddenly fall within two or three hours of the capital. Even more so in the Loire, which was never physically far from Paris, will the lovely countryside and quaint towns come within commuting distance of the centre. Northwestern France is undergoing the biggest influx of the British property-owning classes since the time of the Plantagenets, and now the Loire seems set to be the new playground of weekending Parisians. "The Loire is definitely the place to be buying," says one acquisitive Parisienne. "It's real countryside, but you can get home easily on Sunday evening."

Quick delivery. But the change is important for the people of the area, too. An executive at one Paris communications company makes the point: "We can seriously consider dealing with an enterprise in Angers when we know that time-sensitive material can make the round trip between the two towns in half a day. In fact, we are probably going to do just that, whereas previously we would not have been comfortable working beyond the immediate Paris suburbs."

In a region too close to the centre to permit efficient air traffic (while the rest of the country has been placed within an hour-and-a-half of Paris by the development of regional airlines and airports), the economic benefit of the TGV is bound to follow.

With the decline in commercial use of the waterways in the mid-19th century and the later levelling-off of the agricultural revolution, the Loire region has often watched while the economic progress arriving elsewhere in France passed it by. Indeed, to talk about economic developments in the modern Loire region by reference to its rich, full

history is only natural: for today's Loire seems as much to live by its history than by anything else.

Since the collapse of the Fourth Republic in 1958, French government policy, for all the country's still powerful traditions of centralism, has been aggressively directed towards the regions. New industrial, manufacturing and economic centres have been created across the country, and decision-making spread out from the centre as power was devolved from the capital. But the Loire, that "suburb" of the metropolis, has benefited much less from these moves than more distant parts of the "Hexagon" (as the French

Preceding pages: birthday celebrations at Valle de Courtineau. **Left,** the Loire at peace. **Above,** nuclear power station at Dampierre-en-Burly.

call their large, diffuse country.) Toulouse, Montpellier, Strasbourg, Grenoble, the Languedoc—these have been the towns and regions associated with French economic resurgence in the one-third of a century since General Charles de Gaulle's return in 1958, to shape and head the new Fifth Republic. The new France, pushed through by de Gaulle with the exceptional powers he demanded as a condition of rescuing the country, was committed to growth, revitalisation and regionalism.

But the Loire, half rural community, half historical relic, was during this dynamic period far from the cutting edge of the new France. The area has not been entirely

de la Loire, at over 80 inhabitants per sq. km, is not far from the national average of 100, the 2 million inhabitants of the Centre are spread over nearly 15,000 sq. miles (40,000 sq. km) for a density of less than 60. Of 1,841 communes in the six *départements* of the Centre region, nearly 1,600 have populations of less than 1,500: just nine towns have more than 30,000 inhabitants.

Royal heartland: Politically, the western part tends towards conservatism, particularly in the Maine-et-Loire and the Vendée, the heartland of patriotic, anti-Revolutionary France. It is the heartland, too, of royal France, lopped off by the Revolution, but still resonant in such place names as Orléans,

sleepy, particularly in the far west: in the Pays de la Loire region, comprising the five *départements* between Nantes on the Atlantic coast and Le Mans, one third of the working population is either in the garment trade or in electrical and electronic manufacture.

Le Mans itself has become the insurance capital of France and home to the headquarters of many leading companies. But, to the east, large parts—though not all—of the Centre region, taking in the Loire heartlands stretching from Normandy in the north to the Auvergne in the south, and touching Burgundy in the east, are as quiet and rural as ever. Whereas population density in the Pays

Anjou and Chartres, seats of royalty since the Middle Ages. It is in this region that Louis Alphonse, Duke of Anjou and Bourbon was, in 1989, aged 16, proclaimed Louis XX, rightful heir to the throne.

Louis XX came to his inheritance, such as it is, on the death, in a skiing accident, of his father Alphonse II, the Duke of Anjou and Cadiz. Louis' branch of the family claims as close relatives Juan Carlos (King of Spain), Jean (Grand Duke of Luxembourg, Duke of Nassau, Prince of Bourbon and Parma, Count Palatine of the Rhine and much, much more) and Prince Louis-Gaston (of Orléans and Braganza, head of the Brazilian imperial family—which abdicated in 1889). Indeed, family members with direct experience of autocracy are running thin: cousin Zita of Bourbon-Parma (last Empress of Austria and Queen of Hungary) died in Switzerland in 1989, just short of her 97th birthday.

Obviously, royalists do not stand in elections, so their popular support is difficult to gauge. But they may have been comforted by the fact that Maine-et-Loire was the only *département* among the eleven which comprise the Pays de la Loire and Centre regions to vote, albeit narrowly, for the conservative Jacques Chirac against the socialist François Mitterrand in the May 1988 presidential elections. Further away from the history

regional and national, to boost rural employment and country businesses ranging from farming and viticulture to tourism and craft industries. The most spectacular—and internationally recognised—success has come in the wine industry. It is easy to forget that at the end of the war Muscadet, the staple today of every dining-table and oyster bar, was ranked as a mere white table wine. Now, around 30 million bottles a year are produced in the Pays Nantais near the Atlantic, the best at Sèvre-et-Maine to the east of Nantes, named after two Loire tributaries.

Along a strip 175 miles wide and 50 miles long (280 by 80 km), from Nantes to Pouilly-sur-Loire, some 270 million bottles of *appel-*

trail, towards the southeast of the region, the left has greater strength, dominating the centre-right in the Indre-et-Loire and Indre *départements*. However, the overall political complexion of the region tends to reflect the national picture, and, even when one party seems entrenched, the margins of electoral victory are not great. Political differences in France are serious, but consensus tends to exist in key areas, such as the determination to support the Loire's mainly non-urban population by concerted campaigns, both

Left, spring-time sowing. **Above**, protest against the Loire dam project.

lation contrôlée wine—white, red and rosé, sweet and dry, still and sparkling—plus an estimated 120 million bottles of VDQS and table wine are produced each year from more than 130,000 acres (53,000 hectares) of land under vines. Loire-Atlantique, the Muscadet *département*, has 50,000 acres (20,000 hectares) of vineyards, but the neighbouring Maine-et-Loire, home to Anjou and Saumur wine, has even more—closer to 53,000 acres (22,000 hectares)—and produces nearly 50 million bottles of wine a year.

Further east, Indre-et-Loire and Loir-et-Cher have together almost 60,000 acres (24,000 hectares) of vines, producing some

19 million bottles a year of such *appellation contrôlée* wines as Bourgeuil, St Nicolas de Bourgeuil, Chinon, Vouvray, Montlouis and Touraine, additionally making the VDQS Cheverny wines.

More famous wines are produced in smaller quantities. In the Cher *département*, the extreme east of the wine-making strip, around 750 acres (300 hectares) of land are under vines, producing around 10 million bottles a year of Sancerre and just over a million of Pouilly-Fumé, as well as Pouilly-sur-Loire and VDQS Côteaux de Giennois.

The total wine output of the Loire winemakers is certainly substantial: the region ranks fifth in annual volume production,

behind Bordeaux, the Languedoc-Roussillon, Burgundy (including Beaujolais) and the Côtes-du-Rhône, and ahead of Champagne and Alsace.

Nevertheless, the Loire's *appellation contrôlée* output is only just over one-third of the immense production (three-quarters of a billion bottles annually) of Bordeaux, and wine yields per acre are relatively low, surpassing only Languedoc-Roussillon and the Rhône among the major producers. This smaller scale is reflected in the growers, too: unlike the Gironde, home to Bordeaux, a 50-acre (20-hectare) estate is rare in the Loire, while *domaines* a tenth of that size are com-

mon. Nevertheless, the success of Loire wines in the past quarter of a century has been huge, and continues to grow. Whereas once the region was mainly known, if at all, for its white wines, the reds have become much more commercial. Public demand for lighter reds, often served cool, has coincided with—and been fuelled by—the recent trend towards lighter food.

Today about 12 percent of the working population of the Pays de la Loire region are in the agricultural and food sectors. Those not working vines are in farming, raising cattle, pigs and fowl for the table, as well as vegetables and dairy produce. If the French Revolution gave land to the Loire peasantry, the modern upheavals in agricultural practice have had the effect of taking it away again. The traditional smallholdings of 12 acres (5 hectares) or less which used to characterise farming in the region have been eroded by competition and mechanisation—even when small farmers apparently invested in the future by buying modern equipment, they were frequently taking out credit for machinery which their farms subsequently could not pay for.

The flight from the land has been steady and irreversible. But its effects have not been wholly catastrophic since, for virtually the first time in the history of the region, there has been alternative employment available in those industrial firms which did choose the Loire as the place in which to diversify.

The traditions of winemaking and food production, together with the Loire's obvious scenic and historic attractions, have fed the growth of the tourist industry, which since the 1970s has received much financial support from regional government. In 1985, the Pays de la Loire granted 34 million francs in subsidies to tourism, concentrating on extending infrastructure (camping sites, gîtes and parks), as well as stimulating rural economic activity. The region will pay up to 35 percent of the cost of work on such projects. The direct tourism budget is not the sole source of support, however. In 1987, some 162 million francs were earmarked in the Pays de la Loire for "Quality of Life" programmes, which included 28 million francs for rural improvements.

In creating a tourist industry, the Loire has gained from its obvious strengths of scenery and history. But even these have been augmented by the region's relative economic decline. As elsewhere, enterprising blue-bloods have turned their family pile into places to visit and even stay in. This is not a specially new phenomenon: the 17th-century château at Cheverny—model for Captain Haddock's home in the Tintin books—was first opened to the public in 1920.

But the steady erosion of inherited wealth by inflation and the costs of keeping up old buildings has accelerated the determination of the remnants of the French aristocracy to maintain their mystical links with the seat of their ancestors, whatever socialists and Eurocrats may do to try and make it difficult.

The benefits of tourism in cash terms are

To make a good living in tourism, it helps not to be off the beaten track. This is more difficult than it seems, given the relatively small amounts of good roads in the area. Of about 75,000 miles (120,000 km) of road in the Centre region, around 200 miles (320 km) are autoroutes and 1,000 major Routes Nationales: the rest are lesser departmental and rural roads.

The major attractions tend to follow the major roads, such as the river-hugging N152 which passes from Orléans to Angers through Beaugency, Blois, Amboise, Tours and Saumur, or the other main château drag, the N76, from Tours to Bourges. This is the Loire's Bermuda Triangle, which sucks in

obvious: but they are hard won and not unalloyed. Intense competition between hotels keeps prices low; this is obviously good news for guests, but less so for hotel owners who have to ensure high occupancy rates over long periods to make their businesses viable. The extreme seasonal variations in tourism also hit hard, with a small number of fat months each year being required to sustain hotels and restaurants (not to mention the many shops dependent on tourism) through the lean.

Left, French postman. **Above**, Alexander Calder mobile sculpture at Saché.

tourists who, as far as the rest of the region's trade is concerned, are never to be seen again. "It's difficult to be off the main road," says François de Valbray of Château de Briottières, near Angers. "You don't get any passing trade—people have to seek you out, which means they have to have a good reason to know about you."

The economic fluctuations of the river itself, sharp and frequent since the 19th century, have also been influenced by the tourist trade. Despite the existence of 100 miles (160 km) of navigable waterways in the Centre region alone, pleasure-boat use is still matched by commercial activity. Commercial users of the waterways have begun to campaign for the integration of their river into the European navigable water system, which stretches from the English Channel to the Black Sea but has no connections to the Loire region. But until the navigable part of the river actually goes somewhere, it will inevitably be relegated, almost literally, to a backwater. The river remains part of the scenic heart of the region, with its wide curves and low, silty waters flowing from ancient château to historic town. But the Loire is also treacherous, given on occasions to bursting its banks and flooding the low-lying surrounding countryside. For years, successive national and regional administra-

came, should be allowed to take its course. However, nature is harnessed, not un-leashed, in at least one way: three nuclear power stations, their cooling towers, accord-ing to Norbert Wach, a historian of the Orléans region, "crushing by their gigantic-ism those of the Renaissance châteaux", have been built at Saint-Laurent-des-Eaux, Dampierre-en-Burly and Belleville.

Local resentment stems not only from en-vironmental fears, although these are clearly expressed: "The flora and fauna of the Loire risk being injured by a rise in water tempera-ture [caused by the nuclear stations]," says Norbert Wach. But even more, there is re-sentment that the stations create relatively

tions have proposed a solution: the construc-tion of dams far beyond the valley, near the Loire's source. But after considerable pro-test it now seems that these long-standing proposals have been firmly blocked.

Nuclear power: Despite extensive damage caused by the admittedly infrequent flood-ing, a long and widespread campaign, based on the likely environmental impacts of the proposed dams on wildlife, succeeded in winning widespread support, even among those who had suffered from past floods. A population which, despite two centuries of modernisation and luring from its roots, decided that nature, in whatever form it

few jobs and the power they produce is mostly sucked up by the 10 million consum-ers of the Paris region.

Each day, even before the arrival of the TGV, more than 40,000 people made the round trip between Orléans and Paris. Now these still-growing links between the region and the centre present a challenge to the residents of the Loire: how to exploit its proximity to the capital and still preserve the traditional qualities and beautiful landscape which make the area so attractive.

<u>**Above**</u>, **Orléans street café.** <u>**Right**</u>, **Monsieur and Madame de Valbray.**

THE CHATELAIN

François de Valbray and his wife Hedwige are contemporary châtelains—professional hosts who walk a tightrope between leading their own lives and having their home overrun by strangers. Their home, Château de Briottières, a few miles north of Angers at Champigné, is everything châteaux are meant to be: so much so that it was chosen to represent this uniquely French style of idyll in *Impromptu*, a Warner Brothers movie about Chopin, Liszt and George Sand.

Château de Briottières is a large, spacious 18th-century residence, furnished with 17th and 18th-century antiques and paintings. A long gallery the length of the facade has splendid views across lush lawns, and the grounds extend to 100 acres (40 hectares). *La Vie en Château* aims to provide the visitor with the experience of château living with the comforts of a hotel in a homely authentic setting. All the rooms are furnished differently and guests are also welcome to use the large reception and drawing rooms.

Dinner is provided *en famille* and all the guests sit down at the table together—an ideal arrangement for any one travelling alone or keen to meet others but less likely to appeal to a honeymoon couple wanting to dine à deux. It is a particularly good way to learn more about the area and to practise speaking French.

Château de Briottières has been in Valbray's mother's family for many generations, and passed to her on her mother's death in 1969. She too died only two months later, and for 10 years the château remained empty and vulnerable; in 1975, a furniture van drew up and burglars filled it with everything they could load into it.

By 1979 Valbray was a 23-year-old agriculture student who had grown up not in the Loire but in the sun of Provence—"a real Pagnol life," he recalls—and a decision had to be made whether to keep the château on or let it go. "When you've had a château in your family for six generations, the choice is made for you," he says, dismissing the difficulties.

He started out on a modest scale, taking in British and American students, and in the early years, he was on his own. In 1984 he married Hedwige; the château was part of the package, and she became wife, châtelaine and mother of three children.

They do most of the work themselves; Valbray runs the château and Hedwige takes charge of all the cooking, with the help of a small staff of young people. "We're offering a real château, but one in which people live," says Valbray. "We work hard, which is not to say we work all the time. We'll only do the *table d' hôte* [the common evening meal] perhaps two or three times a week. This is to preserve our private life—we have to pay a lot of attention to that." So, on evenings when meals are not served in the château, it is suggested that the guests should take themselves to local restaurants.

The château is in a quiet rural region and, because of the solitude, the Valbrays do not encourage people to stay more than two or three days. But available at the château are billiards, a library, fishing, cycling and horse riding.

Valbray continues to develop and improve the château. New rooms are being refurbished, including the interior of an adjacent 19th-century farmhouse. He has opened a wine tasting and buying club in another building, giving visitors the chance to try the regional wines.

He has many plans for the future; he may consider turning the château into a private club, catering for small conferences or business retreats. In the meantime the family business is certainly expanding; in 1989, François' brother Charles-Henry, then 23 (the same age that François was when he started out), took over the family château on their father's side, Château de Saint-Paterne, a 15th-century building near Alençon, northwest of Le Mans. He too is now letting out rooms in the château, and providing a similar *table d' hôte* for his visitors.

And in the meantime, in this deeply rural region of Anjou with its wooded valleys and rich farmland, another small château has opened its doors and lit a blazing fire: Château du Plessis near La Jaille-Yvon, also a family-run concern with homemade *beurre blanc* and late night calvados for a real *Vie en Château*.

Panurge — **Massenet**

Haulte Farce Musicale en 3 Actes de M.M.
GEORGES SPITZMULLER
et MAURICE BOUKAY

THE LOIRE IN LITERATURE

It was Rabelais in the 15th century who was the first to call his native Loire valley "the garden of France", and the tag has stuck ever since. Here, just as the mild climate and rich soil bring forth melons and strawberries, asparagus and full-bodied wines, so the serenity and self-confidence of this royal region, so rich in stately châteaux, seem to have been propitious to literary genius too.

Many great writers were born or brought up here—Rabelais himself, Ronsard and du Bellay, Balzac, Alain-Fournier and others. Touraine, the Loire region's heartland, is the quintessence of France, where the most pure and accent-free French is spoken—"Without Touraine, perhaps I could no longer live", wrote Balzac. Henry James, an enthusiastic later visitor, added: "It is the land of good books and good company, as well as good dinners and good houses."

François Rabelais, that rebellious life-loving humanist and scourge of clerics, was very much a product of the jovial *douceur de vivre* of his native Touraine, just as his own writings have since served to promote that tradition. His father, a rich lawyer at Chinon, had a country home in the verdant valley to the southwest, and here the writer was born around 1494. This neat stone manor, La Devinière, is today a Rabelais museum, with period furniture. Its main interest is its view over the châteaux and villages of the valley that Rabelais evokes in *Gargantua*.

Putrid tripe: Parts of this great satiric novel are set precisely in his *pays*—and to visit La Devinière today, with his books as guide, is to gain fascinating insights into how his ebullient imagination worked. Ahead you'll see the meadow of La Saulaie where Gargamelle gives birth to Gargantua, in the best Rabelaisian manner, after eating too much putrid tripe. To the right, a stone tower in a field is all that's left of Seuilly Abbey where Rabelais went to school: in the novel it's the home of the monk Frère Jean, ally of the noble giant Gargantua.

Above all, the valley is the scene of the famous episode of the Picrocholean War,

between the giant's father, Grandgousier, and the brutal King Picrochole of nearby Lerne. This bloody battle was Rabelais' fantasy version of a real but non-violent dispute over fishing rights in the Loire, between his father's clients and a hateful squire of Lerne.

But Rabelais joyfully inflates these villages into great fortified cities: La Devinière becomes Grandgousier's castle with a garrison of 30,000. Picrochole captures the castle of La Roche-Clermault (today a farmhouse by the railway, beside the huge silos of a

local co-operative). But Gargantua then swings into action, combing the cannonballs out of his hair like grape-pips: he is helped by his mare who pisses so copiously at the ford of Véde (near Cinais) that her flood drowns many of the enemy.

The victorious giant then rewards his officers with properties: to Gymnase he gives Coudray-Montpensier château (this stately towered pile, still in fine condition, stands on a hill beside Lerne's new villas; on the Loire near Ussé, Gargantua founds the splendid abbey of Thélème where nuns and monks live freely together, bound only by the rule "Do as you please". Alas, this abbey was fic-

Preceding pages: irises in bloom. **Left**, poster at Rabelais museum. **Above**, Rabelais at work.

titious, though Rabelais might have had in mind nearby Fontevraud Abbey (now a state cultural centre) which was run by nuns but had monks in it too.

The people of Chinon, in whose castle Joan of Arc met the Dauphin, remain hugely proud of their local genius, and they try to keep up his convivial tradition, helped by the renowned Chinon wines. Their bacchic *confrérie*, Les Bons Entonneurs Rabelaisiens, includes such glitterati as Elizabeth Taylor and Paul Bocuse amongst its 5,000 red-robed members, who swear on oath to live up to the Rabelaisian spirit of tolerance and *joie de vivre*. They hold regular banquets in the "Caves Peintes", formerly frescoed caverns

in the castle rock: Rabelais knew them, and they inspired his Temple of the Divine Bottle where Pantagruel seeks truth.

Just after Rabelais' day, the finest lyric poet of the French Renaissance was Pierre de Ronsard. He loved nature passionately, and much of his work reflects his feeling for the gentle poplared valley of the River Loir with its orchards, vineyards and wild woodlands where he loved to roam. Here, near the village of Couture, north of Tours, he was born in his father's handsome manor of La Possonnière, today finely preserved. The banqueting-hall's superb chimney-piece is carved with the Ronsard family motif of

flaming roses (*Ronses Ardentes*). Ronsard was an early Green. He yearned for an "age of gold" when nature would be untainted by man; he hated the cutting of vines or felling of trees and wrote a polemical poem against the woodcutters of his beloved forest of Gâtines. In another famous poem he asked to be buried on l'Ile Verte, a pretty islet in the Loir just east of Couture. But in the end he was laid to rest at St-Cosme Priory, just west of Tours, where he was the prior in his later years. Today this lovely medieval ruin houses a tiny Ronsard museum—worth a visit, despite its odd setting between modern high-rise suburbia and a football pitch, with orange TGVs hurtling close by.

Another priory that was given into Ronsard's charge in his later life is Croixval, near Montoire, also now decrepit. Close by is the famous Fontaine de la Belle Hélène, named by the poet after his dearest love, Hélène de Surgères, a court lady-in-waiting, she of "*Quand vous serez bien vieille…*". So touched was she by the serenading of this half-deaf, gout-racked prior that she asked him to build her a fountain; and his stone paving survives. But today it is a peasant *lavoir* amid messy undergrowth, with no plaque or signpost—no way to honour the greatest of French sonnets? Yet in Ronsard's day, too, these springs may have been little to look at. Steeped in Graeco-Roman poeticism, he peopled his woods with naiads and turned every Loirland trickle into the idyllic Fons Banusiae.

Some way west of Tours is Saumur, where Honoré de Balzac set *Eugénie Grandet* (1833), his masterly portrait of provincial ennui and a girl's youth stifled by her miserly father—it was based on the true story of a local miser. The house that Balzac is thought to have had in mind for the Grandet home still stands, suitably austere, at 7 Montée du Fort, a steep alley just below the castle. Balzac himself was born in Tours, in a house since destroyed.

His parents had come from the Midi, and later he lived in Paris: but it was always Touraine that he loved best, and to which he constantly returned. His feeling for it is rapturously conveyed in *Le Lys dans la Vallée*, a novel set near Pont-de-Ruan on the Indre: "Infinite love… I found expressed by this long ribbon of water streaming in the sun between two green banks, by these lines of poplars guarding this vale of love… Ask me no more why I love Touraine… I love it as an artist loves art."

The valley today is still lovely, even though partly engulfed by the Tours commuter belt. Pont-de-Ruan still has its mill-race and old church. And two of the châteaux described in the book are clearly identifiable. One, the Château de Saché, belonged to landed gentry friends of Balzac's, and here he would go to stay for long periods, when he wanted an escape from his hectic life in Paris and his angry creditors.

This stately 16th-century manor in a pastoral setting today houses a Balzac museum, with portraits of some of his many mistresses

treacherous, he described beautifully in *Rémi des Rauches*, about a fisherman. At St-Denis l'Hôtel is a small museum devoted to him; it evokes his feeling for the suffering of animals. His best novel, *Raboliot*, is set amid the forests and lagoons of the melancholy Sologne country: here, near Brinon-sur-Sauldre, Genevoix had relatives with a hunting-lodge, and he got to know the country people, many of whom went poaching on the big estates. Raboliot is a young peasant who poaches rabbits, hares and pheasants, not only to save his family from starvation but through some inner impulse.

He kills animals, yet feels an instinctive affinity with them; and when hunted by the

and of the great man himself, corpulent and bulbous-eyed. Note the fascinating copies of page-proofs full of those intricate semi-legible corrections that drove his printers so mad that they demanded double pay.

Further up the Loire, beyond Orléans, is the *pays* of Maurice Genevoix (1890–1980), who had a stronger feeling for nature and for animal life than almost any other French novelist, so it is strange that he is not better known outside France. He lived by the broad Loire whose changing moods, serene or

Left, bust of Balzac at Saché. **Above**, Balzac's writing desk.

police, for three winter months he "lives in the woods like a wolf". The descriptions of the Sologne landscape are subtly poetic. Today there is far less poaching in the Sologne, for the peasants are fewer and more prosperous, the rabbits have been wiped out by myxomatosis, and the pheasants are bred behind wire barricades.

Lost domain: A much more famous novel, Alain-Fournier's *Le Grand Meaulnes* (1913), is also set partly in the Sologne—and partly in the rolling Berry country, 60 miles (100 km) to the south. His marvellous book may have its dream-fantasy elements yet is also realistically anchored in the rural world that he knew. But its topography is bewildering, for he chose to jumble the two areas, Sologne and Berry—and unscrambling them makes for absorbing detective work.

Henri Fournier (his real name), son of a schoolmaster, was born at La Chapelle-d'Angillon where his mother's family lived, on the edge of the Sologne. At five he moved with his parents to the primary school at Epineuil-le-Fleuriel, down in the Berry, where he stayed until he was 12 years old.

It was always Epineuil he loved best. In his strange adventure story of children playing at being grown-ups, he mixed his adult dreams and yearnings with his real childhood memories. The school and village

scenes are very precisely Epineuil (Ste-Agathe in the book). But the mysterious forest where Meaulnes finds his enchanted manor is clearly a Sologne landscape. And the manor, *le Domaine sans nom*, is an amalgam of several that the imaginative Henri knew as a boy. One was Loroy, hidden in the Sologne woodlands near La Chapelle.

Another, near Epineuil, was the stately red-brick Château de Cornonçay, set in its own park—and the role that it is thought to have played as an inspiration for the novel is fascinating. In the 1890s it was the home of the Vicomte de Fadate, a benevolent squire who owned 11 farms in the area, providing a living for local peasants and artisans. He had two daughters, and when the second was baptised in 1896 he threw a huge party for the villagers, farm folk and gentry.

The Fourniers were invited, but Henri's father, devout Republican and a state servant, refused to attend a baptismal party where the *curé* would be present—such was the France of those days! So nine-year-old Henri heard about this wondrous fête from his classmates next day—the windows hung with coloured lamps and candles, the party costumes, the carriages crowding the servants' yard. This fired his imagination, and may later have helped to inspire the book's magical *fête étrange* (after all, the narrator, François Seurel, did not attend the *fête* himself but was told about it by Meaulnes).

There is a bizarre epilogue to this tale: Cornonçay today is still owned by a Fadate descendant, who has sold most of the farms but stays wealthy through owning some 200 petrol-stations and garages in the Paris area—there's romance! And of the two baby daughters at the great party, in 1987 the elder was still living at Cornonçay, aged 92! Strange to think that still in that house was a survivor from the long-ago *fête* that germinated Meaulnes' magical venture.

Epineuil, an ordinary little village, today has only 500 inhabitants compared with 1,500 in Fournier's day. But the school is still in use, little changed, though the pupils today wear bright anoraks and jeans, so unlike the dark jackets and smocks of former days. The teacher no longer lives in the modest family home next door, but in it you can visit the tiny attic bedroom where Henri read Dickens by candlelight, and the garret where Meaulnes drew up his plans for finding the "lost domaine".

The village, too, is full of reminders of how Fournier transformed his memories into fiction—the Belle Etoile farmhouse where Meaulnes stole the horse, the fairground where the strolling players came, and the house of the forge where Meaulnes and François watched the fire casting its giant shadows—"I remember that evening as one of the great evenings of my adolescence." Few other French novels are so imbued with poetic feeling for a lost country childhood.

Above, Ronsard. Left, Berry countryside, inspiration for Alain-Fournier.

Wine buffs of the more serious kind tend to divide into claret and Burgundy *aficionados*, either camp reserving for the other the hint of condescension an Oxford graduate might show a product of Cambridge, or vice versa. Their condescension may swiftly turn to pity should you avow a weakness for Loire Valley wines. For if you belong to the Loire wine fan club you do not, on the whole, spend a lot of time with your nose buried in vintage charts or comparing the latest wine auction prices with what you paid for the same wine five years earlier. You are more interested in unearthing unfamiliar *crus*, experiencing new tastes and, when the opportunity arises, combining tourism and good eating with a little wine-sleuthing. You believe wine is to be drunk rather than talked about, and would like to think there was some truth in Rabelais' pronouncement: "*Beuvez toujours, ne mourrez jamais.*"

It is true that only a handful of Loire wines can rival a really big Burgundy or aristocratic claret. They are mostly what the French call *gouleyant*; in other words, they are light and fresh and go down easily (*goule* in old French = "gullet").

But they make up for that shortcoming, if indeed it is one, by possessing several attractive qualities: a very wide spectrum of styles produced mainly by the many different grape varieties used (brought to the area because the Loire was for a long time a major line of communication); a freshness and fruitiness which befit the "garden of France", and which are best brought out when the whites are drunk well chilled and the reds on the cool side; and an ability to combine marvellously with food, both in the kitchen and at table. In addition, they are in general very reasonably priced.

Pouilly-sur-Loire, which lies between Gien and Nevers, produces one of the more expensive wines in the Loire region, the flintily fragrant Pouilly-Fumé. This white wine made from the Sauvignon grape has, at its best, a finesse that fully justifies its steadily rising price. But it needs two or three

years to give of its best. The tendency of the big wine-producing firms which control most of Pouilly-Fumé is to reduce that period to one year, with a corresponding loss of character. Sancerre, another Sauvignon wine produced on the far side of the Loire from Pouilly, has already fallen victim to its own success and suffered from the same syndrome as Beaujolais: standards have been lowered in order to meet demand.

Wine, not war: Sancerre started life as a red wine of some distinction. Henri IV is alleged

to have exclaimed, when visiting the Loire region in 1589: "Gadzooks! This is the best wine I have ever drunk. If everyone in the kingdom tasted it, there would no longer be any wars of religion!"

At the beginning of this century, local production was hard hit by competition from strong Algerian reds, and in the 1920s one or two brave growers tried planting Sauvignon vines. The white wine they produced was excellent, and they successfully promoted it in Paris restaurants. After the wine had become fashionable, they launched with equal success an uninteresting red Sancerre and extended the vineyards. The result today is

Preceding pages: vineyards at sunset. **Left**, wine tasting in Angers. **Above**, vin de Vouvray.

that Sancerre is generally overpriced and extremely variable in quality. In wine expert Michael Broadbent's memorable phrase, "a poor Sancerre is the next thing to drinking neat nitric acid". Sancerre is now facing strong competition from the up-and-coming—and less expensive—Sauvignons made to the southwest: Menetou-Salon (the favourite wine of Charles VII's treasurer, Jacques Coeur, who had a château there) and, on the far side of Bourges, Quincy and above all Reuilly, whose vineyards, after nearly being wiped from the map by the expansion of grain farming, are now producing a delicately subtle wine that is rapidly becoming the talk of the Loire wine trade.

larly, the clean white wines of Cheverny (Romorantin grapes) in Sologne need favourable conditions to give of their best.

Just south of Cheverny, at Oisly and Soings, the first reliable ordinary Touraine *appellation* wines are to be found. The *appellation* is a large one, extending from the edge of the Sologne to beyond Tours; and its range of styles is wide, as is the number of grape varieties used—Sauvignon, Arbois, Chardonnay, Chenin Blanc (also known as Pineau de la Loire, it is native to the Loire Valley), Cabernet Franc, Cabernet Sauvignon, Cot and Gamay.

The Touraine's five major *appellations* are Vouvray, Montlouis, Bourgueil, Saint-

Further down the Loire, the vineyards of the Orléanais have not been so fortunate. They have a long history, and began sending their wines to Paris as long ago as the 7th century. The poet François Villon appreciated them. The area enjoyed the same reputation as the Bordelais does today, until Henri IV, for reasons of political expedience, decided to give preference to the wines produced around Paris.

The few vineyards that survive today, several still surrounded by medieval walls, produce some very pleasant, light *perlé* reds and whites from Gris Meunier and Chardonnay grapes—but only in good years. Simi-

Nicolas-de-Bourgueil (almost indistinguishable from Bourgueil) and Chinon—wines whose praises have been sung by Ronsard, Rabelais, Balzac, Alfred de Vigny and Alexandre Dumas père (all of whom except Dumas, it has to be said, were born in the region).

Two rivals: The vineyards of Vouvray and Montlouis sit staring at each other jealously from either side of the Loire. The rivalry between these two very similar white wines goes back to the time when their respective growers fought a series of court cases over *appellation* just before World War II.

Vouvray is a startlingly uneven wine.

Depending on the grower, the position of the vineyard and the year—not to speak of the *négociant*, who may think solely in terms of meeting the demands of the market—it can vary unrecognisably. A bad Vouvray is flat and lifeless. A good one has an extraordinary wealth of flavours, with hints of almonds, quinces and acacia—certainly the wine Rabelais had in mind when he described Vouvray as "taffeta wine". It shares with few other Loire wines the property to age marvellously in all its forms (sparkling, dry, semi-sweet and sweet).

Although a few wine-growers still have dwindling stocks of very old Vouvray stashed away in their cellars, which run deep

nel—its only TGV tunnel anywhere—beneath the precious vines instead. The growers protested that vibrations from the trains would damage wine slumbering in cellars next to the tunnel. The SNCF eventually got its way by agreeing to lay the railway track on rubber cushions.

During the ceremony in 1989 to inaugurate the bridge that takes the TGV out of the tunnel and over the Loire into Montlouis territory, the Vouvray growers, who had cleverly squeezed as much publicity as they could out of the whole affair, were seen clinking glasses with their fellow *vignerons* from Montlouis, thus ending, for the time being at least, the running battle which had

into the tufa rock beneath the vineyards, it takes more than just a chance visit to cajole a bottle out of them. The easiest way to sample a vintage Vouvray is to dine at Hôtel Jean Bardet, a superb restaurant in Tours: his wine list offers an astonishing 62 vintages.

When the SNCF announced plans not only to route its new TGV railway line straight through the Vouvray area but also to excavate a cutting through the vineyards, the local wine-growers protested vociferously.

The SNCF then suggested driving a tun-

Left, Renaissance grape treading. **Above**, vin de Vouvray harvest.

been going on between the two *appellations*.

Opinion is divided on the question of whether a really good Montlouis can rival Vouvray at its best. Until the court cases of 1938, Montlouis—which relies on the same grape variety (Chenin Blanc), cultivation methods and vinification techniques as Vouvray, and which is grown on almost identical soil—was sold as Vouvray. Some authorities used to dismiss Montlouis as "the poor man's Vouvray", a judgment which is certainly unfair today. Its difference in price with Vouvray, anyway, works very much in the consumer's favour.

Also very attractively underpriced (for the

time being) are the white wines produced in the valley of Le Loir, some 25 miles (40 km) north of Vouvray. The tiny Jasnières *appellation*, yet another of Henri IV's favourite wines, has been making a comeback after a period of decline. Of its little known and hardly marketed neighbours, Côteaux-du-Vendômois and Côteaux-du-Loir, the second is the more interesting: made from the Chenin Blanc grape, like Jasnières, it has the ability to age extraordinarily well, at which point it acquires hints of white peach, toasted almonds and aniseed. It is rumoured that on special family occasions the growers uncork bottles that have been lying in their cellars since the last century.

Bourgueil and Chinon, downstream from Tours, occupy opposite banks of the Loire (Chinon straddles the River Vienne as well), but there is nothing like the same rivalry between these two ancient *appellations* as there is between Vouvray and Montlouis. The mainly red wines they produce, almost totally from the Cabernet Franc grape, can on occasion be very difficult to distinguish at a blind tasting.

This distinction is reflected in the controversy among wine authorities over the associations evoked by the two wines: some swear they detect a taste of strawberry in Bourgueil and raspberry in Chinon, while others (a majority) aver that Bourgueil tastes of raspberries and Chinon has overtones of violets. What is more, both Bourgueil and Chinon vary considerably, depending on whether the grapes come from the plateau, the slopes or the alluvial plain. For some reason Bourgueil was once thought to possess certain powers as a psychological stimulant. The prior of Bourgueil said in 1089 that it was a wine which "gladdened sad hearts"; and 100 years ago doctors prescribed it to women who had "the vapours".

While Chinon wine is very much associated with Rabelais—who was born at La Devinière just outside the town, and whose distinctively hatted, grinning face stares out from every tourist brochure, shop window and restaurant menu—the next wine down the Loire, Saumur-Champigny, used to be the favourite tipple of the gourmet Curnonsky. Although part of the large Anjou-Saumur region, it presents several similarities with Bourgueil and Chinon (the same grape, cultivation and vinification, and a similar soil). It has been described as tasting simultaneously of raspberries, violets and blackcurrant, though others detect a hint of wild strawberries in it.

In the 1970s and 1980s, Saumur-Champigny became extremely fashionable in French restaurants and got sucked into the Beaujolais/Sancerre syndrome (increased yields per hectare, a doubling of the vineyard area, soaring prices). But with steady competition from its peers in the region, in particular from the new Anjou-Villages *appellation*, the wine had returned to a more reasonable price level by the 1990s.

The Saumur *appellation* produces still red, white and rosé wines, like the rest of Anjou-Saumur, but is chiefly notable for the quality of its sparkling whites and rosés, which are produced according to both Saumur Mousseux and Crémant de Loire regulations.

As a large number of white and red grape varieties are permitted (Chenin Blanc, Chardonnay, Sauvignon, Cabernet Franc, Cabernet Sauvignon, Cot, Pineau d'Aunis, Pinot Noir, Malbec, Gamay and Grolleau), this is an area where the art of the blender comes into its own. Sparkling Saumurs, which are all made by the *méthode champenoise*—but are not allowed to say so—of second fermentation in bottle, can at their best vie with good

Champagnes and cost considerably less.

The Anjou part of the Anjou-Saumur region contains a multitude of small *appellations*, some of which produce sweet wines that rank among France's greatest. Most of the output, however, qualifies simply as ordinary Anjou (white, red and especially rosé wines).

The growers of these wines have been particularly hard hit by changing public tastes in the last half century. Before the last war, almost all their production consisted of semi-sweet or sweet whites, except for something called *rouget*, a locally drunk, pink carafe wine. When tastes shifted away from sweet white wine, the Angevin growers

red Anjou. Improved vinification techniques resulted in a generally excellent product for which a special new *appellation*, Anjou-Villages, was created in 1987 (for wines made exclusively from Cabernet Franc and Cabernet Sauvignon grapes). The proportion of total Anjou output accounted for by reds had increased from a tiny 1 percent in 1965 to almost 20 percent by 1989. Although the output of Anjou rosé has declined, the overall standard of what is still being produced by individual growers (as opposed to *négociants*) has improved.

But the four jewels in Anjou's crown, and some of the finest wines the Loire can offer, are Côteaux du Layon-Chaume, Quarts-de-

began to market their *rouget* as Anjou rosé. It proved an immense success—in France partly because the characters in a very popular radio series, *La Famille Duraton*, were constantly knocking back the stuff, and abroad because the cordial-like qualities of semi-sweet rosé made it an ideal wine for the new post-war generation of people embarking on wine-drinking for the first time.

But in the 1960s and 1970s tastes changed again: semi-sweet rosés began to fall out of favour, so the growers tried their third card,

Left, Sologne vineyard. **Above**, a convivial meeting.

Chaume, Bonnezeaux and Savennières, all products of the Chenin Blanc grape. The first three *appellations* produce sweet white wines which can be kept for decades and in which the grape's celebrated "honeyed" quality is allowed to blossom fully. The proximity of the River Layon and the Loire mean that there are frequent morning mists which in some years encourage the formation, at harvest time, of "noble rot" (*Botrytis cinerea*), as in the Sauternes area and also occasionally in the Vouvray vineyards.

Almost the entire production of Savennières, on the right bank of the Loire, consists of dry white wine, despite the fact that the grapes are harvested very late and very ripe. It is notable for remaining "closed" for up to five years, after which it produces an explosion of tastes (quince, honey, lime-blossom and bitter almond are some of the epithets used). The finest example of Saven-nières is the legendary and now virtually unobtainable—except in some local restaur-ants—Coulée-de-Serrant.

As the Loire continues on to the Atlantic it passes through the biggest of all the Loire Valley *appellations contrôllée*, Muscadet. This wine is made from grapes produced by the Melon vine, which had to be imported from Burgundy at the beginning of the 18th century to replace vines that had been killed

by the fierce winter suffered in 1709.

Muscadet has been one of the most suc-cessful of all French wines since the war, and now sells 100 million bottles a year. It is also, partly because of that success, one of the most uneven in quality: at its best, it is a bone-dry white with a touch of flint that is an ideal accompaniment for shellfish, and at its worst an acid, headache-producing concoc-tion ruined by excessive use of sulphur di-oxide as a preservative.

To avoid nasty surprises, go for the *appel-lation* Muscadet de Sèvre-et-Maine *mis en bouteille sur lie* (bottled directly off the lees) and *à la propriété*. The even drier and

sharper Gros Plant du Pays Nantais, pro-duced in the same area from Folle Blanche grapes, is better avoided.

One of the great pleasures to be had in trying to track down unfamiliar wines is visiting the generally very friendly growers. The *vigneron* and sometimes his wife—there are an increasing number of husband-and-wife teams among the younger genera-tion—will proudly explain their cultivation and vinification methods and let you sample a selection of their wines.

The circumstances of such visits—the bonhomie, the attractive mustiness and cool of the cellar, which is frequently hollowed out of the rock, the ritual of the pipette which is plunged into the barrel to extract a sample of wine—can, however, somewhat cloud one's critical faculties.

Often a better idea of a wine's true merit can be gained by sampling a bottle at leisure with food, either in the objective surround-ings of a restaurant (most Loire Valley res-taurants offer a fair to good selection of regional wines bought direct from growers), or else more casually in the course of a picnic, with a bottle bought from a local shop—as long as an ice-box or cooling stream is to hand to prevent the wine from getting overheated.

Vagaries of fashion: If you are ever disap-pointed by a Loire wine—and it can hap-pen—be indulgent. For it is worth remem-bering that growers in the Loire Valley have had to grapple with far more problems than their colleagues in other wine-producing regions of France: their wines can suffer seriously from a bad summer, for although the Loire Valley benefits climatically from the presence of the river it is nonetheless near the northernmost limit for wine-growing. And in some cases (for example, Sancerre, Vouvray, Saumur-Champigny, Anjou and Muscadet) the growers have suffered from—and been tempted to take advantage of—the vagaries of wine-drinking fashion.

And while Loire Valley wines are increas-ingly available everywhere, like so many wines, they fulfill their promise best drunk close to home, and accompanying the excel-lent food, be it fish, fowl or game, the region has to offer.

Above, the budding grape. **Right**, Loire wines and regional delicacies.

On a certain evening in mid-October, after the grape harvest in Touraine is over and the grapes have been transformed into wine, Henry Marionnet can be found in his dining-room at Domaine de la Charmoise, near Soings-en-Sologne, drinking Gamay wine. Usually the most convivial and hospitable of men, Monsieur Marionnet is not to be disturbed, except perhaps by his red-haired wife Marie-Josée, who often joins him. They drink one bottle, maybe another, and possibly a third.

They are not drinking for fun. Henry Marionnet is testing his *primeur*, the first wine of the year, which he has assembled from several recently fermented vats and will release for sale after 15 November. He is searching for the vibrant fruitiness and generosity characteristic of his wines, and he'll keep assembling and tasting until he achieves it.

No spitting: He and Marie-Josée taste, but they do not spit, as many wine tasters do, because Marionnet believes that without drinking a wine—and drinking a fair amount of it—he cannot know if the wine is really good. "Sometimes I get completely loaded when I'm putting together my wines; but to really know a wine, you have to know it physically," he says.

Although Domaine de la Charmoise Gamay and Sauvignon wines are exemplary of Touraine wine at its best—light, fruity and convivial wines that are made to be drunk young—the man who makes them is not at all typical. Nobody in the Loire Valley uses the farming and vinification techniques used by Henry Marionnet.

Marionnet inherited 50 acres (20 hectares) of vines from his father in the late 1960s, as well as several hectares of strawberries and asparagus. His father made ordinary table wine, but Marionnet wanted to make something better, so he decided to teach himself all he could about oenology, while searching for a wine that would be suitable for the region. He discovered the Gamay grape when he was courting Marie-Josée. "I developed a double passion: for my future wife,

and for the Gamay grape," he says, laughing.

Marie-Josée's father, also a winemaker, produced a Gamay wine, and when Marionnet tasted the 1964 vintage, "it was love at first sight". He married Marie-Josée and decided to pull up all of his father's vines and plant Gamay. Three years later he planted Sauvignon grapes as well (his crop is about 25 percent Sauvignon, 75 percent Gamay). The wines he eventually produced with these varieties gave him the right to the Touraine *appellation contrôlée*.

Planting new vines is risky business. It takes four years before new vines yield wine, and meanwhile one has to make a living. Because of their strawberry and asparagus crops, the Marionnets got by those first years; the crops, in fact, were a double blessing, because they gave Marionnet some revolutionary ideas about planting vines. Strawberries are planted under sheets of dark plastic film to protect them from weeds and keep the ground moist around them. Asparagus is planted in raised furrows.

Marionnet realised that if he combined both of these techniques for his vines he could plant vineyards that needed very little tending. He planted the young vines on raised furrows, under dark plastic sheets with holes poked through for each vine. This way the ground around them stayed warm and moist, and no weeds could grow because the sunlight couldn't get through.

With the protection of the plastic, herbicides could be used between the rows, a practice which isn't possible in most circumstances until the vines are four years old, because the young vines can be killed by the herbicides. Twenty years later Marionnet uses the same methods when he plants new vines (he now has about 125 acres/50 hectares of vineyard).

Shooting high: Marionnet also planted the rows of vines much farther apart than the other vines in Touraine, and trained the shoots high, attaching them to wires that he ran down each row. He did this because he was convinced that machine picking would soon arrive in the Loire Valley, and this kind of vineyard would best accommodate it. He was right on all counts; but because of the kind of vinification method he decided to use, he couldn't use machines to pick the grapes; today he is one of the few winemakers in the region not to use them.

After experimenting with different types of vinification, Marionnet settled on a method unheard-of in the Loire but widely used in Beaujolais, where the wines are also made from Gamay grapes. Marionnet is convinced that "carbon dioxide maceration" yields the best Gamay wines. With this method the grapes are left intact to ferment in a vat full of carbon dioxide; the fermentation begins inside the grapes. It takes about eight days, after which time the grapes have lost their dark colour and have begun to burst.

well with meat or fish, and should be drunk slightly chilled.

Every year the winemaking process at Domaine de la Charmoise varies a little. In one year, for example, Marionnet stopped the carbonic maceration after only four or five days; he had an intuition that things were happening more quickly than usual in the vat, and he was right: the wine was almost ready at this point. Marionnet never questions his intuitions; he just follows his hunches, and his good wine is the result. But of course it's a risky business. Many of the unknowns come from the fact that nothing artificial or extra is added—no sulphur or yeasts—to control the fermentation process,

When 30 to 50 percent of the grapes have burst and the juice has coloured, it's time to drain the vat and press the remaining grapes to extract the juice.

Versatile wines: The fermentation finishes in the juice, which is then filtered through a very fine mesh system that only filters out bacteria and yeasts. Fermentation by carbon dioxide maceration is particularly suited, Marionnet believes, to the grapes from the Touraine. "These grapes produce wines full of primary, immediately accessible, fruity aromas, wines to be drunk and enjoyed within the year, not to be laid down." The most versatile of red wines, they go equally

and the wine is only slightly filtered.

Marionnet's Sauvignons are vinified at a low temperature, 15°–18°C (59°–64°F), which produces a fruity, light and aromatic wine. Marionnet is also unique in that he stems the grapes before pressing them, unusual in dry white wine vinification. In so doing he eliminates a strong grassy taste which the French call *pipi du chat* (which means what it sounds like it means).

The harvest and the weeks that follow are an intense time at Domaine de la Charmoise. Because the grapes must be entirely intact for their fermentation, those who pick them have to work extremely carefully, as if they were picking the grapes for display at Harrods Food Hall. Instead of dropping the bunches into buckets, then dumping the buckets into large flats, the grapes are set no more than four layers deep in boxes that rest on stands, which keep the grapes off the ground so that they don't get any sand on them. The boxes are then carefully transferred to the *cave*, where the grapes are placed in the vats. Madame Marionnet does nothing but inspect the grapes as they're picked, during the three weeks of the harvest.

After fermentation Henry Marionnet goes to work assembling the wines and choosing which wines he will release in mid-November as *primeurs*, the best of the young wines,

That taste has won the attention of prominent wine journalists in France and the respect of Marionnet's fellow winemakers. He has received numerous prestigious awards, including the *Gault & Millau* "Loire Man of the Year". Touraine wines are not as well known as the wines produced farther west in the Loire, the Chinons, Bourgueils and Vouvrays, where the wines are made from Cabernet Franc and Chenin Blanc grapes.

Soon after Marionnet began to produce his Gamay, word got around about his winemaking methods and other curious *vignerons* in the region began to come around to taste it. They were impressed. Marionnet started to win prizes at local fairs, and by the

which will be open, fruity and ready to drink. "I shut myself up in my *laboratoire* (a little room off the *cave*) and taste the wines from the different vats, mixing them in different proportions. When I have something I think I like, I take it to the house and taste it in the tranquillity of my living room. Nobody bothers me during this period. Sometimes it takes days to come up with something perfect, and I can get pretty miserable (and drunk) in the process." But Marionnet never stops until he gets the taste he wants.

Left, tending the vines. **Above**, the Marionnets sample the new vintage.

mid-1970s he had enough of a following that he could replace all of his strawberries and asparagus with vines. In 10 years his production has gone from 100,000 bottles a year to between 300,000 and 400,000.

Winemakers are often exceptional, passionate people, and Henry Marionnet is one such. Entirely self-taught, he claims that he benefits from not having had a formal education in oenology. "Otherwise I'd have done a lot of things people told me to do instead of following my own instincts. I do everything differently from the others in the region." And yet he is one of the most esteemed winemakers in the Loire.

The legendary figure of Curnonsky, who was born near Angers in 1872, towers over the history of 20th-century French cuisine. It was he who, in a series of books he wrote in the 1920s and 1930s with Marcel Rouff and Austin de Croze, revealed the glories of French provincial cooking, and who rebelled against the heavy sauces that commonly masked inferior ingredients. He formulated the precept that influenced the sensible mainstream, as opposed to the loony fringe, of the *nouvelle cuisine* school: "In cookery, things should taste of what they are."

It was no coincidence that Curnonsky was born and brought up in Anjou, for the cuisine of the Loire Valley is a remarkable illustration of that precept. Sauces scarcely feature at all in its canon of recipes, and the only one to have gained any renown, *beurre blanc*, is classically simple in style (though not in execution). Local cooks hardly need to disguise their raw materials because they are generally of such high quality. The reasons for this are partly geographical and partly historical. Not only is the Loire Valley fertile for much of its length, but it enjoys a microclimate that protects it against winter frosts and torrid summer weather. It is thus an ideal place for the cultivation of fruit and vegetables. When François Rabelais described the Touraine, where he was born, as the "garden of France" (*Je suis né et ai esté nourry jeune au jardin de France*), he was certainly thinking less of ornamental flowerbeds than of the kitchen garden and its produce.

New arrivals: Down the centuries, new vegetables and fruits introduced from outside always flourished in the Loire Valley. The most important contribution was made by gardeners brought from Italy by King Charles VIII at the end of the 15th century, who revealed globe artichokes, peas, lettuce and other vegetables to members of the court. Their consumption eventually filtered through to the local population.

Other ingredients had always been available—excellent pork and poultry, abundant game and above all a plentiful supply of

freshwater fish from the Loire and its tributaries. Moreover, the light white and red wines of Touraine and Anjou are ideally suited for use in cooking.

By the time Curnonsky came into the world, there was a well-established corpus of Loire Valley cuisine. It varied little from one area to another, though it was perhaps slightly less opulent in the Orléans-Sancerre section and in the Sologne, while Breton influences made themselves felt towards Nantes. It was to be found in its most class-

ical form in the Touraine. "True Tourangelle cooking", Curnonsky wrote, "takes its inspiration from the wit of Rabelais and the genius of Descartes, another famous son of that illustrious province. It is clear, logical and straightforward."

Curnonsky's real name was Maurice-Edmond Sailland. As a young man he moved in the circle of the novelist and poet Pierre Louÿs, the humorist Alphonse Allais, Colette and her husband Willy, and was keen to make a name for himself as a *littérateur*. Allais told him he would need a *nom de plume*, and suggested that as all things Russian were in fashion a name ending in "sky"

Preceding pages: radishes galore. **Left**, fresh garlic. **Above**, *rillettes de Tours*.

might be in order. Sailland, a Latin scholar, murmured: "*Cur non 'sky'*?" ("Why not 'sky'?"). Allais bounded from his chair and said: "That's it!"

When already well advanced in years (he died in 1956), Curnonsky remembered a wedding feast in Anjou he had attended in the early 1890s which "gave some idea of the kind of thing Angevin peasants were eating then". His family owned a number of farms on one of the islands in the middle of the Loire between La Daguenière and Juigné-sur-Loire, just east of Angers. One of their tenant farmers, le père Lardeau, invited Curnonsky to the wedding of his daughter Mathurine. Curnonsky had known her since

they were small: she was, he remembered, "a superb, bold blonde of 20, who had occasionally let me, in the back of the barn, feel the firmness of her fine legs, whose soft and downy skin was turned golden by the Loire's fine sand".

The menu was as follows:

POTAGE
La soupe aux petits pois (avec les cosses cuites dans le bouillon et retirées au moment de servir)
HORS-D'OEUVRE
Les andouillettes chaudes de Saint Hilaire-Saint Florent
Le boudin blanc

POISSONS
L'alose de Loire au beurre blanc
La bouilleture d'anguilles aux pruneaux
VIANDES
Le gras-double "piquerette" au vin d'Anjou
Le cul de veau rôti piqué aux lardons
VOLAILLES
La fricassée de poulet à l'angevine
LEGUMES
La darrée de piochons (choux verts)
La salade aux pissenlits et aux oeufs
GIBIER
Le pâté de lièvre de Saint Georges-sur-Loire
Le pâté de sarcelles de Saumur
FROMAGES
Les caillebottes d'Anjou
Le fromage de Chouzé
DOUCEURS
Les crémets d'Angers
Les boulettes aux amandes et aux noisettes
CONFISERIES
Les biscuits anisés de Saint-Julien
Les croquettes de Château-Gontier

The only concession to non-regional specialities was in the choice of wines with the main courses (Saint Emilion and Burgundy). The greatest wines of Anjou, Quarts-de-Chaumes and Coulée-de-Serrant, were served at the end of the meal.

Although even Curnonsky describes the Lardeau wedding menu as "incredible", such a plethora of dishes was not unusual for special occasions at the time. What is interesting about it is that it consists almost entirely of Loire Valley specialities and makes no concessions whatsoever to the kind of *grande cuisine* which is, and to some extent was, considered more suitable for such exalted occasions as weddings.

Let's look at the courses one by one. The pea soup would have borne little relation to a British dried-pea soup, probably consisting simply of fresh garden peas simmered in broth (with, as the menu points out, the pods thrown in as well to give extra sweetness, then removed before serving).

So many garden vegetables are grown in the lower Loire Valley that at times it looks like an outsized allotment. Appropriately enough, the Ecole Nationale d'Ingénieurs des Travaux de l'Horticulture et du Paysage, a leading agricultural research station which is trying to resuscitate old varieties of fruit and vegetables and develop new ones, is located in Angers. It was in Angers, too, that one of the world's finest pears, the comice, was created, in 1849 in the gardens of the Horticultural Association.

Further upstream, Orléans and Olivet have long been famed for their nurseries and seed merchants (several seed varieties bear the epithets *d'Orléans* or *d'Olivet*); and rare vegetables such as Chinese artichokes, black-skinned potatoes and even bulb chervil can be found on sale in ordinary non-specialised greengrocers there.

Top price: Asparagus thrives in the sandy soil of the upper Touraine and, more particularly, the Sologne, where it enjoys an *appellation contrôlée* and commands a premium price. The local asparagus farmers owe their

After the light overture of pea soup, Curnonsky and his fellow guests got down to the serious business of *andouillettes* (chitterlings) and *boudin blanc* (chicken sausage). These sausages are found all over the northern half of France, but are particularly good in the Loire Valley. Reputedly the best *andouillettes* come from Jargeau, just upstream from Orléans.

The best-known charcuterie specialities to be found in the Loire Valley, however, are the *rillons* and *rillettes* of Tours and Saumur. *Rillons* are chunks of pork breast stewed for hours in lard until tender; they are usually served cold. *Rillettes* are the same thing, but mashed up to the consistency of a soft paste

prosperity to one Charles Depezay.

During the Siege of Paris in 1870, this Sologne-born gendarme was posted just outside the capital in Argenteuil, then the centre of French asparagus production. He noticed that the soil there was similar to that of his own garden, and when demobilised in 1877 he introduced asparagus to the Sologne. This turned out to be a particularly timely idea, for when phylloxera destroyed the local vines in 1885 the wine-growers were able to go over to asparagus farming.

Left, feeding the chickens, Ussé tapestry.
Above, Angevin honey-seller.

and mixed with a little more lard.

Neither sound very interesting, and *rillettes*, especially those sold by charcuteries elsewhere in France, tend to be given a particularly heavy dose of lard. But when made with the proper raw materials, both *rillons* and *rillettes* are very subtle and delicate (though always fatty), and make excellent picnic food. Balzac, a gastronome (not to say glutton) who came from an upper-class Tours family where such rustic food was never allowed on to the table, describes at the beginning of his partly autobiographical novel *Le Lys dans la Vallée* his delight at discovering *rillettes* for the first time at boarding school, when his less aristocratic fellow pupils gave him some to taste from their hampers.

Freshwater fish are one of the glories of Loire Valley cuisine. The *alose* on the Lardeau menu is shad, a sea fish of the herring family which spawns in the Loire. Unfortunately it is now only rarely found in local restaurants (one notable exception is Bernard Robin's excellent establishment at Bracieux); and *beurre blanc*, which consists just of butter and a reduction of vinegar and shallots, nowadays tends to accompany turbot instead.

Other sea fish which spawn in the Loire are salmon and lampreys. Genuine Loire

salmon does not often feature on menus and is expensive; but it is well worth paying a bit extra for it, as it has an incomparable flavour. And you will be very lucky if you come across fresh lampreys (as opposed to tinned ones), which are traditionally sautéed in walnut oil.

But the Loire also offers a wide range of other fish: pike, perch, brill, carp, tench, bream, barbel and the recently introduced *sandre* (pike-perch). Trout and crayfish are bought live by chefs, but under French law they must come respectively from farms or from outside France (usually eastern Europe). One of the most enjoyable gastronomic

experiences in the Loire Valley is a plate piled high with local freshwater whitebait.

Eel is very abundant, particularly in the Sologne, and can be found in a multitude of guises: in a *sauce poulette* (mushrooms, white wine, egg yolk and parsley), grilled, jellied and *en matelote* (stewed in red wine). The *bouilleture* at the Lardeau wedding feast is basically the same thing as a *matelote*. Prunes (once a speciality of Tours) used to be a mandatory accompaniment to eel stews. But such medieval combinations have unfortunately gone out of fashion and few restaurants apart from the great Charles Barrier in Tours are bold enough to put the original dish on their menus.

Gras-double (a meaty kind of tripe) is eaten all over France, and often cooked in white wine. But a characteristic addition in Anjou is a good dash of vinegar (hence the epithet *piquerette*), which cuts through the richness of the dish. Orléans, by the way, has long been a noted centre of vinegar production, and its Guild of Master Vinegar-Makers was created by Henri III in 1580.

No one is quite sure why Orléans made a speciality of vinegar. Some claim that it was the point at which some of the wine being unloaded from boats for despatch by road to Paris was discovered to have gone off; others argue, perhaps more plausibly, that the local Gris Meunier wines were successful only in warm years, and that failed harvests were naturally turned into vinegar.

Cul de veau (rump of veal) is a speciality of Montsoreau, which lies at the confluence of the Vienne and the Loire. With the *fricassée de poulet* (chicken cut into pieces and cooked with onions and white wine) we come to one of the finest ingredients of the Loire Valley: chicken. The most highly prized type of bird, still occasionally found on restaurant menus, is the *géline*, a small black variety with a bright red cockscomb.

At the turn of the century vegetables were hardly ever served with meat, but either before or after it. The *darrée de piochons*, like the salad of dandelion and hard-boiled egg, is a poor peasant's dish found in Anjou and Touraine. It consists of the hearts of young kale boiled and served with butter.

The Loire Valley and the Sologne in particular abound in wild game. It may seem odd for the *pâté de lièvre* (hare) and *pâté de sarcelles* (teal) mentioned by Curnonsky to be served at this point in the meal. But in peasant communities it was quite common until the last war for pâtés to be served just before the cheese course. In the case of the Lardeau banquet, the word pâté would almost certainly have referred to a pie, possibly served hot. It was only in the 1920s and 1930s that pâté generally came to mean terrine—in other words, a crustless pie.

Good game: Many Sologne restaurants specialise in game (venison, young boar, hare, pheasant, quail and partridge). Nowadays the venison and boar that feature on menus are usually the products of specialised farms rather than of the chase—and consequently taste better, as their flesh does not suffer

flower of thistle or with globe artichoke.

Chouzé cheese is nowadays a mild goat cheese of no great interest. The Loire Valley does not boast a great number of cheese varieties, and those that exist have greatly suffered in recent years from industrialisation and pasteurisation. All too often, what you find in the shops are over-salted dairy-made versions, sometimes produced in other regions of France. This is particularly true of two celebrated goat cheeses, Sainte-Maure, which has a piece of straw stuck lengthwise through its middle, and Valençay, a truncated pyramid covered with powdered charcoal. It is best to buy such cheeses at markets, if possible direct from the cheesemaker's

from the build-up of toxins that occurs when an animal is frightened and exhausted. Delicious wild mushrooms—*girolles* (chanterelles), *coulemelles* (parasol mushrooms), *trompettes de la mort* (less offputtingly known as horns of plenty in English) and *cèpes*—are frequently served with game.

Curnonsky, whose appetite was reportedly prodigious, probably still had plenty of room for the cheese course when it was brought on. *Caillebotte d'Anjou* is a kind of junket that used to be "renneted" with the

Left, market day in Sully. **Above**, a cornucopia of fruit and vegetables.

stall, rather than from shops or supermarkets. If there is no market, look for the word *fermier* (farmer) on the label, which is usually a good guarantee. Oversalting is a frequent fault of *crottin de Chavignol*, another famous goat cheese made further up the Loire Valley, even though its manufacture is strictly controlled. When properly made, it goes extremely well with the local wine, Sancerre. It is still occasionally possible to find two other interesting Loire Valley cheeses, Olivet Cendré (covered with real wood-ash) and Olivet-au-Foin (wrapped in hay), both of which have a distinctive flavour. The inhabitants of the Loire Valley seem to have a particularly sweet tooth. *Crémets*, which are also sometimes known as *coeurs à la crème*, are delightfully simple little confections of curd cheese, cream, sugar and whipped egg white. Most restaurants offer an abundance of desserts: fruit tarts, nut cakes, aniseed-flavoured biscuits and, towards Nantes, crêpes and galettes (pancakes made with buckwheat flour) with various fillings. The same specialities are available from many pâtisseries, which also sell tempting confectionery such as prunes stuffed with dried apricot purée and *cotignac*, a hard quince paste which also loomed large in Balzac's fond memories of schoolboy gastronomy. Some confectionery is

Comprehensive though it was, the Lardeau banquet naturally could not include every dish of which the cooks of Nantes, Anjou, Touraine, Sologne and Orléans are proud. Any serious exploration of Loire Valley gastronomy should include, if possible, a number of other traditional local specialities. One of these, which dates from the 17th century when Tours was celebrated for its prunes, is *noisettes de porc aux pruneaux de Tours*, "a bland combination of pork, prunes, cream and the white wine of Vouvray [which] embodies what Henry James described as 'the good-humoured and succulent Touraine'." (Jane Grigson, *Charcuterie and French Pork Cookery*).

extremely localised, such as *aristocrates* (tasty thin plaques of caramel studded with roasted almonds), which are to be had only in Neung-sur-Beuvron in the Sologne.

Much more easily found is *fouace*, a kind of bun half-way between a brioche and a sponge cake that nowadays often accompanies wine-tasting. *Fouaces* have a long history: they are the subject of a dispute between Picrochole and Grandgousier in *Gargantua*. In Rabelais' day they were probably flavoured with saffron. He strongly recommends that they should be eaten with grapes ("*Notez que c'est viande céleste manger à déjeuner raisins avec fouace fraîche*").

Another excellent pork dish is *charbonnée*, a truly peasant concoction made at pig-killing time. In its traditional version, various lowlier parts of the animal (neck, liver, lights) are stewed with onions and spices in red wine and some of the animal's blood, which turns the sauce very dark; hence its name, which derives from *charbon* (coal). In some restaurants classier cuts are used and the blood is omitted, which betrays the spirit of the dish.

Another traditional speciality of the area, and one far subtler and more sophisticated than *charbonnée* though sharing its humble origins, is *beuchelle*. Unfortunately it is now only seldom found on restaurant menus. The dish was elevated from peasant status to something worthy of the grandest tables (though little changed in the process) by the other great gastronome of the Loire Valley along with Curnonsky, the chef and writer of cookery books Edouard Nignon.

Food for thought: Born to a working-class family in Nantes in 1865, Nignon started his career as a kitchen hand at the age of 10 and rose to become one of the most celebrated chefs of his day, cooking for Tsar Nicholas II and Emperor Franz Josef, among others, before running the famous restaurant Larue in Paris, where his customers—and friends—included Anatole France, Edmond

invented towards the end of the 19th century by the Tatin sisters at the Hôtel Tatin et Terminus in Lamotte-Beuvron (there is much evidence to the contrary), it was undoubtedly they who were responsible for making the tart so popular. Its fame spread thence to Paris, probably conveyed by wealthy hunters returning from a weekend's shooting, and it soon found its way on to the menu at Maxim's. In 1907 Claude Monet and his family even motored all the way down from Giverny to Lamotte-Beuvron to find out what all the fuss was about.

There are several versions of *tarte Tatin*: it may be thick and dark, with the apples, and sometimes even pears, heavily caramelised,

Rostand, Sacha Guitry and Marcel Proust.

Beuchelle consists of thin slivers of calf's kidney, calf's sweetbreads and *cèpe* mushrooms, all briefly (and separately) sautéed in butter until crisp on the outside but still soft inside, mixed together with the addition of a little Madeira and plenty of cream, poured into a puff-pastry case, sprinkled with Parmesan and browned in the oven.

One of the most celebrated of all Loire Valley desserts is the upside-down apple tart known as *tarte Tatin*. Whether or not it was

Regional delicacies: fish, *saucissons*, *chèvre* and *confiserie*.

or come in a thinner, lighter version with the butter and sugar forming a kind of butterscotch (two particularly successful examples of the latter version feature on the menus of Bernard Robin at Bracieux, and the Hôtel du Perron at La Ferté-Saint-Aubin).

With the renewal of interest in *la cuisine du terroir*, more and more restaurants at all price levels are offering genuine traditional dishes. So with a little patience the interested gastronome should manage to track down plenty of Loire Valley specialities and possibly even, after several days of exploring and eating, sample all those scoffed by Curnonsky and his fellow guests at a single sitting.

Maurice Genevoix, the author of *Raboliot* who wrote so movingly about wild animals, spent most of his life by the Loire near Saint-Denis-l'Hôtel, 12 miles (18 km) east of Orléans. A member of the Association des Naturalistes Orléanais, he was very familiar with the wildlife of the Loire and the Sologne. In the preface to a world bestiary he published 10 years before his death in 1980 at the age of 90 he wrote: "What I would like to propose primarily to those minded to listen to me is a bestiary—a chance to make friends again with other living creatures, free animals. They are capable of greatly moving and touching us; they can teach, or teach us again, so much. From the bleak [a small carp] to the trout, from the honey bee to the lapwing, they can also accompany us and guide us back to real worlds—the worlds of rustling leaves, of flowing water, of distant murmurs from space that have not yet been smothered by the roar of motor traffic or the bang of supersonic aircraft."

Modern scourges: Had Genevoix been alive today he would surely have added the diktats of technocratic planners to his list of modern scourges. In the hope of taming one of the wildest rivers in Europe, technocrats in Tours concocted an ill-considered scheme to construct a series of dams on the upper Loire and its tributaries that would have resulted not only in the submerging of several villages beneath artificial lakes but also in the disruption of a whole floodplain ecosystem and, consequently, the destruction or banishing of much wildlife. Fortunately the French government stepped in and shelved the plan in 1990, thus preserving the presence—temporarily at least—of spawning salmon and the many rare wild plants, animals and birds that rely for their existence on the Loire's existing ecological niches.

The natural history of the Loire Valley, not surprisingly, is largely dominated by water. The surging current of the Loire does not have the whole show to itself. At the end of its course, the Atlantic plays a role: tides send salt water as far as 25 miles (40 km)

upstream. The ecosystem is also influenced by the Loire's sluggish tributaries and the Sologne's hundreds of lakes.

Many of the animals that are found in the Loire Valley and hardly anywhere else in France rely on a watery environment. The banks of the lower Loire provide shelter for the rare European mink, which feeds on fish, frogs and water rats. Beavers, once quite common in central France (they gave their name to the River Beuvron), disappeared in the 1930s. They returned in 1974 and have

been thriving on the Loire ever since, with an average of one family to every 4 or 5 km of river bank. Otters are also found on the Loire, but only towards the estuary. Another interesting animal is the salamander, a bright black-and-yellow amphibian which is particularly common in the Sologne.

It is in the Sologne that the greatest number of larger wild mammals are found—for the purposes of the hunt. The problem is that its 1.2 million acres (500,000 hectares) are largely private and well patrolled by gamekeepers, so trespassing is not recommended.

But an increasing number of signposted rights of way plunge into the depths of the

Preceding pages: Valençay animal park. **Left,** kingfisher. **Above,** grey heron.

forest, where you are unlikely to see another human soul except during the shooting season (roughly September–February). There is no problem in spotting plenty of squirrels (red only; the grey squirrel has not yet invaded this part of France) and rabbits, though many of the latter suffer from myxomatosis.

But if you sit silently by one of the hidden lakes or fields that your path takes you past, you may see several more exciting animals after a quarter of an hour or so. For the fairly dense, completely flat nature of Sologne woodland means that, just as you can usually see wild creatures only at the last moment, the same is true for them. So there is always that privileged instant between the time they come into view and the point at which they detect your presence.

Wild boar: If you are out bright and early, you may see a bushy-tailed pine marten in the trees, or a ferret or polecat investigating a rabbit hole. It is not uncommon to run into red or roe deer, whose population is maintained at a good level by strict restrictions on the number of animals that may be hunted each year (*plan de chasse*). Wild boar are more retiring than deer, unlikely to be seen in daylight but may be caught in headlights scuttling across the road at night (if you want to see these endearing creatures closer to— but in their tame version—visit one of the many parks that have boars in pens).

The huge Forêt de Chambord is a game reserve where large mammals can be observed at leisure from observation platforms. The best time to visit it is during the red deer's rutting season around the end of September and beginning of October. The Touraine has three large public woods also full of wildlife: the forests of Loches, Chinon and Amboise.

Laurent Charbonnier, France's leading wildlife film-maker, who lives in a half-timbered house on the edge of the Sologne near Bracieux, is relatively optimistic about the prospects for wildlife now that the Loire dams project has been shelved—as long as it stays shelved. In particular, he says, it will mean that the beaver, which returned so recently to the area, will be saved. Interest in wildlife is on the increase in France, and the French birdwatcher, until recently an almost unrecorded species, may now commonly be observed at work, often kitted out with a chic

camouflage jacket and fancy bird-watching telescope. The Sologne is particularly rich in bird life as well as game, says Charbonnier, "despite the pressure of the shooting industry". Although the shooting season disturbs many birds (and in the privacy of their shoots hunters are known to take the occasional potshot at protected "pests" such as owls roused from their daytime roosts), the Sologne remains a sheltered backwater for much of the year.

If you are lucky (and patient), the birds you may spot there, either passing through or breeding, include: two kinds of shrikes (great grey and red-backed), three harriers (marsh, hen and Montagu), osprey (now nesting again after a gap of 50 years), goshawk, merlin, nightjar, woodcock, snipe, the striking great black woodpecker (on the increase throughout France), cirl bunting, brambling, several warblers (reed, sedge, grasshopper, Savi's), kingfisher, three grebes (great crested, black-necked and little), the extraordinary bittern (very rare, according to Charbonnier), heron, crane, water rail, two terns (black and whiskered), greylag goose and an abundance of ducks (shoveler, gadwall, mallard, teal, Garganey, pochard, tufted, goosander and goldeneye).

One bird you are likely to hear before you see it—if you see it at all (it is very shy)—is the golden oriole, with its distinctive, insistent "weela-weelo" song.

But the Sologne does not have a monopoly of interesting bird life in the Loire Valley. In the marshland near the mouth of the Loire the handsome bluethroat is a common breeding bird. The Lac de Rillé, some 25 miles (40 km) northwest of Tours, is a 600-acre (250-hectare) artificial lake that consists partly of a leisure complex; but the rest of the site has been intelligently designed, its variable water levels creating floodlands and mudflats that are ideal for migrating or wintering ducks and waders.

Fishing spot: In addition to the water-loving species already mentioned in connection with the Sologne, birds that frequent the Lac de Rillé include cormorant (which fish there and go to roost on islands in the middle of the Loire), bean goose, pintail, golden plover, various sandpipers, black-tailed godwit, curlew, black stork, spoonbill, hobby, common tern, various divers and swans, peregrine falcon (which uses old tree stumps as perches) and in the surrounding meadows two pipits (rock and tawny), two wagtails (pied and grey) and siskin.

Other important migratory habitats include the floodplains of Baillies, just north of Angers. There, from mid-February to April, the meadows are partly waterlogged (ringed plover, ruff, dunlin, thousands of black-tailed godwit, quail, corncrake, spotted crake, kingfisher, whinchat, various warblers and corn bunting). The plain of Parcé-sur-Sarthe, just south of Sablé-sur-Sarthe, has a combination of copses and very pebbly fields which suit short-eared owl, lapwing, Lapland bunting, stone curlew, quail, ruff, partridge, red-legged partridge, many birds

ring, lesser black-back and great black-back).

The best time to visit the stretch of the Loire around Montlouis, Vouvray, Vernou and Noizay just upstream from Tours is between April and June. Many birds nest on its shingle beaches and sandbanks: terns (common and little), little ringed plover, yellow wagtail, sand martin, Cetti's warbler, willow tit and lesser whitethroat.

Many of the same birds also nest in the section of the Loire between Orléans and Jargeau, where the extraction of gravel has formed islands and pools of water, which is trapped each time the river level goes down. In addition to the terns, ducks and grebes also

of prey, and two rare species, dotterel and little bustard.

The banks of the Loire itself bristle with birdlife too. Invest in very detailed maps of the area (the IGN 1:25,000 series, with a scale of 4 cm to 1 km) to follow all the tiny roads and tracks that run along spits of land, dykes or bridges on to islands. The stretch of the Loire between Langeais and Villandry is particularly rewarding from September to January: there are major colonies of cormorants, herons, large numbers of surface and diving ducks, and gulls (black-headed, her-

Deer grazing at Valençay.

found further down the river, you may see sandpipers, curlew-sandpiper, dunlin and little stint. The sand martins that nest in the river banks are hunted by sparrowhawks and hobbies. In winter cormorants roost in this part of the Loire. Various warblers (melodious, grasshopper, garden and whitethroat) nest in undergrowth alongside the river. The nests of lapwings and stone curlews on the low-lying banks and shingle on the south side of the Loire from Chécy are now reportedly at risk—a fact that would without doubt have greatly saddened that great bird-lover who lived for much of his life near Chécy: Maurice Genevoix.

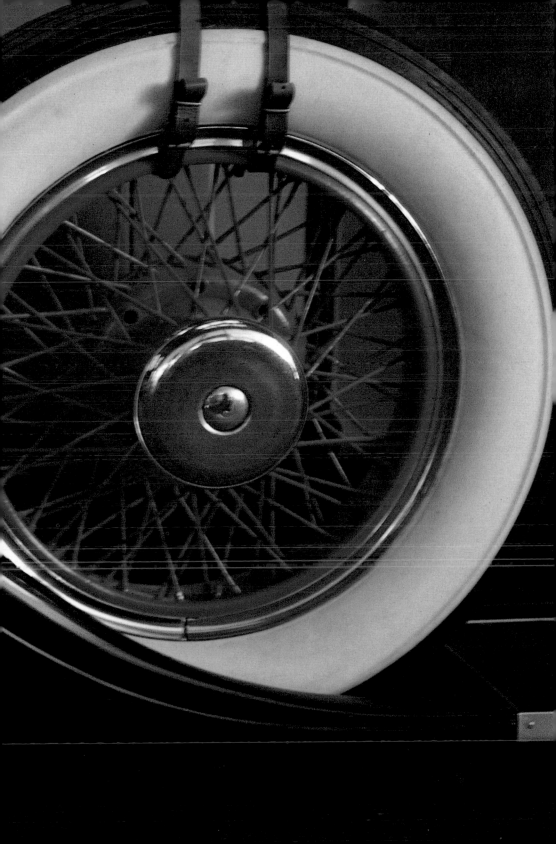

The Loire Valley may be beloved by poets but it is a difficult area to pin down for geographers, and boundary definitions vary considerably. Aware of the riches on offer, we have tried to be as generous as possible with our limits, extending what is usually considered to be the Vallée, between Gien and Angers, to include the whole of Anjou and the Orléanais region.

This stretch of the River Loire, with its magnificent architecture and historic glories, has been covered in detail. But we have not clung too closely to the river, believing that it is often in the backwaters and quiet byways that the true spirit of a region is to be found. Thus you will find areas like the Berry, the Beauce and northern Anjou, which are often rather briskly dismissed, explored at length.

Wherever possible, we have used the familiar names of the areas, such as Anjou, Touraine or the Sologne, instead of the confusingly named *départements* (Indre-et-Loire, Eure-et-Loire, Loir-et-Cher and so on). Each region has its own distinctive character and a visit can swing from the panoply of royal luxury in the great châteaux to the humblest little troglodyte church or cottage. Both are equally rewarding.

Touraine is the region of greatest historical interest; you can follow its literary and royal trails along the Loire and its smaller tributaries, the Vienne, Indrois, Indre and Cher, a landscape full of Renaissance gardens and grand châteaux. Anjou is of central historical importance—both French and English—with its great Romanesque abbey churches and castles. There is also *"la douceur Angevine"* of the poets, a lush, gentle landscape of fertile meadows and soft breezes.

City lovers will be impressed by the fine museums and excellent restaurants of Tours or Orléans, and can enjoy the quiet sophistication of smaller towns like Saumur, Angers or Blois.

But always behind the scenes the rural pleasures of this rich land await; the gentle landscape of the Orléanais with its half-timbered villages and rolling vineyards; le Loir, quiet little cousin of the *fleuve royal*, with its sense of community, its orchards, farms and small villages; the ruined watermills, forests and windswept plains of the Gatine or the Beauce.

Investigate, too, the secrets of the Sologne with its tracts of woodland dotted with little lakes, rare birds and glimpses of hidden châteaux. Further afield is Berry, a region which still represents the good old days to so many French people; an idealised view of the past and of country life to which the whole of the Loire Valley pays tribute; a travel cliché which fulfills its promise.

<u>Preceding pages</u>: Gone fishing; flags at Amboise; Valençay car museum. <u>Left</u>, gardens at Villandry.

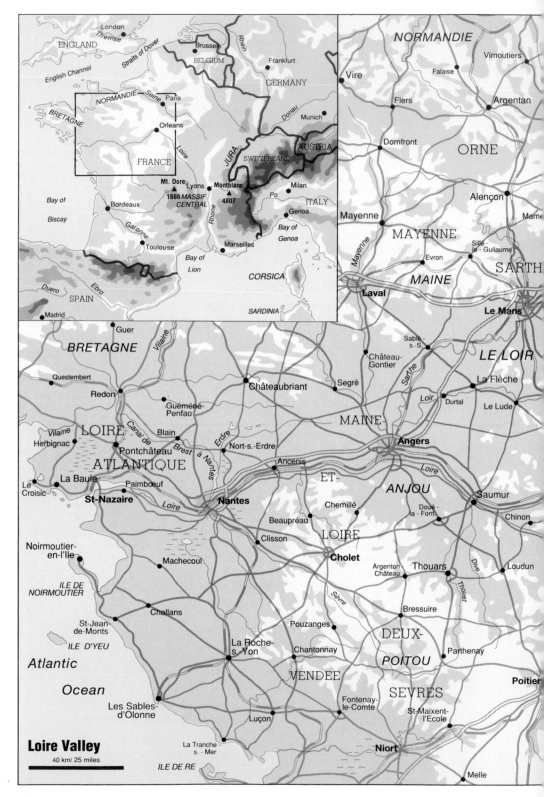

Loire Valley

40 km/ 25 miles

138

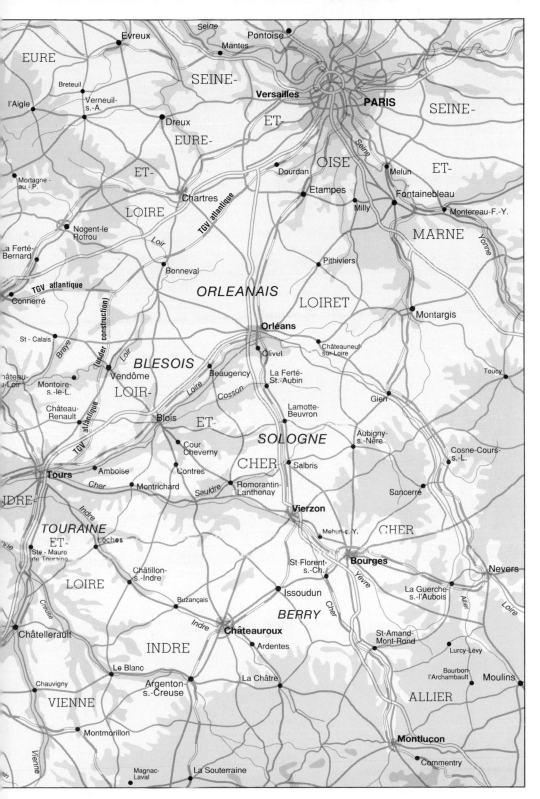

EURE

Evreux

Seine

Pontoise
Mantes

SEINE-

Versailles

PARIS

SEINE-

Breteuil

Verneuil-
s.-A.

l'Aigle

ET-

Dreux

EURE-

OISE

ET-

Melun

Mortagne -
au - P.

ET-

Chartres

Dourdan

Etampes

Fontainebleau

Seine

Milly

Montereau-F.-Y.

LOIRE

TGV atlantique

Loir

MARNE

Yonne

Nogent-le
Rotrou

Bonneval

Pithiviers

La Ferté-
Bernard

ORLEANAIS

LOIRET

Montargis

TGV atlantique

Connerré

Orléans

St - Calais

Braye

(under construction)

Olivet

Châteauneuf-
sur-Loire

Loir

BLESOIS

Beaugency

La Ferté-
St.-Aubin

Toucy

hâteau-
s-Loir

Montoire-
s.-le-L.

Vendôme

LOIR-

Loire

Cosson

Gien

Château-
Renault

TGV atlantique

Blois

ET-

Lamotte-
Beuvron

Cour
Cheverny

SOLOGNE

Aubigny-
s.-Nère

Cosne-Cours-
s.-L.

Tours

Amboise

Contres

CHER

Salbris

Cher

Montrichard

Sauldre

Romorantin-
Lanthenay

Sancerre

IDRE-

Indre

Vierzon

TOURAINE

ET-

Loches

Mehun-s.-Y.

CHER

Ste - Mauro
de Touraine

Châtillon-
s.-Indre

St-Florent-
s.-Ch.

Bourges

Nevers

LOIRE

Buzançais

Issoudun

La Guerche-
s.-l'Aubois

Allier

Loire

Creuse

Indre

BERRY

Cher

Yèvre

Châtellerault

Châteauroux

St-Amand-
Mont-Rond

Le Blanc

Ardentes

Lurcy-Lévy

INDRE

Chauvigny

Argenton-
s.-Creuse

La Châtre

La Châtre

Bourbon-
l'Archambault

Moulins

VIENNE

ALLIER

Montmorillon

Montluçon

Vienne

Commentry

Magnac-
Laval

La Souterraine

139

BLACK ANJOU

The 16th-century poet Joachim du Bellay, who came from west Anjou, wrote that he loved "more than the sea air the sweetness of Anjou." *La douceur angevine* is still the phrase most often used to describe the lush, gentle countryside of the region, where even the black-and-white cows look sweet-natured, the air is soft and a little hazy, the land green and fertile.

The terrain of the area is quite variable, shifting from black schist in the northwest to the white tufa stone further south, both of which lend their characteristic regional tone to the architecture and landscape; hence the terms Black and White Anjou.

Black is a word often applied to the capital of the region, **Angers**. Although the daunting shadow of the château may not be as intimidating now as it was to approaching troops in the Middle Ages, it still eclipses anything built later, and, despite the ubiquitous tangle of motorway intersections, the approach to Angers from the north remains a dramatic experience.

Strategic position: You might choose to stay in one of the many small hotels or châteaux in the area; otherwise, Angers itself makes a comfortable, accessible base for visiting the surrounding region. Its strategic position led the Romans to settle here, and later Foulques Nerra built one of his many strongholds on the present site of the castle.

As one of the capitals of the Plantagenet empire which linked England and France, it was known as the Key to the Kingdom and saw some very fierce fighting during the Hundred Years' War. However, its rich land and the commercial river links meant the town survived and flourished. It suffered badly during World War II and was the regional headquarters of the Gestapo from 1942. As a result, there has been much reconstruction, most of it, however, sensitively done.

Angers today is a substantial town of 200,000 people, enlivened by a young university student population. It is the centre of a flourishing agricultural area, growing vines, flowers and vegetables, much of which can be seen in the huge Saturday market. Local industry includes a thriving electronics sector, as well as the production of the famous Cointreau, a clear liqueur distilled from orange peel; it is manufactured in a large distillery outside Angers which can be visited.

Angers is a civilised and charming place. The wide, leafy boulevards, which were built over the defensive ditches of the original fortress, now surround the old town which is pedestrianised and rich with museums, historical buildings, pleasant cafés and elegant shopping streets. It is a pity that the waterfront is so little exploited, and a road of fast-moving traffic divides it from the rest of the town.

The American writer Henry James, on "A Little Tour of France" in the 19th century, made some very acid observations of Angers, commenting: "There is always an effect of perversity in a town

lying near a great river and yet not upon it." Angers is situated a few miles from the mighty Loire, on the Maine river, which James described rather petulantly as "a meagre affluent".

The 6-mile (10-km) length of the Maine is actually the confluence of the Mayenne, the Loire and the Sarthe rivers, and its position meant that until the advent of the railways, Angers was a very important port, easily accessible from the sea. Today the imposing bulk of the **château** still dominates the town and is the best place to begin a visit; the excellent views from the battlements provide orientation and there is convenient parking usually to be found next to the château walls.

As you approach the drawbridge entrance, look out for the deer grazing in the dry moat, all that remains of a medieval menagerie which included leopards, monkeys and lions. Although the château is described as black, its massive hulk is actually relieved with stripes of white stone and the local blue-black slate. Once inside, take any of the narrow stone staircases up to the battlements and stroll round to get your bearings. From the Moulin tower, so called because it originally had a windmill on the top, there are excellent views, southeast over the black slate roofs of Angers and the cathedral spires, and northwest across the river and beyond.

The original castle was rebuilt by King Louis IX between 1228 and 1238; the 17 towers of the château were originally much taller and complete with pepper-pot roofs, but these were razed by Henri III during the Wars of Religion. Fortunately, Henry IV took a liking to what remained and stopped the destruction going any further.

The medieval gardens introduced by the much-loved King René can still be seen on the battlements, planted with vines, lavender and medicinal herbs. Within the castle walls formal French gardens have been laid out and flocks of white doves flutter among the geometrically arranged topiary.

When you descend, head for the 15th-century chapel built of white tufa stone,

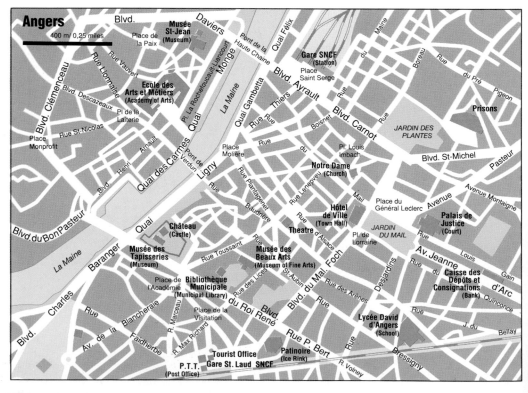

with its beautiful vaulting roof, carvings and delicate wall paintings. The chapel is often used for art exhibitions of contemporary paintings and tapestries which complement and enhance the ancient stones which have been carefully restored after their war-time bomb damage.

The jewel of the château, indeed of Angers, the Apocalypse Tapestry, is housed in an entirely modern gallery, sensitively blended, fortunately, with the original architecture. The Tapestry is truly magnificent, considered to be the oldest and largest tapestry ever woven, 70 huge panels covering over 100 metres of the gallery walls.

It was originally commissioned in 1373 by Louis d'Anjou from a Parisian weaver, Nicolas Bataille, who worked from designs by Hennequin de Bruges, and it was hung in the cathedral to celebrate important ceremonies. But, during the Revolution, the tapestry was thrown into the streets and the good citizens of Angers tore it up for bedspreads and blankets.

It was rescued in 1843 by the Bishop of Angers who managed to find about two-thirds of it and had it painstakingly restored. Still richly hued despite its great age, the tapestry is woven of wool and gold thread, mainly in blues and reds with a background of *millefleurs*, initials interlaced with tiny stylised flowers. It tells the story of the Apocalypse as revealed to St John in the New Testament, with much collapsing of cities and flowing rivers of blood.

Among the gore and damnation there are many humorous little details, like the rabbit disappearing down a hole in one panel and reappearing in the border of another. In one of the images of St John, he is surrounded by exquisite butterflies, their wings decorated with the ermine of Brittany and the arms of Anjou. Another panel depicts Babylon as a prostitute in Satan's service, caught in an intimate moment, arranging her blonde hair in front of a mirror.

Guides, both text and audio, are provided and need to be carefully followed because, when the panels were first

Angers cathedral and château from La Doutre.

restored, some were put together in the wrong order. Also in the gallery are the remains of a Romanesque chapel, recently unearthed. There are more 15th-century tapestries to be seen in the Logis Royal and the Governor's residence, next door to which is a charming little tea garden.

Cathédrale St-Maurice is only a short walk from the château through the quiet byways of the old town: the Rue de L'Oisellerie, Rue St-Aignan and Rue des Filles-Dieu. The narrow streets are still cobbled and winding, with a few old, well-preserved wooden houses, half-timbered with carved beams, stained-glass windows and weathered oak doors.

Alternatively, approach the cathedral from below, climbing up the St-Maurice Ascent. The steep flight of steps is dominated by the cathedral's twin spires, lantern tower and a fine Romanesque facade with beautifully carved frieze and tympanum.

Inside it is exceedingly gloomy, making it difficult to appreciate fully its celebrated nave, considered a 12th-century masterpiece, one of the earliest examples of the Angevin style of Gothic vaulting, spanning a previously unprecedented 64 ft (19.5 metres). St-Maurice is also famous for its glorious, stained-glass windows, some of which date back to the 12th century and have miraculously survived.

Investigate in particular the windows in the north of the nave, one of which tells the extraordinarily gruesome story of St Vincent, the patron saint of vine growers; he was flayed, burned and, while still alive, his body was laid on shards of broken glass.

In Place St-Croix next to the cathedral is the **Maison d'Adam**, a tall 15th-century half-timbered building with elaborate wood carvings. It was formerly known as the House of the Tree of Life after the corner which is fashioned in the form of a gnarled old tree. Pious and profane carved figures mingle merrily on the facade.

Historically, Angevins have been somewhat neglectful of their architec-

Apocalypse Tapestry: Babylon in Satan's service.

tural heritage, and even in 1882 Henry James was complaining about the "stupidly and vulgarly modernized" town, which he sourly described as a "sell". Today, however, the remaining jewels of Angers are greatly cherished, and there are some bold and imaginative attempts at blending old and new.

A brilliant example is the 13th-century **Chapelle Toussaint**, which now houses the David d'Angers Gallery, a large collection of plaster casts donated by the town's famous sculptor. His statue of Duke René can be seen at the crossroads near the château.

The vaulted roof, which collapsed in 1815, and the tall Gothic windows have been replaced by black framed clear glass to elegant effect, the clean lines emphasising the architectural details and white stone of the building.

It more than does justice to the sculptures which seem rather florid and heavy by comparison. The excellent collection of paintings of the Fine Arts Museum is housed in the 15th-century Renaissance palace, the **Logis Bar-**

Cloisters of Hôpital de St Jean.

rault, which is next door to the church.

The church of **St-Martin** is a little difficult to find, tucked away behind the post office in Rue St-Martin, but it is important as a very early 11th-century construction with a dome, built in 1075, considered to be the oldest large French Romanesque dome in existence.

The **Hôtel Pincé** is a well-preserved Renaissance house built between 1530 and 1538, now housing a museum which includes Greek and Etruscan vases, an Egyptian collection, a collection of Chinese and Japanese art and a number of prehistoric artefacts which were discovered locally. The house itself has a beautiful stone stairway and some fine ceilings.

The **Place du Ralliement** is the centre of the town, historically famous as the execution place for Royalists, and a good starting point for exploring the neighbouring shopping streets. Rue St-Laud and Rue St-Aubin both have excellent shops, cafés and restaurants.

In the **Place Pilori** is Notre-Dame-des-Victoires, a neo-Gothic church on

an ancient site which is architecturally unremarkable, but has stunning Art Nouveau stained-glass windows, best seen at midday when the sunlight pierces through, brilliantly illuminating the jewelled panels and dappling the columns of the chancel with colour.

On the other side of the river from the château is the area called **La Doutre** ("Beyond"). Elegant houses front the river where there is a small marina and quiet *quais* pleasant for walking. Cross over by the Pont de Verdun and follow Rue Beaurepaire to reach Place de la Laitierie and the church of La Trinité.

Here a number of carefully restored half-timbered houses surround the square. The 12th-century **La Trinité** is currently under much needed repair, but inside it has beautiful vaulting, and an extraordinary 16th-century carved spiral staircase leading to the organ.

The main reason to cross the river however is the **Hôpital de St Jean**, founded in 1174 by Henry II of England as penance for the murder of Thomas à Becket. It was used as a hospital for seven centuries, the three naves of its vast vaulted hall lined with patients, women on one side, men on the other.

Now the original function of this superb building is confined rather incongruously to a corner, where there is a collection of 17th-century dispensing jars and containers from the original pharmacy, including a huge pewter pot containing a treatment for snake bites. Behind the Hôpital are the remains of 12th-century Romanesque cloisters and the restored granary.

The Hôpital is now devoted to the Lurçat tapestries, created by Jean Lurçat in 1957 and inspired by the Apocalypse Tapestry. *Le Chant du Monde* is his masterpiece and covers the walls of the building. Critical opinion varies about the work itself and it is worth comparing other more experimental examples of Lurcat's painting and tapestry in the museum next door— but Lurçat was responsible for reviving the art of tapestry and it certainly seems appropriate that his modern work should be housed in one of the most

Church carved from rock at Béhuard.

ancient buildings in Angers. The city is famous for its flowers and the **Jardins des Plantes** is a delightful English-style park with lake, trees and ornamental plants. The famous flower market takes place every Saturday, and is best visited early in the morning. As well as exquisitely arranged flowers, plants and vegetables from the surrounding area, there is also a very impressive selection of fish and seafood: crabs, sea urchins, mussels, oysters, snails, shrimps, all piled high and assessed assiduously by traders and shoppers alike. In the nearby Place Pilori there is a flea market, which is lively with music and fun to wander round, though there are few bargains to be had.

West Anjou: Drive out to the south of Anjou through **Ponts-de-Cé** where the Loire starts to divide into tributaries and the Val de Loire comes to an end. From here you can either follow the D751 along the south bank of the Loire, and briefly the Louet tributary which runs parallel, or criss-cross from one side to the other over fairly frequent bridges,

though you do need to plan ahead which bank of the river you want to be on.

Rochefort-sur-Loire is on the Louet, a quiet old village with a 15th-century bell tower, close to the Côteaux du Layon vineyards. This is the only really sweet wine of the Loire, and Quarts de Chaume, sold locally, is the finest to try.

From Rochefort there are signs to Béhuard and Savennières. Both are well worth the detour. **Béhuard** (pronounced *Buard*) is a beautiful island in the middle of the river. At its heart is the church of Béhuard, built high on a massive rock and surrounded by tall, graceful poplars. It began as a pagan sailors' shrine giving thanks for their safety, and later the Christians added a chapel. In the 15th century the devout Louis XI built a church and lodging house next door. The tiny church is very simple and moving, literally carved out of the rock, the north wall of the nave as craggy as a cave.

In the chaplain's house, before you climb up the steps to the church, is an

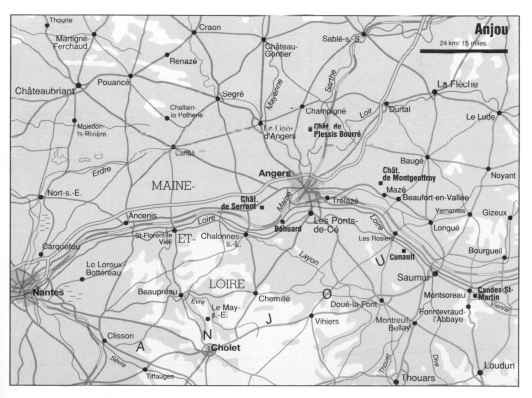

exhibition of photographs, some antique, some as recent as 1988, of the completely flooded village; a very jolly postman is shown doing his rounds by boat. Flooding is a regular occurrence here but the villagers are well prepared, with steps up to all the doorways. Indeed, they seem almost proud of the distinction; a slate marker next to the church records the high water mark of each flood.

Béhuard is a very pleasant place to stop for lunch; there is a restaurant with a good view of the church, and afterwards the quiet fields and sandy beaches of the island can spin out a sunny peaceful afternoon.

Those more dedicated to sightseeing should continue to **Savennières**, which has a delightful old church with a Romanesque apse and intricate red brickwork on the facade surrounding the door. Savennières produces some good wine and its wine cellars are its most treasured facility, visible through narrow arched alleys in the huddled little streets.

Returning to the south bank and the D751, the road begins to wind uphill along the Angevin Corniche, a route less intimidating than it sounds. Much of the road wanders gently through acres of golden vines and huge flower farms where even in the fields the flowers seemed to have been arranged with a discerning eye for design and colour. Stop at **Haie Longue**, where there is a good view across the valley.

Chalonnes would make a delightful spot for a picnic; you can park right next to the church on the riverside where there is a quay with little boats drawn up and large shady plane trees.

It is worth continuing this pretty route downriver as far as **St Florent-le-Vieil**, a small village with an enormous church and a chequered history. It is perched high on the hill overlooking the river. You can drive or walk up the steep streets to the top, where a square full of chestnut trees provides shady respite and a magnificent view.

The Ile Batailleuse below was used by the Vikings as a base for attacking all

Reflections of the Mayenne river.

the Loire villages and it is quite clear what a strategic position it was for marauding invaders.

St Florent was a Roman soldier who came here as a missionary, living in caves in the hillside. Later a Benedictine monastery was built but the monks fled in the 9th century at the threat from the Vikings. A new monastery was eventually established at St-Hilaire-St Florent near Saumur, and thus this St Florent became "le Vieil".

The current church is 18th-century, said to have been designed by Mansard, and it is surprisingly grand for such a small village. You can explore quite freely, climbing the monks' staircase which ascends to a little room from which there is a splendid bird's-eye view of the surrounding countryside.

In the cool white crypt there is a collection of statues, ancient manuscripts and other treasures. Most valuable of all is David d'Angers' monumental mausoleum and statue of Bonchamps, the hero of the Vendéen war, which began in this area.

Returning down the hill, look out for the remnants of much older buildings, a crumbling archway or vestigial carving. Follow the hidden paths, *les ruelles,* between the houses, which wend their way down to the riverbank past the garden *potagers* of the villagers. At the river side there are wooden benches under the trees, a favoured local spot for contemplating the inexorable onward flow of the Loire.

Just a little further along the D751 is **La Bourgonnière**, famous for its 16th-century chapel, and **Liré**, the boyhood home of poet Joachim du Bellay, where there is a good small museum devoted to his memory.

Ingrandes, on the north bank of the Loire, is on the border between Anjou and Brittany. It is best approached along the raised causeway from the south side of the river, from where its origin as a port is clearly visible. Sadly, this function has now ceased and the town is a little forlorn; even its church is an unappealing 1950s construction. Still, the old *quai* is picturesque and pleasant to

Château of Serrant.

wander along, with lots of gaily painted rowing boats thudding against the stone steps and slipways.

Serrant is an important château not far from Angers right on the N23, a beguiling sight with surrounding moat and lake, swans gliding by and violets dotting the bank. Although built over a long period (16th to 18th centuries), it is a homogeneous structure of dark-brown schist and contrasting white tufa, with solid round towers and cupolas. Philibert Delorme, famed architect of the Tuileries and the wing of Chenonceaux whose arches span the river, contributed to the design.

To view the interior, a guided tour is obligatory but it is briskly conducted and the original 18th-century furniture and decoration in the opulent apartments are well worth seeing. The staircase is Renaissance, as are the coffered ceilings and the fireplace in the Grand Salon. There is a bedroom designed especially for Napoleon, with a splendid curved Empire bed and his bust over the fireplace—although in the event he didn't sleep here after all. The most delightful room is the library of 10,000 books, including a complete history of the campaigns of Napoleon. The billiard table and a faint lingering whiff of wood smoke attest to more contemporary occupation.

North Anjou: Stray from the mighty Loire for a while and investigate the charms of its tributaries in the north of Anjou; between the Sarthe and the Mayenne is an enchanting area of rich pasture land, gentle backwaters and quiet roads—a good place to retreat from intensive sightseeing.

Châteaux abound here too—indeed, even the farmhouses have turrets—but they don't flaunt themselves, slipping into the background to be glimpsed on a hillside or through a veil of trees. Many of them are private homes but can be patronised for an authentic *table d' hôte* or an overnight stay to experience *la vie en château*.

Few of the villages here are distinguished by great architecture or must-see sights, which makes wandering **Canoeing on the Sarthe.**

152

around them by car or bicycle all the more delightful and undemanding. Stop wherever appeals for a picnic lunch, a walk along the river bank or just to lean over a bridge and watch the river slip slowly by.

Starting from Angers, follow the D191 along the meandering banks of the Mayenne and head for **Grez-Neuville** where there is a bridge across the river and a quiet marina with lock and weir. Tall poplars reflect golden in a wide stretch of water, shading the grey weathered slate roofs of the cottages with their lovingly tended gardens full of cabbages and roses.

Lion d'Angers (from the Latin *legio*, meaning a military base) is a little further on at the crossroads with the N162 and on the banks of the Oudon. It is a quiet little town specialising in rearing horses; nearby is the racecourse and stud at Château l'Isle-Briand. The church of St-Martin has pre-Romanesque tracery in red brick round the door and 16th-century frescoes.

Returning to the Mayenne, follow the D187 until you reach the pretty village of Chambellay and on to **la Jaille-Yvon**, a sleepy little hamlet at the end of the road. Along the village street and behind the church is a stunning view over the golden wheatfields in the valley, with not a sound to be heard except for birdsong. Continue just a little further to **Daon** along peaceful rural roads bordered by apple trees. Daon supplies a surprising splash of colour among the green and gold of fields and woodland, with jolly pedal boats painted wild colours bobbing about on the water; these plus shady trees on the gently sloping riverbank make it an excellent place to pause with children.

If you take a turn off the D213 just outside Daon towards Menil, there is a very beautiful drive or walk if you have time. The narrow road alongside the Mayenne hugs close to the river with steep woodland on one side and meadows on the other.

The river is so slow moving the reflections of clouds and trees resemble a tapestry, and the silence is broken only

A quiet day's fishing.

by ducks splashing and acorns falling.

Menil is a serious backwater and still has an old-fashioned car ferry to cross the river; it's a shallow raft the size of just one vehicle, manipulated with a great iron chain and pulley wheel. Parts of the village church and its clocktower are Romanesque.

Tiny alleys: To the west is **Segré**, in the middle of *bocage* country, wooded farmland in a gentle landscape, the skyline punctuated by attenuated spires. The buildings are low with slate roofs, built of schist, typical of "Black" Anjou. Segré itself is tucked into the hillside on the banks of the Oudon, and its distinctive hump-backed bridge crosses to the older part of town. Vestiges of its original château may be seen by diligent exploration of the narrow streets and tiny alleyways of the town.

There are any number of smaller châteaux in this area of Anjou, many of which are beautifully landscaped and reward a visit if you are close by. One that is worth a considerable detour, however, is **Château du Plessis-Bourré**. It is both fortified and fairytale, established at a time when houses became more luxurious but their owners still desired adequate protection. It was built between 1468 and 1473 by Jean Bourré, tutor to the Dauphin, the future Louis XI.

The visitor approaches over a long multi-arched bridge across the moat and through the double drawbridge; within is a large interior courtyard and gallery. The interior has a wealth of fine Renaissance furniture and panelling, but its greatest pride is the 15th-century coffered ceiling of the guardroom, its panels richly painted in allegorical scenes and mottoes, which are both moralistic and risqué.

Plessis-Bourré is set like a jewel in flat pastureland to the west of the Sarthe, surrounded by a wide moat which reflects its white walls and blue slate spire and pepper-pot towers to perfection. Like so much of Anjou, what makes it so satisfying is the complementary arrangement of exquisite architecture and a rural landscape civilised over centuries.

WHITE ANJOU

The region flanking the Loire between Angers and Saumur is sometimes known as "White" Anjou because of the predominance of white tufa stone, both in its natural cliff state, carved into troglodyte caves and houses, or used, as in Saumur, to build an entire château. The wedding-cake turrets and pepper-pot towers of Saumur's white-walled fortress thus fulfill the archetypal image of a Loire château. It is perched high on the cliff overlooking a wide sweep of the river, just as it is illustrated in the Duc de Berry's *Très Riches Heures*.

Saumur is a convenient place from which to see the surrounding country—indeed, a good base from which to visit much of the Loire Valley. Although quite a small town, it has some excellent hotels and restaurants, parking is rarely a problem and most of the interesting sights can be reached on foot.

Saumur used to be a much larger town, an important port in the centre of a fertile wine-growing region. During the 16th and 17th centuries it was a key centre for the Protestants, who founded an Academy which drew students from all over Europe. But when the Edict of Nantes was revoked in 1685, stripping French Protestants of their rights, many of them emigrated. Saumur has never had as large a population since. It is now best known for its wines (in particular, sparkling wine), its mushrooms and its cavalry school.

If you can, park right on the *quai* side on the edge of the old town. Here the chestnut trees by the riverside are shady and cool, the river is broad and there are boats, windsurfers and even some swimmers to be seen.

On the Quai Mayaud is the **Hôtel de Ville**, originally part of the town wall which went right down into the river. Only the left-hand side is 16th-century, but later additions have maintained its Gothic appearance. From here you can wander through the windy little streets of the old town and up to the château. Pause first in the **Place St-Pierre** at the

Eglise St-Pierre, whose tall, elegant spire can be seen flanking the château from a distance. Although the exterior and the noted Romanesque door have been under restoration, the building still rewards investigation. Much of it dates from the 12th and 13th centuries but had to be rebuilt after lightning struck in 1674; the Latin inscription *Firmior ex lapsu* (firmer and stronger) on the facade may refer to the building after reconstruction or possibly to St Peter's faith after his three denials of Christ.

Inside, the choir and transept are 12th-century, and there are two greatly treasured 15th and 16th-century tapestries, depicting the lives of St Peter and St Florent, the Roman monk who founded a monastery at the nearby village of St-Hilaire-St-Florent.

In the Place St-Pierre there are a number of very well restored half-timbered buildings. To the right of the church is a narrow street of wooden houses en route to the château. This is Montée du Fort, the location of Balzac's novel *Eugénie Grandet*, a gloomy street "hot

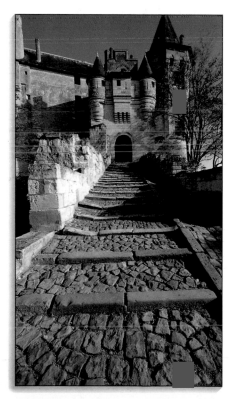

in summer, cold in winter, and in some places dark and overshadowed", according to Balzac. He provides an excellent if sombre picture of how the citizens lived, using the ground floors of the houses as shops or workshops with the top halves of the great wooden doors thrown back and goods laid out on the wall. Like Balzac, "one notes the doors, studded with huge nails, on which our ancestors recorded the passions of the age in hieroglyphs."

Balzac would be surprised by the salubrious nature of these streets today, carefully preserved and enhanced by new and complementary architecture, melancholy completely banished.

The radical reconstruction of many of the buildings in Saumur may not appeal to the purist. Any attempt to preserve Saumur as a museum appears to have been abandoned, and instead a bold effort has been made to recreate houses in a sort of neo-Renaissance style. Around the ramparts of the château is a cluster of new white tufa buildings with beguiling turrets and carved windows, slate spires, even the occasional section of exposed wattle and daub.

The elegant, fairy-tale **château** of Saumur is set in lovely gardens, and it is a pleasure to wander round the outside and enjoy the panoramic view. It is in a perfect defensive position, towering over the curve of the river and visible for miles. Despite the deceptively chocolate-box turrets and decorations of the 14th-century structure, it is first and foremost a well-protected fortress, which has done duty as a prison and barracks as well as a ducal residence.

Instead of the ubiquitous assemblage of furniture and tapestries, the 15th-century interior has wisely been devoted to two highly regarded collections: a Museum of Decorative Arts, particularly Limoges enamel and porcelain, and an Equine Museum devoted to the history of the horse, and including engravings by George Stubbs. Note, however, that the guided tour is 90 minutes long, so unless you have a passion for horses or china you may feel inclined to give it a miss.

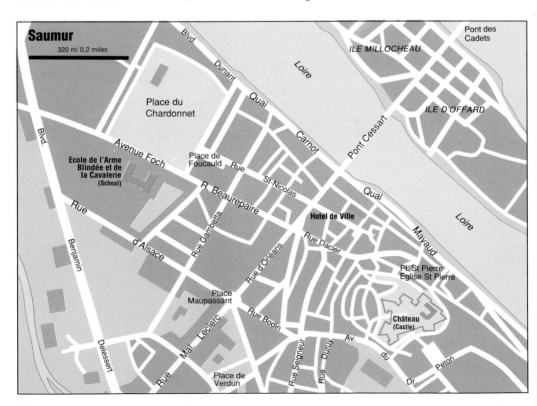

One thing you should look out for is the old iron key hanging inside the castle door; it was stolen by an American soldier in 1918, but he returned it in 1966 after suffering years of guilt, and he was ceremonially pardoned amid great celebration.

If you follow the Grande Rue and little streets behind the châtcau you will discover **Notre-Dame-de-Nantilly**, a beautiful though somewhat neglected Romanesque church with blind arcading and a fine set of gargoyles. It is noted particularly for its oratory and its magnificent tapestries, some of which were made at Aubusson in the 17th century. There is a pleasing continuity in the modern tapestry maker at work in the shop opposite the church.

A leisurely stroll round Saumur does not take long and the town is well provided with elegant clothes shops, second-hand bookshops, *maison du vin* and food emporiums galore. In particular, anyone interested in a radical approach to architectural reconstruction should not miss it.

Saumur cavalry school.

An ecclesiastical route: Downstream from Saumur the river widens further and the drive along its banks, though often busy, has rewarding views as the aspects of the river shift with the seasons and times of day, sometimes blue and sparkling, at other times shrouded in soft pearly mists.

Heading northwest on the D751, you will reach the village of **St-Hilaire-St-Florent** on the banks of the Thouet, famous for its mushrooms, the National Riding School, which can be visited, and its wine—in particular, the champagne method which was developed here. The tufa cliffs are used as cellars by the local growers, most of which can be visited for free *dégustations*.

Continue along the D751 to **Chênehutte-les-Tuffeaux**, pausing to visit its Romanesque church and admire the sweep of the river. A mushroom festival is held here in May. **Trèves-Cunault**, just a little further on, is a charming village of white tufa, built on the site of an old fortress, evidence of which can be discerned in the walls of the village houses. The soft tufa has been used for dwellings, sheds and even garages; if they need a bit more space, they simply hack their way a little further into the rock.

The church here is a movingly simple Romanesque structure with a surprisingly large nave, a barrel vault of wood with oak supports. Note a lovely rood screen and crucifix, the carvings on the capitals, and a porphyry stoup carved with primitive figures.

Cunault is truly stunning, a superb Romanesque church founded by the Benedictines in the 11th century which James Bentley suggests may be the longest Romanesque church in western France. Above the doorway is a tympanum with a Madonna and (headless) Child and the 11th-century bell tower is crowned by a 15th-century spire. Inside, the clean lines and elegant columns of the vast space are awesome.

There are 223 intricately carved capitals, with tender gnomic little figures as well as grotesque monsters, many of which are still painted, and merit close examination with binoculars, if you

MUSHROOM CAPITAL OF FRANCE

They're called *champignons de Paris*, but most of the mushrooms cultivated in France—75 percent of them—come from the Saumur region. That's a lot of mushrooms: about 100,000 tonnes a year, or about one-tenth of the world's production. France is the second largest producer of mushrooms in the world after the United States, and the largest exporter.

Three hundred tonnes of mushrooms are picked daily around Saumur, cultivated in the many dark, damp caves created over the centuries as rock has been quarried to build the great cathedrals, châteaux and towns of the Loire. There are around 450 miles (800 km) of these "Troglodyte Gardens" in the Saumur region alone.

The French began to cultivate mushrooms in the late 17th century. They soon discovered that the quarries around Paris provided the perfect damp, dark, insulated conditions that mushrooms require, thus the name *champignons de Paris*, a name which stuck, even after the Loire Valley became the most important centre of intensive mushroom production in the early 1900s.

Just east of Saumur, in Saint-Hilaire-Saint-Florent, is the Musée du Champignon, devoted to mushroom cultivation, located in caves owned by the winemaker Louis

Bouchard. All you can see at first are flats and bags—mostly bags—of compost with mushrooms at various stages of development. To appreciate what is going on you have to understand something about the process; the mushrooms growing in the flats and bags are the end result of an intense 15-week cycle which starts outside the caves. Mushroom cultivation begins in large compost "factories", where huge, steaming piles of manure and straw soaked with water and mixed with nitrates are left to ferment for a two-week period (one of these composting units produces 1,500 tonnes of compost a week). The compost is then placed in boxes and left in a pasteurisation chamber, a kind of steam bath, where the fermentation is completed, bacteria (as well as the compost's unpleasant odour) are eliminated, and

the mixture becomes ideal as a seedbed for the mushrooms. Meanwhile, scientists at nearby laboratories cultivate mycelium, the mushroom spawn, from spores of the Paris mushroom, the *Agaricus bisporus*. Recently they have also begun to cultivate mycelium from pleurotte mushrooms (oyster mushroom) and the Japanese shitake mushrooms. The spawn is then mixed with the compost at the composting unit, which is taken to the mushroom caves, either in the large wooden boxes where the pasteurisation has taken place, or more often today, in large plastic bags. The Saumur caves provide a perfect atmosphere for incubation, which takes 15 to 18 days. Air circulates freely, and the temperature remains at a constant 12° C (54° F), the humidity at 90 percent.

After incubation the compost is covered with a mixture of crushed limestone and peat (*terre de gobetage* or "casing earth") and in about three weeks the first mushrooms appear. There will be five crops, or "flushes" (*volées*), over the next two weeks, heaviest in the beginning and gradually thinning out. Each 35-kg (78-lb) bag of compost will produce 6–10 kg (13–22 lb) of mushrooms. These will be harvested daily, early in the morning, in time to reach the marketplace by midday. After the last crop of mushrooms has been picked, the bags or flats of spent compost will be removed, the space disinfected and made ready for the next round.

Mushroom production is big business in the Loire, employing about 5,000 people. They are employed as agricultural workers in the caves, by the mycelium labs, the compost production sites, and the mushroom packing plants, where mushrooms are canned, frozen and dried. Almost every major town in the Saumur area has at least one business connected with mushroom cultivation. In Saumur alone there are 12 compost centres and several labs, packing plants (75 percent of the canned mushrooms in France come from Saumur) and shipping depots, not to mention the miles of caves.

It's a wonder, then, that you don't see more dishes in Loire Valley restaurants garnished *à la forestière*, with mushrooms and bacon, and that *beurre blanc* rather than *sauce aux champignons* is the ubiquitous Loire Valley sauce.

have them. There are also large and well-preserved frescoes of St Sebastian and St Christopher, a 16th-century ash chasuble chest, a 16th-century polychrome *pietà*, and a 13th-century carved and painted wooden shrine holding the bones of St Maxenceul, one of the disciples of St Martin. Sundays are a good day to visit since there are often musical performances, and even a practising organist can enhance the medieval atmosphere.

At **Gennes**, drive up to the ruined church from which there is a delightful view of the Loire and a touching monument to the cavalry school cadets of Saumur who died during World War II, defending the hilltop against the Germans. Over the suspension bridge from Gennes, on the right bank of the Loire, is **Les Rosiers**, a small town with an excellent restaurant and a church with a Renaissance bell tower designed by the Angevin architect Jean de l'Espine.

Back to Gennes and just off the D751 is **La Prieure**, a quiet little hamlet built round a beautiful priory with a Roman-

esque tower and surrounded by cedar trees. From here you could continue further west across forested hunting country or return to the river and **Le Thoureil**, once a port for shipping the local apple crop. There is also **St-Maur-de-Glanfeuil Abbey**, a ruined Benedictine monastery founded on the site of a Roman temple, and now restored as a thriving religious centre and welcoming sanctuary.

If time permits, a detour to **Brissac-Quincé** is worthwhile, to visit the Château de Brissac and its magnificent grounds. The château itself is still lived in by the Duc de Brissac and his family but is open to visitors.

If you now head southeast along the D761 you will find distinctly contrasting residences in the troglodyte towns of Louresse-Rochemenier and Doué-la-Fontaine. At **Rochemenier** there is an entire underground troglodyte village, over which the present village has been built. It has been superbly restored, with farms, barns, wine cellars, meeting rooms and even a chapel dug

Left, mushroom farming. Right, the Loire at Gennes.

out of the soft tufa rock. Although this underground existence seems so primitive now, the principle was sound, providing cheap, secure accommodation which was warm and cosy in winter and cool in summer.

Many of the rooms are equipped and furnished and give a very evocative picture of their inhabitants' way of life, congregating in the dark and smoky caves during the winter, to spin and weave and prepare walnuts for pressing. There is also an excellent collection of early photographs of the people at work in their fields and houses.

Above the underground chapel is a little church which was burnt down during the religious wars of the 16th century, when the faithful retreated underground. In the 17th century the church was rebuilt with two massive buttresses, a Renaissance-style doorway, and gravestones used for paving inside. It is a simple, charming building, now used only for burials and an annual service in honour of the village patron saint, Ste Emerance, who had the reputed ability to deflect hail and thunder. Until the 20th century, during a thunderstorm the church bells would be rung until the thunder went away.

Even more evocative than Rochemenier is **La Fosse**, a few miles north of Doué-la-Fontaine, via the D214. (Follow the signs carefully.) Here an enterprising family has taken over an underground hamlet and now lives there permanently, exhibiting its home and way of life to visitors.

From above all that is visible is a narrow "street" with caves off to the side for grain storage, animal hutches, and farm equipment. On one side of a deep pit are little carved doors and windows, bright with geraniums, behind which is a warren of charming cave rooms with little cubby holes dug out of the rock for storage, bedrooms and so on. Each has its fireplace and their chimneys poke cheerfully through to the field above.

At **Doué-la-Fontaine**, which is also built over old cave dwellings and quarries, the sights are a little more difficult

Troglodyte interior at Rochemenier.

to find. But it is worth searching out the Arena which was originally a quarry but in the 15th century was turned into a theatre with rows of seats carved out of the rock. It is still used for musical and theatrical performances and for flower shows of the roses for which Doué is particularly famous.

Follow nearby signs to Les Perrières, which is a sophisticated modern architectural reconstruction of troglodyte caves; the local dogs are, unfortunately, still at a relatively primitive stage so should be treated with caution. Just outside Doué there is an unusual zoo which uses the caves and tunnels of a former quarry to house the animals. At **Dénezé-sous-Doué** there is an extraordinary cave, carved with grotesque figures, thought to be 16th-century and the work of a secret society of stone carvers.

From Doué-la-Fontaine, carry on along the D761 to Montreuil-Bellay on the border of Anjou. Halfway there, take a turn off to **Abbaye d'Asnières**, a romantic ruin with a chancel of Angevin Gothic, accessible via a farm with good honey for sale.

Montreuil-Bellay is beautifully situated, with gardens along the banks of the little River Thouet, overlooked by the tall towers and imposing bulk of the château. The château was one of Foulques Nerra's original strongholds, established in 1025, and still has an intimidating military facade.

Inside, however, Montreuil-Bellay is highly idiosyncratic, and it is well worth visiting the 15th-century interior which includes the large collegiate church of Notre Dame. Summon the keeper by means of the heavy iron bell at the gate; there is a guided hour which lasts about an hour, but it is brisk and entertaining.

There is a superb medieval kitchen, with a round central chimney modelled on Fontevraud and equipped with antique kitchen equipment. Next to it is a curious row of separate little houses for the canons of the chapel, each with its own front door and little turret dedicated to individual prayer. The canons apparently drank more than they prayed, an occupational hazard here since, in 1893, the owner of the château

founded the Confrerie de Sacavins, (brotherhood of wine-growers) who still meet in the magnificent vaulted cellars of the château. Initiation into the brotherhood required a new member to drink vast quantities of different wines, then ascend the spiral staircase without touching the walls on either side.

The château interior is noted for the height of its rooms—and in particular the dining room, which is a perfect cube in proportion and has wonderfully robust Rabelaisian figures carved on the ceiling beams.

In the oratory, 15th-century frescoes completely cover the walls and include musical notations written by a visiting Scottish monk, the music played on tape by the guide. The Grand Salon also has enormous painted ceilings and its rich furnishings include the wedding chest of Marguerite de Valois, as well as more contemporary artefacts of the present residents. Next door is a delightful little music room, with a harp, 16th-century brass and tortoiseshell furniture and an 18th-century crystal chandelier. The

fine spiral staircase of the château is particularly celebrated for the attempt by the Duchess of Longueville to ride her horse to the top.

If the name of Loudon sends shivers down your spine, whether inspired by Aldous Huxley or Ken Russell's version of *The Devils of Loudon,* you may be disappointed by the reality. The square in the centre of the town, where the priest Urbain Grandier was burned at the stake in 1634, is now an unprepossessing pedestrianised shopping precinct and the old church of Ste-Croix has unfortunately been turned into a market hall. However, the Tour Carrée, built by Foulques Nerra in 1040, is still extant, though ruinous, and there is a splendid view from the top over the surrounding country and the little winding streets of the town.

The area to the south and west of Saumur is rich in prehistoric dolmen and standing stones, but they are often rather difficult to find. Easy to locate, and certainly the most spectacular, is to be found just outside of Saumur in the small suburb of **Bagneux** on the D147. It is an enormous burial chamber of 16 upright stones with a roof constructed of four massive stone slabs, all very impressive and mysterious.

But the most curious thing about it is that it completely fills the garden of a small local café, and the only way to see it is by patronising the café. The locals at the bar watch the visitors come and go with amused detachment, and it is hard to imagine they would have stirred very much even for Prince Charles's celebrated visit.

Saumur to Montsoreau: The route between Saumur and Montsoreau on the south bank of the Loire is a potentially bibulous one and worth taking slowly, with frequent stops for sight-seeing troglodyte villages and wine-tasting in equal measure.

First stop, however, on the D947 is **Notre-Dame-des-Ardilliers**, a 17th-century church which was once one of the most important pilgrimage centres in France because of a statue of the Virgin found by a local peasant; during

Market in Loudon.

the 17th century it had more than 10,000 pilgrims a year.

Along this road there are tantalising glimpses of troglodyte houses carved out of the white tufa cliffs and some of the villages are of considerable size once you start to explore. Most are still inhabited and the tufa has been ingeniously transformed into dwellings that range from humble little cottages hacked out of the soft rock to full-blown manor houses with turrets jutting from the cliffside. Narrow but still accessible roads climb up the white tufa cliffsides, above which are the fields and numerous vineyards which produce the excellent local wines.

There are numerous caves offering *dégustations*, and even troglodyte restaurants carved out of the rock. If you follow the signs marked Route des Vins in **Souzay**, the road will take you via the caves and up the hilltop, from which there are wonderful views and quiet pastures and vineyards. A few miles further inland is **Saint-Cyr-en-Bourg**, where the Saumur wine-growers have

their co-operative, and a huge underground complex of stone wine cellars can be visited by car.

Parnay in particular rewards exploration; the village is surprisingly large and you can either drive round it or walk—though discretion is advisable when peering closely into people's backyards and gardens, since the people who still live in the traditional troglodyte manner don't especially appreciate being regarded as a tourist attraction. Parnay even has a troglodyte Chinese restaurant carved out of the rock.

Wine is sold from the château and if you take the road round behind it and follow a sign to the *église* you will arrive on top of the plateau. Here there is an 11th-century church with an intriguingly carved Romanesque doorway and a stone lean-to porch. It is incredibly quiet and peaceful, and there is a splendid view of the Loire and the distant country to the other side.

At **Montsoreau** the river widens out where the mighty Loire meets the Vienne; the banks are broad and sandy

Angevin windmill.

with little punts and fishing boats jostling for mooring space. The château is defensively placed overlooking the two rivers, a superb position which now offers more peaceable visitors magnificent views in both directions.

Mossy walls and sprouting ferns attest to the fact that, once, the château was actually lapped by the river walls with the road running along the other side of it, where you will see it if you walk up and behind the château through steep, narrow streets which more closely resemble a fortified Provençal hill town than many other low lying Loire villages.

The reputation of Montsoreau depends partly on its immortalisation in Alexandre Dumas' novel *La Dame de Montsoreau*—the story of Comtesse de Montsoreau and her infidelities, for which her husband revenged himself by murdering her lover.

The château itself is a good illustration of the transitional architecture of the 15th century, its exterior defensive side has battlements and slit windows but the side facing the village, with its pinnacles and dormer windows, suggests the more decorative developments of the Renaissance. The interior of the château is devoted to the French connection with Morocco.

The village of Montsoreau is an excellent place to stop—and even stay, since it has good hotels and restaurants, is well supplied with pâtisserie and boulangerie, and provides convenient access to the surrounding region.

A little further to the south along the VC3 is **Moulin de la Herpinière**, a 15th-century troglodyte mill typical of the many that once dotted the region. It has now been turned into an excellent small museum devoted to local customs and handicrafts.

Almost immediately next to Montsoreau is Candes-St-Martin, a treat which must be postponed to the next chapter since this is also the boundary between Anjou and Touraine.

Instead, leave Montsoreau on the D147 and head for **Fontevraud l'Abbaye**, allowing plenty of time for a

Interior and exterior of kitchens at Fontevraud.

thorough visit. Fontevraud is distinguished by being one of the most complete collections of medieval monastic buildings anywhere. Now that it has been rescued from the various other functions it has fulfilled, including that of a prison, it gives a fascinating picture of monastic life as well as providing a cultural centre for conferences, musical performances and exhibitions.

It is also noted as the burial place of the Plantagenets, and as such is almost as important in English history as Westminster Abbey. It was founded in 1099 as a group of five monasteries, unusually including both monks and nuns, headed by an abbess. The abbesses most often came from noble families and the abbey became a favourite sanctuary for female aristocracy. These included Eleanor of Aquitaine, one-time queen of England and France, who died at Fontevraud in 1204.

At the height of their power in Anjou, the Plantagenets lavished wealth on the abbey and chose to be buried here rather than in England. The polychrome effi-

gies now lying in the abbey church are contemporary representations of Eleanor of Aquitaine; her husband, Henry II; her son, Richard the Lionheart; and Isabelle of Angoulême, the second wife of Eleanor's son, King John of England.

Take time to wander round the outside of the abbey buildings, especially the medieval gardens, the orangery and the old stables, all of which can be seen without a guide. The abbey church itself is a superb Romanesque building, complete with ambulatory and three apses. Within, the pure simple lines and soaring columns of the immense nave are immediately striking. Note, too, the series of domes and the detailed carvings on the capitals, best appreciated with binoculars.

Continue through to the chapter house with its beautiful vaulting and tiled floor and exquisitely carved doorway, through the nuns' cloisters and the huge refectory with its Romanesque walls and Gothic vaulted ceiling, to perhaps the best building in Fon-

tevraud: the kitchen. It is a classic example of a Romanesque kitchen (similar to the one at Glastonbury) and has been beautifully restored. It is built on an octagonal plan with one large central tower flanked by a cluster of chimneys, all with endearing pepper-pot roofs. Inside are six hearths for the fires which would cook food for the entire monastery. The meals were cooked in whichever niche was opposite the prevailing winds of the day in order to prevent smoke coming down the chimney.

If you have followed the helpful green lines directing you to the car park in Fontevraud, you will approach the abbey via the delightful little church of **St-Michel**; it is worth postponing your visit until after you have seen the abbey, when the intimacy of St-Michel will delight you more.

Spend a franc to indulge in the recorded music and lighting; you can see the little shrines and treasures, richly painted apse, golden altar and a particularly bizarre little collage of saints' relics, all minutely labelled and framed.

Northeast of the Loire: The area of Anjou to the northeast of the Loire is quiet country with few major attractions, all the more welcome as an antidote to the rich fare of the immediate environs of the river. **Beaufort-en-Vallée**, a comfortable small town with a big market-place with cafés and restaurants, provides a good view of the surrounding country from its ruined 14th-century château.

Just off this route—the D147—is **Château de Montgeoffrey**, a fine 18th-century building noted for its furnishings and tapestries, most of which are original and have remained in the place for which they were designed; the kitchen in particular is impressively equipped with a vast selection of copper saucepans and dishes for every conceivable purpose. It must be said, however, that the tour is long, and overly exhaustive, and the proximity of the busy D147 reduces the château's charms.

At first the alluvial plain is flat and rather dull, but by the time you approach **Baugé** and **Fontaine Guérin** it acquires contours which are easier on the eye. Here it is heathland, once forested but much of it now cut down, and the local housing consists mainly of low tufa houses, hugging close to the earth. The horizon is punctuated with church spires but here they have an interesting twist, literally: some of them, like those at Fontaine Guérin, Cuon and Pontigné, curling round like barley sugar sticks.

Further east the **Forêt de Chandelais** rewards exploration, with gentle roads winding through woods of oak and chestnut, tiny hidden hamlets and farms and the occasional manor house. It is deeply rural country, with lots of livestock to be seen, including chickens, goats, cows, sheep and horses. **Mouliherne** is distinguished by its ancient church with its 13th-century bell tower and twisting spire.

Nearby, **Linières-Bouton** is another tiny hamlet complete with small château and a mill with a splendid old iron mill wheel. But we have by now strayed far from the Loire and it is time to return to the more sophisticated attractions of its celebrated banks.

Left, château of Montreuil-Bellay. **Right**, autumn glory.

TOURAINE

The Revolution rechristened Touraine *Indre-et-Loire* and channelled the royal province into a tamer, smaller *département*. But Touraine, like the Loire itself, is not so easily contained. Two hundred years later, the old name is still used to describe the richest province in the Val de Loire. In Touraine, the Loire passes through civilised countryside yet remains the least domesticated of rivers. Since the 9th century, sandbanks and dykes have been built in an attempt to tame the river but plans to construct a series of dams are regularly defeated. The *fleuve royal* remains the wildest of the great European rivers, ready to flood or dry up at any time.

The province of such an unpredictable river in the heart of *la douce Touraine* adds, perhaps, a necessary serpent to this landscaped paradise. Without the Loire, the monk Robert Corillon claims that the inhabitants "would fall prey to indolence, self-satisfaction and excess".

Touraine's literary and royal trails wind along the smallest rivers, the Vienne and the Indrois, as well as the Loire and Cher. The landscape reveals Renaissance gardens, lush meadows, pocket-sized vineyards and old hunting estates. Once owned by kings, abbots and mistresses, the land may now belong to the state or to a rich plastic surgeon rather than to a reclusive marquess. Still, the local authorities are civilised enough to have protected their finest monuments for posterity: by law, every château is entitled to at least 1,650 ft (500 metres) of open space.

Around each bend of the river, architectural visions float into view: a turreted château once owned by Charles VII or Diane de Poitiers; a rose-covered tufa stone villa which once belonged to Ronsard; a vast tithe barn decked out as a concert hall; a water mill converted into an inn; a humble troglodyte dwelling stacked high with vin de Vouvray: all of which make Touraine the bourgeois paradise it is today.

WEST TOURAINE

Considering its glorious heritage, it is unfortunate that, when approaching Touraine from the west, all roads seem to lead to the nuclear power station at d'Avoine-Chinon which blights the surrounding area with its sinister emissions. It apparently pleases the fish at least; they are attracted in shoals to the warmth of the water and so it's a popular spot with fishermen. For those interested in 20th-century architecture, the installation can be visited.

Otherwise there is a good case for avoiding it by following the course of the River Vienne through the gentle rolling hills of southern Touraine, beginning where we left off on the D751, at **Candes-St-Martin**.

Despite the fact that the road is a major thoroughfare, the village has made little concession and traffic is obliged to slow right down for its narrow streets. This is just as well since it is impossible to miss the magnificent church, set a little way back from the road and still very much the centre of the village, summoning the villagers to mass with its mighty bell.

The church was built in the 12th and 13th centuries on the spot where St Martin died in 397, an event which is recorded in a stained-glass window to the north of the nave. It shows a group of monks smuggling his body through a window to a waiting sailboat, because there was considerable controversy over who had the right to his sacred corpse. The interior of the church is unusually light and airy with elegant Angevin vaulting, and a number of small statues still painted in pastel shades of pale rose and blue.

The porch is of special interest because it has just one central support in the middle of the arched doorway and a frieze of statues, many of which have remained unmutilated by religious zealots. They include unidentified heads which Richard Wade suggests may be early portraits of Eleanor of Aquitaine and Henry II.

The cobbled streets behind the church take you up to a panoramic view of the confluence of the Loire and the Vienne. On the other side of the road from the church, narrow alleyways lead down to the *quai* where the houses look out across the Loire as they have done for centuries.

There is a bridge across the Loire at this point, or you can continue along the D751 to Chinon, with the forest of Fontevraud on your right. Innumerable signs make it hard to miss **La Devinière**, the birthplace and childhood home of François Rabelais. Rabelais is an industry hereabouts, and there is even a hospital named after him, though the idea stretches the imagination. La Devinière is a small country manor house with an outside staircase, the steps of which have been worn into deep troughs by devoted pilgrims to the site. The house is a museum to Rabelais, restored and furnished in 15th-century rustic style. The nearby village of **Seuilly** has a number of troglodyte houses and it was here that Rabelais was

Preceding pages: the Loire at Montsoreau. Love-knot garden, Villandry. Left, swans and cygnets. Right, stained-glass window, Candes-St-Martin.

educated at the Benedictine abbey. Return now to the Vienne and the approach to **Chinon**; the grim walls and imposing towers of the château are best viewed from the south. It is a small town with its narrow medieval streets crammed between the river and the château, but there is a lot to see. Allow plenty of time and perhaps schedule lunch here in one of Chinon's numerous excellent restaurants.

The town has been a settlement since pre-Roman times and played a central role in tangled French and English medieval history. The Plantagenets finally lost control of it in 1205. It is most famous for the connection with Joan of Arc; it was here in 1429 that the Dauphin retreated from Paris, and where Joan came to offer him her divinely inspired services.

Purists argue that the town has been over-restored, that its twisted cobbled streets resemble a film set, but it is hard to imagine what else could have been done with a place so popular with tourists. The old town itself is small and can

easily be seen by walking down the **Rue Voltaire**, the main thoroughfare of old Chinon. There are many beautiful houses, some half-timbered wood, some white tufa stone with Renaissance carved windows and doorways.

Just off Rue Voltaire are the famous *Caves Peintes* (the painted cellars), former caves under the castle where Rabelais' character Pantagruel came carousing. Here the *Etonneurs Rabelaisens* still hold their meetings, though the paintings have disappeared and the caves themselves seem somewhat damp and gloomy for such convivial occasions.

Along the **Rue Haute-St-Maurice** is the Hostellerie Gargantua, noted for its elegant turrets, where you can now enjoy a pleasant lunch *en plein air*. The church of **St-Maurice** has a Romanesque tower and nave in the soaring Angevin style.

The **Grand Carroi** is the main crossroads and there are a number of fine half-timbered houses here, as well as the Museum of Chinon, a 16th-century

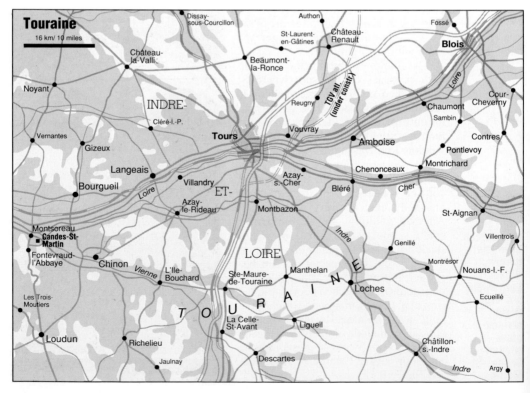

building with a collection of local folk art. Take the **Rue Jeanne-d'Arc**, a steep winding street up to the **château** passing the old stone well where the Maid apparently dismounted her horse. Though very steep, this is the most authentic way to approach the château looming above.

Happily, perhaps, much of this ancient, grim fortress is in ruins, but it is still possible to get a very good sense of how life was lived so completely within its walls. You can wander round without a guide, enjoying the views and exploring the towers and gardens.

Most of the castle dates from the 12th century and is in three parts, divided by deep moats and linked by bridges. A very detailed guide is provided in English. The remains of the throne room where Joan of Arc met the Dauphin can still be seen, and next to it the royal residence has been restored; the rooms have beautiful mullioned windows, enormous fireplaces and spiral staircases, and in the kitchen is a magnificent Aubusson tapestry.

One of the most compelling buildings is the Coudray Keep, a round tower with ogival vaulting, where the Knights Templar were imprisoned in the early 14th century. On the walls and in the window niches it is possible to discern some touching graffiti carved into the stone by the prisoners; there is the plan of a church, a monk's face, a cross and a number of inscriptions. After three years of incarceration, 54 of them were slowly roasted alive.

After the oppressive history of the château, return to the town for a glass of the excellent Chinon wine, and consider a short walk to the **chapel of Ste-Radegonde**. Follow the Rue Jean-Jacques Rousseau and then take a turn up the hill into the Rue des Pitoches which winds past a number of troglodyte houses which are still inhabited; it must be said that it is rather a rough and neglected route and you might feel happier walking with a companion.

The shrine is the 6th-century site of the cave of a hermit, St John the Recluse; Queen Radegonde came to him

View of Chinon from the river.

for spiritual advice and subsequently built a chapel in his memory. The chapel is locked, however, and it is as well to check with the tourist office before making the climb to ensure that a guide will be there to show you round.

Inside there are 8th and 9th-century sarcophagi and 9th-century sculptures on the walls. But the greatest treasures are the wall paintings, 17th-century frescoes of the life of St Radegonde, and a painting discovered only 25 years ago when a piece of plaster fell off the wall. It is claimed to be a painting of the Plantagenets, based on the heraldic designs on the cloaks and depicting the wedding of King John and Isabelle. Whether or not this is true, it is in remarkably good condition, the colours almost as fresh and bright as the day they were painted.

The cave penetrates far into the rock, and the guide will lead you through a gloomy ambulatory carved out by pilgrims to the shrine. Deep into the rock there is a Merovingian holy well with a steep flight of steps leading down to it.

On St John's Day, 24 June, every year, water, reputed to be beneficial for the sight, is fetched from the well. The caves are extensive and were lived in until very recently. They have been maintained just as they were left as a fascinating troglodyte museum.

From Chinon it is worth making a detour to the extraordinary town of **Richelieu**, described by La Fontaine as "the finest village in the universe". You can also get there by the Touraine Steam Train which runs between Chinon and Richelieu during the summer.

It is a planned "New Town" of the 17th century, designed by Cardinal Richelieu as part of his drive for power, and was built according to a classical rectangular plan with all the streets in a grid pattern. It retains a completely homogeneous character with gateways and town squares at each entrance and long streets of fine houses. In the Place du Marché there is a very fine market hall of sturdy oak beams and a slate roof, lively and bustling on market day and a favourite place for skateboarders

Troglodyte house, Valle de Courtineau.

the rest of the time. Opposite is the imposing classical white facade of the church of Notre Dame. Richelieu has a splendid park, also planned by the Cardinal—although most of the fine buildings, including his château, were destroyed during the Revolution. Its long avenues of plane trees and chestnuts provide a delightful place to stroll.

Head now towards **L'Ile-Bouchard**, through rich, rolling pasture land. L'Ile-Bouchard was once an important port on the River Vienne, but is now a quiet little town, nestling comfortably amongst its orchards and gardens.

To the north is the famous forest of Chinon, worth exploring at leisure though watch out for the military boundaries in the middle and hunters everywhere. A little further along the D760, minor roads will take you to St-Epain and a very pretty *Route Touristique* through the valley of the little River Manse, dotted with farms, fields of horses and goats, and the occasional troglodyte house built from the creamy local tufa. You can either return to **Ste-Maure-de-Touraine**, famous for its 17th-century covered market hall and its excellent goats' cheese, or continue on to **Ste-Catherine-de-Fierbois**, a little village dedicated to the memory of Joan of Arc. Saint Catherine was one of Joan's "voices" and it was behind the altar in this church that Joan's sword was found, following her directions. Although her knowledge of the sword was claimed as a miracle, she had in fact visited the church only a short time before and could easily have known of its existence; she herself made no claim to divine guidance.

The church was rebuilt in 1479 in beautiful Flamboyant style, and within is a tribute to Joan in the form of a stained-glass window with Joan in suppliant attitude to Saint Catherine. Next to the church is the Maison du Dauphin, built in 1415, its main distinction being that it was actually here that Joan of Arc arrived, spurred and booted, to hear mass before approaching the Dauphin at Chinon.

Montbazon is the site of one of

Gateway to Richelieu.

Foulques Nerra's original keeps, now in ruins but worth climbing up to for the view. The town is much better known, however, for Château d'Artigny, a luxury country hotel and restaurant in the elegant manor house built in the early 20th century for the perfume manufacturer Monsieur Coty.

From Montbazon it is possible to follow the River Indre on one or other of its banks, almost all the way to the Loire. It is a beguiling route; along wooded valleys, through little waterside villages, the river curves gently along past orchards, hidden châteaux and water mills which have seen little change since they were built. Take it slowly, stopping for gentle walks along the river banks, and allowing for whimsical detours.

Saché is one such rewarding detour, a small village with important connections. The 16th-century manor house at Saché was owned by friends of Balzac and it was here he came to recuperate his health and did much of his writing. The house is now a truly evocative museum

in his honour; because of recent thefts, however, you are expected to follow a guided tour but may be allowed to wander round freely if you don't mind being locked in!

The house is delightful, surrounded by a garden full of oak and chestnut trees. It is kept in the style of Balzac's time, and in particular his bedroom has been maintained just as it was, the bed made up, coffee pot, quill pen and inkwell at the ready on the humble wooden desk. From the window is Balzac's much-loved view of the little village church among the trees. His novel *Le Lys dans la Vallée* is set in this area and in it he describes how it inspired him: "the silence, the great knotty trees and that indefinable air of mystery which filled its lonely valley".

Here he would write, all day and much of the night, coming down to supper in the evening, when he would sometimes read what he had written to the assembled visitors in the drawing room. It is still arranged in early 18th-century style with sofas, little chairs and card tables as if ready to receive guests at any moment, and a real cat is already very much at home, snoozing happily in a cosy chair.

The museum contains a comprehensive collection of Balzac artefacts, including busts and paintings, manuscripts and first editions, and a number of his annotated proofs, so obsessively over-written that the printers had to be paid double time to read them.

The village itself has a fine row of medieval half-timbered houses, a little grey stone church and, amongst these soft muted colours, a wildly coloured Alexander Calder mobile in the middle of the square. Calder was another more recent famous resident.

A gentle drive along the D17 and a further detour will bring you to **Villaines-les-Rochers**, the centre of the local basket-weaving industry. It was founded by the village priest in 1849 as one of the first agricultural co-operatives in France, and now employs 80 local families, weaving according to the traditional methods. The willow rushes are grown beside the Indre, harvested in

Basket weaving at Villaines-les-Rochers.

winter and steeped in water until spring, when they are used for weaving. A huge variety of baskets are made, from little breadbaskets to baby's cradles, and the basket weavers can be seen at work in the cooperative at Villaines, or in local troglodyte houses. Also in the village is a traditional *ferronnerie,* with some simple, elegant ironwork for sale.

The châteaux beat: From here on, as the Loire itself approaches, we are in prime Loire châteaux country. The fact that not the slightest architectural detail or twist of history remains undiscovered is compensated by the sheer wealth of treasures to be appreciated. One of the greatest jewels is **Azay-le-Rideau**, "a many-faceted diamond set in the Indre", in Balzac's description. If you approach the town from the east and park before you get to the bridge, there is a lovely view of the château, glimpsed through a veil of trees, its graceful turrets shimmering in the limpid waters of the Indre forming a natural moat.

The town itself is pleasant, with quiet little streets of white stone with many elegant Renaissance details. The name is derived from the 12th-century noble, Ridel d'Azay, but until the 16th century the town was called Azay-le-Brule because it was burnt to the ground by the Dauphin in 1418.

Apart from the château, do not miss the 11th-century church of **St-Symphorien** and its strange double front which incorporates the remains of a 6th-century Merovingian facade with a row of little statuettes above the doorway. From here you can follow signs to the **château**, entering through its gardens from the Rue de Pineau.

Azay is regarded as perhaps the most perfect Renaissance château, started in 1508 and built by Gilles Berthelot, an important financier, purely for domestic pleasure rather than military defence. Like Chenonceau, it is considered to be very feminine in design, both in its beauty and in the practicality of its living arrangements, due to the fact that Berthelot's wife, Philippe Lesbahy, directed the work, as did Catherine Briçonnet at Chenonceau. It is a truly

Renaissance jewel of Azay-le-Rideau.

lovely, harmonious building, surrounded by tall trees so that the view from every window is private, calming and pastoral; there is no sense of domination over its surroundings.

It is built in an L-shape, with the ornamentation of turrets and dormer windows reflected in the still waters of the moat. It is particularly distinguished by the grand staircase, a major innovation at the time, a zig-zag of three flights with open double-windowed loggias in Italian style on each landing.

The interior is delightful, sumptuously furnished in Renaissance style. The rooms have monumental stone fireplaces, velvet and brocade-draped beds and exquisite tapestries, all the rooms smelling faintly of cedarwood.

The kitchen—which is on the ground floor with plenty of light from the big windows (another female refinement?)—is magnificent, with a vast fireplace, oak carved doors, a great oak table and a fine selection of iron cooking utensils. It was in this kitchen that Prince Frederick Charles of Prussia, billeted at Azay after the defeat of the French army in 1871, was almost killed by a chandelier falling on his head. It took considerable persuasion to stop him burning the château to the ground in retaliation.

From Azay-le-Rideau the road either side of the Indre is a pretty drive, and the attractions on both sides equally beguiling, Villandry in one direction and Ussé in the other.

Sleeping beauty: The D7 to Ussé follows the Indre and hugs close to the Forest of Chinon. Here the smaller river runs parallel before it joins Balzac's "gilded blade" of the Loire, visible now across the fertile alluvial soil of the flood plain between the rivers. In fact, the best view of fairyland **Château d'Ussé** is from the banks of the Loire where it can be seen nestling mysteriously against the cliffside. Ussé is famous as the setting chosen for the original *Sleeping Beauty* story, written by Perrault, and its romantic white pointed turrets framed by the thick dark forest look convincingly romantic.

Ussé, inspiration for *Sleeping Beauty*.

184

Although on an older site, most of the building, including the Gothic towers and parapets, is 15th-century; a Renaissance wing and chapel were added later. It is set in lovely French formal gardens of pools and terraces, and extends to a park which can be visited. The château itself is privately owned and only certain parts are open. It is well worth taking "*La Belle au Bois Dormant*" (the Beauty in the Sleeping Wood) route through the parapet rooms where a *tableau vivant* of the entire story has been elaborately prepared. It is wonderfully, if unintentionally, camp, with good fairies brandishing their wands like cigarette holders.

There is a lovely Renaissance chapel in the grounds, but sadly its treasures are obscured by a rather pathetic wooden picket fence, installed after invaluable Aubusson tapestries were stolen. Notice the carved stalls and a lovely terracotta della Robbia *Virgin*.

From Ussé you might make a detour into the forest, where there are many elegantly restored small châteaux tucked away at the end of leafy lanes, such as the one at Turpenay Abbey. Head for **Huismes**, where there is an excellent view from the slopes overlooking the confluence of the Loire and the Indre. From here the road drops steeply and before you know it the nuclear power station looms again.

Here you need to cross the bridge if you wish to explore the north bank of the Loire, starting with **Bourgueil**, a small and pleasant town, with a fine market hall with stone arches, and an old church with 11th-century Romanesque nave and Angevin vaulting. On the road towards Restigné is what remains of the Benedictine abbey, founded in the 10th century and at one time one of the most important abbeys in the region. Most of the conventual buildings date from the 17th and 18th centuries and can be visited and there are regular musical and theatrical performances held there.

Bourgueil is noted for its delicate high-quality red wines, the most distinguished of which is **Saint-Nicholas-de-**

Shelter from the rain.

Bourgueil, a little village 2 miles (3 km) to the west. The area is covered in thousands of hectares of vines, and there are many *vignerons* offering *dégustations*. At Chevrette to the north of Bourgueil there is a wine museum at Cave de la Dive Bouteille (Cellar of the Divine Bottle) which also offers tastings.

From here on, the Loire is flanked by the rich alluvial plain of the Varennes which grows a wide variety of early vegetables; asparagus, tobacco and sunflowers as well as fruit. The area is protected from flooding by reinforced causeways and it is possible, crossing the river at Langeais, to drive along them and find peaceful little havens such as **Bréhémont**, a quiet little village and an ideal place to stop for tea or a drink under shady trees to the sound of cooing doves.

Criss-crossing from one side to the other of the Loire can sometimes present problems and careful planning is needed to ensure you find yourself on the side you want. By the time you come to investigate **Langeais**, you will probably already be quite familiar with its suspension bridge. Langeais is a grim, primarily defensive castle, in marked contrast to the later, more peaceable Renaissance architecture of Azay-le-Rideau or Chenonceau. It really evokes the atmosphere of castle life in the Middle Ages, with *tableaux vivants*, contemporary furnishings and medieval music. From the walk around the battlement watchtower there is a commanding view of the river and the surrounding countryside and the little half-timbered houses huddled against the castle wall for protection.

Langeais has the ruins of a keep built by Foulques Nerra in 994, one of the first to be built in stone, and it can be seen beyond the gardens, which have been redesigned according to miniatures of Anne of Brittany's gardens at Amboise. The château was rebuilt by Louis XI to protect his borders against Brittany, and its moat and drawbridge, arrow-slit windows, towers and crenellations are everything a castle should be. The interior courtyard, however, is

Grim drawbridge at Langeais.

already in transition from war to peace. The interior rooms too are less austere, superbly furnished in Renaissance style, with a very fine tapestry collection. The guided tour is worthwhile, and provides a good historical summary of the period, along with a complete tableau of the wedding between Anne of Brittany and Charles VIII which is very impressive.

About 5 miles (8 km) further on from Langeais is the oddly named **Cinq-Mars-la-Pile**, its name no stranger than the monument from which it derives, a solid square tower on the clifftop, nearly 100 ft (30 metres) tall with four mysterious little pyramids on the corners. It was built sometime during the Roman domination of Gaul and is referred to as "La Pile" but no one has a clue as to its purpose. The château has two remaining 11th and 12th-century towers with beautiful vaulting; from the roof there is a fine view of the confluence of the Loire and the Cher.

On the side of the Bresme valley is the village of **St-Etienne-de-Chigny**, noted for its church (ask at the *épicerie* for the key) with a very unusual carved hammerbeam roof and 16th-century stained-glass windows. From the N152 there is a good view of **Luynes**, a troglodyte village dug out of the hillside. The village also has a 15th-century oak-beamed market hall and medieval houses, and a gentle walk through the vineyards brings you to the 13th-century château, which is private.

Further to the north, skirting Tours, is **Mettray**, the site of a huge dolmen on a slope above the River Choisille. The dolmen is 35 ft long and 15 ft wide (10.7 by 4.6 metres) with massive vertical pillars, roofed by three great stone slabs; how such a monolith was transported centuries ago remains a complete mystery.

You will need to return to Langeais to cross the Loire again; if you continue on to Tours the suburbs will swallow you up. You can follow the little D16, a pretty route along the side of the river to get to **Villandry**, the final treasure in this region of Touraine. It was the last

Co-ordinated cabbages, Villandry.

great Renaissance château to be built in the Loire Valley (1532) and is a perfect example of 16th-century architecture. It is actually on the banks of the Cher just before it joins the Loire, and is surrounded by a moat on three sides. The interior can be visited, but it is undoubtedly the gardens which have made Villandry famous.

The influence of the Italian Renaissance in France led to the popularity of Italian garden design, from which the French formal, geometric style developed. Both the château and the gardens at Villandry have been returned to their original Renaissance design, due to the commitment of château owner, Dr Joseph Carvallo, earlier this century, and Villandry is still maintained today by his family.

The gardens are arranged in three terraces. On the highest is a large smooth pond, which feeds water to the moat and fountains. On the next level are the ornamental flower gardens, the *jardins d'amour*, each flower bed geometrically arranged using boxwood and yew, in the shape of hearts, symbolising love. All levels are linked by shady walks, pergolas and fountains. On the bottom level are the wonderful ornamental vegetable gardens, a riot of juxtaposed colour at any time of year; red peppers contrasting with golden pumpkins, purple cabbages in full flower, spinach, aubergines and every conceivable fruit or vegetable arranged for maximum graphic effect. There is also a herb garden with a very wide variety of of herbs cultivated, a haven of buzzing aromatic warmth.

The details of the garden are a delight and there are many pleasant flower-trellised bowers in which to sit and contemplate it all, but its full magnificence is best appreciated from a distance, either from the very top of the terraces or the keep of the château itself.

Villandry is as popular with local people as it is with tourists and the gardens appear to have inspired the neighbouring *potagers*, which seem to bristle with pride as they too exhibit splendid displays of lovingly cultivated fruit, flowers and vegetables.

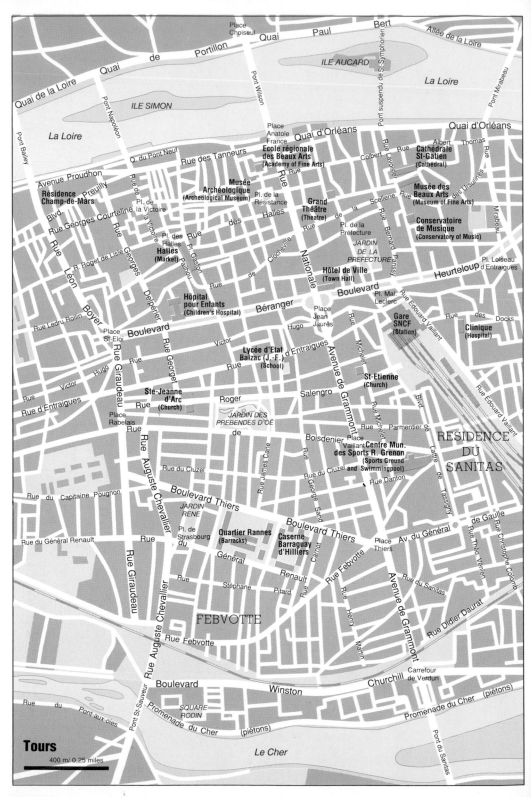

Place Choiseul
Quai Paul Bert
Allée de la Loire
Quai de Portillon
ILE AUCARD
La Loire
Quai de la Loire
ILE SIMON
La Loire
Pont Wilson
Pont Napoléon
Pont Bailey
Place Anatole France
Quai d'Orléans
Quai d'Orléans
Q. du Pont Neuf
Rue des Tanneurs
Ecole régionale des Beaux Arts
(Academy of Fine Arts)
Albert Thomas
Cathédrale St-Gatien
(Cathedral)
Avenue Proudhon
Colbert
Rue des Ursulines
Résidence Champ-de-Mars
Preuilly Blvd.
Musée Archéologique
(Archeological Museum)
Pl. de la Résistance
Scellerie
Musée des Beaux Arts
(Museum of Fine Arts)
Rue Georges Courteline
Pl. de la Victoire
Grand Théâtre
(Theatre)
Conservatoire de Musique
(Conservatory of Music)
Mirabeau
Rue Léon Boyer
R. Roget de Lisle
Pl. des Halles
Halles
des
Rue de la Victoire
Pl. Gaston Pailhou
de
Clocheville
Rue Nationale
Pl. de la Préfecture
JARDIN DE LA PREFECTURE
Pl. Loiseau d'Entraigues
Rue Ledru Rollin
Halles
(Market)
Hôtel de Ville
(Town Hall)
Heurteloup
Clinique
(Hospital)
Delperier
Hôpital pour Enfants
(Children's Hospital)
Rue
Béranger
Boulevard
Pl. Mal. Leclerc
Rue Edouard Vaillant
des Docks
Place St-Eloi
Boulevard
Victor
Hugo
Place Jean Jaurès
Gare SNCF
(Station)
Rue
Rue Giraudeau
Rue Georges
Victor
d'Entraigues
Avenue de Grammont
Michelet
St-Etienne
(Church)
Rue Edouard Vaillant
Victor
Lycée d'Etat Balzac (J.-F.)
(School)
Rue
Salengro
RESIDENCE DU SANITAS
Rue d'Entraigues
Hugo
Ste-Jeanne d'Arc
(Church)
Rue
Roger
JARDIN DES PREBENDES D'OÉ
Place Rabelais
de
Boisdenier
Place Vaillant
Centre Mun. des Sports R. Grenon
(Sports Ground and Swimmingpool)
Parmentier
de Gaulle
Rue du Capitaine Pougnon
Rue Auguste Chevallier
Rue du Cluzel
Rue James Cane
Rue du Cluzel
Rue Danton
Rue Michelet
Blvd.
Latte de Tassigny
Rue Christophe Colomb
Rue du Général Renault
Boulevard Thiers
JARDIN RENE
Pl. de Strasbourg du
Quartier Rannes
(Barracks)
Caserne Barraguay d'Hilliers
Boulevard Thiers
Place Thiers
Av. du Général
de Gaulle
Rue Théo Vernier
Rue Giraudeau
Rue
Général
Renault
Stéphane
Pitard
Carnot
Rue George Sand
Rue Febvotte
Avenue de Grammont
Rue du Sanitas
Rue Didier Daurat
FEBVOTTE
Rue Auguste Chevallier
Rue Febvotte
Rue Henry
Martin
Carrefour de Verdun
Pont du Santias
Boulevard
Winston
Churchill
Rue du Pont-aux-oies
Pont St-Sauveur
Promenade du Cher
SQUARE RODIN
Promenade du Cher (piétons)
Promenade du Cher (piétons)

Tours

400 m/ 0,25 miles

Le Cher

192

TOURS

Balzac, naturally biased in favour of his home town, called Tours, *"une ville rieuse, rigoleuse, amoureuse, fraîche, fleurie, parfumée mieux que toutes les autres villes du monde"*. Other Tourangeaux might not agree with this flowery description but innate good taste would prevent them from openly disagreeing with a fellow citizen from *la douce Touraine*. If the townspeople take after more famous residents, they would be as rational as Descartes, as sentimental as Ronsard, as bourgeois as Balzac, and as earthy as Rabelais. This is not too far from the truth.

The city of Tours has developed from two different poles: Turons, the mercantile Roman town, centred on what is today the area around the cathedral; and Martinopolis, the medieval religious centre connected with the life and work of Saint Martin. St-Gatien cathedral is built over a Roman arena which once seated 12,000 spectators. The neighbouring medieval streets trace rough oval patterns and, in rue Manceau, parts of the old *vomitoria* were recently found in medieval cellars.

Legend has it that one Roman centurion, St Martin, sealed his Christian fate by offering half his cloak to a beggar. Instead of being fed to lions in the arena, St Martin successfully completed his evangelical mission and died of natural causes on 11 November 397. On his death, flowers supposedly blossomed and trees bloomed so, ever since, a warm autumn has been known as *l'été de St Martin*. In medieval times, pilgrims flocked to the Saint's tomb in Tours and the town prospered, not just spiritually. In fact, even today, the Tourangeaux like to think that St Martin's cloak hangs like a blessing over their city.

But it was under the influence of another saintly figure, Joan of Arc, that Tours began its golden century, roughly bounded by the reigns of Charles VII and François I. In 1461, Louis XI made Tours the capital of France and the city

became a manufacturing centre for jewellery, arms and gorgeous fabrics. Tours rivalled Lombardy in the production of silver sheets and embroidered silks, and Flanders in the weaving of tapestries threaded with spun gold. Parallel to this ran a literary golden age, crowned by the works of Rabelais and later Ronsard. After the reign of François I, Tours lost favour with the monarchy and under Henri IV's reign the capital left Tours for Paris.

Without royal cachet, Tours floundered economically, particularly as the River Loire lost its importance as a commercial highway. By no means flavour of the month during the Revolution, conservative Tours benefitted little and the population declined from 80,000 in 1750 to 20,000 in 1800. Largely by-passed by the Industrial Revolution, the city failed to make its silk and textile factories competitive and therefore retained a rural economy until late into this century. As recently as 1961, Tours only employed 1,000 workers in industry and had little to

offer the tourist in the way of well-maintained museums, historic sites, hotels and restaurants.

Tours' dramatically contrasting role in modern politics helps explain this poor economic showing. Bombarded by the Prussians in 1870, an American base in the First World War and a battlefield in 1940 and 1944, Tours has played a key role in modern French history. In June, 1940, the French Provisional Government withdrew to Tours, retreating from an advancing German army. However, in the bombardment of 1944, 9,000 people were killed and 30 acres of Tours were razed to the ground.

Regeneration of the city has been slow but successful, largely due to the popular policies of Jean Royer, Tours' mayor since 1958. Minister of Crafts and Communications under Giscard d'Estaing's government, Royer enthusiastically communicated his belief in a city revived through craft industries, conservation, and the creation of separate industrial zones. The mayor is often praised for his conservative approach,

one in keeping with the bourgeois spirit which reigns in the centre-west of France. However, his attitude to city conservation and restoration was considered little short of revolutionary for pre-1968 France.

By 1960, most of the middle classes had deserted the old city centre: it was a slum with a mixture of bombed buildings, temporary shacks and dilapidated medieval houses. In the attractive quarter now known as Petit St-Martin, tripe sellers worked beside open sewers; there was no sanitation in the seedy bars and an old tannery emptied its waste into the Loire. In the now genteel Place Plumereau quarter, 11,000 Portuguese immigrants lived without running water until the early 1970s. In 1960, in response to the urban ruin, Royer set up the Vieux Tours project which aimed to restore and renovate a 250-acre (100-hectare) zone of Tours. This so-called *Secteur sauvegardé* (protected zone) was one of the first projects of its kind and has been a model for French urban development ever since.

Left, old streets of Tours. **Right**, waiting for a bus.

In essence, the project uses both public and private funds to restore the 15th and 16th-century town houses to their original state. Where too much has been destroyed, the buildings are recreated according to their original design. The success of this initiative means that Vieux Tours is now *bon ton*, a good address for arty intellectuals, yuppies and executives. In 1973, the council wisely decided to site the newly-founded University between the Loire and Place Plumereau, in the heart of the conservation area. The presence of up to 20,000 students has encouraged new enterprise there. Visitors also appreciate the proliferation of stylish bars, art galleries and international *chocolatiers*.

But Royer and his advisers gradually realized that tasteful gentrification had put rents beyond the reach of many citizens. To remedy this, the Petit St-Martin area was created to house poorer families and to help regenerate Tours' dying craft industries. The houses, built in traditional styles and materials, are a mixture of old and new but tend to echo

the past: circular structures are a modern interpretation of the Renaissance model while odd-shaped towers reflect the city's name. Cabinet-makers, jewellers, doll-makers, potters and *sculpteurs en bois* now work in an area around the Carroi-aux-Herbes which was a slum until 1973.

Partly thanks to the regeneration of the city, Tours was able to attract new industries, including publishing, banking and computing. As a result, in the early eighties, Tours was awarded the title of "fastest-growing city in France", a term which, in the nineties, can be redefined as "rich". Most heavy industries are carefully based in Tours-Nord, the industrial zone in St-Symphorien. Factories for plastics, chemicals, tyres and food-processing are kept out of the centre so that locals can enjoy the pleasures of the old city, including the prune tarts Balzac referred to as "the most virtuous of all vices".

Cathedral Quarter: As medieval citizens watched the cathedral rise over the course of two centuries, they had time to

Violin-maker at work.

Santiago Pilgrims

"We will pass through the gentle Vendôme countryside, following the stars to rude Castille and to the beautiful house of Messire Saint Jacques in Galicia." In describing the pilgrims' route to St James's shrine at Santiago de Compostella, the 12th-century monk Aimery Picaud was also writing the first known guide book. Picaud describes the pretty Bords de Loire route as well as the most direct route from Paris or Chartres to northwestern Spain, pointing out attractions ranging from simple metal crosses or chapels to scenic stretches of the river, old Roman bridges, and comments on hospitable monks or disagreeable companions.

The popularity of the pilgrimage was linked to the discovery of St James's relics in the 9th century. Although this "discovery" is now disputed outside Spain, then the evidence was great enough to make Santiago the most popular medieval pilgrimage centre, along with Rome and Jerusalem. By the 15th century the "Way of St James" had been well and truly trodden by saints and sinners alike. Ordinary pilgrims were supported by religious foundations along the route. The Benedictines, Cistercians and the Knights Templar sheltered and fed pilgrims while the Confraternities of St James in Bourges, Montoire and Vendôme also funded hospices and leper houses for those in need of medical care and rest. These early tourists greatly enriched the Loire with new ideas and works of art, religious souvenirs in the form of carved statues of the saint and his personal emblems, the fan-shaped scallop shell, staff and wide-brimmed hat. Two main routes cross the Val de Loire in the general direction of Tours, Poitiers, Bordeaux and Santiago. The Chemin de Paris takes in Orléans, Blois, Amboise and Tours while the Chartres Route travels via Vendôme, Trôo and Marmoutier Abbey, meeting the Chemin de Paris at Tours. Popular alternatives were the Norman Route via Le Mans and an illogical route which travels from east to west rather than north to south. Cynics say that this soft option, known as

the Bords de Loire route, concentrates on scenic views, not religious sites. One rewarding section of the route follows the River Loir from Vendôme to St-Jacques-des-Guerets. Vendôme possesses two of the original four chapels to St James.

Just outside Vendôme, in Villiers-sur-Loir, is a Romanesque church containing a small chapel and statue dedicated to the Saint. Further along the river, at Roches-l'Eveque, is a troglodyte chapel with Romanesque frescoes and at Montoire the Benedictine Eglise St-Gilles is decorated with fine, partially abstract frescoes. At nearby Trôo is the remains of a crypt which once sheltered sick pilgrims while the adjoining village of St-Jacques-des-Guerets contains a church decorated with 13th-century frescoes of the saint as martyr. The church at Lunay has shell-shaped symbols carved beside the doorway. At St-Ouen is a pagan mound which in medieval times was a shrine to St James.

In 1987 the Council of Europe declared the route "one of the oldest signs of European cooperation and enterprise... a key part of our European heritage," and the EC introduced system of signposting, using the St James scallop shell. The Confraternities can take some credit for the fact that in 1989 alone, 9,000 pilgrims walked the route. These societies offer cultural and religious itineraries, or advice on accommodation from priests or local people. Pilgrims who can get their journey authenticated are entitled to the traditional Latin Compostella, the certificate of pilgrimage. The return of the pilgrim to the Confraternity in London or Dusseldorf is a time of great rejoicing, even if the pilgrim drove part of the route or, as was the case of a merchant banker in the London Confraternity, made the journey on a penny-farthing bicycle. The traditional scallop shells, staffs and hats are still in evidence, as are portable stereos, mountaineering macks, and Adidas footwear. Among the civil servants, party hostesses and quiet academics who walk the "Way of St James", there are also the Pope groupies, the eccentrics and the occasional genuine mystic. As in Aimery Picaud's time, the "Way of St James" is a spiritual current that flows through the Loire Valley to the Pyrenees, the plains of Aragon and into the wheatfields of Galicia.

coin the proverb, "It takes as long as the work on St-Gatien". Luckily the congregation is used to waiting because this masterpiece of French Gothic architecture will not be looking its best until 2015, the year its restoration is due to be completed. The building work is necessary because, as Balzac commented a century earlier, "The centuries have thrown a black coat over this great building".

During the restoration, the north tower, the cloisters and the Renaissance domes and staircase will be partially obscured. However, the pride of the cathedral, the Flamboyant Gothic **west facade**, will be visible, as will the vivid 13th and 14th-century windows in the chancel and transepts. These magnificent splashes of red and blue stand out against the weather-worn grey stone. In colour and craftsmanship the windows rival those in La Sainte-Chapelle in Paris or the famous rose windows in Chartres Cathedral.

Less appreciated is the rear view of the cathedral, best seen from the tran-

quil Place St-Grégoire-de-Tours. Birds weave in and out of the flying buttresses and perch indiscriminately on griffin gargoyles and time-honoured saints. This was Balzac's favourite haunt, and where he set one of his novels, *Le Curé de Tours*.

The **Musée des Beaux Arts**, situated beside the cathedral has been through many incarnations. Now the renowned Fine Arts museum, it housed the Archbishops of Tours in the 17th century, while in Roman times it formed part of the city walls, still partly visible from the shady grounds. These French classical gardens are overshadowed by a giant cedar of Lebanon but the elegant building provides an ideal display case for the collection of 18th-century paintings hung against walls of Tours silk. Although the museum is proudest of its two Mantegnas and one Rembrandt, more typical of the collection are the 18th century genre paintings, from landscapes to *scenes galantes*.

Many of these treasures were confiscated from neighbouring abbeys and

châteaux during the Revolution. The Salle de Touraine offers a good display of regional paintings, including 18th-century landscapes and portraits of such local dignitaries as silk merchants and magistrates. From the museum, you can stroll down **Rue de la Scellerie**, an arty street that has long specialised in antiques, old prints, books and paintings. Above the shops, many of the balconies have raised wrought iron to an art form.

The St-Julien Quarter: The area, bounded by Rue de la Scellerie, Rue Nationale and the River Loire represents the heart of the old medieval city of Tours. Although both the riverfront and Rue Nationale were heaps of rubble in 1944, Rue Colbert, the old high street, survived, as did St-Julien church and enough 15th-century town houses to justify the trip. Certainly, a visit to this authentic area is as rewarding as one to the more commercial Place Plumereau.

Just off the bustling Rue Nationale is the first 13th-century island. **St-Julien**, once part of a Romanesque abbey, is a solid Gothic church unshaken by previ-

ous attacks. Used as a stable during the Revolution, the charming interior now holds classical concerts and organ recitals in the summer. But the **monks' cells**, the most intriguing feature, only came to light during the 1944 bombardment. Worth visiting in their own right, the cells have now been turned into a small wine museum. Access to both the Musée des vins de Touraine and to the Musée du Campagnonnage is via two small doorways in Rue Nationale.

Some of the 12th-century cellars may also have been used for wine so the present use is no travesty: the museum aims to explain the folklore and social customs surrounding wine and local growing techniques. A presentation on wine guilds and secret wine-tasting brotherhoods makes a link with the Musée du Campagnonnage downstairs. Under different names, the local *campagnonnages*, or guilds, have existed since medieval times, despite being banned after the Revolution. To this day, the old wine guilds flourish along the Loire, from Vouvray to Chinon.

Dining in Tours.

The crafts museum, certainly unique in France, illustrates the proverb engraved on a beam inside, "*L'homme pense parce qu'il a un main*". As homage to centuries of craftsmen, there are displays of trades, tools and techniques which no longer exist or are dying out.

Slightly further along Rue Nationale, a turning leads to the **Jardin de Beaune Semblançay**, the remains of a splendid Renaissance *hôtel particulier*, chapel and garden. Once owned by Jacques de Beaune, Louis XII's disgraced financier, the house is reduced to its windowless north facade, pierced by protruding branches. Opposite is a pinkish-marble chapel with pilasters topped by classical busts.

In between the chapel and the mysterious facade lies a Renaissance **fountain**, the town's pride and joy. The fountain is a pyramid of white Carrara marble surmounted by a vase; clinging to it firmly are the emblems of Anne of Brittany, two ermines which closely resemble chipmunks. This atmospheric square is best seen at night when light plays on the fountain and illuminates the lion and monkey gargoyles to be seen on the facade.

Just off Beaune Semblançay, the **Rue Colbert** is a workmanlike street running parallel to the river. As well as being a vibrant, slightly raffish area with some of the best restaurants in town, Rue Colbert is also a cross-section of Tours' history. Before saving Orléans, Joan of Arc came here to be fitted with armour. A beamed house bears the name *A la pucelle armée*, but as cynical locals tell you, "*Jeanne d'Arc restait partout*".

In medieval times, there was a toll gate at the bottom of the road and until the 18th-century the street remained the town's commercial centre. This self-important bustle is still present in the early evening as neighbours gossip in the *boulangerie* or exchange cheery insults across 15th-century rooftops. Many of these houses have been converted into old-fashioned family-run restaurants so the smell of woodsmoke is often in the evening air.

Preparing for customers.

At number 66 is the eerie **Passage du Coeur Navré** (the drowned or broken heart). In the 13th-century its name was illustrated with a heart pierced by a spear because the alleyway led the condemned to the gallows at Place Foire-le-roi. Despite the gourmet restaurant next door, it is still a sorrowful place in which drunken revellers can easily be mistaken for child thieves or murderers. At the end of the covered wood and brick passage, the illuminated fountain on **Place Foire-le-roi** is a welcome sight.

Although the square was rechristened Place du Peuple for 50 years after the Revolution, the conservative Tourangeaux prefer the old royal name. It is hard to believe that the tastefully renovated square staged public executions until the 16th century. Luckily, it also witnessed public fairs and, on the occasion of an *Entrée Joyeuse*, held mystery plays in honour of the king.

The St-Martin Quarter: This area is what remains of the religious enclave of Martinopolis. **Tour Charlemagne**, St

Martin's former resting place, lies in Place du Chateauneuf in the heart of Vieux Tours. The original 5th-century church, destroyed by the Normans, was rebuilt under Charlemagne.

The impressive, slightly dilapidated tower is in keeping with the rest of the square: partially renovated buildings stand beside the severe Renaissance residence of the dukes of Touraine; in between is the chic *Bar Américain*, a sign that a more gentrified Tours is just around the corner.

After looking at the broken columns at the foot of the Tour Charlemagne, follow St Martin's body to its next resting place. During the Wars of Religion, the church was pillaged and St Martin's relics were only found in 1860, in the cellars of a nearby house. To celebrate the find, Tours commissioned Victor Laloux to build the **Nouvelle Basilique St-Martin** on the other side of the square. Built in hideous neo-Byzantine style, the church is usually guarded by hopeful beggars, including one who looks enough like St Martin to make pilgrims feel guilty.

Pass quickly by the acres of greyish-white marble and descend to the **Sancto Martino Mausoleum**, placed in exactly the same spot as in the original church. The gloomy tomb is lit only by wavering candles. On 11 November, the mosaic floor is covered with kneeling pilgrims and war veterans waiting their turn to recite St Martin's prayer to the saint's arm. Although the peripatetic saint's body was burnt by the Huguenots in 1562, his head was placed in St-Gatien cathedral and his arm travelled here. No doubt Martin has many more moves yet before his arm can rest in peace.

Considered the finest Renaissance building in Touraine, **Hôtel Gouin** had a miraculous escape from fire and bombs in 1940. This former silk merchant's house is now the city's archaeological museum, an appropriate end for a building built over an old Roman villa. The ground floor is devoted to prehistoric and Gallo-Roman remains, including pieces from Tours' Roman amphitheatre.

Carving in Place Plumereau.

Although there is a passing glance at the Renaissance, the first floor concentrates on medieval statuary, mostly saved from demolished local churches. The exhibits include dramatic gargoyles, a contemporary portrait of Rabelais, a 15th-century tabernacle, and a slightly woodwormed statue of the Virgin and Child.

After visiting the museum, head for **Place Plumereau,** the restored square at the heart of "new" Vieux Tours. While walking along Rue Bretonneau and Rue Briconnet, notice the half-timbered facades, hidden courtyards and crooked towers which typify the authentic medieval city. Sounds of clinking glasses will lead you to Place Plumereau, the place for serious people-watching. In summer, jugglers, tumblers, ice cream sellers and students on bicycles mingle with the regular cliques: black-clad fashion victims, blue-rinsed matrons, anonymous international executives and French intellectuals in olive-green cords.

To avoid the crush, walk under a low archway to the **Jardin St-Pierre-le Puellier,** sunken gardens full of Gallo-Roman remains. Despite the funerary niches in this dimly-lit square, intimations of mortality are quickly dispelled by the aromas coming from the neighbouring streets. Follow your nose to discover such local delicacies as crêpes filled with spinach or asparagus, pork-filled *rillettes* or *rillons,* and *crottin de chavignol,* a rich goat's cheese usually served hot.

However, the last word should go to an early chronicler, Jean Boylesve who said, "If someone asked me to attribute one epithet to Tours, I would ignore for once *rillettes* and *pruneaux* and instead praise Tours, *la ville bien bâtie,* the well-built town".

The surprising suburbs: Once situated on an island in the Loire, the **Prieuré de St-Cosme** is today hemmed in by the Rivers Loire and Cher but is also sadly marooned between a railway line and suburban sprawl. It takes an imaginative leap to see the priory as it was in Ronsard's day. Until the 16th century,

Place Plumereau, Tours.

St-Cosme welcomed pilgrims travelling by boat to the shrine of St-Martin at Tours. The monks also housed, washed and fed the pilgrims following the route to Santiago de Compostella. The creaking refectory and the delightful fountain are reminders of these times.

In 1555, Ronsard and his brother brought their two young mistresses to St-Cosme, no doubt scandalising the monks. Ronsard was then courting Marie du Pin, a 15-year-old girl he called "*douce, belle, amoureuse et bien fleurante rose*". After a happy year, his "*fleur de quinze ans*" left the impoverished poet for richer pastures.

Soon after, however, Ronsard's fortune changed and in 1560 he was appointed official court poet and adviser to Charles IX. Five years later, he was appointed Prior of St-Cosme on condition he finished *La Françiade*, a book of heroic poetry. Once installed in his beloved priory, the new *Prince des poètes françoys* never paid the king in poetry. Instead, he fulfilled his court duties as infrequently as possible and devoted the rest of his energy to managing St-Cosme and his two other priories, Montoire and Croixval.

In particular, discouraged by a series of platonic relationships with women, he preferred to spend time writing love poetry or gardening. It comes as no surprise that his family emblem was a rose, as the peaceful gardens are full of roses to this day. When Charles IX and his mother, Catherine de Médicis, came to visit, Ronsard presented the King with fresh melons from his garden, excusing himself with the words, "*Sire, je vous donne non pas beau, mais tout ce que je puis.*"

Ronsard's last verses: Today, the inviting **Prior's lodge** still stands, surrounded by the ruins of the Romanesque church and cloisters. Despite many alterations, however, the study, overlooking the rose garden, has a real sense of Ronsard's presence. It was here that he dictated his last verses and died, saddened by the Wars of Religion that were tearing France apart. The poet's remains were exhumed in 1933 and his **Hôtel de Ville, Tours.**

body was re-buried under the rose garden. A few streets away, Renaissance gardens and manor houses lie hidden in the suburbs.

Although as royal a residence as any in the Loire, **Plessis-lès-Tours** is a modest, red-brick manor house rather than a full-blown château. Many kings stayed there, from Charles VII's reign onwards, but Plessis was most loved by Louis XI. The King converted this former hunting lodge into a fortified manor house, protected by a drawbridge, two towers, a double set of walls and an inner courtyard.

Naturally mistrustful, Louis surrounded himself by 200 Scottish and Swiss guards, changed his valets often and, in disguise, patrolled the kitchens to eavesdrop on potentially dangerous rumours. Louis' main pleasure was hunting, a pursuit satisfied by the presence of a vast walled park, now engulfed by suburban Tours.

In his old age, Louis stocked the grounds with strange animals from all over Europe: Neapolitan ponies, mini-ature lions from Spain, deer "as large as buffalo" from Denmark and wild hares from Brittany. He also bred a new type of hunting dog, called *souillards*: the spoilt animals wore soft leather collars made in Lombardy and their paws were bathed in mulled wine. History does not relate whether the dogs became drunk in licking their paws dry. In his dotage, the infirm King held rat races or mini-hunts in his bedroom.

In appearance, Plessis is similar to another brick and stone manor house, Clos Lucé at Amboise. The manor once had three wings, connected by galleries, but much was destroyed in the Revolution so now only the King's Apartments and a few outbuildings remain.

Still, even if some of the grander reception rooms no longer exist, Louis' austere bedroom remains much as he left it. The Flemish tapestries depicting hunting scenes are also a reminder of his happier days. From Plessis, you can follow the Loire to Amboise or visit the Gatine, the windswept plains to the north of Tours.

Prieuré de St-Cosme.

EAST TOURAINE

The inhabitants of East Touraine are not averse to presenting their charms in a bottle or on a plate. Any *Carte du jour* would feature the two most famous white wines in the Val de Loire, Montlouis and Vouvray. Apt accompaniments would be three of France's most celebrated châteaux: Amboise, Chenonceau and Loches; not forgetting rural stretches of four great rivers, the Loire, Cher, Indre and Indrois. As visitors or residents, Balzac, Flaubert and Voltaire all succumbed to many dinner invitations and lived to tell the tale of over-indulgence in the rich provinces.

By contrast, Touraine *à la carte* is an acquired taste, far from the popular *Route du Vouvray* along the Loire. The unappealing top notes consist of windswept plains, sleepy backwaters and a forest of long-dead monks. However, a bitter-sweet keynote soon develops with the realisation that workmanlike villages, ruined water mills and a deserted charterhouse are fitting preludes to, say, Montrésor, the most evocative of Tourangeaux villages.

Healthy walks: "Valleys are rich and plains are poor—and so it shall ever be," says Bernard Briais, the well-known local historian. The scrubby plains of the **Gâtine** stretch unpromisingly from La Loire to Le Loir and are neglected by Tourangeaux and tourists alike. However, when "châteaux country" begins to pall, the plains offer healthy walks across heath and woodland and quirky rural architecture, from tithe barns to fortified farms and many converted water mills.

Once a great forest, the Gâtine was felled from medieval times onwards—hence the origin of the name from *gâstée*, meaning "spoilt" or "devastated". The poet Ronsard protested in vain against the destruction of the oak and elm forests, "*Escoute, bucheron, arrête un peu le bras*" ("Take heed, woodcutter, and raise your axe no more.") But the wood was needed for barrels, carts and barns, and the new land was gradually covered with today's rye and wheat fields. Since the poor, sandy soil is difficult to cultivate, there is little incentive for farmers to cut down the remaining woods, and agriculture is far less mechanised than in the huge Beauce region, further north.

Most of the area immediately north of Tours belonged to the Abbey of Marmoutier from the 11th century to the Revolution and, as a result, many of the older buildings in the area have religious links. The finest of these is the **Grange de Meslay**, a huge tithe barn and gatehouse surrounded by attractive walled gardens. This is all that remains of the priory, chapel and dovecotes which were built here in 1220. The Prior's house was destroyed as recently as 1944, when a munitions depot exploded in the woods nearby.

The 200-ft (60-metre) barn itself is magnificent, proudly referred to as "a cathedral for corn" by its owner, Patrick Lefebvre. In the 15th century, the roof was redone in chestnut timber-work and the structure is divided into five naves

by four rows of vast oak supports. However, as Lefebvre says poetically, the main structure dates from the 13th century "when the Romanesque and the Gothic styles rose side by side in the region". In summer, the barn becomes a real cathedral for Tours' prestigious music festival. Sviatoslav Richter, the musical director, is fond of quoting Nietzsche, "Without music, life would be a mistake" and is delighted that he can attract stars to a mere barn.

Signs of the Abbey of Marmoutier are ever-present, not least in the small, scattered vineyards on the slopes. This is the northernmost area of *appellation Vouvray* so your last chance to try this dry white wine, perhaps accompanied by a picnic of *rillettes de Tours.*

An unusual way of exploring the Gâtine is to visit old water mills on the rivers Ramberge, Brenne and Choisille. As late as 1939, there were hundreds of working mills in the region but now there are only eleven.

On the River Ramberge, north of Amboise, two atmospheric mills can be seen at **St-Ouen-les-Vignes**. Here, the Moulin de Pont Chalet crushed chestnut wood, used in the tanning process. In fact, it is known as the *Moulin Rouge* because the tanning process turned the water red.

The Gâtine is not an area dotted with historic châteaux but a place to make chance discoveries, following small roads and streams north. However, Touraine's more sceptical residents, the majority, cannot be tempted to live on the plains. Generally speaking, a visit to the Gâtine confirms sophisticated valley dwellers in their prejudices towards their "backward" northern neighbours. The view of the River Loire, east of Tours, is a welcome sight.

From Tours to Amboise: Following the north bank of the Loire, you soon come to the remains of the legendary **Abbey of Marmoutier**, now a private school in Tours' bourgeois suburbs. Founded by St Martin in 372, attacked by Normans in the 9th century, occupied by Cluniac monks from the 10th century, this celebrated place of pilgrimage finally gave

Tithe barn at Meslay.

up the ghost after the French Revolution, when it was sold as a *bien national* to local builders.

Superficially, all that remains is a Romanesque gatehouse, flanked by the Prior's lodge, a watch tower and belfry. However, carved into the rock are the so-called *hermitages* a network of underground cells and chapels originally used by hermits and early Christians, including St Gatien. Although not a silent order, the Benedictine monks were encouraged to withdraw for long periods of prayer. Nowadays, these peaceful cells are sometimes home to truanting teenagers, there to avoid the *cours de philosophie* and other intellectual pursuits. The monks would turn (silently) in their watery graves.

Cave-dwellings of a less spiritual kind are a feature of the next village, **Rochcorbon**, and, in fact, follow the Loire to Vouvray. Since this is the heart of wine-growing country, the caves are used primarily as private or commercial wine cellars. The caves, like the vineyards stretching above them, face south, to the Loire and to the sun. The area is dotted with marked walks past historic manor houses, troglodyte caves and, of course, vineyards.

From the *Mairie* (Town Hall), a 5-mile (8-km) walk (signposted yellow) follows a stretch of old Roman road to the Abbey of Marmoutier via the Romanesque St-Georges chapel and the *lanterne*, a strange tower that dominates Rochcorbon. Perched on the clifftop, the *lanterne* remains a mystery, like the one at Cinq Mars, near Langeais. It is either all that remains of Rochcorbon's château, a watchtower, or a river lighthouse to guide boats or send coded messages to embattled allies.

Rochcorbon and Vouvray have long provided refuge. In 1914, the low-life writer, Georges Courteline, escaped the war by settling here. Although originally from Touraine, he dismissed Tours as "a third-rate town" whose citizens did little but sing patriotic songs and squander money on interminable bridge parties and riverside dinners where the locals "sipped white Vouvray

wine and ate fried fish at St-Avertin".

Just north of Rochcorbon, the river Bédoire leads to a couple of intriguing water mills, the Moulin de la Gravotte and the **Moulin de Touvois**. Because the water level of the Loire fluctuates so greatly, no water mills were ever built on the Loire, only on the small tributaries. From Rochcorbon, a 4-mile (6-km) walk (marked white) leads past vineyards and woods to the Touvois mill, an idyllic spot, equally accessible by car.

Part mill, part manor house, Touvois was built under the reign of Louis XIII and converted in the 1930s. Now privately owned, this enchanting mill is a favourite location for French film directors. A version of "The Beauty and the Beast" was shot beside the old weir and rose-covered turret. Once back in Rochcorbon, follow the Loire to Vouvray, the self-proclaimed heart of the white wine region. En route, admirers of Balzac can stop at **Moncontour**, the château beloved by the local author. In 1846 he wrote to his mistress, Madame Hanska, "You're going to jump for joy—Moncontour is for sale. My 30-year dream is about to come true... if we had Moncontour, all my plans would change... we could live there forever".

In fact, the long-suffering Madame Hanska did not jump for joy. Tired of paying off Balzac's debts, she said nothing and Balzac never bought the place he called, "A charming little Tourangeau château, its towers embroidered like Mechelen lace". With the passion of an unfulfilled estate agent, Balzac contented himself with befriending the new owner. He later gave the château a starring role in his novel, *La Femme de Trente Ans*.

Tiers of vineyards signal the approach of **Vouvray**. Legend has it that St Martin himself promoted the local wine industry by encouraging the proper use of fertilizer. His faithful donkey is said to have made a small contribution. Since the wine harvest is often late, the troglodyte caves only become hives of activity in late October. Then, smoke curls out of the tall chimneys; inside the tufa rock, whole

Véretz from the river.

families or knights of the ancient wine guilds are huddled over the secrets of the new wine.

A number of walks and drives interlace the vineyards: by car, follow the route signposted *Route du Vouvray*; on foot, follow the blue and white *Vouvray les vins* signs through cherry orchards and vineyards. A good time to try the renowned dry, demi-sec or sparkling wines is at the Vouvray wine-tasting fair in mid-August.

On the other bank of the Loire is **Montlouis**, another wine growing village riddled with wine cellars. From Montlouis, a choice of walks leads to the Duc de Choiseul's old hunting lodge, to Henri IV's bachelor quarters (Belle Roche), and to La Bourdaisière, the park and château once occupied by Gabrielle d'Estrée, Henri IV's mistress. Sadly, it is now an old people's home, an inappropriate end to the reign of the *Vert Galant*, the evergreen monarch.

La Bourdaisière has a long romantic history. It was built in 1520 by Philibert Babou, François I's great financier for his wife, known as *la belle Babou*. If contemporary letters and sonnets can be believed, her lovers included François I, Charles V and the Pope! If your energy is flagging, visit these places by car and then sample the Montlouis wine with a Touraine apple turnover at a local brasserie. Although the wines are rated slightly less highly than *appellation Vouvray*, they are reputed to take after *La Belle Babou* in maturing and travelling well.

Royal Amboise: Amboise is rightly considered the most royal of Loire châteaux, home to five kings and, if legend can be believed, one Roman Emperor. Julius Caesar is supposed to have established winter quarters at Amboise; certainly his Roman tower acted as a river lighthouse until its demolition in the 17th century. In the Middle Ages, Amboise was one of only five châteaux on the Loire between Gien and Angers and dominated the route to Spain. In 1440, Charles VII confiscated the château from the Dukes of Amboise and its royal fate was sealed: for over a

Indre farmhouse.

century the history of Amboise became the history of France.

Louis XI gave Amboise to his pious wife, Charlotte de Savoie, but preferred to live at Plessis-lès-Tours, alone but for 200 Scots and Swiss guards and his mistresses. Louis XI had seen the great influence of Agnès Sorel over his father and therefore resolved not to mix pleasure and politics: no wife or mistress had any significant influence. According to Brantôme, the court chronicler, while the King, "changed his mistress as often as his nightshirt", the Queen walked and prayed at Amboise, "as badly dressed as a peasant girl".

By contrast Charles VIII and his wife, Anne of Brittany, ushered in a bright era of enlightened attitudes and Italian splendour. Brought up at Amboise and inspired by his sumptuous visits to Italy, Charles transformed Amboise from a feudal domain to a Renaissance palace. From here, the Renaissance spread to the rest of the Loire.

The reign of Louis XII began on a sour note with the annulment of his marriage to Jeanne de France in order to marry Anne of Brittany. Howèver, Amboise soon reverted to its new-found role as the intellectual and artistic centre of France and a new wing was added to the royal château. Renaissance splendour, however, reached its peak under the reign of François I, with a renewed building programme at Amboise and magnificent masked balls designed by Leonardo da Vinci. After the Wars of Religion, and, in particular, the Amboise Conspiracy the château ceased to play centre-stage in French history.

Appropriately enough, royal Amboise is now run by a public trust set up by the Comte de Paris, the Pretender to the French throne. The chateau is only a disappointment if you dwell on the loss of the Queen's Apartments, the Renaissance gardens and the southern and eastern wings. Instead the Renaissance St-Hubert chapel, the arcaded galleries, the Gothic *logis du roi* and the ingenious riders' ramp provide enough clues to the original design. The spiral ramp opens onto a surprisingly wide terrace,

Left, the Loire at Amboise. **Right**, self-portrait by Leonardo da Vinci in old age.

LEONARDO'S LAST YEARS

The enlightened François I recognised Leonardo da Vinci as the greatest artist of his reign and unsuccessfully tried to obtain Leonardo's *Last Supper*; when the fresco could not be wrested from the walls of Santa Maria delle Grazie in Milan, François decided to settle for the painter rather than the painting. In 1516, the King invited the careworn artist to leave the turbulent atmosphere of Italian City-state rivalry for the relative peace of Clos-Lucé, François' childhood home. Leonardo was "resting" between patrons and looking for a less warlike retirement and lured by an annual position of 700 ecus, a household of servants, and a charming manor house beside Amboise. In 1516, Leonardo crossed the Alps on a mule, accompanied by his most famous works, including the *Mona Lisa*, *St John the Baptist* and *Saint Anne*. In his lifetime, the paintings and cartoons were hung in his sunny studio in Clos-Lucé. The artist's official title as *Premier peintre, architecte and mechanicien du Roi* was whatever Leonardo chose to make of it. The young King indulged the wayward genius so that Leonardo's status was one of honoured guest rather than court functionary. But whether through guilt or gratitude, Leonardo willingly acted as court jester, impresario or confidant.

Leonardo knew how to sing for his supper and, as master of ceremonies, staged mechanical pranks, firework displays and masked balls to entertain the court. Apart from sketching the festivities, Leonardo designed all the costumes and special effects. At one *son et lumière*, thousands of candelabra flooded the night sky and the heavens were represented by mechanical replicas of the sun, moon and stars. On another occasion, Leonardo made such a realistic lion that ladies fainted; when the King touched the lion's muzzle with his ring, the beast yawned and a *fleur de lys*, the royal emblem, dropped at François' feet.

In his long, light studio, now decorated with bright yellow Louis XV furniture, Leonardo reworked the head of *John the Baptist*, painted abstract works, landscapes, and portraits of old people's faces, including his own. One expressive landscape depicts the view from Leonardo's studio, a misty scene of Renaissance gardens, trees and, in the distance, a small tower.

As a master of all elements, Leonardo did not restrict himself to painting at Clos-Lucé but pursued his fascination with air and water, trying to codify the laws of motion. As a respected civil engineer, Leonardo planned a canal to link Tours to Lyons via Romorantin. He also drew up plans to redesign Amboise along the Venetian model, creating a series of canals and futuristic walkways. Although no buildings in the Val de Loire can be attributed with certainty to Leonardo, some architects wonder if his drawings inspired the revolutionary Renaissance staircases at Blois and Chambord. Certainly, Leonardo designed a new palace and classical gardens for the Queen Mother at Romorantin; the project was abandoned only when malaria was found to be rife in the marshy area. In an attempt to bring some physical stability to an itinerant French court, Leonardo designed prefabricated, collapsible houses, an idea whose time had not yet come.

The ground floor of Clos-Lucé is a museum in honour of Leonardo's technical achievements. The 40 models, constructed according to Leonardo's drawings, represent a constant ebb and flow of ideas, 400 years before their time. On display are models of a cannon, car and helicopter, as well as a tortoise-like tank, linen parachute and fire-resistant ship. As a scientist, Leonardo had cinematographic vision—his mechanics are all conceived in movement. For ordinary mortals, however, it is a relief to find the occasional crackpot scheme: a likely candidate is the horizontal windmill, designed to sweep assailants off the battlements!

The museum at Clos-Lucé celebrates Leonardo the scientist; the house itself celebrates Leonardo the artist. His last drawings depicted swirling patterns of water; abstract designs partly inspired by bad dreams. In *Deluge* and *Vision of the End of the World*, all the elements are unleashed and appear to defeat the rational, scientific world. Ultimately, then, in Leonardo's vision, the scientist is submerged by the artist.

once an inner courtyard but now planted with azaleas.

The interior has, in places, been over-restored but the furnishings are authentic although, given the itinerant nature of French courts, not necessarily from Amboise originally. In the dining room, the transition between Gothic and Renaissance styles is apparent in the collection of chests and chairs: the medieval ones are usually heavier and built of oak whereas the Renaissance fashion was for lightly-carved chestnut. The tapestries are less impressive than those at Langeais or Chaumont but coincide with Amboise's period of glory; notice that, with age, the green tint becomes blue, while yellow turns green.

Imprinted on the château's fabric and furnishings are royal symbols such as the *fleur de lys*, ermine or salamander. As for religious symbolism, the most striking are the gargoyles, particularly the snarling griffins, which look threateningly at the river.

The **St-Hubert chape**l, built by Charles VIII for Anne of Brittany,

forms part of the ramparts. This delicate stone chapel is adorned with a finely sculpted hunting scene; above is a frieze of Anne and Charles at prayer, with the Virgin and Child interceding. Many of the interior friezes were destroyed in the Revolution; those remaining are fine enough to decorate what is now the tomb of Leonardo da Vinci.

The grounds are far more spacious than in Charles VIII's time: apart from additional wings, there were also stables, a granary and a menagerie stocked with monkeys, parrots and even lions. It is difficult to remember that the court was once a self-sufficient citadel of 1,000 dependents. Louis XI's personal retinue included two confessors, two silversmiths, an official court painter, 200 French and Scottish retainers and an astrologer.

For an impression of the original scale of Amboise, look out of the tower galleries in the north wing. On a hot summer's day, your attention will float across the medieval rooftops to the dehydrated Loire, gradually turning into one long sandbank. Once the most royal of châteaux, Amboise, like the *fleuve royal* is also adrift today on a historical sandbank.

River Cher to Chenonceau: The **Cher**, just south of Amboise, is often dubbed "the poor man's Loire". But even though it rises in rustic Berry, by the time it reaches *la douce Touraine*, the Cher is positively rich. Apart from geographical advantages, such as good soil, safe swimming and natural sun traps, the Cher is also an estate agent's paradise. There lies the problem: most of the châteaux on this stretch of river are privately owned. Unless your car comes equipped with a stepladder, you are unlikely to see much behind duplicate sets of walls. However, with the right *carte de visite* or an American Express card, doors may open and elderly counts may cancel appointments to dine with you.

Larçay is a hamlet dominated by the imposing château-hotel on the hill. As an inducement to stay, signs praise the local wine, stacked in wine cellars built into the rock. **Véretz**, a tumbledown

Amboise, detail of tapestry.

village wedged between the river and the vineyards, was where Madame de Sévigny conducted her *al fresco* summer salons. Still privately owned, this slightly forbidding château boasts classical statues and fountains. From the terraces, underground galleries lead to wine cellars hidden in the rock.

Facing the village of St-Martin-le-Beau, the **Château de Nitray** conceals a large 16th-century château behind serious walls. However, as the *Vin de Touraine* sign suggests, you are welcome to call if you buy the local wine. At **Bléré**, a small market town with a Romanesque church, cross the river and travel on the north bank to Chenonceau. All along the Cher, small side turnings lead to picnic spots and landing stages by the river; while quicksand and swift currents make the Loire dangerous, swimmers are quite safe in the Cher. As the magnificent Chenonceau comes into view, it is a relief to put the stepladders away and explore the second most visited monument in France.

Chocolate-box Chenonceau: To many visitors to the Val de Loire, **Chenonceau** is the icing on the cake, the quintessential château. In fact, it comes as no surprise that its present owner is *un chocolatier*, Gaston Menier. According to Flaubert, an enamoured visitor, this frothy concoction floats "on air and water, its calm never boring and its melancholy without bitterness". For such a famous château, Chenonceau has little historical importance: compared with Amboise and Blois, it was never a political pawn; unlike Chinon or Loches, it staged none of the set pieces of French history. Joan of Arc did not visit: if she had, she might have taken off her armour and gone for a swim.

Chenonceau was designed as a pleasure palace and private theatre, fought over by a series of female owners but always loved for itself. Catherine Briconnet and her husband, Thomas Bohier, gradually bought parcels of the Chenonceau estate as the land became vacant. Between 1513–21, the couple demolished the feudal castle and old watermill on the site, leaving only the

Nightfall at Amboise.

Marquis tower, which remains today. Bohier, treasurer to the king, had fought at Marignano and had seen enough of Renaissance architecture to wish to employ Italian workmen to rebuild Chenonceau. In his long absences, his wife oversaw the work and improvised as she watched the château grow from its new centre. Balanced on two enormous pillars in the River Cher, the compact new building represents the nucleus of Chenonceau today.

Perfect gift: At war with his financiers, François I confiscated the château on the grounds that Thomas Bohier had been guilty of embezzlement. To François, Chenonceau was just another hunting lodge but to Henri II it was a perfect gift for his favourite, Diane de Poitiers, "*sa parfaite amie*" and companion for 22 years. Ironically, the gift, along with financial help, was made in recognition of her "good, kind and amiable services to the Queen", Catherine de Médicis. In some respects, this was an unconscious irony on Henri's part since Diane, as the senior lady-in-waiting, was given total responsibility for the royal household, even including the well-being and education of the royal children. During Henri's lifetime, therefore, Diane was too powerful to be usurped, even by the Queen herself.

Diane's key contribution to Chenonceau was to build a bridge connecting the château to the left bank of the Cher; she also designed a classical park, complete with flower, herb and vegetable gardens, a maze, pools and fountains, all fed by a complex irrigation system which still exists. For her first few years in residence, Diane encouraged visitors to bring gifts of nut, apricot and pear trees. Although the gardens at Chenonceau are still fine today the gardens at Villandry actually follow Diane's design more closely.

Following Henri II's death, Catherine's revenge was to force Diane to accept **Chaumont** in poor exchange for Chenonceau. But when the sweetness of victory faded, Catherine also learned to love Chenonceau and, using Diane's builder, Philibert Delorme, enclosed

Gardens of Chenonceau.

the bridge with a long gallery, doubled the number of windows and decorated the bedrooms with sculptures. Catherine also planned an identical château on the other bank, but this was never built so she contented herself with the classical banqueting gallery and turned her hand to the grounds.

Catherine, the Florentine, aimed to transform Chenonceau into a cross between a French palace and an Italian villa. As Regent of France, she was anxious to dazzle the court with exotic novelty and lavish receptions. With grand *fêtes champêtres* in mind, she created grottoes and concealed fountains in her new park. One *jardin vert* was filled with orange and olive trees, a patch of Mediterranean colour under a northern sky. Chenonceau quickly acquired an aviary, a silkworm farm and rock pools filled with turtles and water snakes. One artificial grotto contained a statue of Catherine entwined with serpents, a symbol of her eternal power.

Under Catherine's influence, Chenonceau became the haunt of her 200 "ladies of honour", known as the *escadron volant* or "flying squad". This secret weapon was used in dubious romantic intrigues to further Catherine's political ends. Members of the "flying squad" were loyal and *galantes*, often a euphemism for promiscuous. *La Belle Rouet* was one of the unofficial ambassadors sent to neutralise an enemy during the Wars of Religion. In 1562, she was despatched to charm Antoine de Bourbon, the Protestant King of Navarre; partly as a result of Louise Rouet's amorous efforts, a successful truce was eventually negotiated.

More openly, Catherine used Chenonceau as a public palace, the natural choice for lavish receptions. In 1571, the Queen Mother summoned the fairest members of the "flying squad" and commanded them to prepare for a "transvestite ball". The women, theoretically dressed as men, were barebreasted, while Catherine's favourite son, Henri III, made a passable woman, with heavy make-up, pearl earrings, a decolleté rose damask dress and a

Chenonceau from the river.

purple wig. The court alternated between shouting *"vive le roi"* and *"vive la reine."*

On Catherine's death, the château went to Louise de Lorraine, bereaved wife of Henri III, who spent the next 11 years there dressed in white, the colour of royal mourning. In 1733, after a succession of royal links, Chenonceau fell into the hands of Monsieur Dupin, whose enlightened wife used Catherine de Médicis' gallery as a literary salon for such philosophical guests as Montesquieu, Jean-Jacques Rousseau and Voltaire. Rousseau fared badly at Chenonceau since, despite composing trios, putting on plays and "becoming as fat as a monk", he was a science tutor to the Dupin's insupportable son.

If Chenonceau today is little changed since Renaissance times, its 19th-century owner, Madame Pelouze must be thanked since she blocked up Catherine de Médicis' "extra windows" and gave Diane de Poitiers the last word. But to see Chenonceau through a châtelaine's eyes, visit early on a winter morning; at

any other time, ownership must be shared with the milling crowds. Even then, this conjuring trick of a château is still dazzling.

Visible at the end of a long line of plantain trees, a solid white cube comes into sight, guarded by two sphinxes. But as you approach the château, it shimmers into a facade; this is the first illusion. Then, perfectly-proportioned bay-windows and balconies stretch across the water and the château becomes a bridge. Just when it seems most real, Chenonceau glides away like a cruise liner, its illusion complete.

Apart from the gardens and the exquisite setting, the highlights include the long gallery, Catherine de Médicis' quarters and the straight staircase, an innovation for its time. Catherine's library, bedroom and study make a harmonious unit, preserved exactly as she left it: the ornate ceiling in the library and *cabinet vert* (study) have not been touched since 1521. Her bedroom, complete with an elegant fireplace, original tapestries and a magnificent four-poster bed, is a model of Renaissance good taste.

Diane de Poitier's bed, as if vindicated by history, has been moved into the *chambre des cinque reines*. When Flaubert stayed with Madame Pelouze at Chenonceau, he playfully commented: "Even empty, Diane de Poitier's canopied bed inspires many palpable realities".

The gallery spanning the River Cher has a black and white tiled floor which, in Louise de Lorraine's time, was echoed by a black-and-white ceiling symbolising her mourning. Elsewhere in the château are black-and-white motifs which were also Diane de Poitier's colours, chosen to enhance her pale complexion, rather than to symbolise genuine widowhood. The gallery played an important role in both world wars: in 1914 it was a hospital for over 2,000 soldiers; between 1940 and 1942, the north door of the gallery was in occupied territory, while the south door led to Vichy France.

Before leaving for a boat trip on the Cher below, pay your respects to

Royal bedroom at Chenonceau.

Chenonceau's three great châtelaines. In the François I room, look at the portrait of Diane as legendary huntress. Catherine Briconnet's epitaph appears on a door nearby, "*s'il vient à point me souviendra*" (if this château is finished, remember me). As for Catherine de Médicis, her memorial was once written on a pillar in the gardens, "*fin al cielo n' andara la fiamma*" (the flame of royal glory will rise to the heavens); the pillar is no more but the memorial is still there in stone and water.

From Tours to Loches: The Indre, once a tributary of the Cher, comes from Lower Berry and meanders through Touraine. Compared with the Loire and the Cher valleys in this part of Touraine, the Indre is quieter and gentler, more what Balzac had in mind when he praised his *douce Touraine*.

By pottering along minor roads, you can trace the path of the river quite closely, while making time for investigating mills and manor houses. Riverside picnics, fishing and even swimming are possible if you don't mind the reeds or inquisitive cows as spectators.

Slightly south, **Corméry** and **Truyes** face each other across the river and are surrounded by walks from Corméry's stark watch tower, dilapidated mill or ruined abbey to the dairy farms just south of Truyes. At **Reignac**, the river narrows and a lush rural scene unfolds. Tracks wind down to the river past small allotments and an old mill half-hidden in the trees. Against a backdrop of nonchalant cows and upturned boats, young boys fish from a wooden platform overhanging the river.

Azay-sur-Indre, is where the rivers Indre and Indrois divide: the Indrois, a smaller version of the Indre, can be followed upstream to Montrésor while the Indre goes on to Loches. Just outside Azay is **La Follaine**, an attractive 15th-century gabled manor house which, in pre-Revolutionary days, was Lafayette's hunting lodge. This is a reminder that the river now borders the Forest of Loches, for long a popular hunting zone with local landowners. In the forest, four strange pyramids still remain from

Reflected glory, Chenonceau.

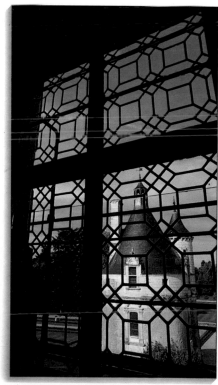

the Duc de Choiseul's time: built in 1778, these markers could be seen from afar and were used by hunters as landmarks or meeting points.

The name **Loches** could derive from an archaic word meaning "light in the forest" or "clearing". Loches' most famous son, poet Alfred de Vigny, is lightly condemnatory about his native region, referring to the countryside as "varied in its monotony, light and gracious but with a beauty which caresses without capturing, charms without seducing". His impressions, however, were coloured by a 49-year absence and a preference for city sophistication.

Loches is backward-looking in the nicest sense of the word. The town reached its apogee in the 16th century when its royal connections and cloth industry made it an important trading post on the route to Spain. Soon after, the Spanish route switched to Tours and Loches became a sleepy backwater until the arrival of the railways in the last century.

Even then, Loches still relied heavily on dairy farming, a declining silk-growing and textile industry, and on a traditional arts and crafts market. For a clear impression of rural crafts and folklore in the 19th century, visit the **Musée du Terroir** in the Porte Royale. The view from the roof clearly shows the interdependence of town and castle.

Although more recently Loches has diversified into mushrooms and pâtisserie, the arts and crafts tradition has continued to expand. In mid-July, a *marché paysan* celebrates the old crafts with a sale of hand-made products ranging from rough hoes to delicate pots. The finale is a public ball which soon turns into a chaotic street party to which all are welcome. There is some inkling of this bonhomie on market day every Wednesday when normally chic bars are full of amiable farmers haggling over crates of chrysanthemums and mushrooms. Even the occasional chicken on the loose fails to interrupt the proceedings.

Jacques Lefeque, the regional director of tourism, says that if a simple **Fortifications at Loches.**

adjective had to be applied to each of the Loire château, he would choose "royal" for Amboise, "historical" for Chinon, but "the most moving" for Loches. In this, he could be thinking of the "reign" of the beautiful Agnès Sorel, the uncrowned Queen of France; or of Joan of Arc's impassioned plea to Charles VII, in which she reminded him of his promise to go to Reims to be crowned. Even the local tourist guides, normally a hardened species, are not immune to emotion about Loches.

In describing the atrocities of the English during the Hundred Years' War, tears come into the eyes of the young castle guide. Observant listeners notice, however, that while addressing a patriotic French audience, the guide's descriptions of English perfidy are much freer. Not that the fairytale turrets of Loches lack a rich historical or royal past: in the Middle Ages, Loches was one of France's most vital fortresses.

Protected like a Russian doll by raised rings of medieval streets and three tiers of city walls, the citadel itself is surprisingly vulnerable. Once inside the Porte Royale, the first feeling is one of space: the church, château and dungeons make three very separate focuses. The citadel is a mixture of styles and periods: the church, dungeon and watch tower date from the 11th century while the château is essentially a Gothic hunting lodge with Renaissance facades. A walk around the ramparts reveals how all these different styles interlock.

Before Amboise and Blois became the royal favourites, Loches was considered the safest base for a largely itinerant court. Although both Charles VIII and Louis XII lived there, the château is most closely associated with Charles VII and his mistress Agnès Sorel, the first "official favourite" in French history. It is often forgotten that Charles also had a wife, Marie d'Anjou, by whom he had 14 children, most of whom died.

La favorite was present at all major occasions and in return for loyal support to the King, received ermine gowns, oriental silks and gold brocaded Egyptian sheets. Both a trendsetter and a fashion victim, she wore the highest *hennin* (pointed head-dress) and had the longest train in the kingdom. She is credited with starting a new fashion for semi-nudity in dress. The bishop Jean Juvenal raged against her bare-breasted gowns to no avail: *la dame de beauté* usually prevailed.

Copies of two famous portraits of Agnès Sorel adorn the château. In one, painted by François Clouet, Agnès is shown in a gauzy head-dress and ermine train, her pale complexion and bare breast are set off by a sombre black robe. In the other portrait, painted by Jean Fouquet, a bare-breasted Agnès poses as the Virgin Mary in much the same way that Brigitte Bardot and Ines de la Fresange, the top Chanel model, posed for portraits of Marianne, the female embodiment of France.

As far as her impact on the course of French history is concerned, her influence over Charles VII was considerable, but Joan of Arc's intervention was more crucial. Agnès died in 1450, supposedly of a "stomach upset", but some

Agnès Sorel as the Virgin Mary by Jean Fouquet.

historians believe she was poisoned by the Dauphin, the future Louis XI. In keeping with royal custom, she was cremated and her heart and entrails placed in a casket. These were then buried in a black marble tomb over which a statue of Agnès, carved out of purest white marble, rests on two lambs, embodiments of peace, beauty and her own name.

The *logis royal*, or château, is sparsely furnished but has unusual architectural details, including graceful turrets and Renaissance fireplaces, including one in Anne of Brittany's chapel, the only one known to exist in a church. Since the pious Queen Anne spent so much time here, mourning the deaths of Charles VIII, her first husband, and three children, a fireplace was essential. The chapel was once painted azure blue and was covered in Anne's personal emblem, silver ermines. These, along with much in Loches, were obliterated in the Revolution, when the château was used as a prison.

After leaving the château, look at the Romanesque **St-Ours church** opposite. The unique roof takes the form of four turrets: two towers enclose two octagonal pyramids, below which is an impressive vaulted ceiling. The **watch tower**, **keep** and **dungeon** are an essential part of Loches, as interesting as the château itself. Begun in 1005, these are the work of Foulques Nerra, the pitiless but eccentric Duke of Anjou. After each massacre along the banks of the Loire, he went on a penitential pilgrimage to Jerusalem or founded another abbey, and then began a new cycle of extortion, pillage and plunder. As a military architect, however, he had no rival and this is his finest work.

Certainly the prisons are the most intact in the Loire, ironically because they were in use until 1926. The guide is only half-joking when he warns visitors against wandering off down the myriad side passages, many of which emerge outside the city walls. In June 1940 when the Wehrmacht occupied the town, there was little opposition, partly because citizens had already fled down

Ladies gossiping.

the passages and were hiding there or in wine cellars, troglodyte dwellings, or even old hermits' caves hidden at the end of the tunnels.

The most intriguing prison is in the **Martelet tower**, which was home to Ludovic Sforza, Louis XII's most valuable prisoner. He was treated well, however, and even allowed to paint his well-furnished quarters. It is just possible to make out Sforza's signature on the walls, in the form of the message, *"Celui qui net pas contan"* ("He who is unhappy"). The official version of Sforza's death is that he died the day after he was released from prison because, after so many years in the dark, the shock of broad daylight was too great. Local tradition, however, suggests that Sforza's food was poisoned the night before his release.

After escaping into the sunlight, it is a shock to find that prison images persist: on the city walls are replicas of *fillettes*, iron cages invented by Louis XI, perhaps as a reaction to his unhappy childhood in Loches. As King, he is reputed to have suspended Cardinal Balue, a traitor, over this wall for many years. For more ghostly and gory stories about Loches, try the "Loches by night" guided walking tour.

If exploring the town by day, make a point of looking at architectural details on facades in the Rue du Château and Rue St-Antoine. Locals refer to many of these as Renaissance facades but the guiding spirit of Loches is definitely late Gothic. Although the Hôtel de Ville boasts François I's salamander emblem and the elegant proportions of true Renaissance architecture, much more typical of Loches are the two late-Gothic gateways, Porte des Cordeliers and Porte Picois.

Loches has been slow to realise its tourist potential and therefore the citizens have not yet lost their local pride, so enjoy it while it lasts. In 1989, the town elected Christine Mora as its first woman mayor and first left-wing leader. For sleepy, royalist Loches in Bicentennial year, this was little short of revolutionary!

Men playing boules.

From Loches to Montrésor: Even though Loches and Montrésor are not far apart, a local expression says, *"de Loches à Montrésor, 18 kilométres sans boire"*, a reminder that in the monks' time it was an alcohol-free zone. Without a village en route, this remains true today. Between Loches and Montrésor stretches the forest of Loches which, from the Middle Ages until the Revolution, was a religious domain ruled by the Abbots of Beaulieu and the monks of the Chartreuse de Liget.

Facing Loches, on the other bank of the Indre, lies **Beaulieu-lès-Loches**, an old abbey town. The quaint Beaulieu tourist brochure introduces itself as "a small city who keeps in his houses as many legends and ghosts as an old Scottish burg" (*sic*). In fact, this odd translation conveys the right atmosphere of haunted and troubled times. Historically, conflicts between the crown and the church were highlighted by the presence of a strong king on one side of the river and of a powerful abbey on the other. As a result, Beaulieu is an independent-minded town with little affection for its royal neighbour.

Beaulieu is reached by a street called **Rue Brûlée** with good cause: the street and much of the town was burnt down by the English during the Hundred Years' War. The town still has enough dilapidated remains to conjure up these war-torn times. The **abbey**, now ruined, was founded by Foulques Nerra. Although destroyed by the English in 1412, the abbey was rebuilt in the 15th century and still retains its original Romanesque bell tower and part of the original abbey church.

In the old, rather battered, streets nearby are a number of 15th and 16th-century houses built from recycled abbey stone. In particular, look at the **Maison de Justice** which was once a law court but became the Hôtel de Ville after the Revolution. Of the earlier religious buildings, the most interesting are the **Maison des Templiers**, a 13th-century lodge belonging to the Knights Templar, and **La Léproserie**, a 12th-century house used either for healing

Beaulieu-lès-Loches.

the sick or as a shelter for lepers. Before continuing your journey, it is worth checking facts with the villagers, some of whom are keen local historians. As the Beaulieu tourist brochure puts it in its own inimitable style, "We have a solid will-power to revive this patrimony and we don't disregard the economics" (*sic*). You can always help by showing an interest in the local mushrooms and pottery.

In the forest halfway between Beaulieu and Montrésor lies what was once the most important religious foundation in Southern Touraine, the **Chartreuse de Liget**. This Charterhouse was founded by Henry II of England in 1178 in atonement for the death of Thomas à Beckett. His penance did not end there, however, and the **Chapelle St-Jean**, half-a-mile (800 metres) from the Chartreuse, was also built at his request. Set in an isolated field, this white Romanesque chapel contains some of France's finest 12th-century frescoes.

Although only a shadow of its former self, the Chartreuse is still impressive, helped by an idyllic location in a clearing in the wooded valley. A series of ornamental arches leads to a gateway and a lodge once reserved for female guests and residents. A cluster of outbuildings once housed the monks' workshops for carpentry, furniture-making and glasswork. Sadly, only one section of the cloisters remains but the encircling walls and mini-watchtowers give some sense of the importance of the Charterhouse. The grounds also contain fish ponds once stocked with fish from the River Liget. Eleanor of Aquitaine is said to have been taught how to fish by the local monks.

During the Revolution, the Chartreuse was sold as a *bien national* and the new owner demolished the religious buildings and sold the stone to local farmers. As a result, Chartreuse stone has not travelled far and can be seen, for instance, in the farms near **Sennèvieres**, a well kept village with an ivy-covered church and fields full of brown goats.

A number of walks lead from the Chartreuse to the animal-filled Forest of

A royal steed.

Loches. In endowing the Charterhouse, Henry II, King of England and Anjou, sacrificed the rich hunting grounds of the forest to the monks of the Order of St Bruno.

Once back on the Montrésor road, you soon see **La Corroierie** on your left, a mysterious, fortified farm which also belonged to the monks. This *ferme-manoir*, fortified during the Hundred Years' War, served many functions: it was where the monks hid in times of danger and it was where the noisy, heavy trades, such as tanning and forging were carried out. The material and spiritual worlds were theoretically kept apart but for the sake of convenience exceptions were made. One such, is the ruined Angevin chapel adjoining the dilapidated, windowless farm. La Corroierie is not safe to visit but a gentle walk around this atmospheric site is an ideal prelude to a picnic, possibly by the lake a short walk away.

It is odd to reflect that this empty stretch of woodland was, on the eve of the Revolution, a thriving community of 1,000 people. The 18th-century gateway leading to the Chartreuse has an eerie frieze of priest, cross and skull which has no explanation.

From Azay to Montrésor: The River Indrois has wound its way into the heart of literary Touraine, from Descartes to Balzac. At times the most rural of rivers, its trick is to disguise poverty as romance, helped by a succession of Romanesque churches, ruined abbeys and more water mills than anywhere else in Touraine. The Indrois meanders past the Forest of Loches, carving a narrow path between small orchards and lush meadows. The banks are lined with willows, alders and poplars. Although unfortunate for the local economy, the rural exodus makes this indolent stretch of river a joy to visitors.

The Indre and the Indrois merge north of **Azay-sur-Indre**, but between Azay and Montrésor the Indrois flows through a number of small villages, of which **Chédigny** is the best-known. A quaint bridge leads to **St-Quentin**, a sprawling village with a partly Roman-

Cows in the Cher valley.

esque church and an old water mill.

Genillé, the next village upriver, is worth visiting, if only to see the clinically neat château and the remains of a 17th-century abbey.15th and 18th-century houses compete for gentle river views as do the troglodyte caves at Genillé, and the fate of two very different mills is on display: the Moulin de la Roche has been well-restored while the Moulin du Pont is quietly rotting by a dry weir, its "For Sale" sign blowing in the breeze.

Chemillé, the closest village to Montrésor, curves into a loop of the river. In summer this stretch of water attracts anglers and rowers, as does the large lake bordering the village. This scenic valley is also popular with riders and ramblers so riverside trails lead to troglodyte dwellings, landing stages and to the inevitable decrepit water mill. Before going on to historic Montrésor or rushing to the new leisure complex on the lake, visit the well-restored village church, topped by a Romanesque belltower. Inside is the ancient bell from the Chartreuse de Liget; it used to summon recalcitrant monks to prayer from the fishponds and fields.

Set in one of the most heavily wooded spots in the Loire region **Montrésor** lives up to its poetic name. It is regularly labelled one of the loveliest villages in France and this subjective judgement does at least confirm that Montrésor has all the right ingredients. Centre stage is a crenellated château mirrored in the placid Indrois; in the foreground Norman cows pose indolently as if for a pastoral painting; in the middle distance, the watery plains are empty, heralding rural Berry to the south.

Set on a rocky promontory, the château was built by the feared Foulques Nerra, but his only visible legacy is the fierce watchdog which guards the grounds at night. Apart from the 12th-century gateways, most of the château is 15th-century and a mixture of Gothic and Renaissance styles. From 1493 onwards, it was owned by Basternay, a counsellor to four kings of France, from Louis XI to François I. In

La Corroierie near Montrésor.

Basternay's hand, the château lost its original defensive function and became a pleasure palace, planted with the terraced gardens you can see today.

In 1849, however, the château was given to Count Xavier Branicki, a friend of Napoleon III. Since then it has been a Polish island in rural France. The eclectic Polish Count furnished it with treasures which once belonged to the 17th-century Polish king, Jean Sobieski. The Branicki family restored the château, damaged in the Revolution, but added a few neo-Gothic flights of fancy, such as the crenellated turrets.

The same family owns the château today so do not be surprised at the Polish silver and paintings depicting Polish history—nor at the occasional Polish street name. In addition to Polish memorabilia, however, there is a fine collection of paintings, including some by Holbein, Raphael, Veronese and Caravaggio.

From the shady terraces, there are views through the cedars and sequoias to the medieval old town below and to

the watery meadows beyond. A walk around the ramparts confirms this harmonious impression: mellow stone, verdant countryside and indolent river blend into another pastoral cliché.

A number of steep alleys lead down to the medieval quarter and the river. On the way down, you pass wine cellars and carpentry workshops built into the 13th-century walls. Tucked into niches in the walls are religious statuettes placed at odd angles. In Rue Branicki, the head of John the Baptist looks more like a medieval impression of a Saracen.

Look out for the 17th-century **Halles**, a barn used both for storing grain and for carding wool, an activity which survived until the end of the last century. Since Montrésor depends on crops, cattle and woodcarving, the medieval economy shows no sign of being replaced by tourism.

The population currently stands at 500, the lowest in its history, and is still declining despite the efforts of the local council and church to generate interest in fishing clubs and other similar activities for sprightly pensioners of the *troisième age*.

The local church is, however, proof that the Renaissance did reach Montrésor. Built by the Basternay family to house their tombs, the church has 16th-century windows, Gothic turrets but a fine Renaissance facade. The family tombs were broken during the Revolution but, now restored are inside the church once more.

Near the church is a well leading to an underground river 46 ft (14 metres) below the old quarter. Legend has it that hidden treasure was discovered here in early Christian times, thus explaining Montrésor's name. True or not, Montrésor has enough tangible treasures to draw your eyes from the cows, neatly arranged under a line of poplars, to the top of the flamboyant Polish turrets and the Berry skyline beyond.

Like the River Indrois itself, the spiritual values of old Touraine spill over the bureaucratic boundaries and tinge neighbouring regions with Tourangeaux qualities, from charm to complacency, and even sheer indolence.

War memorial at Montrésor. Right, château walls.

BLESOIS

An aerial view of **Blois** reveals a town hemmed in by forests: the only opening is made by the plains of the Beauce and by the Loire itself. Before the feudal counts of Blois conquered the land, this was an inhospitable forest infested with wolves. It is no coincidence that the oldest city emblem is the wolf, nor that the city name comes from *bleiz*, a Celtic word for wolf. This *pays à loups* still feeds off its forests, particularly in the hunting season when Parisians flock to restaurants full of feathered and furry game. Every autumn, wild boar, roebuck and partridges are suspended from butchers' shops or appear on menus with other forest delicacies such as *cèpes* and *chanterelles* mushrooms.

Arrival by train is sweetened by the overpowering smell of chocolate: the Poulain chocolate factory next door is a major employer. It also confirms the city's collective sweet tooth, a tradition going back to the days when cocoa was shipped here from the East Indies via Nantes. As an important market town, the city marches on its stomach. Cereals from the Beauce, asparagus and goat's cheese from the Sologne, game and mushrooms from the forests: all are processed or simply eaten here.

In the broadest sense, the local economy lives off the land, converting cattle into *Kickers* shoes or exploiting the decentralisation of Paris in the 1960s to provide civil servants with cosy patches of land. Few can resist the quality of life in Blois, which can only be improved by the appointment of Jack Lang, François Mitterrand's Minister of Culture, as mayor in 1989.

This was equally true for the city's original rulers, the Comtes de Blois. From the 9th century, the counts ran a fiefdom embracing Chartres, Champaigne and most of Touraine. The dynasty lost control only in 1397 when the last count sold the land to Louis d'Orleans. From then until the Revolution, the history of the town followed the fortunes of the Château and the royal house. It is thanks to such historical continuity and minimal industrialisation that Blois has retained so much medieval and Renaissance architecture.

The historical richness also makes the old centre seem bigger than it is. Blois is only a quarter the size of Tours yet, thanks to its insignificance as a military target in modern times, has a greater concentration of historical curiosities, from its Jewish ghetto to grand *hôtels particuliers*, hidden inner courtyards and airy Renaissance loggias. However, Blois is a town of exteriors not interiors: its museums and churches are secondary to the essential experience of traipsing the hilly streets and unpromising alleys for courtyards, stone emblems and cosy restaurants.

The city turns its back on the river: few fine houses, restaurants or shops lie on the banks of the Loire. Instead, the town's identity lies curled up in the old quarter, a semicircle bounded by the château, Porte Chartraine, the cathedral and the former Jewish ghetto.

Set protectively high above the town,

Preceding pages: stained glass, church of St-Nicholas, Blois; Blois at sunset. **Left**, open skies of the Beauce. **Right**, statue of Joan of Arc, Blois.

the cathedral and the Town Hall represent the moral and civic heart of Vieux Blois. During the Occupation, both buildings were landmarks for aviators who risked their lives making secret landings. Nearby, the sober, classical Hôtel de Ville and surrounding Jardins de l'Eveque witnessed nocturnal gatherings of Resistance workers. Today, the peaceful gardens rarely see anything more dramatic than an impromptu game of *boules*.

Once the Bishop's Palace, the Town Hall faces an ecclesiastical building adorned with a splendid sundial. It is inscribed with the Latin motto: "Time moves on, our works stand still; while we have the time, let us use it to the good". The liberal Blesois interpret this as a pretext for charity *boules* matches or masterly inactivity. Beside the Town Hall, sunny terraces stretch towards the Loire. A warlike statue of Joan of Arc on horseback surveys the valley, the saint's moral indignation at odds with this quietly sensuous scene.

St-Louis Cathedral, backing on to the gardens, has a chequered history but is a disappointment. The present building dates back to the 10th century when a church housed the tomb of the Bishop of Chartres. Only the Romanesque belltower and crypt remain from these times as the rest of the church was rebuilt under François I. However, in 1678 a hurricane ruined three facades and destroyed the windows. The spooky crypt is now the most atmospheric spot: while you admire the vaulted ceiling and stark Romanesque columns, a disembodied voice echoes through the gloom, reciting the history of the crypt as a pilgrimage centre.

Back in the sunlight, **Place St-Louis**, on the other side of the cathedral, is an assymetrical yet elegant square, the town marketplace until the 18th century. The harmonious *hôtels particuliers* have well-restored facades and wrought-iron railings. The finest half-timbered house is the **Maison des Acrobates**, carved with characters taken from medieval farces: a chivalrous knight bends down on one knee,

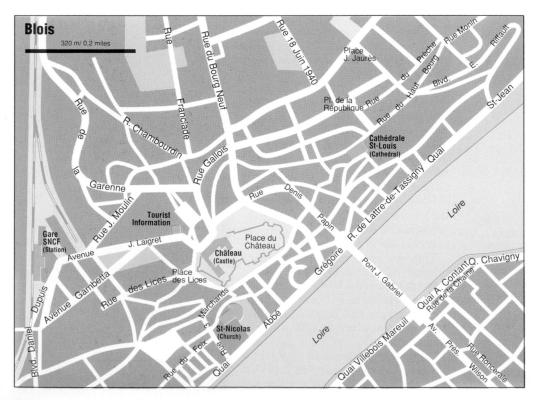

surrounded by jugglers and acrobats. On the left, a cobbled alley leads downhill to Rue de la Pierre de Blois and the 14th-century Jewish ghetto. En route, notice the **Hôtel de Villebresne**, with its covered Gothic passage linking two medieval houses. The Rue des Juifs has three fine hotels, all kindly labelled by the Town Council. In particular, notice the galleried **Hôtel de Condé**, with its Renaissance archway and deep inner courtyard. Judging by the names and plaques in the doorways, Jewish psycho-analysts are much in demand with today's angst-ridden citizens.

But in the adjoining streets there is little evidence of angst in the chic galleries, bistros and bars. Where Rue des Juifs meets Rue des Papegaults and Rue Degres St-Louis, a photogenic half-timbered house straddles both medieval streets. In the 14th century, the narrow **Rue des Papegaults** was the main link between the upper and lower town. Named after the wooden parrots used as target practice, the street is now target practice for pigeons swooping into courtyards in search of scraps.

The most striking courtyard is **Hôtel Belot**, a 16th-century house adorned with an external spiral staircase, barrel-vaulted loggias and *fleur de lys* designs. In keeping with other grand houses, the dingy ground floor was the preserve of chefs and guards while noble salons were held upstairs. Rue Grenier à Sel is a short cut to an impressive 15th-century barn. This is now an exhibition centre overlooking **Place Vauvert**, the most appealing square in Blois, not just because it is the gastronomic centre. On summer evenings, the square is carpeted with competing restaurants but nothing detracts from **Hôtel Sardini**'s floodlit Renaissance facade, dominating one side of the square. From Rue Vauvert, a small doorway leads to a sweet-smelling herb garden which, like the barn, once belonged to the Sardini, the prominent Italian bankers.

From here, you can stroll to the other old quarter, a network of steep streets radiating from the château to Rue Chemontin and Rue Beauvoir. After walking along Rue Papin, the main street, to the foot of the château, follow the well-marked Rue Royale tour through Vieux Blois. Alternatively, if it is a hot summer's night, walk up the steps to the château and watch a memorable *son et lumière*. Although the plot owes much to Hollywood, so did the antics of the original cast of royal Blois.

Historical pageantry aside, the *son et lumière* is an ideal opportunity to appreciate the **château** in all its architectural diversity. The light sweeps from the feudal Charles d'Orleans wing to the Gothic Louis XII wing, highlighting the Renaissance spiral staircase on the François I wing and lightly brushing over the classical Gaston d'Orléans wing. Blois, unlike Chambord or Chenonceau, is not a unified masterpiece but a haphazard configuration of contrasting styles and tastes. However, as a resumé of French architectural styles it is unequalled.

Seen from different angles, it is hard to piece the château together. Viewed from Place du Château, the impression is one of an uninviting feudal castle,

enlivened only by the sculpture of Louis XII on horseback, erroneously carved so that the horse is raising both legs on one side, a physical impossibility. By contrast, seen from the Victor Hugo gardens, the Renaissance wing is an airy concoction, glimpsed through fountain spray and weeping willows. The galleries, jutting out like boxes at the opera, overlook the town as if it were a spectacle for the court's amusement.

For long the property of the legendary counts of Blois, the present château dates from the 13th century but only the feudal hall remains from then. In 1397 the grim fortress passed to the Orléans dynasty. However, under the civilising influence of Charles d'Orléans, the poet prince, Blois became a comfortable palace, celebrating courtly love with poetry tournaments. Charles's son, the future Louis XII, added a new wing and chapel, along with Italianate gardens which once stretched all the way to the station quarter.

François I, the archetypal Renaissance king, demolished part of the Gothic château but re-used the bricks and stones in more harmonious designs. However, although his wife loved the Blois, he infinitely preferred Chambord or any other hunting lodge. Yet despite François' long absences, historians have praised him for creating "The Versailles of the Renaissance" at Blois.

As the century drew to a close, the interminable Wars of Religion meant that all building work at Blois came to a standstill. But Blois then witnessed a dramatic turning point: the murder of the Duc de Guise by Henri III in 1588. With Henri IV's reign, the court moved to Paris and Blois lost its historical importance, used only as an occasional royal prison, pleasure palace or military barracks. Its last architectural flowering was in the 17th century when Louis XIII's brother, the exiled Gaston d'Orléans, built the classical wing. The creation of Versailles meant the final eclipse of Blois.

The **feudal wing**, sandwiched between the grander Louis XII and François wings, was used as a council **Blois river view.**

and court. Flaubert, paying a visit in 1847, called this part, "the most bare, the roughest, the most entrenched in the Middle Ages". In fact, this feudal hall is an elegant space and the best preserved Gothic hall in any Loire château. Since the place was a barracks in Flaubert's time, the writer may have been influenced by the rough, drunken soldiers milling around.

The **Louis XII wing** is an uneasy blend of Gothic design tinged with Renaissance inspiration. Despite assymetrical windows and statues of grimacing medieval monks, the gallery is full of Renaissance motifs, from candelabra to the king's own porcupine symbol and motto, "From near and afar, I can defend myself". As an absolute monarch, the king felt little need to defend himself and this is reflected in the openness of windows and balconies. As a sign of confident times, the arrangement of the rooms places privacy and convenience above safety: where once rooms opened on to one another, here galleries divide rooms and separate

staircases give access to different floors. The wing was clearly intended as a place for receptions and administration—defence was secondary.

The château's masterpiece is undoubtedly the **François I wing**, described by Flaubert as "the final explosion of Renaissance architecture before the Renaissance degenerated into bastardised Greek design under Marie de Médicis". Stretching between the feudal and Classical wings, this wing resembles an Italian palazzo, with no Gothic elements save the high slate roofs and tall chimney pots. Running under the roof are two floors of Italianate loggias with views of the Victor Hugo gardens and the *Pavilion Anne de Bretagne*, once a chapel where Louis XII's wife used to pray for a son. Just beyond is the royal orangery, now the city's most exclusive restaurant.

But the highlight is the **spiral staircase**, superior to its rival at Chambord. Facing the inner courtyard, the staircase is enveloped in a sculpted octagonal tower. Flaubert referred to both as

"chiselled by the liveliest scissors and cut out like the high collars of the *grandes dames* who walked the stairs 300 years ago." Here and elsewhere are Renaissance motifs including cherubs, plants and François I's own symbol, the salamander promising to "encourage good and snuff out evil".

Compared with many Loire châteaux, Blois is sparsely furnished but truer to its historical origins. The Renaissance and Gothic motifs have been well-restored or recreated, while paintings reflect Blois' troubled history, including the death of the Duc de Guise. Damaged by wood smoke and years of neglect, the château was repainted in its original design a hundred years ago but luckily these garish colours have softened with age.

The most intriguing rooms are the Queen's Apartments, especially Catherine de Médicis' study, carved with 237 wooden panels, all containing secret cupboards. What they concealed is open to speculation: probably jewels, letters and state papers; romantics prefer Alexandre Dumas' conviction that the Queen hoarded poisons and secret potions. Still, nothing had any visible effect as she lay dying in the royal chamber, ignored by family and friends. According to Pierre de l'Estoche, the court chronicler, "No more notice was taken of her than of a dead goat."

Despite the château's grisly history, Blois is a town for arrivals not departures and is an ideal base for visiting neighbouring châteaux. On returning, you will find the town much as Victor Hugo celebrated it in 1825. Arriving in style, Hugo saw Blois at sunrise from his stage coach, "I opened my eyes and saw thousands of windows at once, an irregular and confused cluster of houses, belltowers and the château; and on the hills, a ring of huge trees while on the river bank lay gabled stone houses: a complete town built like an amphitheatre" he wrote.

Lucrative meetings: Originally François I's hunting lodge, **Beauregard** feels more classical than Renaissance, despite the 16th-century arcaded

Beauregard glinting gold.

galleries on the main building. Beauregard is currently being restored but its manicured grounds have been achieved by converting the orangery into a lucrative conference centre.

The entrepreneurial du Pavilion family lives in one wing and anxiously guards the unique portrait gallery, subject to a spate of unsuccessful burglaries. This *gallerie des illustres* contains famous historical paintings including ones of Joan of Arc, Savonarola and the entire Valois dynasty. Apart from this magnificent time capsule, appreciated by Louis XIV and Richelieu, the other historical treasure is the Cabinet des Grelots, a panelled study with secret cuboards and ornate Italianate ceiling.

With its neat avenues, ruined chapel and classical statues, Beauregard lives up to its name. The château is best seen at sunset when the light glints gold on the main facade. Visitors should not linger, however, since the grounds are then patrolled by fierce Alsatians.

On to Chaumont: From Blois, the most direct way to the lofty white **Château de Chaumont** is to follow the River Loire, a pleasant but busy route.

After crossing the river at Onzain, you reach a pretty village by the sandbanks. From there, a steep walk leads to the cliff-top Château de Chaumont. On top of this windy cliff, the initial impression is one of space and wildness, reinforced by the swishing sounds of the surrounding trees, and the sweeping views over the valley. The hilly grounds are unkempt and exciting, especially the forest trail leading from the old stables: a high, narrow bridge leads through a gnarled tree trunk into the sweet-smelling cedar wood.

A fortified château has existed on the spot since the 10th century, protected by defensive moats, deep valleys and the river itself. Originally owned by the Amboise family, Chaumont was "lent" to Charles VII in 1431 and thereafter became the property of the Valois dynasty. Louis XI and XII largely rebuilt the present château, softening the grim, windowless facade with Renaissance terraces on the east wing. Nonetheless,

Loire and bird's-eye view of Chaumont.

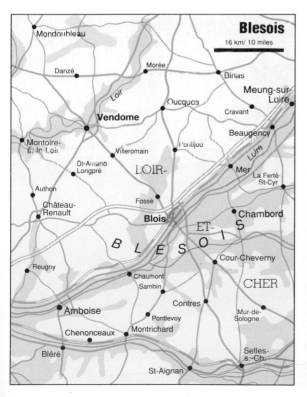

its feudal character reasserts itself in the four round towers, sturdy drawbridge and severe Gothic south and west wings. In the 18th century, the north wing was demolished and replaced by terraces in response to the French fashion for river views.

Despite its undoubted beauty, Chaumont has rarely brought its inhabitants much pleasure. Catherine de Médicis, Henri II's widow, used it as a political pawn to humiliate her rival, Diane de Poitiers, the late king's mistress. By forcing Diane to accept Chaumont in exchange for her beloved Chenonceau, Catherine triumphed: Diane declared Chaumont heartless and retired to her ancestral château in Normandy. But Catherine herself experienced little happiness at Chaumont: in her turreted observatory, she and Ruggieri, her Florentine astrologer, plotted both the stars and the downfall of royal detractors. Legend has it that here Catherine read the grim destiny of her three sons, all to die violent deaths. She also foresaw the end of the Valois dynasty, her Machiavellian plotting routed by the accession of Henri IV.

In 1810 the political writer, Madame de Staël was exiled "40 leagues from Paris" so the "empress of the mind" came to Chaumont with her constant companion, Bernard Constant. She was busy writing her famous work on Germany at the time; so as not to be distracted she forbade her guests to talk in the drawing room and they were obliged to communicate using little notes which they called, "la petite poste". The interior now is tastefully decorated with Aubusson tapestries and Renaissance trunks from the Prince de Broglie's Sicilian collection. Chaumont contains a portrait of Catherine de Médicis but her magnetic presence is felt most in her shadowy observatory. As light relief, step into the sunny courtyard where musicians and singers, dressed as Renaissance courtiers, give summer classical concerts.

From Chaumont to the Cher: From Chaumont, the D 114 leads south to the river Cher and rural Berry. However, a **Stables at Chaumont.**

more leisurely route zig-zags across woodland to the castle of **Fougères-sur-Bièvre**, cuts through the plains to the market town of Pontlevoy and, just before the river Cher, reaches the eccentric **Château de Gué-Péan**.

Built on the edge of the Sologne, Fougères is surrounded by birch trees, asparagus beds and marshes. The castle keep dates from the 11th century but the rest was added in the 15th century by Louis XI's chancellor. Unlike the king, Pierre de Refuge did not believe in user-friendly homes but designed this castle in the old feudal style. After living through the English invasions, de Refuge only had faith in moats, drawbridges, arrow slits and battlements. Although his son-in-law made it more graceful by adding windows and galleries, the spirit of the castle is Gothic. An octagonal tower, narrow windows and pinnacles complete the anachronism.

From Fougères, a direct route leads past wheatfields and occasional goat farms to **Pontlevoy**, a small provincial town with a rich religious heritage.

Despite pockets of commuters living in the prettified villages along the river Bièvre, this is a sleepy patch of rural France with local farms offering goat's cheese and *vins de Touraine*.

The **abbey**, founded in the 11th century, is Pontlevoy's main claim to fame. Unfortunately, it was pillaged and burnt down during both the Hundred Years' War and the Wars of Religion. Although the monastic buildings were partly rebuilt in the 17th century, the original abbey church was never finished, resulting in a strangely truncated Gothic chancel.

With the foundation of an abbey, Pontlevoy acquired prestige as an artistic and educational centre. In the 17th century, an important college was established in the abbey grounds and, until the Revolution, provided a civic and military education to the *petite noblesse*. After the Revolution, the college educated the *haute bourgeoisie* instead, hardly revolutionary. Now it is a technical college.

Without the abbey or college,

Chaumont: astrologer's room.

Pontlevoy is today just a sprawling village aspiring to the status of a provincial town. But in the **Musée Municipal** is a more fitting tribute to the town's history: an illuminating collection of local photographs representing a slice of village life at the turn of the century. Taken by Clergeau, the village clockmaker, the photographs reveal such scenes as eccentric mechanical inventions, stern-faced local dignitaries and dumpy stall-holders in full Solognot costume.

On the slopes of an isolated valley just south-east of Pontlevoy lies **Gué-Péan**, its individuality and odd inhabitants at home in this wild and wooded setting. Across a deep valley comes the first sighting of the château, with its three pepper-pot towers and distinctive bell-shaped keep. Although the keep dates from the time of Foulques Nerra, most of the château is late Renaissance, built at the same time as Chambord. However, unlike its famous rival, Gué-Péan was unfinished: "*troubles revolutionnaires,*" mutters the old retainer elusively. Even the "finished" structure is studded with architectural errors, typified by the orangery which was never used as such because it was built facing north. The château owes its original name to the words for "gap" and "tax" because in François I's time Gué-Péan bordered seven water mills and operated a toll on grain delivered through a passage in the water. Today, there is little sign of water because the moats are dry and only one ornamental pond remains from the once resplendent classical gardens. However, Gué-Péan does not rely on conventional charm to attract paying guests: although the lush grounds and the adjoining riding school play a part, much is due to the personality of the owner, the Marquis de Keguelin de Rozieres de Sorans.

The château has been in the family for over 300 years and, if you stay overnight, the elderly marquis will enlighten you on his family tree, including the Polish connection. Visitors may be humbled to learn that illustrious house guests have included Alexandre Dumas, Mary Stuart, Georges Sand and

Salon at Gué-Péan.

Chopin, the late Shah of Iran and Alain Delon. All have left souvenirs which have found their way into the marquis' inimitable collection: Persian paintings, war memorabilia, embroidered saddles, family flags, indifferent watercolours, a valuable piano, and historic letters are all in this magpie's nest.

After dinner, the marquis and his bassett hounds may escort favoured guests around the library, inviting them to read Marie Antoinette's last letter or to admire his war memorabilia. The marquis is modest about his role as a Companion d'honneur Resistance hero. The family retainer has no such scruples: according to him, the marquis singlehandedly saved Paris in 1944 and was rewarded by membership of the General's postwar Government.

Over liqueurs, General de Gaulle's name crops up frequently: "The General wanted all Frenchmen to eat chicken on Sunday" is the marquis' highest accolade. The marquis himself, now in his eighties, can manage the chicken dinner but is inclined to fall asleep in the middle of relating a key exploit with Generals Leclerc and de Gaulle. However, even if you do not stay overnight, few visitors are allowed to leave before seeing the old retainer's comic de Gaulle impression. Be warned: any praise results in repeat performances.

Vendôme and the north: By TGV, the fast new train service from Paris, Vendôme is only 40 minutes away yet occupies the "green heart of France" much as it did in Ronsard's day. The poet described this provincial capital as enriched by a *"source d'argent toute pleine/ Dont le beau cours éternel/ Fuit pour enrichir la plaine/ De mon pays paternel."* ("A silver stream overflows, and bubbling eternally, to enrich the meadows of my native country.")

Vendôme truthfully calls itself *"une cité d'eau et de fleurs"*. The little river Loir forms a greenish-grey grid through the white stone city while baskets of geraniums sprout from medieval facades. On a rainy day, it is difficult to distinguish between reflection and watery reality: mills, wash houses and watergates are duplicated downstream. Overlooking the twists and turns of the Loir is a decapitated fortress on a rocky promontory, a reminder that the name "Vendôme" originally stood for "white mountain". It is also a reminder that this peaceful scene is a modern myth.

Vendôme was an English fiefdom in the Hundred Years' War and at times both a Protestant and a Catholic stronghold during the Wars of Religion. Since Henri IV's time, the town's future was linked to the fortunes of the royal dynasty and suffered for its allegiance in the Revolution, when the old city walls were destroyed. As recently as June 1940, Vendôme was a battlefield when German troops occupied the town while in the late 1980s there were disputes between environmentalists and executives over the building of the TGV line in green belt land. With such a warring past, it comes as no surprise that Vendôme should have produced Rochambeau, leader of the Yorktown victory in the American Revolution. But until the time of the French Revolution,

Vendôme statue of Rochambeau, hero of the American Revolution.

most visitors to Vendôme were there for religious as well as military affairs. The town became a major pilgrimage centre in the Middle Ages, thanks to its renowned abbey, its place on the Santiago de Compostella pilgrimage route and its possession of a great relic, St George's arm, in the castle itself.

Dating from the 11th century, the feudal **castle** was built by counts of Vendôme but, by the 13th century, was run by the Knights Templar as a sanctuary, hospital and bank for pilgrims on their way to Spain. Three medieval towers still remain, along with St George's chapel which once contained the saint's arm, a gift from the Emperor of Constantinople. A walk along the steep ramparts reveals views over the well-stocked castle gardens to the watery maze below.

On a windy day, the castle and tiered troglodyte caves are best viewed from the **Hôtel du Château** at the foot of the cliff. At night the hotel's seedy low-life bar attracts an odd mixture of tourists and locals to its *spectacles du soir*: these range from sedate *thé dansants* to the raunchy *Patrice Rat*, Vendôme's belated answer to punk rock.

Higher-minded visitors might continue their investigations of religious Vendôme in the abbey church just over the river. The **Eglise de la Trinité** is the finest Gothic church in the Loir-et-Cher region and the remains of the once great Benedictine abbey. The abbey was used as the regional military headquarters from the Revolution until 1940: in Vendôme, religious and military functions often intermingle.

Legend has it that the abbey was founded after a vision in 1034: standing on the castle ramparts, the Comte d'Anjou and his wife saw three shooting stars fall into a fountain beside the river. The abbot of Chartres interpreted this event as a sign that the couple should found an abbey on the spot. La Trinité became so powerful that its abbots were automatically appointed cardinals and were accountable only to Rome.

In the shadow of the ornate west fa-

Vendôme Castle.

246

cade is a 12th-century belfry which provides a sober counterpoint, relieved only by grinning animal sculptures. Although built four centuries apart, both the Romanesque belfry and the Flamboyant Gothic facade were the architectural inspiration behind their counterparts at Chartres cathedral. Inside the church, the highlights include the graceful vaulted ceiling and the choir stalls decorated with signs of the zodiac and angelic musicians. The stained-glass windows span five centuries of different styles but the finest is the Romanesque *Majesté Notre-Dame*. This stylised Madonna and Child are crowned with sky-blue haloes, the hallmark of Loir valley glass designs.

Damaged in the Wars of Religion and disbanded after the Revolution, the abbey and its precincts are reduced to the monk's private granary, one arcade of cloisters and the chapterhouse, now a museum. One section is dedicated to medieval murals, glasswork and Romanesque statuary. However, folklore is present in a section showing dying regional crafts, from ironwork to tanning, wine-making and barrel-making.

A walk along the main street, the **Rue du Change**, shows that such crafts still survive in the form of dry white wines, wrought-iron work, antiques and leather goods. Kid gloves have been made here since Renaissance times and were then considered a great luxury. Catherine de Médicis used to present two bejewelled caskets, each containing one Vendômois glove, to favoured members of her "flying squad", who furthered her political ends by seducing royal adversaries.

Further along the Rue du Change, now a pedestrian precinct, you pass **Place St-Martin** with its 16th-century belltower which chimes the litany associated with Joan of Arc's journey: "Orléans, Beaugency, Notre-Dame-de-Cléry, Vendôme, Vendôme". Memories of two other famous figures lie in wait in Parc Ronsard, just off the Rue du Change. Here, the Vendômois would have us believe, Ronsard wrote love poetry and Balzac, three centuries later,

Vendôme,
La Trinité
Church.

played truant from an unhappy childhood. As a young boarder in the bourgeois Collège des Oratoriens, Balzac enjoyed none of the kayak races today's schoolchildren indulge in but hid behind disused warehouses or watched the washerwomen by the river. His schooling was as strict as these severe 18th-century buildings suggest and although the old name lingers on, the building is now the Town Hall.

The Parc Ronsard used to be the monks' vegetable and herb garden before it became a *jardin à l'anglaise*, which, in French terms, represents a stream, winding paths, romantic undergrowth and an air of neglect. The park has cultivated all this but here and there French classicism reasserts itself in the form of a scowling statue or a manicured ornamental garden.

Around bends of the Loir, heavy plantain trees appear rooted in the river while, on the other bank, willows droop over medieval courtyards and the river washes against the ground floor of former tanneries. Many of the tanners left for Château-Renault after Henri IV sacked the town. A rare *lavoir-séchoir*, a timbered two-storey washing and drying room, overhangs the river. Here 15th-century pilgrims washed their clothes on the ground floor and dried them on the floor above. This recently restored washhouse backs onto the Romanesque **Chapelle St-Jacques**, a pilgrims' church which is now an exhibition centre.

If you can face any more watery sights, visit the **Porte d'Eau**, the atmospheric old weir on the other side of the Rue du Change and choose from a variety of surprisingly sophisticated restaurants. For such a small provincial town, Vendôme runs the gamut of high life and low life, from chic Michelin-starred restaurants to sawdust-floored bars. However, a visit to Le Vieux Moulin appeals to insatiable water-lovers: while watching the old mill-wheel turn, you can enjoy such regional specialities as goat's cheese, mushroom dishes and *charcuterie*, all washed down with Côteaux de Vendômois. If you have any

Windswept plains of the Beauce.

energy left, remember the *thés dansants* or punk rock at Le Château.

Bleak Beauce: From Vendôme another watery experience follows the course of the river and an old pilgrims' route to Montoire. If, however, you decide not to carry on down the Loir, an entirely different landscape awaits you to the east. Known as the granary of France, these vast cereal-growing plains stretch north and east to Chartres, and produce higher yields than the North American prairies.

Legend has it that the name Beauce was coined by Rabelais. During Gargantua's first journey from Touraine to Paris the author recounts Gargantua's pleasure at the sight of the flat plains: "I find this beautiful" ("*Je trouve beau ce*"). The Beauce is best seen in spring when the wild flowers still manage to bloom between the patchwork of fields filled with young maize and wheat.

But before daring to leave the river, it is well to know what the area is not: the architecture is functional rather than decorative, while the landscape is bleak rather than beautiful. With one notable exception, Talcy, the grander châteaux remain locked behind feudal gates, their keys remaining in the hands of privacy-conscious landowners. If the manor houses look slightly forbidding it is because they have to sing for their supper as working farms. Naturally enough, local farmers measure their wealth in hectares, not in lovingly re-stored mullioned windows or in repointed Renaissance facades.

The pleasures of the Beauce lie in the broad vistas, the neglected churches, watchtowers and windmills isolated against the skyline. The low sky and sense of space flatten the architecture, shrinking its impact by magnifying the rigours of the elements. But if this sounds oppressive, the compensation is that, until you cross the plains and rejoin the Loire at Beaugency, tourism, as such, does not exist. On a sunny day, there is pleasure enough in admiring the yellow fields from a belltower, picnicking by a trout stream or even pottering

Village of Talcy.

around a farm on the pretext of buying fresh goats' cheese.

From Montoire, a rambling route takes you east past the hamlets of Sasnières and Chapelle-Vendômoise to the isolated farm and dolmens near Mézières and from there to the magnificent Château de Talcy and the medieval town of Beaugency. After seeing the faded frescoes in the church at **Sasnières**, ignore the Château d'Ambloy in favour of the Eglise St-Martin, a church attached to one of the sturdy wooden galleries that are a feature of the Beauce.

On the way from Ambloy to Chapelle-Vendômoise the road passes through sprawling, workmanlike villages and farms adrift on a sea of yellowing fields. Outside the low stone farms, chickens amble across the road to eat corn on the cob drying against the barns. Even the most dilapidated barns are bursting with the latest harvesters and tractors: farming in the Beauce is highly mechanised and there are few hedges or copses to impede the machin-

ery, nor to stop the wind howling across the plains. In winter, the forlorn landscape makes for sombre reflections on the problems of depopulation and an ageing community which cannot keep its youth from migrating to the hi-tech industries in Tours and Orléans.

Life on the plains has always been harsh, from the medieval land clearances to the cereal riots here in the last century. In fact, the feudal sharecropping system existed until after the Second World War and the effects of this inequality remain today: land ownership remains largely in the hands of the wheat barons, just as it did in Emile Zola's day. In *La Terre*, Zola cast a clinical eye over the Beauce: "This flat, fertile plain, easy to cultivate but requiring constant care, has made its inhabitants cold and reflective—their only passion is for the earth". Despite such reserve, the people have a reputation for sudden outbursts of emotion, not just about family feuds and land inheritance. In the words of a local proverb, the inhabitants tend to "*s'emporter comme une soupe au lait*" (boil over like a milk soup).

Between Chapelle-Vendômoise and Maves, there are glimpses of impressive manor houses, crab-shaped dolmens, lone water-towers, deserted chapels and a brackish lake. In the hamlet of **Mulsans**, look at the Romanesque church with its adjoining wooden gallery. It is a chilling thought that despite the proliferation of roadside chapels, crucifixes and shrines, the Beauce has the highest suicide rate in France. A team of sociologists from Tours university is currently studying the problem but the lay observer need only visit the Beauce in a wintery storm to empathise with those who could face no more.

At **Maves**, one of the bleakest spots on the plains, stands a 15th-century windmill, one of those described by Zola as "idle sails perched on timber frames". Such windmills have existed on the plains since the 6th century but, predictably, are considered a poor relation to the grander water mills in the lush Loir, Cher and Indre valleys. Now restored, the **Moulin de Maves** is no

Talcy: Sophie Louise Bernard, 1737.

longer idle on Sundays. Even on a wind-swept day, Maves is just the place for contemplating the meaning of life before passing on to a semblance of civilisation at the **Château de Talcy**.

Seen from outside its imposing gateway, Talcy is dark, severe and atmospheric, the product of a fertile Gothic imagination. Yet this feudal castle is, in fact, an anachronism, or at least a Renaissance masquerade. Talcy was built in 1517 by Bernardo Salviati, an Italian merchant who had been brought up in Florentine *palazzi*, a Renaissance style he rejected in favour of moody French Gothic. The square keep is in archetypal Gothic style with a forbidding, crenellated entrance pierced only by two narrow doorways. Nevertheless, there are a few Renaissance touches to lighten the medieval tone. Salviati wanted to be near the royal court at Blois but perversely chose these inhospitable plains on which to build his home. Even then, the Beauce was spiritually remote from court life but Salviati, a part-time courtier, used the location to transform Talcy into a model of self-sufficiency, at once an innovation and a necessity.

In addition to vineyards, orchards, herb, vegetable and pleasure gardens, Salviati introduced cattle, sheep, goats and pigeons. Talcy and its system have stood the test of time. In the rear courtyard is the original dovecote, complete with two revolving ladders and space for 3,000 pigeons. In the barn opposite lies a wine press which, after 500 years of service, can still produce ten barrels of juice at one pressing. Behind the back gate, tiered gardens were once well-stocked with "new" Italian herbs and exotic fruits such as oranges.

The front courtyard shelters a small rose garden, le rosier de Cassandre, where Ronsard is reputed to have courted Salviati's 15-year-old daughter, Cassandra. Ronsard met her at a ball in the Château de Blois and his unrequited love soon inspired some of his most poignant poetry, including "*Mignonne, allez voir si la rose...*". Although bound by the conventions of courtly love, Ronsard's flowery im-

Salon at Talcy.

agery conceals genuine pathos. Since Salviati did not favour an alliance between his beautiful daughter and the impecunious poet, Ronsard never got further than the rose garden.

Luckier visitors, however, can explore a sumptuously furnished Renaissance château, thanks to the protectiveness of its former occupants. In 1932, the last owners sold Talcy to the state on condition that the interior remained intact. The furniture in the château spans the reigns of Charles VIII to Louis XV and is at its grandest in the royal apartments. More charming, however, is Cassandra's boudoir, decorated with a Venetian mirror and romantic Aubusson tapestries. Elswhere, the Renaissance marquetry, rosewood dressers, oriental ceramics and quaint bidet present a highly sophisticated contrast to life on the surrounding plains.

Talcy's strange location and quirky architecture make it the most individualistic of the smaller châteaux in the region. Its charm puts one in a happier mood to cross the final stretch of the Beauce to Beaugency. If the season and light are right, you may recall Zola's uncharacteristically aesthetic description of the countryside in late spring. "Then the wisps of corn have thickened out until each plant took on its special hue; he could pick out from afar the yellowy green of wheat, the blue-green of oats, the grey-green of the rye, in fields stretching out in all directions as far as the horizon amid the red patches of clover". Still, when the compact medieval town of Beaugency looms on the horizon, you will probably welcome the cuisine, warmth and comforts of city life. The bleak beauty of the plains is not for all seasons.

Down the Loire to Blois: Sandwiched between the Beauce and the Sologne, **Beaugency** was once a frontier town between the fiefdoms of Orleans and Blois. Until modern times, the town possessed the only Loire bridge between the two rivals. Beaugency's strategic importance made it a pawn in the Hundred Years' War, when it fell into the hands of the English four times, only

Bicycle at rest.

to be delivered by Joan of Arc in 1429. During the Wars of Religion the three tiers of medieval walls were breached, the castle and Notre Dame church damaged. In June 1940 and 1944, the north of the town was bombarded but the Gothic bridge spared.

As a river fortress, Beaugency owed its prosperity to the Loire fleet until the advent of the railways in 1846 forced it to turn its back on the river and face its agricultural hinterland. Now a quietly attractive market town, Beaugency is gradually realising that its rich medieval architecture, understated charm and simple restaurants make it popular with discerning visitors. The medieval centre is constructed around rectangular *îlots*, pockets of houses clustered around small courtyards which follow the outline of the former moats. This private style of architecture gives the town a sense of mystery confirmed by such chance discoveries as the Caves d'Igoire, a vaulted Romanesque cellar or occasional sightings of the enclosed River Ru.

In a town with so many low-key pleasures it is difficult to single out highlights. **Place Firmin** makes a self-contained medieval unit, particularly when the gas lamps cast a ghostly light on the Romanesque tower, the statue of Joan of Arc, and the beheaded keep, its roof destroyed by English fire. In an adjoining square, and also cast in a pool of light, are the 14th-century fortress and the old abbey church. But even in daylight, the quirky backstreets do not disappoint: the half-timbered Renaissance **Hôtel de Ville** is decorated with shields, salamanders, saints and lambs while the refuge of the Knights Templar is decorated in herringbone brick, a style more common in the Sologne than in the Val de Loire.

Following the northern bank of the Loire to Blois is a scenic route past fields of chrysanthemums and asparagus beds. From Beaugency to Cour-sur-Loire, country lanes wind past workmanlike villages, secretive châteaux, Romanesque churches and old washhouses. **Suèvres** and **Cour-sur-Loire** are perched on the Beauce but have

rejected wheat-growing in favour of cultivating flowers and asparagus. Just north of Suèvres is a graceful moated château with an octagonal tower while the village itself has two attractive Romanesque churches, a turreted gateway and, in Rue des Juifs and Rue des Moulins, a cluster of medieval houses beside willows and fast-flowing streams. **Cour-sur-Loire** borders the loveliest stretch of the river Loire and is, unsurprisingly, home to local gentry and wealthy Blois commuters. The ivy-covered stone village boasts a sloping Gothic church, a picturesque washhouse in the main square and, behind heavy gates, Madame de Pompadour's château. At weekends, the sandy river banks attract strollers and picnickers as well as boys fishing from traditional black boats.

Just before Blois is **Ménars**, a magnificent château once owned by Madame Pompadour's brother. Views of the orangery, sphinxes, terraces, rock pools and grottoes are restricted to disappointing views from the gates.

Springtime wisteria.

CHAMBORD

North of Cheverny and Villesavin, watery Sologne evaporates into the woods. From here, the Domaine de Chambord, dissected by elegant avenues, stretches as far as the eye can see. Through the trees are hazy glimpses of the Loire's largest and grandest residence, a Renaissance château built for posterity by a fickle king.

Poet Alfred de Vigny likened this skyline of dove-grey domes and delicate cupolas to an oriental town in miniature. Prosaic Charles V, not normally given to fulsome praise, called Chambord, "a summary of human endeavour" while Châteaubriand, more attuned to the fate of the château, saw a neglected woman with windswept hair. Vivian Rowe in "Châteaux of the Loire" calls Chambord, "The skyline of Constantinople on a single building."

In keeping with its romantic image, Chambord's medieval past is suitably mysterious, inhabited by a succession of feudal owners, including the feuding Comtes de Blois. Chambord was a stylish backdrop against which the black-clad Comte Thibault le Tricheur, accompanied by black dogs and steeds, pursued captives and game. But in 1519, the humble hunting lodge was demolished by François I, Chambord's most significant owner.

In its place, the young king created an airy pleasure palace as an escape from his stifling marriage, the inward-looking château at Blois and the restrictions of court life. But as the château grew in splendour, so too did the king's aspirations. By the end of his life, Chambord was François' bid for immortality, prefiguring Louis XIV's relationship with Versailles. It is no surprise, then, that Chambord foreshadows Versailles in its scale of conception and sheer size. With false modesty, François used to invite favoured guests to "come back to my place", a cosy hunting lodge with a fireplace for every day of the year.

Significantly, the architects' names are unknown, although Leonardo da Vinci, the King's guest at Amboise, is reputed to have drawn the first plans or guided the master builders. Nearly 2,000 craftsmen worked on the site over the next 25 years, producing a vast palace containing over 450 rooms, 365 windows and 70 staircases. Yet, despite the sumptuous apartments, Renaissance court life was an outdoor affair, revolving around hunting and feasting in the grounds.

After François' death, the court left for Chenonceau and Blois while Chambord was inhabited fitfully, like a guest house out of season. Henri II, François' son, tinkered with the architectural design but the chapel and west wing were only finished in Louis XIV's time. But until Versailles emerged from its chrysalis, Chambord remained a favoured location for the grand summer balls and *son et lumière* spectacles pioneered by François I. In the galleried ballroom, Molière first staged *Le Bourgeois Gentilhomme* and *Monsieur Pouceaugnac* for Louis XIV. One performance was narrowly saved from

Preceding pages: Maves windmill. Left, riding display at Chambord. Right, roof of Chambord.

royal disapproval by the timely action of Lully, the composer, who jumped off the stage and smashed a harpsichord in order to make the King laugh.

Slapstick humour often greeted artistic endeavour at Chambord: Maréchal de Saxe, its 18th-century owner, created a star vehicle for his actress-mistress, Madame Favart. Spectators wickedly reported that the Marshal played "the triple role of director, author and cuckold." Under such eccentric custodianship, Chambord also housed the Marshal's private army, a motley crew of Tartar and West Indian cavalry officers atop Ukrainian horses.

After de Saxe's death in 1750, the unlucky château fell into a musty decline until recent times. Flaubert, visiting in 1847, saw Chambord as "an abandoned inn where the travellers have failed to leave even their names on the walls." On a rainy day, the novelist prowled through "the long, empty galleries and abandoned rooms in which spiders spin webs over François I's salamanders."

However, thanks to restoration work during Giscard d'Estaing's presidency, the château is no longer an exquisite piece of lost property. The once insalubrious moats were re-dug, the sculpted royal emblems restored and the interior furnished with Renaissance hunting scenes and 18th-century fabrics.

Exotic birds: Apart from the majestic double spiral staircase, the hunting room and the ballroom (*salle en croix*), the interior is remarkable less for its Renaissance design than for its 18th-century style. While Chambord's early tapestries and coffers were absorbed by Versailles, de Saxe's floral furnishings remain or have been faithfully restored. In particular, notice the *salle à l'indienne*, decorated with a vivid design of exotic birds and goats.

Yet, under the vibrant furnishings, the fabric of the king's original château is clearly visible: the square-within-a-square design is formed by a central keep flanked by four towers, in turn enclosed by a courtyard and four corner towers. Chambord embodies a château

"The skyline of Constantinople on a single building."

258

in transition: Renaissance ideas grafted on to a Gothic model and slowly cast in a classical mould.

For all this apparent disunity, the château looks harmonious from the ground floor to the terraces. However, while the ground floor is dull and heavy, the upper levels become progressively lighter and more high-spirited. On the roof-top terraces, the exuberance of the architecture can be restrained no longer. Dormer windows, sloping gables, elongated chimney pots, miniature spires and bell turrets like minarets are all competing for sky-space.

From this airy village, courtiers gathered to watch tournaments or hunts until nightfall. At intervals, enthusiastic parties, laden down with trestle tables and portable banquets, were despatched to join the hunters. An irate English ambassador complained that these French courtiers were "bohemians and gypsies, never in their quarters when one went to visit them". Despite their elevated vantage point, courtiers readily sank to low intrigue, idle gossip or romantic assignations among the chimney pots.

From this airy platform are magnificent views of the vast estate, the majority of the 13,600 acres (5,500 hectares) forming part of the National Hunting Reserve. Reassuring signs claim that *"Cerfs, biches et sangliers vivent en liberté"* but in fact most sensible deer keep a low profile and the boar are positively invisible, not just in the autumn mating season.

Perhaps old race memories die hard: here François I would trap and kill a stag single-handedly to impress female admirers on the terraces. One evening, François, wounded by a particular *liaison dangereuse*, used his diamond ring to scratch a message on a pane of glass: *"Souvent femme varie, bien fol est qui s'y fie"* (Every woman is fickle, he who trusts one is a fool). This complaint finds a poignant echo in Chambord's experience of neglectful male owners—or even in Claude de France's disappointment in a faithless husband who had hunted too long on the estate or the terrace.

LE LOIR

The Romans had the right idea. They called the Loir *Lidericus* and the Loire *Liger*. Today, in French, only someone attentive to grammar immediately knows which is which (the masculine *Le Loir* and the feminine *La Loire*). Physically and historically, however, the two rivers have little in common. The former extends for only slightly more than 185 miles (300 km) and has never been of any great strategic or commercial importance, while the latter is more than three times its length, serves as a means of dividing France into North and South, and has been a major trade route since the Middle Ages. The Loir Valley can claim, however, to be famous. Its praises were sung by one of France's most celebrated poets and visitors are constantly reminded that this is the *Pays de Ronsard*. Pierre de Ronsard (1524–95), whose birthplace, La Possonnière, can be still be visited, referred to himself as Vendômois and his poetry contains many references to his native province. His love poems and odes are considered masterpieces and he did much to promote the use of French in poetry instead of Latin which was still common practice in his day.

Though the Loir River runs from just below Chartres to just above Angers, its presence is only discreetly felt when visiting the valley. Though on occasion it can be an impressive sight (at Châteaudun or Trôo for example), visitors might crisscross it endless times without noticing that these small rivulets are in fact the Loir.

The Loir Valley is, above all, a land of orchards and hilly farmland; villages, churches and even châteaux tend to be small. There is a sense of community here, as though the valley were actually situated somewhere much more remote. Indeed, tourists are still something of a rarity and often experience a sense of discovery here quite different from that encountered on the well-worn routes of the Loire. A visit to the Loir Valley, in short, provides a charming contrast to travelling down its famous homonym to the south.

The Loir is a more plebeian river; instead of châteaux, this neglected route offers glimpses of village life in closely-knit communities. Following the fast-flowing Loir downstream from Vendôme to Montoire is an effortless way to discover troglodyte settlements, ruined fortresses and Romanesque frescoes. And this stretch of the river unravels a well-trodden spiritual trail, leading eventually to Santiago de Compostella in Spain.

The pleasant uniformity of the passing landscape is not the whole truth: most of the vineyard-covered slopes conceal a honeycomb of cave dwellings, wine cellars, mushroom farms and even the occasional pagan chapel. The woods are protection for the tumble-down priories, churches and hospices which once lined this historic pilgrimage route. At **Villiers-sur-Loir**, the macabre 15th-century murals in the dilapidated Eglise St-Hilaire make a refresh-

Preceding pages: rusticity, valley of Le Loir. **Left,** Le Loir at Durtal. **Right,** a favourite pastime.

ing change from staid religious imagery. In the dimly lit church, the faded *"Dict des Trois Morts et Trois Vies"* is both a social parable and a pictorial dialogue on the vanity of human wishes. While out hunting falcons, three noblemen are reproached by three decomposing corpses which represent the traditional social orders: the aristocracy, church and common people.

Since the pigment was traditionally applied with glue made from fish or rabbit skins the tawny colours have faded. Still, as sharp social comment, the murals are unique in French churches and it is hardly surprising that such subversive images were whitewashed over and only discovered in 1925.

Les-Roches-l'Evêque is a fortified village sandwiched between the river and the cliffs. As a celebrated troglodyte village, Les Roches boasts a number of chic cave dwellings covered in lilac and wisteria. However, the number of *chiens méchants* signs and parked Peugeots suggests that the caves are now second homes belonging to

weekend *vignerons*. If you feel like clambering inside the damp rock, call in at the 15th-century Chapelle St-Gervais or, if permitted, visit the crumbling Hypogée-des-Roches, a secret pagan chapel carved with cabalistic rites.

Following signs for the *Route Touristique*, you come across more orthodox religious cults in **Villavard**, a medieval hamlet. Apart from Le Temple, a former priory on the Santiago trail, the local church displays curious murals and a painting of the *Vièrge Noire*. Religious festivals are celebrated with a pilgrimage through cornfields and vineyards to venerate this black Madonna.

Just downstream, sleepy **Lavardin** announces itself as the home of *le douceur de vivre* and indeed the village is often praised as "the most French of French villages". Nestling into a bend of the Loir, Lavardin is dotted with half-timbered houses, a former priory, a Gothic bridge as well as a Romanesque abbey church, decorated with stylised murals. High above the village looms the jagged silhouette of the feudal for-

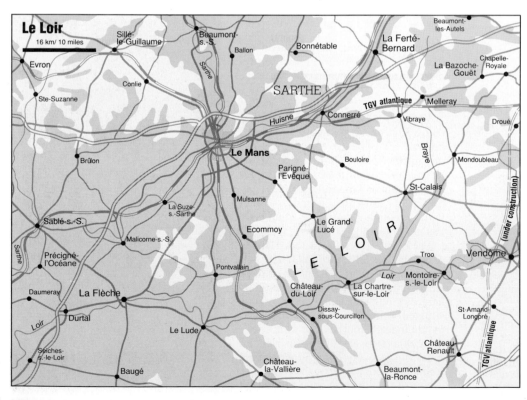

tress. During the Hundred Years' War, this *château-fort* marked the border between the French Capets and the English Plantagenets. But after the Wars of Religion, the château was dismantled by Henri IV as a deterrent to future opposition.

While the château is being restored, the dramatic interior is closed but the three rings of ramparts, high 12th-century keep and medieval gates are impressive sights, not to mention the drawbridge stretching over a deep ravine. Just outside the village, those on the alternative religious trail can call in at the *grottes des Vièrges*, an erstwhile haunt of druidesses.

Vineyards, dairy farms and mushroom cellars signal the relative prosperity of **Montoire-sur-Loir**: unlike Lavardin, the medieval château is ruined but the village has thrived off its land. Visitors are given a taste of the good life in the local wine-tasting pavilion, open every summer weekend. The wide range of *Côteaux du Vendômois* makes it difficult to choose between a light white wine, a peppery rosé or a full-bodied red.

Romantics can hire rowing boats and attempt to stay afloat while consuming a picnic of local *cendré* cheese, game pâté and wine from the hills. There may well be sightings of canoe racing or fishermen looking for trout and perch in the river or carp and bream in the local lakes. With 13 regional fishing clubs, it is oddly optimistic for the authorities to declare, "No more than six salmon may be fished per person per day".

From the stone bridge over the river there are sweeping views across willows by the river to the tumbledown castle on one bank and to the higgledy-piggledy village on the other. A walk from the foot of the château to Place Clemenceau passes a number of Renaissance houses, decorated with mullioned dormer windows, gabled chimney stacks, statues of horses and saints and, on one facade, a fine sundial.

Only the streets with military names recall Montoire's more recent past, particularly its historic role in the Sec-

Gentle Lavardin, "most French of French villages."

ond World War. On 24 October 1940, Marshall Pétain, head of the Vichy Government, secretly met Hitler in a special train. While Messerschmidts circled overhead and German roadblocks sealed off the village, Hitler tried in vain to persuade Pétain to take up arms against Britain.

In the Loir valley, however, it is hard to escape religion for long, especially since Montoire's Chapelle St-Gilles houses the finest Romanesque frescoes in the Loir et Cher. Founded in the 7th century, St-Gilles was originally a priory, hospice and leper hospital for pilgrims. A Romanesque arch leads to a meditative chapel set among cypresses, yews and sloping riverside gardens. The frescoes, dating from the 11th century, are painted in seemingly modern abstractions. Although the white, blue and ochre colours have faded, the bold brushstrokes look much as Ronsard recorded them during his time as resident prior.

From here, tired visitors may just decide to slip downstream to Trôo,

ignoring all troglodyte caves and chapels in favour of a fishy dinner.

Trôo to Le Mans: Trôo looms up as a rounded hill of greenery and cliffs topped by a squat church. In spring, the pink and white blossoms of fruit trees mingle with pale green and red leaves to make it a lovely sight. A troglodyte village, Trôo has been an historic monument since 1886.

Trôo is best visited on foot, so leave the car in the parking lot next to the stone bridge in the centre of town, and climb the narrow staircase leading up to the troglodyte dwellings and the church. The path takes you across roofs and between chimneys pots and the view is splendid. On a clear day one can just make out Vendôme, 15 miles (25 km) away. At the top of hill is the small Collégiale St-Martin, a simple building with a square belltower and wooden pews in the Angevin Gothic style. It dates from the 12th and 13th centuries and has the intimate feeling of a country chapel. On the far side of this hill is the "talking well" ("*le puits qui parle*") so-called because of its impressive echo.

Before leaving Trôo, visit the Grotte pétrifiante located on the main road in the centre of town. The *grotte* is a small, humid grotto draped in limestone curtains deposited by the constant "rain" that has fallen inside it for 4,000 years. Some 400 years ago, a stone baptismal font was placed in the grotto and the result is a strange limestone creation that combines elements of the man-made and natural. Visitors have occasionally deposited objects of their own in the grotto in hopes of "petrifying" them as well... a practice frowned on by the present owner and, in any case, rather unlikely to produce visible results within anyone's lifetime.

Across the Loir from Trôo is the little church of **St-Jacques-des-Guérets**. Enter the grounds through the small cemetery gate at the back. Inside the church, the wooden vaulting, typical of this region, is well preserved and still shows traces of decorative painting along the spine and crossbeams. 12th-century wall paintings cover the apse, the inside of the choir window and

La Possonnière, birthplace of Ronsard.

about half of the nave (turn the knob to the left of the entrance door to light the murals). Subdued hues of brown, gold and blue dominate and the "Byzantine" style is not unlike that of the paintings in the church at Montoire. The 16th-century polychrome wooden sculptures still visible here are also worthy of note.

Leaving Trôo, follow the *Route Touristique de la Vallée du Loir* toward Artins and Couture-sur-Loir. This is an area of rich farmland and vine-covered houses with steeply slanted tile roofs. **Couture** itself is not particularly beautiful, though the sculpted tombstones of Ronsard's parents in the local church do attract visitors (the Ronsards have been further immortalized by the baker across from the church who sells *Ronsardises*, delicious "R"-shaped hazelnut biscuits well worth sampling).

Turn left in front of the church and follow signs to **La Possonnière**, the birthplace of Pierre Ronsard. Although it is officially open to visitors in July and August, if you are lucky (and for the usual entrance fee), the gatekeeper's wife may show you around. Although little of the original 14th-century building in which Ronsard was born remains, the manor house, remodelled in the 16th century by Ronsard's father, is still intact. Inside the house is a giant stone fireplace decorated with the Ronsard family seal and emblem of burning rose bushes, pictorial renderings of the family name—RONSes ARDentes— meaning Ronsard.

Troglodyte caves, the only parts of the original dwelling that remain, line the interior courtyard on the left. Over each door is a Latin inscription describing the use to which these cavernous rooms were put: a kitchen, with ovens and chimneys carved out of the rock, a wine cellar, a pantry, and so on.

From La Possonnière, return to Couture then follow the D917 to **Poncé-sur-le-Loir**. The château here has a remarkable Renaissance staircase with decorative carved coffered ceilings. The 18th-century gardens, with their arbour and labyrinth, are worth a visit, as is the dovecote with its 2,000 pigeon-

Ronsard, meaning "ardent roses".

holes, crossbeams and pivoting ladder. In the courtyard, you can visit a small museum with an interesting collection of locally made farm tools, pottery and basketwork. Nearby is a *Centre artisanal,* housed in an 18th-century water mill, where glassblowers, potters and woodworkers can be seen at work.

From Poncé, route D305 leads to La Chartre and Château-du-Loir. Just after passing through Ruille-sur-Loir, you may want to make a detour toward Dauvers to visit the Loir's most prestigious vineyard: Jasnières.

After La Chartre, the Loir continues its sinuous course to **Le Lude**, about 16 miles (27 km) downstream. The château here is a massive structure with four circular corner towers. Built during the 15th and 16th centuries by the Daillon family on the foundations of a medieval fortress, the severe military air of the original fortress was softened by Italianate ornamentation: mullioned windows with floral decorations replace the military loopholes, and a series of large medallions adorned with busts break the monotony of the wide expanses of wall. The 18th-century east wall, however, looks strangely out of place—it now joins the north and south towers, replacing a series of arcades that originally connected them. The medieval moat was drained and transformed into a "low garden" (*jardin bas*), originally planted with vegetables.

The interior of the château has as many styles as the exterior. From the large Renaissance hall with thick, richly coloured, wood-panelled walls, you pass into an airy, pale-grey 18th-century sitting room.

During the summer months, at nightfall, a spectacular sound and light show with fireworks brings the château to life as hundreds of townspeople in period costumes re-enact the history of Le Lude. Halfway between Le Lude and La Flèche is **Luché-Pringé**. Its church, built between the 13th and 16th centuries, is unusual for its many gables, as well as bands of humorous gargoyles and portraits that adorn the facade; a bas-relief of St Martin on horseback is

Château of Le Lude.

above the main portal. Inside, on the right, is a remarkable 16th-century wooden *pietà:* Mary expresses her sorrow with a downturned mouth while Mary Magdalene wipes her eyes with a handkerchief.

From Luché-Pringé the D13 goes through Pringé and past the **Château Gallerande**, a magnificent 15th-century building with high corner towers; across the way, a beautiful old farm complex with its tall dovecote and round turret can be seen from the road.

La Flèche is a bustling town that spans the Loir and the bridge in front of the Hôtel de Ville offers an excellent view of the city. The town's main attraction is the Prytanée National Militaire, originally built as a Jesuit College in the 17th century; it became a military academy in 1762. Among more illustrious graduates of the College are the philosopher René Descartes and Jérôme le Royer de la Dauversière, one of the founders of Montreal. The grounds of the academy and the Chapelle-St-Louis may be visited. To enter, ring at the small door to the right of the main entrance. The buildings, of a very simple classical style, surround a series of large courtyards; the chapel is in the second courtyard to the left. Built by the Jesuits, its sober exterior is in stark contrast to the exuberant baroque style of the altarpiece that dominates the columned and vaulted space inside. A golden, crowned heart placed high up in a niche to the left of the altar is said to contain the ashes of the hearts of King Henry IV and Queen Marie de Médicis. On the end wall, opposite the altar, is a magnificent organ built during the 17th century and remodelled during the 18th.

Though less well known, one of the most memorable sights in La Flèche is the tiny **Chapelle Notre-Dame-des-Vertus** located behind the cemetery just off the road leading to Sablé. Once inside this small 11th to 12th-century building, the visitor feels the wonderment of a child opening a box of jewels. The rounded wooden ceiling is covered with paintings depicting biblical scenes ("Noah's Ark" or "The Ladder to

Serious business of shopping in Baugé.

Heaven") and the walls are lined with magnificently carved wood panels dating from the Renaissance. The door that once was the entrance to the chapel is sculpted with a life-sized warrior carrying a shield decorated with a fierce head whose mouth cleverly surrounds the keyhole, with comic effect.

Interesting sights in the vicinity of La Flèche include the Zoological Park at Tertre Rouge and the church at Pontigné. In the latter town, the familiar Angevin church spire was literally given a curious twist in the 17th century. Instead of having the usual angular facets rising straight up to the tip, the black slate tiles were laid at a slant so that the flat surfaces curve around the spire, creating an eerie "witch's hat" effect. Several churches in the area were remodelled in this way at roughly the same time, and other "twisting spires" can be see in Vieil Baugé, Mouliherne, and Fontaine Guérin.

Inside the church at Pontigné are traces of 13th-century wall paintings whose red floral and sun motifs are still visible on the ribs of the Plantagenet vaults. The best preserved paintings are in a niche to the right transept: Christ is surrounded by the four Evangelists; underneath, on the left, Lazarus rises from his tomb while, on the right, people kneel in prayer. A short distance from Pontigné, **Baugé** boasts an 11th to 15th-century château that houses the museum, devoted to local history and folklore. Open only from June through September, or by special appointment, its displays centre around everyday objects made here in the past (china and pottery, utensils, *coiffes*, jewellery, and coins). The museum also contains a substantial collection of arms dating from the 14th to the 20th centuries.

Not far from the château is the **Chapelle de la Girouardière** were the bejewelled Croix d'Anjou is kept. This small, double-armed cross is claimed to be made from the wood of the True Cross of Christ. It was brought back from the crusades in the 13th century. The ornamentation on each side of the cross was added by a Parisian goldsmith at the end of the 14th century for the Duke of Anjou. It became the Cross of Lorraine and the symbol of the Free French during World War II.

On the opposite side of the château from the Chapelle de la Girouardière is the **Hôpital St-Joseph**. Here, a 17th-century pharmacy has been perfectly preserved as a reminder of the institution's past. Ask for a guide at the office of the *Services Administratives* in the building facing the entrance to the hospital proper. The walls of the pharmacy are lined with hatbox-like containers, glass vials and porcelain pots still containing *simples* dating back 200 years. The ceiling of the pharmacy is decorated with squares and other geometrical designs painted in *trompe l'oeil* pink marble, set against a grey background strewn with stars.

The last town of any size on the Loir before the river meets the Sarthe just north of Angers is **Durtal**. A busy crossroads in Roman times, Durtal is now a centre for the manufacture of pottery and brick with a lively fruit and vegetable market on Tuesday mornings. Its

Baugé: St Joseph's pharmacy.

imposing château has an east wing with a tall keep and two pepper-pot turrets with machicolations dating from the 15th century; the bulk of the building dates from the 16th century and the west wing from the 17th. Today, the château serves as a rest home, but it may be visited in July and August; it is entered through the courtyard at the back.

Other sights in Durtal include the **Porte Verron**, a vestige of the old city wall flanked by two 15th-century towers and the old bridge into the city which offers a beautiful view of the river and town.

If travelling from Durtal to Le Mans, stop to visit the **Abbaye St-Pierre**, a Benedictine monastery in the town of **Solesmes**. Only the abbey church is open to the public, but it is remarkable for the theatrical Renaissance sculptures in the transept. On the left, close to 100 figures are crowded on three levels which depict scenes from the life of the Virgin Mary. In the right transept is a monumental *Entombment of Christ* dating from 1496 and a terracotta *pietà*,

Solesmes on the River Sarthe.

also from the 15th century. Visitors are welcome to attend services in the church, held four times a day and sung by the monks in Gregorian Chant.

Arriving in **Le Mans**, one is immediately struck by the contrast between this sprawling industrial city and the peaceful Loir valley so very nearby. Famous for its 24-hour automobile race, its version of a common Loire valley pâté (*rillettes du Mans*) and emasculated chickens (*chapons*), Le Mans might not appear have a rich cultural heritage. This impression is quickly dispelled when the visitor discovers the magnificence of the **Cathédrale St-Julien** high on a hill in the centre of the city. Coming upon it from behind, with its lacework of inverted Y-shaped flying buttresses, one marvels at its design and it is difficult to imagine the effect it must have had on the simple minds of medieval countryfolk.

Leave your car in the parking lot behind the cathedral and climb the wide staircase that leads up to it from behind. At the top of the stairs is the wall of the

south transept; further on is the 12th-century south portal with a tympanum that pictures Christ surrounded by the symbols of the four Evangelists and columns with statues of Saints Peter and Paul and the Kings and Queens of Judea. Continue along this wall to the main entrance (note the pink sandstone menhir leaning against the corner of the cathedral, a curious reconciliation of the pagan past and the Christian present). The main portal itself is simply designed, and decorated with signs of the Zodiac surrounding a seated figure, most probably Christ. On Sundays, this door is open, but on other days of the week, enter the cathedral through the door in the transept.

Inside, the Romanesque side aisles, with their black and white rounded arches and columns, contrast sharply with the Angevin arches of the central nave, raised in the 12th century after a fire destroyed the original wooden ceiling of what had been hailed as "the most beautiful church in the West". The Romanesque decoration of the capitals is particularly interesting, including portraits of the artisans and workers who built the cathedral, and the stained-glass *Ascension* window in the second bay of the right-hand aisle is not only magnificent but also well preserved. Its central panels, which date from 1120, are the oldest stained glass still in place in France today.

The choir, with its double ambulatory, is one of the tallest in France at 103 ft (34 metres) and, fortunately, most of the original 13th-century stained glass windows are still intact. The construction of a new choir was a daring and ingenious undertaking: part of the old city wall had to be demolished in order to extend the church to its present length, and the flying buttresses were built in such a way that they virtually never cast a shadow on the windows. Although the choir was consecrated in 1254, final work was not completed until the 1270s.

With the raising of the choir, the transepts, which were the same height as the nave, looked out of proportion. Plans to **Le Mans' old quarter.**

raise them as well were made, but the Hundred Years' War greatly slowed construction. In 1392 work on the south transept was finally finished and the north transept was completed 40 years later. The rose window in the north transept is contemporary with its construction, while the magnificent organ that spans the entire width of the south transept was added later, in the 16th century. A fascinating series of wooden models on permanent display in the left-hand aisle of the nave traces the cathedral's history from its very beginnings to today.

Old Le Mans covers the south side of the hill that descends from the cathedral. The narrow cobblestone streets are best visited on foot. They are lined with buildings dating from the 15th to the 17th centuries, beautifully preserved and restored, many of which are now restaurants and shops. Of particular interest are the half-timber and tufa dwellings with carved colonnades in the Rue de la Reine Bérangère. The three buildings at numbers 7–11 are now a

museum which displays interesting collections of local ceramics (plates and pitchers, often in the form of animals and people) and pewterware. The sculpted wooden entrance door to the museum is particularly lovely.

About a third of the way down the hill, the street changes its name to La Grande Rue. On the left, at number 71, note the tufa Maison d'Adam et Eve from the Renaissance: Adam and Eve are sculpted in a wreath over the door while, above them, a centaur carries away a hapless maiden. A little further down on the left, in the Rue St Honoré, are several more half-timbered houses; across the street at number 86 Grande Rue, the picturesque Cour d'Assé leads to a 17th-century section.

Also in Le Mans is the **Musée Tessé**. This small art museum possesses what is considered to be the largest enamel plaque produced by European workshops in the Middle Ages, a champlevé portrait of Geoffroy V, founder of the Plantagenet dynasty and father of King Henry II of England. It is discreetly displayed in an alcove in the room to the left of the entrance hall.

The museum also has a small but fine collection of paintings from all periods. The medieval Primitives include some excellent Italian works and paintings by lesser known regional artists. On the top floor is a collection of Egyptian artefacts including sarcophagi, mummies and jewellery, some fine Roman and Greek pottery and a few well-preserved pieces of embroidered cloth.

Also in Le Mans is the **Eglise Notre-Dame de la Couture**. The columns and arches of the 12th-century nave, decorated with a leaf and tendril motif, look strikingly like a stand of palm trees. The church has several 17th-century tapestries from Aubusson, some 16th-century paintings on wood (toward the front of the nave), and a white marble statue of the Virgin and Child by Germain Pilon (1571).

While in Le Mans, try to visit the large open-air market held on Sunday mornings behind the cathedral. It is ablaze with colour and the excellent local produce will prove hard to resist.

Le Mans open-air market.

TROGLODYTES

"This hill is a warren of dwellings inhabited by vignerons. In more than one place, there are three tiers of houses carved into the rock and linked by dangerous tufa-stone staircases." Balzac was referring to the troglodyte caves at Vouvray, near Tours but this 19th-century description could well apply to cave dwellings along the Loire.

Although simply the Greek term for cave-dweller, the word troglodyte conjures up a vision of a swarthy Neanderthal man dressed in a bear-skin. In the overly civilised Val de Loire, the truth is different but not disappointing. The dwellings are bound up in the persecution of the early Christians, medieval quarries, beseiged cities, Devil-worship and magic mushrooms. The caves themselves are a storehouse of French history, as well as stores of real wine and *champignons de Paris*.

At first, the appeal of a sunless, damp, badly-ventilated and uncomfortable cave is unclear, but as the most ancient dwellings in the region, the caves have proved extraordinarily versatile, not just duplicating the functions of "normal" accommodation but serving defensive or storage purposes, ranging from apple cellar to nuclear shelter. Over the centuries, the caves have been used as hermitages, chapels, prisons, refuges, schools, workshops, wine cellars, farms, barns as well as homes.

The caves are found all over the region, wherever soft, porous limestone rock exists. Known as *tuffeau* or *falun*, this yellowish stone has long been exploited by any farm, manor or hamlet lucky enough to find the tufa-stone on its territory. For the visitor, however, the main areas of interest are along the Valley of the Loir, from Vendôme to Trôo; south of Saumur, near Doué-la-Fontaine; and along the Loire, particularly from Saumur to Montsoreau or from Langeais to Vouvray. These areas contain traditional troglodyte villages which, like a do-it-yourself building site, are in a constant state of development. But there is a distinction between cave dwellings on ... ide and those on the plain. To locals, the ... stigious settlements are built into the low riverside cliffs, as at Trôo, Montcontour and Vouvray. In Balzac's day, over half the 800 homes at Vouvray were modest two-roomed cave dwellings owned by wine-growers. The writer waxed lyrical about "these rock caves dressed in coats of ivy" and noted the dreamy views of white sailing boats on the Loire. Inside the caves, the constant temperature of 13°–15 °C (56°–60°F) is perfect for wine, though less so for wine-growers.

Often built around a three-sided square open to the river, the rocky caves have been quaintly domesticated. Clifftops double as rooftops; unmatching doors and windows sprout from odd angles; baskets of geraniums hang down the cliff face; and trees protrude from the mossy "roofs". In the grander dwellings, comfortable conservatories and sunny extensions are a sign that these once modest caves are now *residences secondaires*, highly desirable second homes. By contrast, cave dwellings on the plain can look rather comical, their chimneys protruding like periscopes from a muddy field. Access is usually at a lower level, on the road or further down the field.

Such caves are a feature of the plains south of Saumur, particularly near Fontevraud Abbey and the village of Rochemenier. Many are carved into former quarries dotted with concealed entrances. At Rochemenier, the honeycomb village beneath the rock is almost twice the size of the village above ground. Here, two underground farms are carefully preserved, along with the original oil and wine presses and rustic furniture. Often the use of caves as dwellings developed in disused medieval quarries. But the concept of sheltering in caves is universal and the early Christians sought refuge in natural and man-made caves.

In the 9th and 10th centuries, the Norman invasions prompted the nobility to build elaborate underground defensive systems, linking the local château or citadel to fortified cave dwellings. Connected by narrow passages, these *caves fortes* were pierced with camouflaged air vents which doubled as spyholes through which arrows could be fired. In the most sophisticated fortifications, the besieged inhabitants could escape down false wells, travel along underground galleries to temporary shelter and, eventually emerge safely in deep woods. Such systems are still in place at Amboise and Loches, while at Chinon the tunnel networks provided for escape under the river Vienne. These dwellings were used during feudal conflicts, the Hundred Years' War and, in the case of Loches, during both World Wars. Although these galleries are generally closed to the public, sections can still be visited at Loches.

As late as the 19th century, large numbers of troglodyte villages continued to be inhabited by artisans, weavers, carpenters, farmers and basket makers, as well as vignerons. Balzac romanticised one such community at Langeais, describing it as a pleasing patchwork of caves and vineyards set amongst wild lilies and irises. He did not see the harsh living conditions: inside the caves, water conduits drained the porous rock while outside trenches, like mini-wells, were used for sewage. In the front room, niches were used as cupboards for food, tools or candles. Carved stone seats faced the fireplace and an adjoining bread oven. Given the cold, the fire would be kept ablaze, fuelled by bundles of twigs collected from the nearby vineyards at Bourgeuil. But there was a more comforting side to communal living: having to group together for work, warmth and comfort made for a more intimate, supportive way of life.

This is typified by the *veilloirs*, the village gatherings which represent the folkloric essence of cave behaviour. At a typical fireside scene, the community squeezed into the largest cave. While the women sorted flax or knitted in the firelight, the men made wicker baskets and crates. Depending on the season, the whole village also hulled barley, shelled walnuts or removed pumpkin seeds—all produce precious for their crushed oil. In the half-light, the young danced, sang rounds or ate nuts and goat's cheese. As the night wore on, wine was passed around and the cave echoed to the sound of joking and clog-dancing.

Elements of this merrymaking still exist in the harvest celebrations organised by the local vignerons, either for families and friends or among the wine-growing brotherhoods at Angers, Chinon and Vouvray. In the past, the grapes were tipped down funnel-like chutes into the vast cellars below. Now the grapes are delivered more conven-

tionally but the best *crus* are still often marked by slate in the traditional way; and the celebrations also end in dancing.

The caves have also been used for less innocent pleasure, whether as secret love nests or as mysterious places for witchcraft, sorcery or satanic rites. There is evidence of heretical sects meeting at caves in La Roche, near Saumur: inside, the 11th-century sculptures feature nudes, cats and magic mushrooms, suggestive of orgies or initiation rites. In response to the growth of heretical sects, the Council of Toulouse ordered the destruction of all caves in 1226. But by the 16th century there were signs that Devil-worship had not died out.

In Dénéze-sous-Doué, excavations have unearthed 200 enigmatic sculptures which depict sexual antics, with symbols and numbers associated with black magic. Some modern scholars link these scenes with the "diableries de Doué", Satanic versions of 16th-century mystery plays mentioned in Rabelais' work. Local guides prefer to attribute the sculptures to the fertile imagination of a bored carpenter.

A surprising number of caves are still inhabited and many have been converted into *residences secondaires* by city dwellers nostalgic for the good old days. From Langeais to Vouvray, weekend residents indulge their simple tastes for do-it-yourself, fire-making, home-baking and even wine-growing. In an inhabited but unconverted cave, your impressions may be different; the front room lit by a paraffin lamp and warmed by a permanent fire; crockery, tobacco and garden tools tucked into stone niches. A simple wooden table and chairs will have replaced the original stone benches. In the background, an old wireless and this year's agricultural calendar may provide signs of 20th-century living. Passageways leading off the front room lead to a couple of sparsely-furnished bedrooms, a small kitchen with a larder carved deep into the rock, and a wine store, either in the deepest part of the dwelling or in a separate cave.

If you wish to become a temporary troglodyte, you could stay in Hautes-Roches in Rochcorbon, once a dormitory for the monks of Marmoutier, and now France's only cave hotel.

SOLOGNE

Bounded by the sleepy River Cher to the south, and nestling in the arm of the powerful Loire as it veers from northwest to southwest at Orléans, the Sologne is a secret—and secretive—area that has remained relatively little-known even to the French. As a glance at the map reveals, it consists of a plain covered with large tracts of woodland and dotted with innumerable small lakes. Not far beneath its poor and sandy topsoil there are impermeable beds of clay which prevent rainwater from sinking deep into the ground, thus causing the formation of lakes and wetlands. This geological configuration has had a crucial bearing on the history and culture of the area and on the nature of Solognot society.

Throughout its chequered history, the Sologne has been at threat from its high water table. After a period of agricultural prosperity in Gallo-Roman times—the name Sologne derives from the Roman Secalonia, an area where much *secale* (rye) was grown—it once again became an impenetrable expanse of marshland and undergrowth until monks in the 10th century began to channel the water into lakes and streams, make clearings in the forest and redevelop farming.

In the 16th century, the prosperity of the Sologne was boosted by the establishment of the French court at nearby Blois and the building by François I of the massive Château de Chambord. In François I's wake, several members of the royal court built, rebuilt or enlarged châteaux in the surrounding area.

Brutal suppression: But a number of factors conspired to cause the decline of the Sologne. In 1585 two thirds of the inhabitants of its largest town, Romorantin, died of the plague. The royal court moved from Blois. The uprising against crippling taxes during the so-called Clogmakers' War (1658–59) was brutally put down. Many Solognot peasants and craftsmen who had converted to Protestantism fled to other provinces or left the country after the Revocation of the Edict of Nantes in 1685. By 1700, the Sologne was already "a wretched and poor region", in the words of Christian Sauvageon, prior of the little village of Sennely.

During the 18th century, the Sologne was left in a state of almost total neglect. The water trapped by underground clay began to exert its hold again. Without proper drainage or dredging, lakes reverted to semi-stagnant marshland and rivers became clogged. High humidity spoiled grain harvests and caused *ergotism*, a disease contracted from cereal poisoning, also called "St Anthony's fire". Malaria too became rife.

The Sologne did not really come to life again until the mid-19th century, when the Paris-Vierzon railway line was built and Napoleon III, who had bought some large estates near Lamotte-Beuvron and Vouzon, undertook large-scale drainage and reafforestation work. Others followed suit. It was at about that time that the Sologne began to attract wealthy hunters. They

Passe martin

built the hundreds of hunting lodges, imitation châteaux and follies that are so characteristic of the landscape, and were responsible for turning hunting into a veritable industry which, until recently at least, played an important role in the local economy.

The Sologne took on its pre-Revolutionary aspect again. Châteaux were once more occupied by aristocrats—some of them genuine, others newcomers to their class who had bought their "nobiliary particles" (the preposition *de* indicating that their name derived from landed property). Many of the châteaux provided a livelihood for the peasantry, most of whom lived in small, one-storey cottages (the reason for there being only one storey was that it was expensive to construct proper foundations on a subsoil of wet sand and clay).

Except in the more agricultural southwestern corner of the Sologne around Contres, there were relatively few big farmers or representatives of the middle-classes. This social structure, which persisted until recently, is perfectly illustrated in Jean Renoir's masterpiece, *La Règle du Jeu* (which at one point was going to be called *La Chasse en Sologne*). Two plots run side by side, then intertwine; one involves the de la Chesnaye family and aristocratic friends, and the other their gamekeeper, his wife and a poacher.

The film also captures beautifully the landscape of the Sologne, an area whose most idiosyncratic quality is its mystery. This is because it is a wooded plain: your view is nearly always blocked off by vegetation, and there are almost no landmarks except church spires, no hills or valleys to lend perspective. You round a corner and suddenly discover a hidden lake. A glance down a woodland track, which in summer becomes a tunnel of foliage, may reveal a tantalising glimpse of a château at the other end.

Often a stroll through the woods will take you to a solitary little field bounded on all sides by dense undergrowth, like some stage that has been set for an event that may never happen.

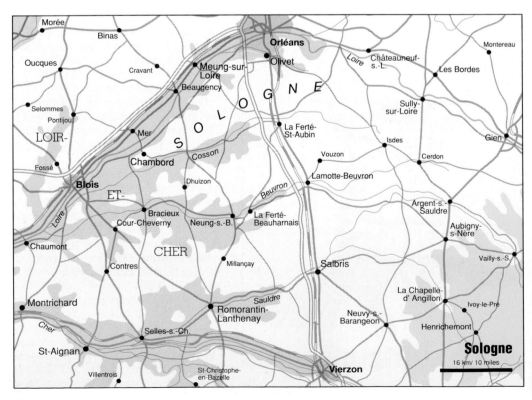

This atmosphere of mystery and theatricality is exploited by two excellent French novels, Alain-Fournier's *Le Grand Meaulnes*, with its evocation of an enchanted château deep in the woods, and Maurice Genevoix's *Raboliot*, which tells the story of a poacher who has an almost mystical relationship with the Solognot landscape and its game animals. Fournier's vision, though loosely based on his own experience in Sologne, is largely imaginary, whereas Genevoix based the character of Raboliot closely on the poachers he talked to when staying near Brinon-sur-Sauldre.

Raboliot rebels against the estate-owners and gendarmes who represent an external authority. He is a cunning loner with a mentality which is fairly typical of the Sologne—and a product of its history. It was in the 16th century, when the Solognots were squeezing as much advantage as they could out of the French court at Blois, that the expression *"niais de Sologne"* was coined. Literally "a Sologne dimwit", it refers to someone who pretends to be stupid in order to outwit others.

The prior of Sennely noted in 1700 that the Sologne was "a little republic of self-sufficient folk" and that "both the people and the region are quite different from the rest of France." He went on: "They are interested neither in news nor in fashion nor in anything happening in the rest of the world, as though they were somehow detached from it." It was apparently not uncommon at the turn of the last century for Solognots to wear flared frockcoats of the kind sported by the subjects of Louis XV some 150 years earlier.

It would seem that present-day Solognots have remained true to character. In 1989 the magazine *La Sologne* sent a questionnaire to the mayors of all the *communes* in the Sologne. One of the questions was: how would you describe the character of a typical Solognot? Answers received from some mayors included such epithets as "crafty", "cunning", "sly", "uncommunicative", "distant", "stubborn", "dis-

Cows in the Sologne.

trustful" and "stay-at-home". Fortunately for the tourist, however, most mayors described their fellow villagers as "affable", "hospitable", "generous" and "fun-loving".

The Sologne is not a part of the Loire Valley much frequented by tourists, mainly because it has few "major" sights apart from Chambord and Cheverny. But its apparently monotonous yet subtly varying landscape has a great deal to offer those who like to get away from the madding crowd. Unfortunately for the hiker, most of its woodland is private property; and it is as well not to risk a barrage of abuse from a gamekeeper—or worse from a hunter during the shooting season—by straying off the beaten track. But there are now many well-signposted rights of way through the woods.

Follow one such sandy path and you will be unlikely to meet another living soul apart from birds or rabbits. A typical walk will take you through plantations of feathery silver birches, stately woods of ancient oak and dark, serried ranks of spruce, past fields of buckwheat (food for pheasants), maize (cover for game) and occasionally asparagus (which thrives in the sandy soil), over expanses of springy heather, past placid carp-filled lakes covered with waterlilies and bordered by clumps of bullrushes.

The Sologne has an ecosystem that is particularly rich in wildlife, largely because nature is kept under control by mechanical rather than chemical means on the shooting estates that account for much of its total area of 1.25 million acres (500,000 hectares). The non-use of pesticides guarantees an abundance of butterflies and wild flowers, while the woods, largely undisturbed except during the shooting season, harbour a large and varied bird population.

Particularly memorable are the changing colours of the Sologne from season to season: bluebells, purple heather and mauve ling, banks of blackthorn whose bright white flowers appear before its leaves, yellow broom and gorse, orange-yellow *chanterelle*

Sologne château.

mushrooms and red-and-white fly agarics, the startlingly clashing reds of the fruit of the spindle tree and, of course, the full range of autumn colours provided by a wide variety of tree species. And there are sensations for the nose as well as the eyes—wild thyme crushed underfoot, the acid odour of leafmould, mushroomy fragrances, the baked resin of conifers in the summer sun, the sweet smell of bracken and the marshiness of the lakes.

Back of beyond: The impenetrability and self-contained nature of the Sologne is no doubt responsible for the fact that although it is not far from Paris its "remoteness" is legendary: people commonly refer to places in the back of beyond as being "like Romorantin". **RomorantinLanthenay** (usually abbreviated to plain Romorantin) is the largest town in the Sologne (with all of 18,000 inhabitants), and one that will certainly repay a careful visit.

Its moment of glory came in the early 16th century, when the young François I brought Leonardo da Vinci to France.

Da Vinci looked at ways of draining the Sologne and produced designs for a palace that François I wanted to build at Romorantin for his mother, Louise de Savoie. The king abandoned his plans on the deaths of both his mother and da Vinci. The existing **Château Royal**, of which only one wing and a tower have survived, was the birthplace of Claude de France, who became François I's wife and gave her name to the *reine-Claude* variety of plum (it was introduced to England by Sir William Gage in the 19th century—and thus called the greengage).

The **Hôtel Saint-Pol**, an elegant early 16th-century building with a delicate lozenge-shaped pattern of glazed bricks on its façade, was the scene of an incident in 1521 that almost cost François I his life: during some horseplay, he was hit on the head by a burning log thrown from a window of the building. It is said that in order to hide his scars he grew a beard—and set off a fashion for beards at court.

There are a number of other interest-

ing buildings in Romorantin in addition to the Hôtel Saint-Pol. They include the **Chancellerie**, a delightfully lopsided Renaissance construction with an over-hanging upper storey and (again) a loz-enge pattern, formed this time by criss-crossed beams. Near it stands another half-timbered building, the **Carroir d'Orée**, which has some fine carved cornerposts and now houses an arch-aeological museum. But Romorantin's most interesting museum is undoubt-edly the **Musée de Sologne**, which is housed in the Mairie. Its intelligently presented ethnographical collection il-lustrates Solognot life and lore down the centuries, and there are vivid recon-structions of a typical peasant family's living quarters and of craftsmen's workshops (there is a similar museum in Château de Ciran, near La Ferté-Saint-Aubin).

Romorantin can be regarded only very loosely as the "capital" of the Sologne, for the Sologne is not an administrative entity. It straddles three *départements*, and there is not even general agreement on what its precise borders are. But for convenience's sake it can be divided up into three broad areas: an eastern zone to the east of the A71 motorway (and the older Orléans-Vierzon road, the N20), a central zone, and a western zone to the west of a line from Chambord to Romorantin.

Of the three parts of the Sologne the eastern zone is historically the least affluent (because farther from the royal court), the wildest and the highest in altitude (a modest maximum of 100 ft/ 300 metres). It is there that the three main rivers which flow across the Sologne at leisurely pace from east to west—the Cosson, the Beuvron and the Sauldre—take their source. Its main town, and the second largest in the Sologne with 6,000 inhabitants, is **Sal-bris**, on the N20, whose name is of Celtic origin ("bridge on the Sauldre"). Its church, the Eglise St-Georges (mainly 15th and 16th-century), con-tains a striking early 17th-century stone *pietà* and some remarkable keystones.

One of the few large-scale old

Asparagus farming.

châteaux to be found in the poorer eastern part of the Sologne is at **La Chapelle-d'Angillon**, the village where Alain-Fournier was born. The château, which contains a museum devoted to Alain-Fournier, forms a large quadrangle and overlooks a lake. It has a massive square 11th-century keep and a Renaissance central section.

The cult of Alain-Fournier has become something of an industry in the Sologne (which is hardly surprising given that it is an area with few big tourist attractions). To the west of La Chapelle-d'Angillon, at the village of **Nançay** where the writer was a schoolteacher for a time, there is an interesting if small Musée Imaginaire du Grand Meaulnes housed in the Grenier de Villâtre, one of the outbuildings of Château de Nançay.

The 9 miles (14 km) of road from La Chapelle-d'Angillon to **Aubigny-sur-Nère** form one of the many absolutely straight lines that are such a common feature of Sologne topography. (The lack of sharp twists and turns makes driving easy in the Sologne—but there are dangers for the unwary motorist: because of the high water table, almost all roads have very deep drainage ditches on either side.)

Aubigny-sur-Nère is a well-preserved little town with many ornately decorated half-timbered houses. The seigneury of Aubigny was given to John Stuart of Danelay by Charles VII in 1423 as a reward for services rendered against the English during the Hundred Years' War. A number of Scottish noblemen and craftsmen settled in Aubigny and established a cloth-manufacturing industry there that thrived until the 19th century.

Another long stretch of straight road leads northwest to **Clémont**, a charming village with several half-timbered houses, which boasts one of the finest churches in a region not noted for its ecclesiastical architecture. Uncharacteristically for the Sologne, where churches tend to be built of brick, Clémont church is a massive stone building with some beautifully sculpted

Typical low-roofed Sologne architecture.

doors. The use of large and expensive blocks of stone was made possible by gifts from Jean, Duc de Berry, in the 14th century. The church's spire, an extremely slender slate-covered construction, is typical of the Sologne.

The next village, **Brinon-sur-Sauldre**, has a church which possesses another characteristic Solognot feature, a kind of open wooden gallery at one end where the congregation would assemble after mass to hear official announcements and discuss the affairs of the parish. The gallery is aptly known as a *caquetoir* (from *caqueter*, a French word meaning to chatter).

Maurice Genevoix often stayed with relatives near Brinon-sur-Sauldre, and the melancholy heathland and lakes just to the north of the village were the model for his moving evocation of the Solognot landscape in *Raboliot*. The Sauldre Canal, a favourite haunt of local anglers, runs through the area. Its towpath is a very congenial place for a picnic, stroll or even bike ride (bicycles can readily be hired in the Sologne,

whose topography is ideally suited to none-too-strenuous cycling). If you prefer the pleasures of a larger expanse of water complete with a beach, pedalos and boats, make for the 435-acre (175-hectare) **Etang du Puits** near Clémont, which once served as a reservoir for the Sauldre Canal.

Also north of the canal is the village of **Souvigny-en-Sologne**, whose church has a particularly fine 16th-century *caquetoir*, and whose erstwhile mayor was the noted author of farces, Eugène Labiche (1815–88). Northwest of Souvigny, and on the border between the eastern and central zones of the Sologne, is the busy little town of **La Ferté-St-Aubin**. Its château is a majestically proportioned 17th-century redbrick and stone building surrounded by a wide moat of running water diverted from the nearby Cosson. The interior of the château, which was opened to the public in 1987, contains a wealth of furniture from various periods, as well as an intelligent reconstruction of what life must have been like in the château

Souvigny-en-Sologne, 16th-century *caquetoir.*

during the 18th and 19th centuries (it includes a linen-room, games room, kitchen, billiards room and chamber-maid's bedroom as well as grander rooms). Château de la Ferté-St-Aubin was used by Jean Renoir as a location for the exterior scenes of the de la Chesnaye's mansion in *La Règle du Jeu*.

Until the mid-1980s, La Ferté-St-Aubin was well known to French radio listeners as a notorious cause, during holiday weekends, of tailbacks on the N20 road (its central street is long and narrow). But since the opening of the A71 motorway all that has ended, and life in the town has reverted to a more civilised pace. The motorway, although cutting a swathe through the forests of the Sologne, was designed with the interests of wildlife in mind: there are special bridges and tunnels for the use of deer and migrating toads (*cerviducs* and *crapauducs* respectively).

Brinon-en-Sologne. A very little-known château, **Château du Lude** (not to be confused with its namesake in the Sarthe *départe-*ment), is to be found in a beautiful setting by the River Cosson just off the road from La Ferté-St-Aubin to **Ligny-le-Ribault**.

Only the grounds may be visited. Although the size of a pocket handker-chief, this 15th and 17th-century château has a moat and a drawbridge, and is the sort of place one could, with a little wishful thinking, imagine living in oneself (it is indeed inhabited by a gentleman who may perhaps emerge and inquire after your identity).

Healing springs: On the far side of the Cosson, which feeds the château's moat, there is a small shrine devoted to Ste Corneille, who was thought to be able to cure children of "listlessness". The Sologne contains many such shrines and healing springs bearing the names of saints, and the Solognots remain very superstitious even today. There are several local legends which tell of maidens dressed in white dancing at night on ancient tumuli.

As in the Berry region to the south, the practice of witchcraft (which nowa-

days consists chiefly of casting spells or exorcising spirits) is fairly widespread in the Sologne, and villagers usually know of the existence of one or more witching oaks in the vicinity.

Also near Ligny-le-Ribault is another château which can be seen only from the outside, **Château de Bonhôtel**. It is one of the few buildings dating from the later wave of château-building (the 19th and 20th centuries) that is worth looking at. With its slightly overhanging upper stories and various features echoing Chambord, including the turrets and windows, the château would not be out of place in an illustration for a Grimms' fairy tale.

The road to **Jouy-le-Potier**, whose church has a 12th-century porch, leads on to **Cléry-St-André**. This village boasts a church of almost cathedral-like proportions, **Notre-Dame-de-Cléry**. First constructed in the 14th century, it was rebuilt and greatly enlarged by Louis XI. Although not a very harmonious building—its square belltower, the only part of the original church to es-cape destruction by the English in 1428, is set incongruously against the later nave, which dwarfs it—Notre-Dame-de-Cléry is a good example of Flamboyant Gothic architecture and has numerous features of interest. These include the Chapelle St-Jacques, which contains some fine vaulting, Louis XI's mausoleum, and a delightful spiral staircase without a central pillar leading up to the private chapel where the king could follow the service without being seen by the congregation.

It was the establishment of the royal court in the Loire Valley, and more particularly at Blois, that prompted noblemen, financiers and other courtiers to build their own châteaux or enlarge existing ones in the western part of the Sologne between Blois and Romorantin. It is there that the relentlessly flat heath and forest of the two zones already described begins to give way to a more fertile, rolling landscape of farmland, copses and vineyards. The châteaux dotted over this area range from the grandiose, such as Chambord,

Château du Moulin, "pearl of the Sologne".

to buildings that are scarcely larger than manor houses.

Château du Moulin, at **Lassay-sur-Croisne** near Romorantin, deserves its nickname "pearl of the Sologne". It is a charming red-brick Renaissance building set among attractive grounds. Its military features (moat, corner towers, drawbridge) are decorative rather than truly defensive. Its architecture of patterned red and black bricks with white cornerstones demonstrates a decided Italian influence.

The same influence can also be detected in **Château de Villesavin**, near the compact village of **Bracieux**, which has a fine 16th-century covered market. The château, the drive of which runs through a magnificent stretch of woods, offers a striking combination of architectural exuberance and classicism. Built by François I's financial secretary, Jean Le Breton, on the site of a Roman villa (Villa Sabinus), Villesavin has two symmetrical wings built round a courtyard, in the middle of which stands a remarkable Florentine vase of white Carrara marble. An unusual feature of the château is its huge and perfectly preserved 16th-century dovecote. It has its original revolving ladder and space for 3,000 birds in 1,500 holes. The right to own doves was one of the historic privileges abolished in the Revolution, a right restricted to abbots and aristocrats and directly linked to the extent of one's land. The downtrodden peasants were not allowed to kill the birds even when the doves destroyed their own meagre crops. As a result, most dovecotes were destroyed in the Revolution so this is one of the finest remaining, superior to those at Talcy and Cheverny.

The 16th-century **Château de Troussay** near the village of Cheverny is an attractively small manor which contains various elements (stained glass, sculptures, a door) that were salvaged from other Renaissance buildings in the area by the historian Louis de la Saussaye during the 19th century. The delicate architecture of the facade contrasts piquantly with the sturdy ver-

Cheverny.
Following pages: gateway to the past; boar hunt; feeding time at **Cheverny.**

nacular style of the château's outbuildings (which house a small museum devoted to Solognot life).

The only château in the Sologne that has the feel of a medieval castle, with its small windows, forbidding turrets and low-slung arches, is **Château de Fougères-sur-Bièvre**. But only its square keep is 11th-century; the rest of the building was built in the late-15th and early-16th centuries in the "old" style, with a judicious sprinkling of Renaissance details.

Château de Cheverny, without any doubt the most impressive historical monument in the Sologne along with Chambord, was constructed from 1604 to 1634, a century after the golden age of château building. A perfect specimen of Louis XIII architecture, it has a unity of style and harmony in its proportions that take one's breath away when it first comes into view. It is particularly notable for the subtly contrasting rhythms of its bright white facade and four grey slate roofs.

The interior of the château is equally rewarding. Its rooms are decorated with a riot of gilt, marble, painted panelling and sculpture, and lavishly furnished with pieces from the 17th century and later. In the king's bedroom is a coffered ceiling, 17th-century tapestries and a bed covered in a 16th-century embroidered Persian canopy. The kennels in the grounds house a pack of 70 hounds, (watching the dogs at feeding time is a popular tourist event) and every winter deer hunts are held in the surrounding woods. On display in another outbuilding is a collection of 2,000 deer antlers—an eloquently silent token of the area's huntin' and shootin' tradition that produces a gasp of admiration in many people visiting the château.

The splendour and wealth of Château de Cheverny perfectly epitomise one aspect of the Sologne. But there is another, less spectacular side to the region which may well leave a more lasting impression on the visitor—the Sologne of secret lakes, timid wildlife, slender-spired churches, one-storey cottages and, invisibly present everywhere, the ghost of Raboliot.

LA CHASSE

The Sologne is France's most important region for organised hunting and shooting (both of which are embraced by the French term *la chasse*). Its 1.2 million acres (500,000 hectares) provide ample cover for all sorts of game, from deer and boar to pheasant, duck, hare and rabbit, not all of which qualify as truly wild.

There are a number of liveried hunts complete with horses and hounds, the most famous of which is based at Château de Cheverny. While these are very popular with the lesser aristocracy and *nouveaux riches* that are well represented in the Sologne, they are less so with farmers (whose crops get regularly trampled on) and mayors (for some reason, hunted deer have a tendency to take refuge in *mairie* courtyards or school playgrounds, where they are illegally despatched by the hunters).

More often, though, a deer will seek salvation by plunging into one of the Sologne's many lakes. The hounds then swim after the animal and drown it by clambering on to its back. This explains the cryptic—to the non-initiate—remark that may be heard tripping from the lips of the exultant hunters after a successful chase: "*On a noyé le cerf!*" ("We drowned the stag!").

But by far the commonest form of *chasse* is shooting. Many shoots are owned by or rented out to companies, which use them as a marketing tool: many a crucial contract with a client is clinched in the relaxed, clubby atmosphere of a weekend's shooting.

Hunting and shooting are important for the economy of the Sologne, providing employment for gamekeepers and beaters and pumping money into the tills of local shops, hotels and restaurants. But many Solognots who used to earn a living from *la chasse* are having to find alternative sources of employment because of the decline in the number of hunters (their number nationwide went down from 3.5 million in 1960 to 1.8 million in 1989).

On the remaining big estates that can afford a live-in gamekeeper thousands of pheasants are raised in vast aviaries. The pheasants, bought as chicks, or from eggs, are looked after exactly like farmyard fowl. Some time before the opening of the season, the tame pheasants are released into the woods. There, the gamekeeper will often go on feeding them: when he hoots his horn, they dart out of the bracken, eager for the treat.

When the pheasant shooting season starts in September, lines of beaters and guns begin to comb the woods, pausing for refreshment between *battues*. Although still semi-tame, the birds learn after an hour or two of blitzkrieg that man is no longer their friend. The cannier pheasants refuse to take to the air, scampering instead through the lines of hunters, who are not allowed to fire at a bird on the ground (for obvious reasons of safety; but they sometimes get carried away, which partly explains the 20-odd fatal shooting accidents that take place each year in France).

Extra pheasants may be released a day or two before an important shooting weekend, to ensure a big bag. On the new mini-shoots, which have neither aviaries nor resident gamekeepers, the last-minute release of bought-in game is the only option available.

Sometimes pheasants are even let out of sacks during the *battue* itself in the line of fire of an important guest. This latter technique of release in batches is regularly used for duck shooting. The guns position themselves round a lake and blast away enthusiastically at the small flocks of ducks that fly past every minute or so.

But since even the dullest hunter cannot fail to realise that there is something "unnatural" about the groups of ducks that mysteriously appear from nowhere, some estates use a diabolical machine to maintain the fiction of *la chasse*: the ducks are fed one by one into the base of a small tower-like construction with a spiral ramp inside; after waddling up to the top they emerge on to a perch, off which they are pushed by the duck that is following behind. As a result, a solitary duck flies past the guns every 10 seconds or so. Absurd though such practices may be, they are probably less so than official French hunting legislation, which allows more species of bird to be shot than in any other EC country; no less than 95 species including some rare birds. *Ca, c'est du sport*!

BERRY

"It is difficult to be sure you have arrived in Berry yet the Berrichon always knows when he's home; Berry's boundaries are emotional not physical." The writer, François Gay, represents the traditional French view of this complex region. In fact, Berry is two lands, one on the map, the other in the head. Real Berry spans the *départements* of the Indre and Cher, a vast wheat and barley growing region; mythological Berry exists only in the French subconscious.

Fantasy Berry is where all good French citizens would like to go home to die. It is the land of *braves gens*, simple honest folk, happy to till the hard soil, down full-bodied wine, exchange earthy jokes and, when required, don baggy blue shirts, red kerchiefs and funny hats. In the meantime, sophisticated Parisians can get on with normal lives, secure in the belief that Berry almost exists, like the good old days that never were.

The two conceptions of Berry come closest to collusion in the Brenne, the southern "region of a thousand lakes and legends." Elsewhere, Berry has enough grand châteaux, famous rivers, royal links and economic prosperity to make it a quieter version of Touraine or Anjou. That said, if you spend too long in the lake district or attend too many agricultural fairs or traditional festivals, the seduction of the Berry myth takes its toll. If so, it is time to hang up your red kerchief and go home.

Mushroom farms: Built on a promontory overlooking the river Cher, **Montrichard** is protected by two valleys and a sweep of forest. As a border town, Montrichard has a foot in many camps: historically linked to Touraine to the east, technically part of Loir-et-Cher to the north, yet economically the gateway to Berry in the south. Montrichard was once known for its excellent *tuffeau* stone but the former quarries at Bourré are now equally successful mushroom farms. Today Montrichard is a comfortable market town known for its wine,

mushrooms and goat's cheeses. The goats which once roamed the southern slopes still provide *crottin de Chavignol* but the hills are also dotted with rest homes, a newer industry.

Montrichard is visible from afar, distinguished by its jagged tower, church and cluster of medieval houses below the ruined castle. Seen in close up, the scene is a snapshot of small town life. In the foreground is a market in which sombre, cloth-capped farmers haggle over the price of purple pansies. An elderly Berrichon rests his newish motor bike against La Vieille France, a rustic bar as old as it sounds. Beside this gabled *brasserie* is a *boulangerie*, its clients buying a *baguette* to accompany their evening glass of *Gamay* or *Pineau de Loire*. In the background rises the castle keep and narrow church spire, quiet counterpoints to the bustle.

The keep is all that remains of Foulques Nerra's feudal **castle**, destroyed by Henri IV to punish local Catholic dissenters. A steep bank leads to the keep, past terraces, outbuildings

Preceding pages: boar hunt, and feeding time at Cheverny; the Berry landscape. **Left**, St-Aignan. **Right**, gone fishing again.

and the remains of three sets of encircling ramparts. A precarious climb to the top of the keep is rewarded with sweeping views of the Fôret de Montrichard to the north, the domaines of Amboise and Chenonceau to the west, the banks of the Cher to the east and, to the south, the first sign of rural Berry.

Adjoining the château is the Romanesque **St-Croix** church, surmounted by a 19th-century belltower. A walled stone path leads to this narrow church, apparently balanced on spindly columns. Although over-restored in places, the church has a serious atmosphere in keeping with its history: here Louis XI's daughter, the 12-year-old Jeanne de Valois, married the future Louis XII. Louis later divorced the deformed, retiring Jeanne and married Anne de Bretagne, Charles VIII's widow. In the church, Jeanne's statue shows a grave-looking woman dressed in pale blue and red, perhaps already realising that she would spend the rest of her days in a nunnery in Bourges.

Nearby are a number of historic houses which survived both 19th-century expansion and 20th-century bombardment. In **Rue de la Juiverie**, close to the 18th-century town hall, is a pointed, gabled house, reputed to be the former synagogue. Montrichard was not alone in expelling its entire Jewish population in accordance with the edict of the mad King Charles VI.

A few streets away lies the fine Renaissance **Hôtel d'Effiat**, reached by the Porte aux Rois, the medieval gateway to the city. The 18th-century Marquis d'Effiat bequeathed the mansion to the town on condition that it was used as a hospice. Recently, however, the charms of the ornate windows and exotic *Ginkgo biloba* tree were outweighed by the impracticality of the turreted staircases and narrow passage ways. The house is now a community centre and the former residents have moved into a rest home over the river.

Just round the corner is **La Chancellerie**, a 15th-century hotel with a pentagonal tower and a domed Renaissance well. Equally striking is

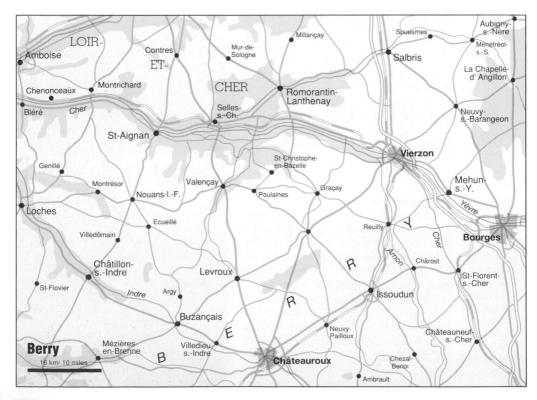

the **Maison du Prêche**, a Romanesque lodge which once belonged to the Knights Templar but was used for Protestant meetings after 1563. Particularly charming is the half-timbered **Maison Ave Maria**, now the Tourist Office. The sculpted beams depict monsters, angels, virgins, saints and pearls in a confusing design. From here, the narrow Passage du Saumon leads across the Gothic bridge to the **Parc Plage**, the finest "beach" on the Cher. The stone bridge was originally built of wood so that it could be dismantled quickly in times of war.

After admiring the landscaped riverside gardens and the fishing and boating lake, you could visit the wine cellars in the nearby troglodyte **Caves Monmousseau** or, a little further downstream, watch the "champagne method" at cellars in **St Georges-sur-Cher**. A more unusual taste lies just downstream at the **Fraise d'Or**, a strawberry distillery in **Chissay-en-Touraine**. There you can sample fruit liqueurs, eaux de vie or elixirs made from over 40 plants. Visitors who prefer to drink in style could try the 17th-century Château de Chissay, a grand hotel-restaurant on the hillside.

Naturally Montrichard itself has no shortage of wine so *Touraine Primeur* can be enjoyed in the town's sole chic piano-bar or in the rustic Vieille France. This stretch of the Cher is a good place to begin the quest for simple Berrichon dishes, from creamy vegetable soup to stuffed rabbit or *poulet en barbouille*, a chicken *flambé* with a rich sauce. After a surfeit of prune tarts and honey doughnuts, it is time to explore the Cher itself.

From Montrichard to Vierzon: Compared with the Loire, the Cher is a tamer, channelled, unpretentious river. However, the landscape between Montrichard and Vierzon is exceptionally rich, varying from the white cliffs pitted with cave dwellings near Montrichard to woodland and vineyards near St-Aignan and the marshy Sologne landscape near St-Loup. En route, there are enough neglected châteaux and wine-tasting opportunities to make this jour-

Montrichard village and view from the river.

ney upstream pass only too quickly. The route from Montrichard to **Thésée** follows the old Roman road which linked Tours and Bourges. At Thésée, a white château contains a collection of Gallo-Roman statuettes, bowls and jars. Apart from the museum, vaulted cellars and a 16th-century wine press are also visible but the rest of the château now houses the town hall.

A few kilometres east is a turreted château just visible behind stone walls and vineyards. At **Mareuil-sur-Cher** the Lorriere farmhouse waylays visitors with a tempting display of sheep's and goat's cheeses and local wine. Once at **St-Aignan**, you have to make do with a wine museum, a Romanesque church and a cluster of gabled houses. The grand château only allows visitors a glimpse of the L-shaped Renaissance building, with its octagonal tower, crenellated keep and terraced gardens. After standing wistfully in the courtyard, turn your attention to the Romanesque murals in the church, particularly the *Christ in Majesty*.

From St-Aignan, the D675 leads to the **Beauval** tropical bird sanctuary, home to flamingoes, emus, macaws and cockatoos. However, without even straying from the Cher, you can catch sight of a range of indigenous birds flying over from the Sologne lakes.

Between St-Aignan and Selles-sur-Cher are views of vineyards on the sunny slopes and occasionally the asparagus beds heralding Sologne. Unlike the mechanised plains further south, these patches of meadow are often still ploughed by horse. En route, at **Chatillon-sur-Cher**, is the St-Blaise church, celebrated for its paintings of St Catherine and angels, painted by pupils of Leonardo da Vinci. The delicacy of the hands and the luminous expressions show the master's touch. From here signs point to the *Route Touristique du Vignoble;* but, for another fine Romanesque church and château, continue to **Selles-sur-Cher**, a village nestling into a curve in the river.

In the village, the St-Eusice church and a few cloisters are all that remain of

Berrichon farm.

the abbey desecrated during the Wars of Religion. This Romanesque and Gothic church is decorated with sculptures of mis-shapen people on the apse while in the crypt is the gloomy 6th-century tomb of St Eusice.

The château is really two châteaux in one: a graceful 17th-century residence imposed on a 14th-century castle built by the Black Prince. Aesthetically, this is an unsatisfying château because the demolition of key facades has resulted in a clash of medieval authenticity and Renaissance grace. However, the interior has been intelligently restored, particularly the huge 17th-century fireplaces and the panelled ceiling decorated with allegorical scenes. The triangular-shaped grounds are criss-crossed by four bridges over the Cher and moats. In the right light, this awkward château drowns in its own watery reflection, leaving behind lush gardens of geraniums, dahlias, mulberry trees and a giant cedar of Lebanon.

From Selles, it is worth making a detour south to **Valençay**, the finest château in Berry. The route leads through a mixture of rolling countryside, plains and woodland, all of which belonged to the domain of Valençay until the last century. Although Valençay is geographically in Berry, spiritually it belongs to the Val de Loire. In fact, the scale, period and design point firmly to the château of Chambord as a role model.

Valençay was built in 1540 by Jacques d'Estampes, a local châtelain wishing to impress his new wife, and had a succession of aristocratic owners of whom the most notable was the Prince de Talleyrand, the skillful statesman. Despite its remote location and distance from Paris, Valençay was the château most in vogue in the early 19th century. Napoleon put pressure on Talleyrand, his Foreign Secretary, to acquire an estate suitable for entertaining ambassadors and foreign dignitaries. Conveniently, the Comte de Luçay had narrowly escaped the guillotine and was only too willing to sell his château in return for official approval.

The pleasure palace of Valençay.

In 1803, Talleyrand and his wife spent three days trotting around their new estates, taking stock of the 100-roomed château, the village, forests, meadows and 99 farms. However, after helping Talleyrand purchase one of the largest feudal domains in France, Napoleon exacted swift compensation. At the Emperor's request, the exiled Spanish princes were invited to live at Valençay for six years and Talleyrand was obliged to house the vast Spanish retinue as well as adding a theatre and concert hall especially for the princes' amusement.

After the Congress of Vienna, Talleyrand finally regained control and became a model owner, renovating the château, starting up mills and foundries, and importing both merino sheep and efficient agricultural methods from England. The interior decoration of the château was masterminded by the Duchesse de Dino, Talleyrand's vivacious young niece and lover.

As a pleasure palace, Valençay is as much fun as Chambord, if not as inno-vative. Since the château took three centuries to complete, a number of Renaissance features have disappeared, including the 16th-century east wing. Unlike at Chambord, the corner towers are topped with domes rather than authentic Renaissance "pepper pots". However, Valençay is exciting enough to dismiss the charge of faulty Renaissance design: with its low-slung mansard roofs and symmetrical columns, the château represents a positive step towards classical design. Valençay plays games with different styles: the gatehouses, for instance, have purely decorative crenellations.

Even the grounds appear to go along with the game: bad-tempered peacocks weave in and out of topiary which has been teased into comical animal or abstract designs. The quirky topiary was part of Talleyrand's desire to transform the classical French park into a wilder English garden. However, his conception of an English garden also included a Chinese bridge, an Egyptian temple, a Russian *dacha*, and a dancing

Acorn harvest, November, *Les Très Riches Heures du Duc de Berry.*

pavilion; sadly, only the ballroom remains. It may even be part of the joke that while docile llamas, zebras and kangaroos are firmly enclosed in a paddock, the main grounds are patrolled by assertive, free-range black swans and child-molesting peacocks.

The interior is decorated in Empire style so expect chandeliers, ornate chairs and clashing colours, especially lime green, pillar-box red and turquoise blue. In the *grand salon,* pride of place is given to the round table used at the Congress of Vienna; notice the chairs decorated with images of all the leaves found on the Valençay estate. Other highlights include Talleyrand's private theatre and his lover's music room, complete with a harp, lyre and music seats. Your last sight of the château will probably be of a peacock plummeting from a great height on to the head of an unsuspecting child.

After rejoining the Cher at **Chabris**, on the south bank, visitors may be tempted by the dairy produce on sale at local farms. This high road leads through patches of woods and scrubland until the reward of fine views over the Cher valley at St-Loup. After glancing at the strangulated spire of the St-Loup church, cross the river to **Mennetou-sur-Cher**. From here, the the old Canal du Berry follows the path of the Cher, a route once plied by *berrichons*, traditional narrow barges. Mennetou itself is a compact medieval town, partially enclosed by 13th-century ramparts, three towers and three town gates. The Gothic and Renaissance *hôtels particuliers* in the Grand Rue are particularly impressive. Before leaving, sample *beignets au miel*, the famed honey doughnuts.

The river widens at **Chatres-sur-Cher**, an attractive sprawling village with views of marooned sandbanks. Since the river laps the Sologne on the north bank, kestrels and hawks occasionally hover overhead. The road passes several well-concealed châteaux before reaching **Vierzon**, the meeting place of three rivers: the Arnon, Cher and Yèvre. Despite its potential as gateway to the Sologne and Berry, Vierzon

sees itself as a self-contained commercial town, shaped by its old industrial heritage. Foundries flourished here in the 19th century while, more recently, light engineering, food processing and, above all, ceramics, have taken over. However, the town is gradually realizing that commercial single-mindedness need not exclude urban conservation or "green tourism" in the rural valleys.

Although limited in size, the nucleus of the old town is atmospheric in a slightly dingy way. Set high on the hill, the old quarter is dominated by the Gothic belfry which, along with sections of the ramparts, is all that remains of the feudal castle. The view of the well-restored belfry is somewhat marred by the ugly 1960s tower block behind it, an error of judgment characteristic of Vierzon.

As if by way of apology, a short stroll downhill reveals higgledy-piggledy gabled houses, although many are in need of restoration. A little lower down is the Romanesque church of Nôtre-Dame with its finely sculpted doorway.

Joan of Arc visits Mehun-sur-Yèvre.

Nearby, a staircase leads to gardens with views over the rooftops to the valley. Given Vierzon's insouciance, the black Victorian lamps around the Nôtre-Dame church may well be genuine rather than a recent gimmick.

Mehun-sur-Yèvre: If a night in Vierzon does not appeal, press on to **Mehun-sur-Yèvre**, the historical capital of northern Berry as well as the gateway to the plains of modern Berry. Mehun's reputation is entirely due to its château, depicted in all its glory in the *Très Riches Heures du Duc de Berry*, the famous book of miniatures depicting medieval prosperity.

A medieval clock tower points the way along Rue Jeanne d'Arc to the château perched on a spur overlooking the river. A narrow drawbridge leads across a deep ravine to two towers, all that remains of the château rebuilt by Jean de Berry in 1386. Here King Jean le Bon's son created an alternative royal court which, in its heyday, rivalled even Chinon and Loches. In fact, given the habitually itinerant nature of French courts, Mehun provided a southern home for the Valois dynasty until the 15th century.

Looking at the crumbling château, it takes an imaginative leap to recall that in Jean de Berry's time this was the intellectual centre of France, a brilliant court of writers and miniaturists, sculptors and architects. Sadly, there is little left of the scenes painted by Holbein: the château was dismantled during the Wars of Religion and allowed to crumble until 19th-century Romanticism made it fashionable once more. However, Mehun has active historical and archeological societies which are currently restoring the château and excavating the grounds.

One of the two remaining towers is sliced in half, revealing a cross-section of arches and chimney breasts; by contrast, the Charles VII tower is relatively intact. Despite its grim appearance, this was an intellectual hothouse in Charles VII's day, containing the most remarkable library in France and a school of illuminated manuscript design. Al- **Goat's cheese.**

306

though the historical museum inside gives little sense of intellectual high-living, the architecture indicates that Mehun was not just another feudal château: airy hexagonal rooms are lit by high, Gothic windows, not mere arrow slits. From the château, there are views of meadows, streams and the river Yèvre. On the castle square, a statue of Joan of Arc is a reminder of her visits to Charles VII in 1429 and 1430. The statue quotes her famous threat to the English, her desire to "*buter les estrangers en dehors de la France*".

But in Mehun today there is little need to "kick foreigners out"; there are too few visitors to justify the effort. The lack of tourism also means that the charming Romanesque church by the château is full of genuine Christians, more intent on prayer than admiration of the 15th-century reliquary. The town, built over the Yèvre river and the Berry Canal, offers shaded waterside walks and views of washhouses and an old mill. However, despite a little kayak racing along the many streams, the town

Berry goats.

is still blissfully unaware of its tourist potential. Mehun's fortunes are bound up in the local porcelain industry and in agriculture. As a result, the hearty cuisine on offer is designed more for the appetites, style and pockets of passing lorry drivers than Parisian intellectuals. Expect large steaks and copious helpings of stuffed rabbit, all washed down by Gamay.

Before travelling south, it is worth revisiting the château at night. The spotlights illuminate the griffin gargoyles on the Charles VII tower while its eerie, ruined twin, looking like a 19th-century industrial mill encircled by vociferous crows, is home to a pair of marauding owls. Locals say that the owls represent the unsettled spirit of Louis XI who, as Dauphin, spent many years at Mehun plotting the death of his father.

From the Cher to the Indre: Mehun borders the Champagne Berrichone, an expanse of cereal plains stretching south to Châteauroux and Bourges. However, agriculture is smaller-scale

and less mechanised than in the northern Beauce. As a result, the geometric neatness of barley, rape and wheat fields is broken up by grassland covered in poppies or bright sunflowers, pools of water, patches of peatbog, and even some vineyards.

Far from being a cultural desert, the southwesterly route from Mehun to Buzançais includes unusual châteaux and market towns which once thrived on the medieval wool trade. Although most of the flocks have gone to southern pastures new, enough sheep and goats remain to provide delicious cheeses, including *Pouligny, Valençay* and *St-Maure*. In addition, the profusion of village wines provides the perfect excuse for a picnic.

The messy village of **Quincy** is not an inspiring beginning, rising as it does, out of the swamps. However, after glancing at the solid manor house and square-shaped church, incongruously close to a gypsy encampment, try a glass of Quincy or wait until **Reuilly**, a more significant village and an *appellation controllée* wine. Apart from a Romanesque abbey church, a 15th-century priory and a few gabled houses, Reuilly boasts the moated château of La Ferte, now a grand riding school.

Vatan, due west of Reuilly, is a small wine-producing town with enough picturesque alleys to justify a visit. As well as an 18th-century corn exchange and 17th-century stables, the highlights include a late Gothic church, a medieval chapter house and a chantry topped by a domed tower.

Vatan is also a typical Berrichon market town, from its full-blooded wines to the wearing of traditional berets by local farmers. Here muddy labourers down serious drinks, even in the early morning: in Vatan, real men drink Pernod, not wine. Visitors with more fragile digestive systems might stick to the *pinôt gris* with a local honey cake or a crunchy *galette de pommes de terre*.

Bouges-le-Château is an isolated village centred on a classical château. Bouges borders two very different landscapes, the woods reaching north to

A morning read.

Valençay and the plains stretching south to Châteauroux. The 18th-century château is equally anomalous, an Italianate model of the Petit Trianon in the middle of nowhere. The decor, furniture, stables and gardens echo the classical theme and so could not be further from the perceived idea of Berry.

Royal town: Across a stretch of yellowing cornfields lies **Levroux**, the most royal town on the plains. Although François I, Henri II and Catherine de Médicis have left their marks, modern Levroux is rather dilapidated and wears its history with little pride. In the Middle Ages, Levroux was well-known for its charitable endeavour and hospices. Cynics say that such charity also helped the local economy recover: the fitter patients were used as cheap labour in the parchment and leather workshops. Now on a more reputable footing, these trades still exist and a visit to the workshops can be arranged.

The old quarter is clustered around the Romanesque St-Sylvain church, intended for pilgrims on the way to Santiago de Compostella but also used as a refuge for serfs, fugitives and the sick. The main doorway is heavily sculpted with *Last Judgment* scenes and the scallop shell emblems of St James. Inside are 52 choir stalls representing the vices and virtues popular in medieval design. The local craftsmen modelled the faces on friends and enemies but the occasional Arab or Ethiopian face represents the imagined or remembered faces from pilgrimages to distant lands.

Just in front of the church is the Pilgrims' House, built by the young Henri II for his wife, Catherine de Médicis. She stayed here when visiting her nearby estates but, in turn, offered it in perpetuity to all pilgrims. This gabled house is emblazoned with the arms of Henri II, three lilies borne by angels. But the finest feature is the central wooden post, carved with a constipated-looking figure: either a court jester carrying a rattle or a leper covered in scabs. It is unclear whether sick pilgrims were supposed to be entertained or chastised.

From Levroux, head south to **Ville-**gongis, the most authentic of French Renaissance châteaux. Built by Pierre Trinqueau, Chambord's presumed architect, Villegongis echoes its grander contemporary. Two wings and the Cour d'Honneur were demolished in the 18th century but what remains is exquisite: a long, narrow facade completed by two corner towers and mirrored in the decorative moat. The château is topped by pinnacled chimney stacks, carved with geometric designs of lozenges, circles and squares.

Owned by the Baronne de Montesquieu, the château is decorated entirely with furniture and tapestries that have always been part of the family *patrimoine,* an exception amongst Loire châteaux. In spring, the small, unfussy grounds burst with wild flowers. The noisy ducks are a feature at all times of year but the Montesquieu family loses a number of them in the hunting season.

From Villegongis, a short drive through the woods leads west to **Argy**, a 16th-century château rebuilt by one of

Louis XII's knights. Today Argy is being restored by the *Club du Vieux Manoir*, an efficient but authoritarian local charity. The turreted 15th-century keep has already been restored as has the Louis XII gallery and Renaissance tower of the château.

However, despite lovely Renaissance fireplaces, Argy feels more classical, partly because the ivy-covered main facade has gracious windows added at the time of the Revolution. Sadly, the moat was filled in at the same time but the rest of the grounds are attractively unkempt, including the moss-covered statues of winsome muses. From Argy, a short drive leads to the lush landscape of the river Indre.

Down the River Indre: **Buzançais** is a small, sluggish town nesting within its medieval ramparts and tumbledown towers. After glancing at the Gothic church and Romanesque chapel, walk past turreted towers to a riverside picnic, conceivably eaten on porcelain, the town's mainstay. Just down river is **St-Genou**, a ramshackle village with its fair share of medieval houses and a fine Romanesque church, once part of a Benedictine abbey. Although the interior is distinctly damp, the carved Romanesque columns, decorated with monkeys, angels and distorted human heads, appear to express their disapproval at the dilapidation. Outside the church is a striking war memorial of a soldier staring into space, his back to the church.

A small turning south leads to another intimation of mortality, the **Lanterne des Morts**, an isolated funerary tower which can also be seen as a symbol of eternal life.

After regaining St-Genou, a scenic route leads across the river to **Palluau-sur-Indre**, a medieval town built like a wedding cake. The icing is undoubtedly the Gothic château, surrounded by two tiers of ramparts and magnificent views over the valley. Built by Foulques Nerra's father, the pointed castle and heavy drawbridge are misleadingly austere. Inside, the present owners enjoy rich Renaissance furnishings, in-

Palluau-sur-Indre.

cluding a series of tapestries given by Louis XII to the Comte de Palluau. From the château, the improbably named Ha Ha passage leads down the flank of the hill to the village.

On the first level below the château is the Gothic St-Sulpice church, renowned for its 15th-century choir stalls, carved with the faces of sad sheep. High above is a collection of painted polychrome statues, including one of St Roch with his guardian angel and a dog with a strong resemblance to the cartoon character, Snoopy. Further down the hillside is St-Laurent, an even more celebrated church, renowned for the Romanesque frescoes in the crypt. The finest is the *Virgin in Majesty*, sitting on a throne carved with dragon heads. The colours of the Virgin's green veil and purple dress have lost little of their freshness despite its age.

Following the marshy south bank leads past a Romanesque church and fortified farms at **Clion**, followed by the château of **L'Isle-Savary**, marooned on an island. Also at L'Isle-Savary is a fortified manor house with a Gothic chapel as well as an impressive water mill, still in use.

Facing L'Isle-Savary on the other bank of the Indre is the feudal castle of **Le Tranger**, complete with moat and impressive fortifications. From here, the road clings to the north bank until the turreted castle keep at **Chatillon-sur-Indre** comes into view. On market days, the narrow streets are packed with farmers selling sheep, cattle, dairy produce and agricultural equipment. Apart from dramatic views near the ruined 13th-century fortress, Chatillon offers a marked walk through the old quarter, passing a 15th-century priory and picturesque gabled houses before reaching the river again.

However, the town's greatest treasure is the Romanesque Notre-Dame church near the river. The doorway is decorated with mythological and Biblical scenes: a sphynx battles with a phoenix; a man eats a monster's tail; and Adam and Eve are chased from the Garden of Eden. From Chatillon, a di-

L'Isle-Savary Château.

rect road leaves the river for the quirky château of **Azay-le-Ferron**. Situated on the borders of rural Touraine and the lake district of the Brenne, Azay is equally unsure of its architectural identity: a 15th-century crenellated tower adjoins wings added over the next three centuries. The juxtaposition of styles is surprisingly harmonious, enhanced by grounds overflowing with streams and geometric topiary. Shaped like witches' hats, the topiary echoes the hat on the medieval tower of the château.

Inside the château, Empire furniture predominates, the preference of its last private owner, Madame Hersant Luzarche. The highlights are the parquet floor inlaid with a rose design and the Hollywood bed, shaped like a swan. The view from the crenellations reveals woodland gradually fading into the flat wetlands characteristic of the Brenne.

Land of a thousand lakes: As you approach Mézières-en-Brenne, the landscape gradually slides into seascape or, as the **Brenne** tourist brochure expresses it, "Instead of huge castles and

cathedrals, the Brenne oozes out a history closely clinging to a wild nature". These low-lying lakes are largely man-made, however, created by enterprising 13th-century monks from the abbeys of **St-Cyran, Meobecq** and **Fontegombault**. The monks channelled the marshy swamps into pools in order to provide a reserve of fish during the lean period of Lent. The land drainage was continued by Napoleon III and new pools are created every year, used as fish-breeding grounds, boating lakes or experimental nature reserves.

The name **Mézières** comes from the Latin for "old stones", stones which are still in evidence in the Gothic church and towers of the ruined fortress. As a *seigneurie* of the Brenne family, Mézières had a vast medieval fortress which stretched between the river Claise and the old canal. The waterways still encircle the town but the fortress is reduced to a 10th-century porch and two towers, now forming part of the Hôtel de Ville and a local history museum. Not far away is the Marie Madeleine church, with its square belltower, fine Gothic windows, Renaissance chapel and small canon's house.

In the 19th century, the local economy was fuelled by the iron foundries in Corbançon and horse-racing in Mézières. George Sand, in Mézières for the races, complained of being bitten by fleas, "but we sleep where we can in this one-horse town". She felt no embarrassment at forcing the chief of police to give up his bed to herself and Chopin.

Luckily, there are now flealess beds available in the historic Boeuf Couronné, one of the few hotels in the region. Mézières is the only logical base from which to explore the Brenne wetlands; judging from the number of wellingtons and waxed jackets in evidence, most visitors are intent on serious sport: bird-watching, animal-spotting or fishing.

The local economy is heavily dependent on fish-breeding as the shallow pools, quickly warmed by the sun, provide good conditions for the breeding of carp, tench, eels, pike and roach. 500 tonnes of carp alone are sorted, processed and sold annually. In the prairies

Roosting cormorants.

and heathland, goats, white charollais cattle and isolated herds of horses provide a difficult living, given that the land is bone dry in summer and sodden in winter.

The agricultural fairs at **Rosnay** are the best place to appreciate traditional Brenne. However, Berry, as always, runs against the popular stereotype. In the 19th century much of the Brenne was defaced by ugly iron works and mills but today has a flourishing high-tech image, from the production of gliders and telecommunications equipment in the Brenne to Exocet missiles manufactured nearer Bourges.

The Brenne is not without historic sights, from the three abbeys to the Romanesque church at **Paulnay** or the old forges at **Corbançon**. Nevertheless, it is best known for its scenery, often tinged with legend. Berry is reputed to be one of the most folkloric places in France but only in the Brenne are traditional festivals really kept alive.

In Mézières alone there are several major festivals. On the Sunday after Mardi Gras, children dress as Berrichons, the girls donning bonnets, aprons and long dresses while the boys wear blue serge tops and red kerchiefs. The children hold aloft blazing *brandons*, torches made from straw and twigs, often twisted into the shape of a cross. A procession leads to the *Champ de Foire* and a feast of doughnuts, cider and *pinôt gris*.

Mid-Lent is enlivened by the *grande foire aux poissons et aux echaudés*, a festival celebrating fish. Naturally great quantities of fish are sold and eaten outdoors. Visitors are also encouraged to sample carp mousse, carp sausage, *terrine de carpe* or, for variety, stuffed carp. The fish is followed by *echaudés*, local pastries.

Wetlands attractions: Just south of Mézières is the Chérine nature reserve, where the wetlands begin. The Chérine is a mosaic of willow plantations, meadows, *landes*, peatbogs and lakes. Walks and observation points afford the patient visitor views of resident or migrating birds, including ducks, her-

Lake in the Brenne.

ons, black kites and buzzards. In the reedbeds are occasional sightings of a slippery water turtle or of a purple heron with a distinctive geometric plumage.

Even if you fail to see the rare moustached titmouse perched on a wispy reed, there is consolation in the profusion of bright swamp orchids, white lilies, yellow water irises or even the yellow and mauve bird-shaped orchid. Although less visible, deer, boar and even American mink lurk in the undergrowth and woods.

From Mézières or the Chérine, a number of marked walks and drives lead south and east through the Brenne. The watery landscape is open and varied, dotted with *depatures*, button-shaped hillocks said to have been made by the giant Gargantua as he scraped his boots by the pools. On summer nights, the pools vibrate with the croaks of mating toads or the sounds of frogs plopping through the acquatic ferns.

Sound and sudden storms are a feature of the Brenne: "It all begins with a shiver and the Brenne quivers, the rushes flatten with a sigh and the lake's calm surface wrinkles with a thousand ripples...Oaks crash in the reedbeds; shrieking herons, cranes and curlews are swept into the storm." Jacqueline Pelletier d'Oisy's description is given a special twist in local legend. The storms are thought to represent a curse on the region, personified by the ghost of an impious landlord who prefers to hunt wolves on Christmas Eve rather than attend Midnight Mass. Even now, Brennou fishermen protect themselves from storms by making the sign of the cross or drawing a magic circle in the air.

Due south from the Chérine is one of the largest lakes, **l'Etang de la Mer Rouge**, named by a 13th-century crusader. Apart from watching the kingfishers in the lake and the falcons overhead, visitors can view the Château du Bouchet, built on a rocky reddish spur overlooking the lake. This dramatic medieval château has been inhabited by the Veronne family for 200 years but visitors can still stand on the watchtowers and terraces to admire the panoramic views of the Brenne.

Secret base: Just east of the château is **Rosnay**, a small village once feared as "the parish of sorcerers" but now better-known for its colourful agricultural fairs and secret military base. Glowing pylons, transmitters and warning signs indicate the base, used for communicating with submarines *"en mission"*. Submariners on leave in Rosnay claim that the damp atmosphere is conducive to the effective transmission of messages. The mystery of the Brenne however, is not so easily unravelled.

Unlike the Sologne, which is characterised by interlocking woods and clearings, the Brenne appears an endless, free-flowing vista of brackish lakes. Jacques des Gatons writes of the Brenne as "blue grasses, pink heather, dark woods, flowery meadows and silver lakes". In not mentioning the storms or the paradoxes, he follows in the tradition of sentimental French writers whose eyes mist over when they talk of Berry. It is well to remember that Gerard Départieu is both a typical Berrichon and a consummate actor.

Left, Mézières-en-Brenne. Right, Berry homestead.

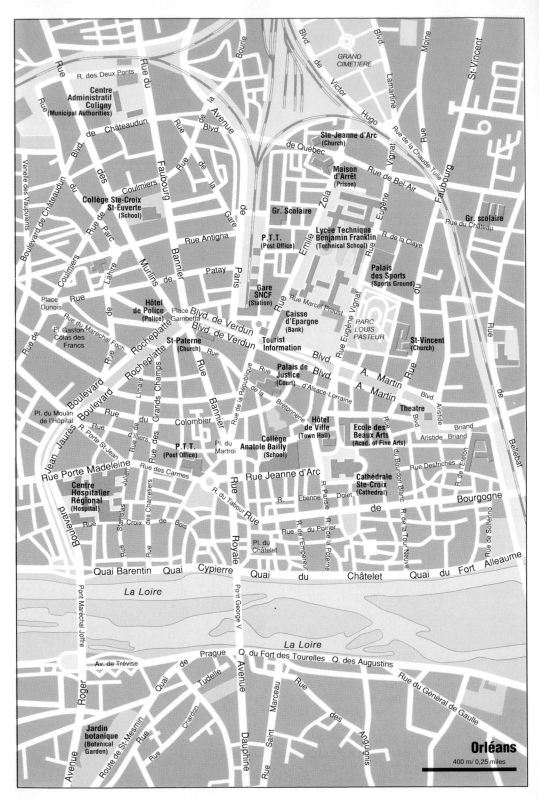

Orléans

400 m/ 0,25 miles

ORLEANS

Orléans is France's 33rd-largest city, just below Perpignan, just above Rouen. But unlike these two, each of which has a single, distinctive persona, Orléans has at least four. The one that may first strike you as you drive through its suburbs is its industrial persona. It manufactures textiles, machinery and motor accessories. Its processing plants are responsible for much of the canned or frozen food eaten in France. It makes nearly half the vinegar used by French housewives. It is the nexus of road and rail networks with the SNCF junction at Fleury les Aubrais one of the biggest in the country.

Naturally, being a French city, it also has its commercial persona of seductively attractive shops. It is certainly a good place to eat, not surprisingly since it has such a range of superb, fresh ingredients on its doorstep: fruit and vegetables from the market gardens of St-Marceau across the river; meat, poultry and local cheeses from the farms of Beauce; game from the Forest of Orléans; fish from river and sea.

You can see all these, as well as the terrines, *rillettes*, pâtés and other delicacies made from them, in the shops. But to discover them in their truly cornucopian profusion, visit the **Nouvelle Halles**, off the Rue Royale, if possible early in the morning. Sample them too in restaurants, ranging from the expensive to the surprisingly reasonable, to be found particularly in and around the **Rue Ste-Catherine**.

Orléans' third persona is, of course, that of the city of Joan of Arc. She was actually there for just 10 days, not, as you might be forgiven for supposing as you walk the streets, most of her career. But that short period represented an historic turning point and its drama is recaptured in dioramas and exhibits, which include the only sketch of her drawn from life, in the **Maison Jeanne d'Arc**, where she lodged after her clandestine arrival in the city.

Besides its Maison, the city also has a

Rue and a Lycée Jeanne d'Arc. The courtyard of the town hall has a statue of her at prayer, scarred with bullet-holes from World War II. Another within shows her guiding her horse's hooves away from a wounded English soldier lying on the earth. Her story is told in stained glass in the cathedral of **Ste-Croix**. Most arresting is Denis Foyatier's idealised equestrian statue of her in the **Place Martroi**.

Yet even industrialisation and Joan of Arc's omnipresence has failed to obliterate the fourth persona: that of the royal city. By a tradition dating back to the 14th century, the title of Duke of Orléans was borne by the second son of the king. And, despite 200 years of often militant republicanism, the city's coat-of-arms still bears the *fleur-de-lis* of French royalty.

It seems to have been particularly favoured by kings as a place to accommodate mistresses. The Duchesse d'Étampes was installed in one mansion by François I and Diane de Poitiers in another by his son, Henry II. Among

frequent visitors was the Marquise de Pompadour. Louis XV's lavish spending on her did not escape the attention of the Orléanais, whose reputation for acid wit had earned them the nickname of "Les Guépins" (the wasps). Observing her crossing its principal bridge in her carriage, they were said to have commented that it must be very strong to have borne France's heaviest burden.

But the city's ancestry is reflected in more than its reminders of royal infidelities. It can also be seen in spacious, harmonious planning and elegant buildings, both at their most glamorous after dark when they are floodlit. It is true that there is a characterless modern shopping precinct near the main railway station in the Boulevard Verdun, but on the whole the centre has been spared the developer's hand. It is not difficult to understand why. In 1940 it was heavily and pointlessly bombed by the Italians and, in 1944, was the scene of heavy fighting. In the process it lost many of its most treasured buildings so that what now exists is largely a piece of amaz-ingly seamless reconstruction. Having gone to so much expense and trouble to achieve this the Orléanais would hardly want to see it demolished.

The city is divided into two parts by the Loire. To the south lies Olivet and Orléans-la-Source. **Olivet** is an elegant (and expensive) residential suburb. **La Source** is a magnificently laid-out park surrounding the 17th-century Château de la Source; from the time it opens to the public in May until it closes for the winter in mid-November it is ablaze with flowers. Its feature is the roses for which Orléans is famous and more than 400 varieties are on display, but, in addition, there are flamingoes in its lake and deer roaming its glades.

Much of the work of designing the gardens, as well as reconstructing the château, was undertaken by the English statesman Henry Bolingbroke, who angered George I by some imprudent dealings with the rebel Jacobites and fled to France where he married the owner of La Source, the Marquise de Villette. La Source is also the site of the

Left, Hôtel de Ville, Joan of Arc day. **Right**, Joan of Arc at the stake, Ste-Croix, Orléans.

University of Orléans, a recent successor to the medieval one, abolished during the Revolution, where the religious reformer John Calvin once studied. It is claimed that, in establishing it on the outskirts, its founders were imitating the American campus universities. Cynics with sharp memories of the 1968 Paris student riots say that it was to keep rebellious youth off the streets.

Old Orléans, still the hub, is an area forming a rough semi-circle north of the river. The centre is the **Place du Martroi**, with its fountains, splendid buildings and Foyatier's *Joan of Arc*. It looks like a pedestrian precinct, but do not be deceived by appearances. Not only cars and delivery vans, but those enormous French buses, actually two buses joined in the middle by a concertina-like corridor, drive over what appears to be pavement.

Two of the most imposing buildings, both in a restrained classical style, are the **Chancellerie** and the **Chamber of Commerce**. The Chancellerie, built in the 18th century, and now an up-market brasserie, once housed the archives of the Duchy of Orléans. The Chamber of Commerce, which might strike envy in most of its British counterparts, was built in 1860 as its twin.

Beneath the Place an underground car park has been installed, one of several such in the city. Despite this attempt at relief, parking problems remain formidable, an inconvenience to the visitor aggravated by the fact that most of the underground car parks close at 9 p.m. and do not allow cars to remain overnight. In practice you may find you have to leave your car some distance from your hotel.

As one would expect of a hub, the Place Martroi is the point from which other streets radiate. Southward are the arcaded Rue Royale, with its smart shops, and the Rue de Notre-Dame de la Recouvrance, both of which take you to the Loire. Halfway down the second is the Hôtel Toutin where François I housed his *belle amie* and in whose ivy and Virginia-creeper clad courtyard he sits in stone looking extremely pleased

Orléans river view.

with himself. At the bottom of both streets are the quays and the bridge that Joan of Arc crossed to inflict her first defeat on the besieging English. To the east of the Place Martroi, via the narrow Rue Ste-Catherine is the **Rue Jeanne d'Arc**, a man-made canyon of three-storied, classical facades which opens on to the Place Ste-Croix and on to the west front of **Ste-Croix** cathedral.

Marcel Proust called **Ste-Croix** "the ugliest cathedral in France" and its twin towers have been compared to triple-tiered wedding cakes. Though both observations are less than fair, it is certainly a hodge-podge of styles as a result of the reconstructions following the various misfortunes which befell it through its history, among them its destruction by Protestants in 1568.

For all this, the interior has a certain soaring majesty and, like even the most modest Loire churches, contains splendid wood carvings. In its treasury are 11th-century Byzantine enamels, examples of 12th-century goldsmiths' work and a number of valuable paint-ings including *Christ bearing the cross* by the 17th-century Spanish master Francisco de Zurbarán.

Midway along on the right is the little Place de la République with its flower-sellers' stalls. Behind them, in the Hôtel des Créneaux with its belfry-tower, is the Orléans' Music Conservatoire and a small shopping precinct leading into the **Rue Ste-Catherine**. The remains of the Church of Ste-Catherine, destroyed during the Revolution, have been incorporated into the Credit Municipal which forms the corner.

In the nearby **Place Abbé Desnoyers** is Diane de Poitiers' former home, the Renaissance **Hôtel Cabu**, now the Museum of History and Archaeology. Among its treasures is some superb Celtic bronze sculpture, including human and animal statuary, from a pagan temple site at Neuvy-en- Sullias.

Parallel with Rue Jeanne d'Arc is the **Rue d'Escures** with its 17th-century mansions, ending in the little **public garden** behind the Renaissance Hôtel Groslot, now part of the town hall. The facade of the former Chapel of St-Jacques has been set up in one corner of the garden, the benches beneath its gothic stone arches a night-time rendezvous for lovers. It was amid the carved woodwork, tapestries and tooled leather of the Hôtel Groslot's salons that, in 1560, 16-year-old François II died after attending a meeting of the French Parliament, the Estates General, with his pretty young bride, Mary, Queen of Scots. As this suggests, the Place de l'Etape and its adjoining Place Ste-Croix, on to which the Hôtel Groslot faces, was once the city's centre

Opposite is the modern block of the present municipal offices. Round the corner, facing the north side of the cathedral, is the **Museum of Fine Art**, containing works by French and Italian masters, as well as more modern artists such as Gauguin, Boudin and Rouault.

Further along, in the Rue Dupanloup, is the former **Bishop's Palace**, now the public library with its formal garden flanking it. From here, you get one of the most attractive views of the cathedral and its lacelike flying buttresses.

ORLEANAIS

If, like most travellers, you enter the Orléanais from the upper Loire, this is the moment for mental adjustment. You are leaving an area where the challenge is to pack as many châteaux as possible into however many days you happen to have allowed yourself. You are entering one whose delights are of a different order: those of a landscape varying from cornfield, meadow and vineyard to forest or rolling downland.

Of course, the Orléanais has its châteaux too, but they are more separated, more modest in scale and ornamentation. Above all they are more at one with the half-timbered towns and villages in which they stand. They are altogether less importunate. The failure to inspect one or other of them need not leave you, after your return, with a nagging sense of an opportunity missed. You are free to abandon the tyranny of set itineraries and respond instead to the distant beckoning of turret or steeple.

There could be no better introduction to the area than **Meung-sur-Loire**. The 14th-century poet Jehan de Meung lived among its sloping and crooked streets when he penned his 18,000-line addition to the *Roman de la Rose*, which Geoffrey Chaucer so admired that he translated it into English.

To another poet Meung proved less hospitable. François Villon wrote his magnificent *Testament* in 1461 while under sentence of death here. The graceful, slender-towered château, former home of the bishops of Orléans, which served as Villon's prison, stands near the 13th-century abbey church of St-Liphard, amid horse chestnuts and grassy banks and can be visited during most of the year.

Across the river from Meung, the basilica of **Cléry St-André** is associated with the king to whose pardon Villon owed his life, Louis XI. Destroyed by the English in 1428 it was rebuilt by Louis in fulfilment of a vow to Notre-Dame de Cléry, whose interces-

sion he regarded as responsible for his victory over the enemy at Dieppe in 1443. Such was his attachment to the church that he chose it as the final resting place for himself and his queen in preference to the traditional royal tomb in the cathedral of St-Denis in Paris. The elaborate monument in the rather barn-like interior, which shows him kneeling at prayer and attended by cherubim, was said to have been designed according to his instructions and built under his personal supervision.

From Cléry the D951, which runs along the Loire's south bank, passes through the St-Marceau outskirts of Orléans to **Jargeau**, a little town clustered round its bridge, with tree-lined, riverside walks.

As her banner-flourishing statue in its square testifies, Jargeau was also the scene of one Joan of Arc's victories over the English invaders. Every June and October it becomes the meeting place for the Confrérie des Chevaliers du Goûte Andouille (roughly the Knights of the Tripe-Sausage Fanciers'

Society), a body which, as its name suggests, is not to be taken too seriously, despite the splendid red robes of its members.

Crossing to the north side of the river, over Jargeau's bridge, you will come to **St-Denis de l'Hôtel**. A leper colony in the Middle Ages, it is now a pleasant village with its 12th-century church built so close to the river that it looks in danger of toppling in. St-Denis was the home of the novelist and animal lover Maurice Genevoix, best known for *Raboliot*, the story of a poacher; there is a small exhibition devoted to the writer at the Maison Maurice Genevoix.

Further along the river's north bank is the town of **Châteauneuf-sur-Loire**, climbing through cobbled streets to its white château and its grounds. The building, despite the indisputably French bell-shaped roof on its single tower, resembles the summer palace of some princeling in a Russian novel. Now the property of the town, it houses a museum dedicated to the Loire's past as a maritime highway; the gardens

have become a public park with a lake, an arboretum and rhododendron walk.

Both St-Denis and Châteauneuf are in good walking country, surrounded by footpaths. You can get free maps from the Tourist Office in the Place Aristide Briand, just across the road from the château's main gate. In any case, either town is a good base for further exploration of an area rich in sights.

Among these is the 9th-century church of **Germigny-des-Prés**, south east of Châteauneuf. Its distinctly Mediterranean Greek cross form and its surrounding cypresses make it something of an incongruity in its present setting and, in fact, it was actually built by a Catalonian bishop of Orléans, St Theodulphus.

The southern feeling continues inside. Light is subtly diffused by alabaster panes in the windows of a lantern tower supported on robust, square, round-arched columns which give the appearance of an arcade. The cold stone expanses of the interior are dramatically relieved by the gold tesserae of a mag-

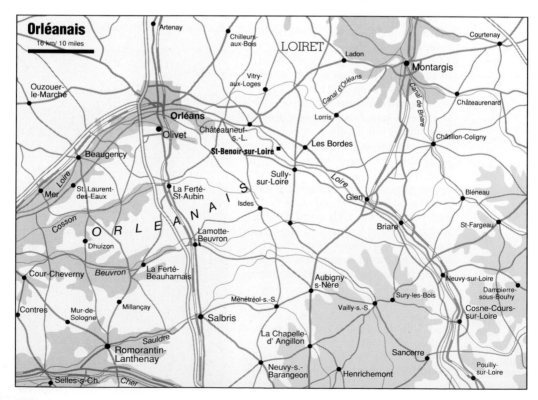

nificent mosaic over the east apse. The church's other treasures include a 16th-century carved wood *pietà* and a 12th-century reliquary in Limoges enamel.

More traditional in form is the abbey of **St-Benoît-sur-Loire**, resting place of Europe's patron saint, the 6th-century St Benedict, who now lies in its crypt. It has been called "a ship of stone" and, as one first sees it standing above the surrounding plain, there is certainly something reminiscent of a moored vessel about it. Unadorned, even stark lines emphasise both its proportions and such decorative details as have been incorporated. Notice the Biblical scenes, often touched with humour, ingeniously carved into the stone capitals of the porch colonnade and the charming little angels round the archway of the north door.

This classical simplicity is even more remarkable within. The high nave, supported on plain columns, is lit by unadorned windows in the clerestory. The only touch of colour comes from the multicoloured marble floor of the choir.

Notre-Dame de Cléry, misericord carving.

If St-Benoît is an outstanding example of ecclesiastical architecture, continuing south east from the abbey and recrossing the river at St-Père-sur-Loire will bring you to an equally impressive secular example. Ideally the great château of **Sully** should be seen twice: once by bright day and again by night when flood-lighting transforms it into a fairy-tale castle. Its early owners included the La Trémoîlles who were so opposed to Joan of Arc's influence on the king that they once held her a virtual prisoner here. In 1606 it was acquired by Henry IV's finance minister who had taken the title of Duc de Sully.

It was under his proprietorship that its conversion from fortress to mansion was undertaken. His embellishments, external and internal, are open to public view and include its tapestries, paintings and painted ceilings. Not all its original features have been lost, however; for example, the great keep's amazingly intricate medieval roof-timbering remains.

From Sully the D951 will take you to

Gien. If you have a spare moment or two take a look at the 12th-century church at **Lion-en-Sullias** with its *caquetoir*, or "gossiping place", outside the main porch.

Instead of going straight to Gien, by recrossing the bridge at Sully on to the D948 you can get to rose-red **Bellegarde**. (It can be also be reached from Châteauneuf on the N60.) The château, rising from what was once the moat but is now an ornamental lake, was home to Madame de Montespan, mistress of Louis XIV, whose involvement with the notorious witch, Madame Lavoisin, at one point threatened the monarchy.

Her son, the Duc d'Antin, was responsible for disguising its 14th-century origins by, among other additions, building the surrounding pavilions, one of which serves the little town as *mairie*.

You can continue your perambulations by taking the D44 to **Lorris** with its half-timbered houses and its oak-roofed, 16th-century market square. It was here that France's oldest legal code, in force until the 19th century, was drawn up and it was the birthplace of Guillaume de Lorris, who shared with Jehan de Meung the authorship of the Roman de la Rose. Among its sights is the organ, clinging spider-like midway up the wall of the nave of the 12th-century Church of St-Eloi.

On its outskirts a Museum of the Resistance and the Deportation, installed in the town's former railway station, has recently been opened. Lorris is also the home of the light, fruity but little-known Gris-Meunier wine.

From here either continue along the D44 to Gien or take the D961 going south, through the Forest of Orléans, turning left at Les Bordes on to the D952 which goes to Gien via Dampierre-en-Burly. Whatever route you take to it, **Gien** remains, as it has been for most of its history, an important Loire town— its Leather Fair is said to date from the 6th century. It is also another good strategic base from which to explore further into the lower Loire.

For the most attractive view of its plane-tree-sheltered walks, the houses, **Farm, St Fargeau.**

shops and cafés lining its river-front and its château on the rising ground behind them, approach, if possible, from the Loire's southern bank, crossing over by the 16th-century hump-back stone bridge. The château claims to be the first in the Loire valley, with an ancestry going back to Emperor Charlemagne in the 9th century. The present stone and red-brick building dates back to 1484 when it was erected on the orders of the ambitious and unscrupulous Anne of Beaujeu, eldest daughter of Louis XI and effective regent during the minority of her brother, Charles VIII.

Appropriately, with the Forest of Orléans, one of the richest game areas in France, nearby, it is now a hunting museum. Besides trophies of the chase, its great upper hall with its impressive wooden roof-structure contains 100 works by the leading painter of the subject, François Desportes.

The terraces, where Anne of Beaujeu must once have strolled as she hatched her plots, give commanding views of the river, especially spectacular when it is gilded by the setting sun. The town is also the centre for the manufacture of faience china. Both the factory and a faience museum can be visited.

The D952 continues downstream to Briare. From the road you can see the turrets of its 12th-century château of St-Brisson-sur-Loire across the river, but to reach it and the unspoilt village in which it stands you will have to make a detour as the only bridge after Gien is some miles on at Châtillon-sur-Loire.

Briare is the junction of a canal system started in the 17th century by Henri IV which, by linking the Loire with the Seine, the Saône and the Rhône, provided a flowing highway from the Channel to the Mediterranean.

It contains one curiosity to justify the vexation of trying to park amid its remorseless traffic. This is the late 19th-century **Briare Pont-Canal**, a 2,000-ft (610-metre) iron aqueduct over the Loire joining the Briare and Loire Lateral Canals. Its foundations were laid by the engineering company established by Gustave Eiffel of tower fame.

The French do it by bike.

Engineering marvel that it undoubtedly is, its Art Nouveau design is more appropriate to *fin-de-siècle* Paris than to an unassuming Loire country town. It remains in use by, among other vessels, a *bâteau mouche*, which not only conveys visitors along it and through the surrounding waters, but also tempts the hungry with a five-course meal.

From Briare, it is worth making a foray into the lovely countryside by turning north on to the N7. Its highlights include two châteaux. One is **La Bussière** with its angling museum and gardens by Jean Lenôtre, father of André, designer of Versailles, and the other the late classical **Pont Chevron** with a 2nd-century Roman mosaic in its park.

The town of **Châtillon-Coligny** is closely identified with French Protestantism and one of its leaders, Gaspard de Coligny. Its former Protestant College still stands in the Place Coligny. It was also the birthplace of the Nobel laureate Antoine-Henri Becquerel who has given his name to the unit of measurement of radiation.

From Châtillon the D93 (which changes to the D90) goes to St-Fargeau. If you take this road on a fine day stop at **Rogny les Sept Ecluses** to admire a feat of 17th-century engineering. The *sept écluses*, or seven locks, capable of raising a vessel over 100 ft (30 metres), came into service in 1642 and continued in use until 1887.

The heart of **St-Fargeau**, medieval capital of the Puisaye region, is its old town, entered through an archway in the 15th-century Tour de l'Horloge or clock-tower. It is dominated by its vast, squat pentagonal château, its round-bellied brick tower crowned by structures like miniature bandstands. Built about the same time as the clock-tower, like most châteaux it has been fundamentally changed over the centuries.

One of those primarily responsible was the Duchesse de Montpensier, who passed her time in this activity when banished here in 1652 for her part in the Fronde civil wars in which she twice took command of the rebel forces. Its magnificent grounds are the backdrop

Briare aqueduct.

to a spectacular re-enactment of scenes from history by a cast of 600 actors.

The château's immensity has reduced the rest of the old town to a fringe round it. It includes the town cemetery in whose rather derelict little chapel are a collection of 15th-century frescoes; these can be seen by borrowing the key from the Maison de la Puisaye, opposite the château's main entrance.

St-Fargeau is the gateway to several other places worth seeing. Not to be missed is Moutiers reached by taking the D85 from the town and turning off to the right at Moutiers' signpost.

Moutier is old French for a monastery and the hamlet, set among lakes and farmland, is centred round the 8th-century monastery of St-Pierre. In 1982, flakes of whitewash falling off its walls revealed a fresco in shades of brown and ochre beneath. As more and more of the whitewash was carefully removed it was found that the entire walls had been decorated with frescoes. Though restoration is still in progress, their age—some date back to the 12th century—

and their remarkable artistic quality has already attracted international interest.

Further along the D85 is the pretty hilltop town of **St-Sauveur-en-Puisaye**, birthplace of the novelist Gabrielle Colette (1873–1954) perhaps best known for *Gigi*, the basis of the highly successful musical. There is a museum dedicated to her in the town.

On the D955 from St-Sauveur, is **St-Amand-en-Puisaye**, which with its single main street and its tall trees rising above the roofline, is not unlike an English country town. It is also the leading centre for the satisfyingly rugged pottery made from *grés*, the local clay, which is on sale in at least half-a-dozen shops.

The road continues to **Cosne-sur-Loire**, where the anchors and cannons for the French navy were once produced. Remains of the royal foundry can be found in the Rue des Forges, a stone's throw from the chestnut tree-lined Allée des Marroniers beside the river. Cosne boasts three museums devoted, respectively, to local history and

Sancerre vineyards. _Following pages_: the Loire at Sully. Surveying the Loire from Amboise.

prehistory, the Loire and its past as a commercial highway, and to rural vitality down the ages.

From here the D955 goes to Sancerre, but a detour on to the D55 via Subligny takes you through rolling hills with villages and farmsteads towards **Jars** with its manor house and 15th-century church. From here take the D74, through Les Noyers, to **Château de Boucard**. Set back among fields at the end of a long avenue, it gives a feeling of life not always to be found among historic buildings—there is a farm in the grounds, for example—and it contains a fine collection of 17th-century furniture.

Daunting hill: From Boucard take the D85 to Menetou-Râtel and the D923 to **Sancerre**. The town should be explored on foot, leaving your car in the park below. The steep trudge up a hill which, on a hot day, can look almost vertical may be daunting, but is preferable to the hazards of negotiating and trying to find parking places in the constricted streets of the town.

Sancerre has a long and troubled history. It found itself in a strategic position during the Hundred Years' War. In 1573 it was a Huguenot stronghold which surrendered to the besieging Catholic forces only when, all supplies consumed, its citizens were reduced to eating leather and even powdered slate to keep themselves alive.

It is true that it is not a place of notable buildings. The 15th-century Tour de Fiefs, a landmark for miles round, is all that remains of the château of the Counts of Sancerre. Apart from this there is only the 16th-century tower which now serves as belfry for the church of Notre-Dame, but was formerly the tocsin or alarm bell.

Its charms lie in its character, its winding byways, its jumble of ancient red roofs above timbered gables, carved doorways and sculptured lintels. Because of its high elevation it also offers commanding views of the surrounding landscape with a motley of neat little vineyards where the Sancerre wine grapes are grown, and the Loire river winds off into the distance.

INSIGHT GUIDES
Travel Tips

FOR THOSE
WITH MORE THAN
A PASSING INTEREST
IN TIME...

Before you put your name down for a Patek Philippe watch *fig. 1,* there are a few basic things you might like to know, without knowing exactly whom to ask. In addressing such issues as accuracy, reliability and value for money, we would like to demonstrate why the watch we will make for you will be quite unlike any other watch currently produced.

"Punctuality", Louis XVIII was fond of saying, "is the politeness of kings."

We believe that in the matter of punctuality, we can rise to the occasion by making you a mechanical timepiece that will keep its rendezvous with the Gregorian calendar at the end of every century, omitting the leap-years in 2100, 2200 and 2300 and recording them in 2000 and 2400 *fig. 2.* Nevertheless, such a watch does need the occasional adjustment. Every 3333 years and 122 days you should remember to set it forward one day to the true time of the celestial clock. We suspect, however, that you are simply content to observe the politeness of kings. Be assured, therefore, that when you order your watch, we will be exploring for you the physical—if not the metaphysical— limits of precision.

Does everything have to depend on how much?

Consider, if you will, the motives of collectors who set record prices at auction to acquire a Patek Philippe. They may be paying for rarity, for looks or for micromechanical ingenuity. But we believe that behind each $500,000-plus

bid is the conviction that a Patek Philippe, even if 50 years old or older, can be expected to work perfectly for future generations.

In case your ambitions to own a Patek Philippe are somewhat discouraged by the scale of the sacrifice involved, may we hasten to point out that the watch we will make for you today will certainly be a technical improvement on the Pateks bought at auction? In keeping with our tradition of inventing new mechanical solutions for greater reliability and better time-keeping, we will bring to your watch innovations *fig. 3* inconceivable to our watchmakers who created the supreme wristwatches of 50 years ago *fig. 4.* At the same time, we will of course do our utmost to avoid placing undue strain on your financial resources.

Can it really be mine?

May we turn your thoughts to the day you take delivery of your watch? Sealed within its case is your watchmaker's tribute to the mysterious process of time. He has decorated each wheel with a chamfer carved into its hub and polished into a shining circle. Delicate ribbing flows over the plates and bridges of gold and rare alloys. Millimetric surfaces are bevelled and burnished to exactitudes measured in microns. Rubies are transformed into jewels that triumph over friction. And after many months—or even years—of work, your watchmaker stamps a small badge into the mainbridge of your watch. The Geneva Seal—the highest possible attestation of fine watchmaking *fig. 5.*

Looks that speak of inner grace *fig. 6.*

When you order your watch, you will no doubt like its outward appearance to reflect the harmony and elegance of the movement within. You may therefore find it helpful to know that we are uniquely able to cater for any special decorative needs you might like to express. For example, our engravers will delight in conjuring a subtle play of light and shadow on the gold case-back of one of our rare pocket-watches *fig. 7.* If you bring us your favourite picture, our enamellers will reproduce it in a brilliant miniature of hair-breadth detail *fig. 8.* The perfect execution of a double hob-nail pattern on the bezel of a wristwatch is the pride of our casemakers and the satisfaction of our designers, while our chainsmiths will weave for you a rich brocade in gold *figs. 9 & 10.* May we also recommend the artistry of our goldsmiths and the experience of our lapidaries in the selection and setting of the finest gemstones? *figs. 11 & 12.*

How to enjoy your watch before you own it.

As you will appreciate, the very nature of our watches imposes a limit on the number we can make available. (The four Calibre 89 time-pieces we are now making will take up to nine years to complete). We cannot therefore promise instant gratification, but while you look forward to the day on which you take delivery of your Patek Philippe *fig. 13,* you will have the pleasure of reflecting that time is a universal and everlasting commodity, freely available to be enjoyed by all.

Should you require information on any particular Patek Philippe watch, or even on watchmaking in general, we would be delighted to reply to your letter of enquiry. And if you send us

fig. 1: The classic face of Patek Philippe.

fig. 4: Complicated wristwatches circa 1930 (left) and 1990. The golden age of watchmaking will always be with us.

fig. 6: Your pleasure in owning a Patek Philippe is the purpose of those who made it for you.

fig. 9: Harmony of design is executed in a work of simplicity and perfection in a lady's Calatrava wristwatch.

fig. 5: The Geneva Seal is awarded only to watches which achieve the standards of horological purity laid down in the laws of Geneva. These rules define the supreme quality of watchmaking.

fig. 7: Arabesques come to life on a gold case-back.

fig. 10: The chainsmith's hands impart strength and delicacy to a tracery of gold.

fig. 2: One of the 33 complications of the Calibre 89 astronomical clock-watch is a satellite wheel that completes one revolution every 400 years.

fig. 11: Circles in gold: symbols of perfection in the making.

fig. 3: Recognized as the most advanced mechanical regulating device to date, Patek Philippe's Gyromax balance wheel demonstrates the equivalence of simplicity and precision.

fig. 8: An artist working six hours a day takes about four months to complete a miniature in enamel on the case of a pocket-watch.

fig. 12: The test of a master lapidary is his ability to express the splendour of precious gemstones.

PATEK PHILIPPE
GENEVE

fig. 13: The discreet sign of those who value their time.

Reality check. Call home.

—— *AT&T USADirect® and World Connect®. The fast, easy way to call most anywhere.* ——

Take out AT&T Calling Card or your local calling card.** Lift phone. Dial AT&T Access Number for country you're calling from. Connect to English-speaking operator or voice prompt. Reach the States or over 200 countries. Talk. Say goodbye. Hang up. Resume vacation.

Austria*†††.....................022-903-011	Luxembourg...........................0-800-0111	**Turkey***............................00-800-12277
Belgium*.........................0-800-100-10	**Netherlands***..................06-022-9111	**United Kingdom**.............0500-89-0011
Czech Republic*.............00-420-00101	Norway................................800-190-11	
Denmark............................8001-0010	**Poland**†♦¹....................0◊010-480-0111	
Finland...........................9800-100-10	**Portugal**†........................05017-1-288	
France....................................19-0011	**Romania***.......................01-800-4288	
Germany............................0130-0010	**Russia***†**(Moscow)**...............155-5042	
Greece*...........................00-800-1311	**Slovak Rep.***...................00-420-00101	
Hungary*.......................00◊-800-01111	**Spain**♦.............................900-99-00-11	
Ireland...........................1-800-550-000	**Sweden**...........................020-795-611	
Italy*....................................172-1011	**Switzerland***........................155-00-11	

AT&T
Your True Choice

**You can also call collect or use most U.S. local calling cards. Countries in bold face permit country-to-country calling in addition to calls to the U.S. World Connect® prices consist of USADirect® rates plus an additional charge based on the country you are calling. Collect calling available to the U.S. only. *Public phones require deposit of coin or phone card. †May not be available from every phone. †††Public phones require local coin payment during call. ♦Not available from public phones. ◊Await second dial tone. ¹Dial 010-480-0111 from major Warsaw hotels. ♦Calling available to most European countries. ©1995 AT&T.

For a free wallet sized card of all AT&T Access Numbers, call: 1-800-241-5555.

Getting Acquainted

The Place

Area: 32,000 sq. km/12,350 sq. miles (Pays de la Loire)
Language: French
Religion: Roman Catholic (90 percent)
Time zone: one hour behind Greenwich Mean Time (GMT) for most of the year.
Currency: French franc (FRF)
Weights and measures: metric
Electricity: 220/230 volts and 50 cycles. (110 volts in some areas).
International dialling code: (33)

From its source, way down in the Ardèche, the Loire, at well over 620 miles (1,000 km), is the longest river in France. The region known as the Loire Valley is a lush fertile plain, frequently referred to as "the Garden of France". It forms a natural divide between northern and southern France.

Important though it is (although no longer commercially viable), the Loire is by no means the region's only waterway. Other rivers – for example, the Cher, Indre, Vienne, Mayenne and Loir – also contribute much to the landscape, and it is perhaps not surprising that the area is prone to flooding. Lacking mountains and other geographical extremes, a striking feature of the countryside is the chalk cliffs which flank the river in places, most commonly in the west of the region. Even more unusual is the fact that many of these cliffs were (and in some cases still are) used for dwellings and storehouses. They also provide an ideal atmosphere for the cultivation of mushrooms.

Climate

North of the Loire, the climate is much the same as in southern England, but once past the river the temperature rapidly heats up. The region itself enjoys mild weather which helps to attract visitors practically all year round. In spring and autumn the average temperatures are around 17° C (60° F), which can climb as high as 26° C (80° F) in July and August. Late autumn and winter bring frequent fog and mists.

The Economy

While traditional agriculture still flourishes in the region – flowers and mushrooms are notable products, and wine is very important – Maine-et-Loire (Anjou) has now become the second most industrially developed county in western France, with electronics, textiles, pharmaceuticals, car parts and perfume being the main businesses.

Some famous names are to be encountered in the region – the Poulain chocolate factory is based in Blois and Cointreau, the liqueur makers, are in Angers where, incidentally, they have a museum. Because of the region's proximity to Paris and its central position geographically in the country, it has benefited from companies that have chosen to relocate their headquarters outside the capital; Thomson, Cibié, Bull and Motorola are all based here. Another very important contributor to the wealth of the area is, naturally, the ever increasing number of tourists.

Government

For years the French put up with a very centralised form of government, but under the Socialists (1981–86) the Paris-appointed *préfets* lost much of their authority as the individual *départements* (or counties) gained their own directly elected assemblies for the first time, giving them far more financial and administrative autonomy. Each *département* still has a *préfet*, but the role is now much more advisory. The *préfecture* is based in the county town of each *département*: Bourges in the Cher, Tours in Indre-et-Loire, Blois in Loir-et-Cher, Orléans in Loiret and Angers in Maine-et-Loire. These offices handle most matters concerned with the social welfare of their citizens.

Each French *département* has a number which is used as a handy reference for administrative purposes; for example, it forms the first two digits of the postcode in any address and the last two figures on vehicle licence plates. The *département* numbers for the Loire Valley are as follows: Cher–18, Indre-et-Loire–37, Loir-et-Cher–41, Loiret–45, Maine-et-Loire–49.

Each *département* is divided into a number of disparately sized communes whose district councils control a town, village or group of villages under the direction of the local mayor. Communes are now responsible for most local planning and environmental matters. Decisions relating to tourism and culture are mostly dealt with at regional level, while the state still controls education, the health service and security.

Planning the Trip

What to Bring

Maps

A first essential in touring any part of France is a good map. The *Institute Géographique National* is the French equivalent of the *British Ordnance Survey* and their maps are excellent; those covering the Loire Valley are listed below:

Red Series (1:250,000, 1 cm to 2.5 km) sheet 106 covers the whole region at a good scale for touring.

Green Series (1:100,000, 1 cm to 1 km) are more detailed, corresponding roughly to individual *départements* – sheet numbers 25 and 26 cover most of the region.

Also available are the highly detailed 1:50,000 and 1:25,000 scales. The Michelin regional maps are published at a scale of 1:200,000 (1 cm to 2 km). The whole region is covered on three maps: sheet no. 232 for the western Loire, 237 and 238 for the centre and east, but there is also an excellent map, showing almost exactly the area covered in this guide, called *La Vallée des Rois* (Valley of the Kings). Michelin also publish town plans, as do Blay, but local tourist offices frequently give away town plans free of charge.

Stockists in London are Stanfords International Map Centre, 12–14 Long Acre, Covent Garden, London WC2.

Tel: 0171-836 1321; The Travel Bookshop, 13 Blenheim Crescent, London W11 2EE. Tel: 0171-229 5260; Travellers' Bookshop, 25 Cecil Court, London WC2N 4EZ. Tel: 0171-836 9132; and The European Bookshop, 5 Warwick Street, London W1R 5RA. Tel: 0171-734 5259.

World Leisure Marketing, 9 Downing Road, West Meadows Industrial Estate, Littleover, Derby DE21 6HA. Tel: 01332 343332, are the UK agents for IGN and offer a mail order service. To order from IGN's Blue Series tel: 01629 826262.

Compass Books, 32 Bertie Ward Way, Rash's Green, Dereham, Norfolk NR19 1TE. Tel: 01362-691623, offers a mail order service (7-day money-back guarantee) and carries a wide range of maps and guides for whole of France.

France House, Digbeth Street, Stow-on-the-Wold, Glos. GL54 1BN. Tel: 01451-870871; fax: 01451-830869, carries the most comprehensive stock of French publications in the UK.

In France, most good bookshops should have a range of maps, but they may cost less in hypermarkets or service stations. Motorway maps can often be picked up free of charge at rest areas.

Entry Regulations

All visitors to France require a valid passport and a visa (except nationals from EU countries, Andorra, Monaco and Switzerland. If in any doubt check with the French consulate in your country, as the situation may change from time to time. If you intend to stay in France for more than 90 days at any one time, then a carte de séjour must be obtained (again from the French consulate) – this also applies to EU members until restrictions are relaxed.

Customs

All personal effects may be imported into France without formality (including bicycles and sports equipment). It is forbidden to bring into the country any narcotics, pirated books, weapons and alcoholic liquors which do not conform to French legislation. Certain items (e.g. alcoholic drinks, tobacco, perfume) are limited as to the amount you may take in or out, and these amounts vary for those coming from countries in

the EU, other European countries or outside Europe. From 1 January 1993 customs barriers within Europe for alcoholic drinks and tobacco (bought and duty paid in France) practically ceased to exist, but for goods bought at duty-free shops on the ferry or aeroplane the old restrictions still apply. The current allowances are shown below (with on-board duty-free shop allowances in brackets), although these can be exceeded, provided proof is shown that the goods bought are for personal consumption (e.g. a family wedding, and not for resale). If in doubt, check with your local customs office (In the UK HM Customs and Excise, Dorset House, Stamford Street, London SE1 9NG. Tel: 0171-928 3344 or any Excise enquiry office.)

Customs allowances, for each person over 18 years of age:

10 litres (1 litre) of spirits or strong liqueurs, over 22 percent vol.

20 litres (2 litres) fortified wine.

90 litres (2 litres) wine (of which no more than 60 litres may be sparkling wine).

200 cigars (50 cigars); or 400 cigarillos (100 cigarillos); or 800 cigarettes (200 cigarettes).

Animal Quarantine

It is not advisable to take animals to France from the UK because of the six-months' quarantine required by the British authorities on your return. However, if you do wish to take a pet you need to have either a vaccination certificate for rabies, or a certificate to show that your country has been free of the disease for 3 years. No animal under 3 months of age may be taken into the country. For further information, contact the French consulate in your country.

Health

The International Association for Medical Assistance to Travelers (IAMAT) is a non profit-making organisation which anyone can join, free of charge (although a donation is requested). Benefits include a membership card, entitling the bearer to services at fixed IAMAT rates by participating physicians, and a Traveller Clinical Record, a passport-sized record completed by the member's own doctor prior to travel. A directory of English-speaking doctors

belonging to IAMAT and on call 24 hours a day, is published for members' use.

EU nationals should check before leaving for France that they qualify for subsidised treatment under the EU (most British nationals do: check with the Department of Health and acquire from them the form E111). The E111 does not cover the full cost of any treatment so you may find it worthwhile to take out private insurance too.

IAMAT offices:

US: 417 Center Street, Lewiston NY 14092. Tel: 716-754 4883.

Canada: 1287 St Claire Ave, W Toronto, M6E 1B9. Tel: 416-652 0137; or 40 Regal Road, Guelph. Ontario N1K 1B5. Tel: 519-836 0102.

New Zealand: PO Box 5049, Christchurch 5.

Switzerland: 57 Voirets, 1212 Grand-Lancy, Geneva.

Money

The franc is divided into 100 centimes – a 5-centime piece being the smallest coin and the F500 note the highest denomination note.

Banks displaying the *Change* sign will change foreign currency and, in general, at the best rates (you will need to produce your passport in any transaction). If possible, avoid hotel or other Independent bureaux which may charge a high commission. Credit cards are widely accepted, but Visa is by far the most common and can now even be used in hypermarkets and some supermarkets. Access (MasterCard/Eurocard) and American Express are also accepted in some establishments. Eurocheques, used in conjunction with a cheque card, drawn directly on your own bank account, can be used just like a cheque in the UK and are commonly accepted. Apply for these, or if you prefer, travellers' cheques, from your own bank a couple of weeks before your departure.

Credit cards and cash cards from many European banks can also be used to withdraw cash from automated cashpoint machines outside banks, using a PIN number. Check the validity of your own cash card with your home bank prior to departure.

A list of major public holidays is given below. It is common practice, if a public holiday falls on a Thursday or Tuesday, for French businesses to *faire le pont* (literally "bridge the gap") and have the Friday or Monday as a holiday too. Details of closures should be posted outside banks, etc., a few days before the event but it is easy to be caught out, especially on Assumption Day in August, which is not a holiday in the UK.

New Year's Day (1 January); **Easter Monday** (but not Good Friday); **Labour Day** (Monday closest to 1 May); **Ascension Day**; **Whit Monday** (Pentecost); **Bastille Day** (14 July); **Assumption Day** (15 August); **All Saints' Day – Toussaint** (1 November); **Armistice Day** (11 November); **Christmas Day** (25 December), but not Boxing Day (26 December).

Getting There

Apart from its obvious cultural attractions, the Loire Valley is very popular with British visitors as it can easily be reached within a day's travelling.

By Air

Air France is the main agent for all flights to France, including those operated by the region's own airline, TAT, based in Tours. It operates a regular flight (Monday and Friday) from London (Gatwick) to Tours, as well as hotel and fly drive packages. Brit Air offers daily flights from Heathrow to Nantes as well as seasonal flights from Cork to Nantes; reservations can be made through Air France.

Although there are good scheduled services from the UK direct to the region, travellers from other countries need to travel via Paris, or London (which may well work out cheaper). Numerous companies offer flights to these two cities; Nouvelles Frontières offer some of the most competitive fares on both scheduled and charter flights to Paris and London from the US and Canada. Availability of charter flights is variable; details from their offices at:

London: 11 Blenheim Street, London W1Y 9LE. Tel: (0171) 629 7772.
New York: 125 West 55th Street, New York, NY 10019. Tel: (212) 247 0100.

Montreal: 800 Boulevard de Maisonneuve Est., Montreal, Quebec H2L 4M7. Tel: (514) 288 4800.

Students and young people can normally obtain discounted charter fares through specialist travel agencies in their own countries; in the UK try Campus Travel, 52 Grosvenor Gardens, London SW1W OAG. Tel: (0171) 730 3402 for your nearest branch. Campus is part of the international group USIT, whose main US address is the New York Student Centre, 895 Amsterdam Avenue, New York, NY 10025. Tel: (212) 663 5435. From Paris, there are regular flights to Nantes operated by France's internal airline, Air Inter. Reservations can be made through any office of Air France.

By Sea

There are several ferry services operating from the UK, Eire and the Channel Islands to France. All of them (apart from hydrofoil services) carry cars as well as foot passengers. The ports of Caen, St-Malo, Le Havre and Dieppe bring the motorist closest to the region.

Brittany Ferries: sails direct from Portsmouth and Cork (Ireland) to St-Malo. Alternative crossings are Portsmouth to Caen, to Roscoff, or, by its cheaper Les Routiers service, from Poole to Cherbourg (summer only). Details from The Brittany Centre, Wharf Road, Portsmouth PO2 8RU. Tel: (01705) 827701, or from Millbay Docks, Plymouth PLI 3EW. Tel: (01752) 221321.

P & O European Ferries: has services from Portsmouth to Le Havre and Cherbourg, and also operates the shorter sea routes from Dover to Calais. Fares and schedules from Channel House, Channel View Road, Dover CT17 9TJ. Tel: (01304) 203388.

Stena Sealink Line: its Newhaven – Dieppe service brings the motorist within easy reach of the Loire Valley, but the Dover to Calais route is quicker. Details and reservations of all services are available from Charter House, PO Box 121, Park Street, Ashford, Kent TN24 8EX. Tel: (01233) 647047 (reservations).

Hoverspeed operates hovercraft from Dover to Calais and Folkestone to Boulogne. Crossings take just 30–40 minutes. Details from: Hoverspeed Ltd., Marine Parade, Dover CT17 9TJ. Tel: (01304) 240241.

Irish Ferries: sails to Normandy with a year-round service from Rosslare to Le Havre and Cherbourg, and ferries in July and August, once a week, to Le Havre from Cork. Contact them at 2/4 Merrion Row, Dublin 2. Tel: 661 511.
Emeraude Lines: runs a ferry from Jersey in the Channel Islands to St-Malo, daily or twice daily in season, and less frequently the rest of the year. Information from Albert Quay, St Helier, Jersey, Cl. Tel: (01534) 74458; New Jetty, White Rock, St Peter Port, Guernsey, Cl. Tel: (01481) 711414; Gare Maritime du Naye, 35400 St-Malo. Tel: 99.40.48.40.

By Rail

For visitors travelling from Paris, the train is a fast, efficient way to reach the region, especially with the high-speed train (TGV) which has an average journey time of 42 minutes to Vendôme, 57 minutes to Tours and 90 minutes to Angers. All services leave from Paris-Montparnasse. Travel around the region by train is pretty good too. Car and bicycle hire is available at most main stations – as a package with your rail ticket if you prefer (details from French Railways, *see Useful Addresses*).

Tickets may be booked for through journeys from outside France. In the UK tickets can be booked from any British Rail station, including ferry travel. BR travel centres can supply details of continental services, or contact British Rail International Enquiries, International Rail Centre, Victoria Station, London SWI. Tel: 0171-834 2345. Students and young people under 26 can obtain a discount. Eurotrain, tel: 0171-730 3402, offers 30 percent off standard two-month return tickets for those under 26.

French Railways has opened a new telephone service, Rail Shop, in London to provide an instant booking service. The lines, however, are usually very busy and a little patience is required. A second Rail Shop is to be opened in Manchester. The service includes ferry bookings, discounted tickets for young people, a "Carte Vermeil" for senior citizens, which also gives a generous discount on tickets and Eurodomino rail passes (*see below*). Lines are open Monday–Friday and Saturday morning. Tel: 0891-515477 (providing information only) or

0171-495 4433 (reservations only).

Any rail ticket bought in France must be validated by using the orange automatic date-stamping machine at the entrance to the platform. Failure to do so incurs a surcharge.

RAIL PASSES

There are several rail-only and rail combination passes available to foreign visitors. These must always be bought before departing for France. In the UK a Eurodomino Pass offers unlimited rail travel on any 3, 5 or 10 days within a month. This can also be purchased in conjunction with an Air France-Rail ticket (see By Air).

Visitors from North America have a wider choice of passes, starting with the basic France Railpass which offers four or nine days' unlimited travel within a month. Then there are various types of Eurail Pass which offer varying periods of first-class travel throughout Europe; the Eurail Youthpass offers a similar deal for young people under 26. The France Rail 'n' Drive pass offers a flexible rail and car rental package, while the Fly Rail and Drive Pass combines internal flights on Air Inter with train travel and car hire.

Similar passes are available to travellers from other countries, although the names of the tickets and conditions may vary slightly.

SCNF has a central reservation office in Paris. Tel: (1) 45 65 60 60, and an information service in English tel: (1) 45 82 08 41, in French tel: (1) 45 82 50 50. The SNCF office in Paris is at 10 place de Budapest, 75436 Paris Cedex 09. Tel: (1) 42 85 60 00.

Most French railway stations accept payment by Visa and Amex.

CHANNEL TUNNEL

The long-awaited Channel Tunnel offers fast, frequent rail services between London (Waterloo), Lille (2 hours) and Paris – Gare du Nord (3 hours) – for connection to other destinations. Rail passenger services are operated by a consortium of the French, British and Belgian railway companies and tickets are bookable through French Railways or British Rail (see above).

Le Shuttle is the name for the service to take cars and their passengers from Folkestone to Calais on a simple drive-on-drive-off system, with a jour-

ney time of 35 minutes. Payment is at toll booths (which accept cash, cheques or credit cards). Prepaid tickets are available, but no booking is necessary as you just turn up and take the next available service. Le Shuttle runs 24 hours a day, all year round, with a service at least once an hour through the night. The toll-free motorway link between Rouen and Neufchâtel has been extended to Abbéville to make this a reasonable alternative for motorists to the longer ferry crossings.

By Bus

Eurolines European coach services operate a regular service to Tours (daily in summer) from London (Victoria). The ticket includes the ferry crossing (via Dover) and there are connections to London from most major towns in the UK. Discounts are available for young people and senior citizens. For details contact Eurolines UK, 52 Grosvenor Gardens, London SW1W OAV. Tel: (0171) 730 0202.

By Car

Angers is 124 miles (200 km) from St-Malo, and although there are no motorways down to the region, it is still an easy drive. If speed is not of the essence, follow the green holiday route signs to your destination – these form part of a national network of bison futé routes to avoid traffic congestion at peak periods. The first weekend in August is usually the worst time to travel, so avoid it if you can. For further details about driving in France, see Getting Around.

Travelling with Children

In France, children are generally treated as people, not just nuisances. It is pleasant to be able to take them into restaurants (even in the evening) without heads being turned in horror at the invasion. It has to be said, however, that French children, being accustomed to eating out from an early age, are on the whole well-behaved in restaurants, so it helps if one's own offspring are able to understand that they can't run wild.

Many restaurants offer a children's menu for around FF35; if not, they will often split an adult's menu between two children. If travelling with very

young children, you may find it practical to order nothing specific at all for them but just to request an extra plate and give them tasty morsels to try from your own dish. It is a good introduction to foreign food for them, without too much waste. French meals are generally generous enough (nouvelle cuisine excepted!) to allow you to do this without going hungry yourself, and you are unlikely to encounter any hostility from le patron (or la patronne). Another alternative is simply to order an omelette as a main course – even if it does not appear on the menu most chefs will happily oblige for children.

Most hotels have family rooms so children do not have to be separated from parents and a cot (lit bébé) can often be provided for a small supplement, although it is a good idea to check availability in advance.

In other respects, children are well provided for. Touring châteaux is not much fun for them until they develop an interest in history or art. However, many other pursuits are possible for an active holiday – see the Sports section for ideas.

It is fairly common for French children to take holidays away from their parents in colonies de vacances (holiday camps or villages). This type of holiday offers children a wide range of activities, including horseriding, water or other sports. The Gîtes de France organisation offers farm holidays for unaccompanied children; there are several in Loir-et-Cher (bookable through the Loisirs Accueil Service – see Useful Addresses) and also in Indre-et-Loire (bookable through Gîtes de France de Touraine, 38 Rue Augustin-Fresnel, BP 139, 37171 Chambray-lès-Tours). These are ideal for parents who want to have a touring holiday without a car full of bored children, but it is essential for children to have some knowledge of French so that they do not feel isolated.

Students & Young People

Students and young people under the age of 26 can benefit from cut-price travel to France and rail cards for getting around the region – for details see Getting There.

If you wish to have a prolonged stay in the region, it may be worth finding out about an exchange visit or study holiday. Several organisations exist to provide information or arrange such visits. In the UK, the Central Bureau for Educational Visits and Exchanges, Seymour Mews House, Seymour Mews, London WIH 9PE, produces three books; *Working Holidays* (although opportunities in the region are limited); *Home from Home* (a wealth of useful information about staying with a French family), and *Study Holidays* (details of language courses).

Organisations in the USA include the **Council on International Educational Exchange** (CIEE), 205 E. 42nd Street, New York, NY I00I7. Tel: 2I2 66I I4I4. A wide range of services, including travel; **American Council for International Studies Inc.**, I9 Bay State Road, Boston, Massachusetts 02215. Tel: 617 236 2051; and **Youth for Understanding International Exchange**, 3501 Newark Street, NW, Washington DC 20016. Tel: 202 966 6800.

Study Tours and Language Courses: there are several French tour operators which organise study tours in the region, and language courses. The first two are national organisations, the others based in the region.

Accueil des Jeunes en France: 119 Rue St. Martin, 75004 Paris. Tel: (1) 42.77.87.80; fax: (1) 40.27.08.71. Offers French study programmes, inexpensive accommodation (or with a family), and tours for individuals or groups.

Centre des Echanges Internationaux: 104 Rue de Vaugirard, 75006 Paris. Tel: (1) 45.49.26.25. Sporting and cultural holidays and educational tours for 15–30 year olds. Non-profit making organisation.

Institut d'Etudes Françaises de Touraine: 1 Rue de la Grandière, BP 2047, 37020 Tours Cedex. Tel: 47.05.76.83; fax: 47.20.48.98. Offers full-time and summer courses in the French language for all levels, with accommodation at the university or with local families. There is also an office in Chémery (Loir-et-Cher). Tel: 54.79.51.01; fax: 54.79.06.26.

The **Langue et Culture Françaises** association regulates quality in seven other centres in this region. For details write to them at BP 214, 37402 Amboise Cedex. Tel: 47.23.10.61; fax: 47.30.54.99.

Once in France, students will find a valid student identity card is useful in obtaining discounts on all sorts of activities, including admission to museums and galleries, cinemas, theatres, etc. If you do not happen to have your ID card with you, reductions may sometimes be allowed by proving your status with a passport.

The **Centre d'Information et Documentation de Jeunesse** (CIDJ), based at 101 Quai Branly, 75015 Paris. Tel: (1) 45.67.35.85, is a national organisation which disseminates information pertaining to youth and student activities. It also has an office in Nantes which handles enquiries for Maine-et-Loire, at 28 Rue du Calvaire, 44000 Nantes. Tel: 40.48.68.25.

In Tours, an important university town, there are two or three bureaux which welcome and give advice to foreign students. These are:

Accueil aux Etudiants Etrangers: 1 Rue Grandière. Tel: 47.0548.93.

Stanford in France: Foyer Universitaire, 13 Rue Grandière. Tel: 47.05.63.55.

Service Universitaire des Etudiants Etrangers: 3 Rue des Tanneurs (Université François Rabelais). Tel: 47.36.66.00.

For individual holidays, the cheapest way to stay is generally under canvas, or in a hostel, but if communal living does not appeal, then there are plenty of one-star hotels where you can find very reasonably priced, simple rooms. *See Where to Stay.*

Travellers with Special Needs

Most less able travellers will be keen to book accommodation in advance rather than arriving "on spec". Most of the official list of hotels (available from the FGTO or the regional tourist office – *see Useful Addresses*) include a symbol to denote wheelchair access, but it is always advisable to check directly with the chosen hotel as to exactly what facilities are available. Balladins is a chain of newly-built, budget-priced hotels throughout France which all have at least one room designed for disabled guests and restaurants and all other public areas are accessible. For a complete list, contact Hotels Balladins, 20 rue du Pont des Halles, 94656 Rungis Cedex. Tel: (1)-49.78.24.61, fax: 46.87.68.60.

An information sheet aimed at disabled travellers is published by the French Government Tourist Office; for a copy, send an SAE. There is a guide, *Où Ferons Nous Etape?* (published in French only) which lists accommodation, throughout France, suitable for the disabled, including wheelchair users, but again if you have specific needs you would need to double check when booking. It is available (for FF40 by post) from the Association des Paralysés de France, Service Information, 17 Boulevard August Blanqui, 75013 Paris. Tel: (1) 40 78 69 00. This organisation may also be able to deal direct with specific enquiries and can provide addresses of their branches throughout France. The *Rousseau H Comme Handicapé* guide may also prove useful. It is available from Hachette bookshops or at SCOP, 4 Rue Gustave-Rouanet, 75018 Paris. Tel: (1) 42 52 97 00.

The Michelin *Red Guide France*, for hotels and their *Camping-Caravanning – France* both include symbols for disabled welcome.

The Royal Association for Disability and Rehabilitation (RADAR), 25 Mortimer Street, London WIN 8AB. Tel. 0171-637 5400, has some useful information for tourists, including a guide book, *Holidays and Travel Abroad*. This is a general country by country guide and provides information about France as a whole, including hotel chains offering suitable accommodation, and tour operators offering specialist holidays.

France's sister organisation to RADAR, the Comité National Français de Liaison pour la Réadaption des Handicapés (CNFLRH), is based at 38 Boulevard Raspail, 75007 Paris. Tel: (1) 45 48 90 13. It offers a good information service for visitors with special needs to France, although they do not have an specific information about the region itself.

The Holiday Care Service offers free information on travel, accommodation and counterpart associations in France. Send a large S.A.E. to them at 2 Old Bank Chambers, Station Road, Horley, Surrey RH6 9HW. Tel: 01293-774535; fax: 01293-784647; Minicom (for hearing impaired): 01293-776943.

For young people, the Centre d'Information et de Documentation Jeunesse, 101 Quai Branly, 75740

Paris Cedex 15 provides information on services for young less able travellers. It publishes *Vacances pour Personnes Handicapées* and annual leaflets on acitivity and sports holidays for young disabled people. Parents may also find the following organisation helpful: Union Nationale des Associations de Parents d'enfants Inadaptés (UNAPEI), 15 Rue Coysevox, 75018 Paris. Tel: (1) 42 63 84 33.

The Comité de Liaison pour le transport des personnes handicapées, Conseil National des Transports, 34 avenue Marceau, 75009 Paris publishes a booklet called *Guide des Transport à l'usage des Personnes à Mobilité Réduite*. This gives brief information on the accessibility and arrangements for less able passengers on all forms of public transport and contacts for special transport schemes throughout France.

Some concessionary ferry fares are available for members of the following organisations: The Disabled Driver's Association, Ashwellthorpe, Norwich NR16 16X. Tel: 01508-41449; Disabled Driver's Motor Club, Cottingham Way, Thrapston, Northants NN14 4PL. Tel: 01832-734724; and the Disabled Motorist's Federation, Unit 2a Atcham Estate, Shrewsbury SY4 4UG. Tel: 01743-761889.

In the US, the following organisations offer services to disabled travellers:

Travel Information Service, Moss Rehabilitation Hospital, 1200 West Tabor Road., Philadelphia, PA 19141-3099. Tel: 215-456 0600 – has general information for would-be travellers.

Society for the Advancement of Travel for the Handicapped (SATH), 26 Court Street, Brooklyn, New York 11242. Tel: 718-858 5483 – offers advice and assistance in travel matters.

Accessible Journeys, 35 W Sellers Avenue, Ridley Park, Philadelphia, 19078-2113 – offers tours using wheelchair accessible transport in Europe.

In Canada the following organisation may be of help:

Canadian Rehabilitation Council for the Disabled, 45 Sheppard Avenue E, Toronto, Ontario, M2N 5W9. Tel: 416-250 7490 – national organisation producing some material relating to travel.

Air France: 177 Piccadilly, London W1. Tel: (017I) 750 4306.
• 29–30 Dawson Street, Dublin 2. Tel: (I) 77-8272; reservations (1) 77-8899.
Consulat Général de France: 21 Cromwell Road, London SW7 2DQ. Tel: (0171) 838 2000; fax: (0171) 838 2001; visa section, 6A Cromwell Place, London SW7. Tel: (0171) 838 2050; fax: (0171) 838 2046.
French Government Tourist Office (Maison de la France): 178 Piccadilly, London W1V 9DB. Tel: (0891) 4244123.
French Railways (SNCF) Rail Shop, 179 Piccadilly, London W1V OBA. Tel: (0171) 495 4433 (reservations); (0891) 515 477 (information).

USA & Canada

Air France: 666 Fifth Avenue, New York, NY 10019. Tel: (212) 315 1122.
• 850I Wilshire Boulevard, Beverly Hills, Los Angeles, CA. Tel: (213) 688 9220
• 979 Ouest Boulevard de Maisonneuve, Montreal. Tel: (514) 284 2825.
• I5I Bloor Street West, Suite 600, Toronto, Ontario. Tel: (416) 922 3344.
French Government Tourist Office (Maison de la France): 610 Fifth Avenue, Suite 222, New York, NY 10020-2452. Tel: (212) 757 1125; fax (212) 247 6468.
• 9454 Wilshire Boulevard, Beverley Hills, Los Angeles CA 90212-2967. Tel: (310) 271 7838.
• 645 North Michigan Avenue, Suite 630, Chicago, Illinois 60611 -2836. Tel: (312) 337 6301.
• 1981 McGill College, Tour Esso, Suite 490, Montreal H3A 3W9, Quebec. Tel: (514) 288 4264.
• 30 Patrick Street, Suite 700, Toronto M5T 3A3, Ontario. Tel: (416) 593 4723.

For information on railways, contact the following offices:

In the US: Raileurope Inc. at the following locations: 226-230 Westchester Ave, White Plains, NY 10604; 360 Post Street, San Francisco, CA 94102. Tel: 415-982 1993; 100 Wilshire Boulevard, Santa Monica, CA 90401. Tel: 213-451 5150; 11 E Adams Street, Chicago, IL 60603. Tel: 312-427 8691; 800 Corporate Drive, Suite

108, Fort Lauderdale, FL 33334. Tel: 305-776 2729; 6060 N Central Expressway, Suite 220, Dallas, TX 75206. Tel: 214-691 5573.
In Canada: Raileurope Inc: 2087 Dundas East, Suite 100, Mississauga, Ontario L4X IM2. Tel: 416-602 4195; 643 Notre Dame Ouest, Suite 200, Montréal, Quebec H3C 1HB. Tel: 514-392 1311; 409 Granville St, Suite 452, Vancouver, BC V6C IT2.
In Australia and **New Zealand** details are available from Thomas Cook offices.

For tourist offices and other useful addresses in France *see Practical Tips*.

Practical Tips

Business Hours

Office workers normally start early – 8.30am is not uncommon – but often stay at their desks until 6pm or later. This is partly to make up for the long lunch hours (from noon or 12.30 for two hours) which are still traditional in banks, shops and other public offices. Many companies, though, are beginning to change to shorter lunchbreaks as employees appreciate the advantages of getting home to families earlier in the evening.

Tipping

Most restaurant bills will include a service charge, but if in doubt ask – "*Le service, est-il compris?*" In any case, it is common to leave a small additional tip for the waiter, if service has been good. Please remember to address waiters as *Monsieur* never *garçon* and waitresses as *Mademoiselle* or *Madame* (according to age). It is usual to tip taxi drivers 10 percent of the fare.

Weights & Measures

The metric system is used in France for all weights and measures, although you may encounter old-fashioned terms such as *livre* (roughly one pound weight – 500 grams) still used by small shop-keepers.

For quick and easy conversion remember that 1 inch is roughly 2.5 cm, 1 metre roughly equivalent to a yard, 4 oz is just over 100 gm and a kilogramme is just over 2 lb. As a kilometre is five-eighths of a mile, a handy reckoning whilst travelling is to remember that 80 km = 50 miles, thus 40 km = 25 miles. Accurate conversions are given below:

Weight: 100 grammes (gm) = 3.5 oz; 500 grammes = 1.1 lb; 1 kilogramme (kg) = 2.2 lb.

Length: 1 centimetre (cm) = 0.39 in; 1 metre (m) = 1.094 yards; 1 kilometre (km) = 0.62 mile.

Liquid: 1 litre (l) = 2.113 pints; 1 litre = 0.22 Imp gallon or 0.26 US gallon; 10 litres = 2.2 Imp gallons or 2.6 US gallons.

Temperature: temperatures are always given in Celsius (Centigrade). For conversion to Fahrenheit: 0° C = 32° F; 10° C = 50° F; 15° C = 59° F; 20° C = 68° F; 25° C = 77° F; 30° C = 86° F.

Doing Business

Business travel is now such an important part of the tourist economy that the French Government Tourist Office in London and Chicago (see Useful Addresses) has a department set up just to deal with business enquiries. They will help organise hotels, conference centres and incentive deals for any group, large or small. The Loire is a very attractive area for British executives – easy to get to and now with a growing industry in luxurious châteaux vying for the conference trade, Blois, Chambord and Amboise are just three which offer facilities. The Relais et Châteaux chain of hotels includes some of the best in the region for luxury business travel. Its handbook is available from the French Tourist office.

On a more mundane level, several hotel chains have offices in the UK which will take bookings. These hotels are usually modern, and do not have the charm of a little family-run *auberge*, but they are practical from a business point of view, normally being situated on or near motorways or business centres. A selection follows:
Ibis/Arcade: Shortlands, Hammer-

smith, London W6 8DR. Tel: (0171) 724 1000; fax: (0181) 748 9116.
Inter-Hotels, Voyages Vacances Int., 34 Savile Row, London W1X 1AG. Tel: (0171) 287 3231; fax: (0171) 434 1870.
Mapôtel, Best Western Hotels: Vine House, 143 London Road, Kingston-upon-Thames KT2 6NA. Tel: (0181) 541 0050; fax: (0181) 546 1638.

Apart from tourist offices, the best source of business information and local assistance is provided by the Chambres de Commerce et d'Industrie in the individual départements. Here you can obtain information about local companies, assistance with the technicalities of export and import, interpretation/translation agencies and conference centres – indeed, most chambers of commerce have conference facilities of some kind themselves. Angers has developed business tourism to the extent of providing a "Welcome in Anjou" service for business travellers in the county and the town's new Centre de Congrès offers excellent conference facilities.

The region's Chambres de Commerce et d'Industrie are located at the following addresses:
Cher: Route Issoudun, 18000 Bourges. Tel: 48.50.48.08.
Indre: 24 Place Gambetta, 36000 Châteauroux. Tel: 54.27.01.16.
Indre-et-Loire: 4 bis Rue Jules Favre, 37000 Tours. Tel: 47.66.61.11.
Loir-et-Cher: 16 Rue Vallée Maillard, 41000 Blois. Tel: 54.44.64.00.
Loiret: 23 Place Martroi, 45000 Orléans. Tel: 38.53.24.24.
Maine-et-Loire: 8 Boulevard Roi Réné, 49000 Angers. Tel: 41.88.23.11.

There is also a French Chamber of Commerce in London (Tel: (0171) 225 5250) which exists to promote business between the two countries, and at the same address is French Trade Exhibitions, 2nd floor, Knightsbridge House, 197 Knightsbridge, London SW7 1RB. Tel: (0171) 225 5566.

Media

Newspapers

Regional newspapers, containing national and international as well as local news, have a far higher standing in France than in the UK and are often read in preference to the national dai-

lies such as *Le Monde*, *Libération* and *Le Figaro*. In fact, the Loire's major regional daily, *Ouest-France*, has the largest circulation of any in France. English-language papers, notably *The Times* and the *International Herald Tribune*, are available in the larger towns and cities of the region.

Television

Television viewers in the region can receive the two main national channels, TF1 (commercial) and Antenne 2 (state-owned but largely financed by advertising), as well as FR3 which offers regional programmes. French houses are also beginning to be defaced by satellite dishes at about the same rate as their British counterparts.

Radio

France Inter is the main national radio station (l892m long wave); it broadcasts English-language news twice a day in summer (generally 9am and 4pm). BBC Radio Four and World Radio can also sometimes be picked up in the region.

Postal Services

Post Offices – Postes or PTTS (pronounced *pay-tay-tay*) – are generally open Monday –Friday 9am–12 noon; 2 –5pm and Saturday 9am–12 noon (opening hours are posted outside). Inside major post offices, individual counters are marked for different requirements – if you just need stamps, go to the window marked *Timbres*. If you need to send an urgent letter overseas, ask for it to be sent *par exprès*, or through the Chronopost system which is faster, but very expensive.

Stamps are often available at tobacconists (*tabacs*) and other shops selling postcards and greetings cards. Letters within France and most of the EU go for F2.80 for up to 20gm, (F4.30 for airmail to Ireland, the USA and Canada). F5.10 for Australia.

Telegrams can be sent during post office hours or by telephone (24 hours); to send a telegram in English. Tel: (16-1) 42.33.21.11.

For a small fee, you can arrange for mail to be kept *poste restante* at any post office, addressed to Poste Restante, Poste Centrale (for main post office), then the town postcode and name, e.g. 45000 Orléans. A passport is required when collecting mail.

Many post offices have coin-in-slot photocopying machines.

Telex, the Minitel information service (useful for directory enquiries) and fax facilities are now available in the main post office in most major towns.

Telecommunications

The French telephone system is generally very efficient. That is not to say that you can be guaranteed to find telephone boxes (*cabine publiques*) that are always operational, but most are. Telephone numbers have been rationalised to 8 figures, given in sets of two, e.g. 99.44.63.21. The only codes necessary are for dialling into or out of Paris (put 16 before the rest of the number) or overseas.

International calls can be made from most public booths, but it is often easier to use a booth in a post office – you have to ask at the counter to use the phone, then go back to the counter to settle the bill; the only unnerving thing is that you do not have any record of how much you are spending whilst on the phone.

Coin-operated phones take most coins, and card phones, which display the Télécarte sign, are now so common and simple to use that it may well be worth purchasing a phone card (currently F40 or F96) if you are likely to need to use a public call box. Cards are available from post offices, railway stations, some cafés and *tabacs*.

If you use a phone (not a public call box) in a café, shop or restaurant you are likely to be surcharged. Some hotels and cafés now have computerised public telephones whereby the caller receives a printed statement of the details of the call on payment of the bill at the bar, a useful asset for people travelling on business.

To make an international call, lift the receiver, insert the money (if necessary), dial 19, wait for the tone to change, then dial the country code, followed by the number (omitting any initial 0).

International dialling codes:
Australia 61
Canada 1
Ireland 353

UK 44
USA 1

Useful numbers:
Operator services 13
Directory enquiries 12

Note that numbers will be given in pairs of figures, unless you ask for them to be given *chiffre par chiffre* (singly).

If using a US credit phone card, first dial the company's access number: Sprint. Tel: 19 00 87; AT&T. Tel: 19 00 11; MCI. Tel: 19 00 19.

Main post offices in France have now replaced their traditional telephone directories with the computerised Minitel system. Members of the public can use this free of charge to look up any number in the country. The instructions (albeit in French) are fairly simple to understand, and you simply tap in the name of the town, county and person (or company) whose number you seek for it to be displayed on the small screen, connected to the telephone. It can also be used in the same way as yellow pages to find, for example, all the dry cleaners listed in a particular town.

If you need to make a phone call in rural areas, or in small villages with no public phone, look out for the blue plaque saying *téléphone publique* on private houses. This means the owner is officially required to allow you to use the phone and charge the normal amount for the call.

You cannot reverse charges (call collect) within France but you can to countries which will accept such calls. Go through the operator and ask to make a PCV (*pay-say-vay*) call.

To take advantage of the cheapest rates, use the phone weekdays between 10.30pm and 8am, after 2pm on Saturday, and all day Sunday.

Tourist Information

Air France: 119 Champs Elysées, 75384 Paris, Cedex 08. Tel: 1-44.08.24.24; central reservation: Tel: 1-44.08.22.22.

Les Halles de la République: Place Mondain-Chalouineau, 49000 Angers. Tel: 41.87.60.79; 4 Rue de la Cerche, 45000 Orléans. Tel: 38.54.82.10; 8–10 Place de la Victoire, 37000 Tours. Tel: 47.37.54.54.

Maison de la France: 8 Avenue de l'Opéra, 75001 Paris. Tel: 1-42.96.10.23; fax: 1-42.86.08.94.

Comité Régional du Tourisme: 9 Rue St-Pierre-Lentin, 45041 Orléans Cedex, 1. Tel: 38.54.95.42; fax: 38.54.95.46.

Départmental tourist offices (Comité Départemental de Tourisme):

Cher: 5 Rue de Séraucourt, 18000 Bourges. Tel: 48.67.00.18; fax: 48.67.01.44.

Indre: 31 Rue Saint-Martin, BP 141, 36003 Châteauroux cedex. Tel: 54.22.91.20; fax: 54.22.31.21.

Loiret: 8 Rue d'Escures, 45000 Orléans. Tel: 38.54.83.83; fax: 38.77.04.12.

Loir-et-Cher: 5 Rue de la Voûte du Château, BP 149, 41005 Blois cedex. Tel: 54.78.55.50; fax: 54.74.81.79.

Indre-et-Loire: 9 Rue de Buffon, BP 3217, 37032 Tours cedex. Tel: 47.31.42.60; fax: 47.31.42.76.

Maine-et-Loire: Place Kennedy, BP 2147, 49021 Angers cedex 02. Tel: 41.23.51.51; fax: 41.88.36.77.

The **Service Loisirs-Accueil** is well organised in this region. It is a complementary service to the tourist offices and arranges bookings for gîtes and often activity holidays.

For information, write to the département concerned.

Cher: (as tourist office). Tel: 48.67.01.38; fax: 48.67.01.44.

Indre: (as tourist office).

Loiret: (as tourist office). Tel: 38.62.04.88; fax: 38.77.04.12.

Loir-et-Cher: (as tourist office).

Indre-et-Loire: 38 Rue Augustin-Fresnel, BP 139, 37171 Chambray-lès-Tours. Tel: 47.48.37.27; fax: 47.48.13.39.

Maine-et-Loire: (as tourist office).

Embassies & Consulates

In most cases, the nearest consular services are in Paris.

American Consulate: 2 Rue Saint-Florentin, 75001 Paris. Tel: (1) 42.96.14.88.

Australian Embassy: 4 Rue Jean-Rey, 75015 Paris. Tel: (1) 45.75.62.00.

British Consulate: 16 Rue d'Anjou, 75008 Paris. Tel: (1) 42.66.38.10 and in Nantes at L'Aumarière, 44220 Coueron. Tel: 40.63.16.02.

British Consulate: 35 Rue du Faubourg St Honoré, 75383 Paris. Tel: (1) 42.66.91.42.

Canadian Embassy: 35 Avenue Montaigne, 75008 Paris. Tel: (1) 44.43.29.00.

Irish Embassy: 12 Avenue Foch, 75116 Paris. Tel: (1) 45.00.20.87.

Emergencies

Security & Crime

Sensible precautions regarding personal possessions is all that should really be necessary when visiting France. Theft and other crime exists here as elsewhere but it is not a serious problem as far as tourists are concerned. Drivers should follow the rules of the road and always drive sensibly. Heavy on-the-spot fines are given for traffic offences, such as speeding, and drivers can be stopped and breathalysed during spot checks. Police are fairly visible on the main roads of France during the summer months.

To report a crime or loss of belongings, visit the local *gendarmerie* or *commisariat de police*. Telephone numbers are given at the front of local directories, or, in an emergency, dial 17. If you lose a passport, report first to the police, then to the nearest consulate (see Useful Addresses). If you have the misfortune to be detained by the police for any reason, ask to telephone the nearest consulate for a member of the staff to come to your assistance.

Medical Services

For minor ailments it may be worth consulting a pharmacy (recognisable by its green cross sign); these have wider "prescribing" powers than chemists in the UK or USA. They are also helpful in cases of snake or insect bites and identifying fungi!

If you need to see a doctor, expect to pay a fee for a simple consultation, plus a pharmacist's fee for whatever prescription is issued. The doctor will provide a *feuille des soins* which you need to keep to claim back the majority of the cost (around 75 percent) under the EU agreement. You have to attach to the *feuille* the little sticker (*vignette*) from any medicine prescribed to enable you to claim for that too. Refunds have to be obtained from the local *Caisse Primaire*.

In cases of medical emergency, either dial 15 for an ambulance or call the *Service d'Aide Médicale d'Urgence* (SAMU) which exists in most large towns and cities – numbers are given at the front of telephone directories.

The standard of treatment in French hospitals is generally high, and you should be able to find someone who speaks English to help you. Show the hospital doctor or authorities your E111 and you will be billed (once you are back home usually), for approximately 25 percent of the cost of treatment.

Getting Around

Public Transport

Bus and rail stations are often found together and details of routes and timetables are generally available free of charge. If you intend to travel extensively by train it may be worth obtaining a rail pass before leaving home (*see Getting There*). These tickets can be used on any journey, otherwise individual tickets need to be purchased, but check on any discounts available, e.g. the Carte Couple for married couples travelling together on off-peak services. Children under 4 travel free, from 4 to 12 for half-fare.

All tickets purchased at French stations have to be put through the orange machines at the stations to validate them before boarding the train. These are marked *compostez votre billet*.

Private Transport

A private car is probably the most convenient way of touring the Loire – you can stop exactly when and where you choose. Car hire, however, is very expensive, but bikes are fairly readily available. Most railway stations have them for hire at around F50 per day and they do not necessarily have to be returned to the same station. Bikes can be carried free of charge on buses and some trains (Autotrains); on other,

faster services you will have to pay. Travelling by a combination of bike and bus or train can be an excellent way of touring, and relieves you of some of the legwork.

Driving

Car hire is expensive if rentals are organised locally, but bikes (*vélos*) are fairly readily available for hire, often from cycle shops. Local tourist offices keep information on hire facilities. French Railways have them for hire at several stations in the region; they do not necessarily have to be returned to the same station. Bikes can be carried free of charge on buses and some trains (Autotrains), on other, faster services you will have to pay. Travelling by a combination of bike and bus or train can be an excellent way of touring, and relieves you of some of the legwork. For further information *see Sports & Leisure*.

British, US, Canadian and Australian licences are all valid in France and you should always carry your vehicle's registration document and valid insurance (third party is the absolute minimum, and a green card – available from your insurance company – is strongly recommended).

Additional insurance cover, which can include a get-you-home service, is offered by a number of organisations including the British and American Automobile Associations and Europ-Assistance, Sussex House, Perrymount Road, Haywards Heath RH16 1DN. Tel: 01444-442211; in the US Europ Assistance Worldwide Services Inc., 1133 15th Street, Suite 400, Washington DC 20005. Tel: 202-347 7113. The Automobile Club National is the umbrella organisation of France's 40-odd motoring clubs. They will assist any motorist whose own club has an agreement with it. Contact them at 9 rue Anatole-de-la-Forge, 75017 Paris. Tel: (1) 42 27 82 00, fax: (1) 40 53 90 52.

Rules of the Road

Britons must remember to always drive on the right: it doesn't take long to get used to, but extra care should be taken when crossing the carriageway, for instance, to use a service station. It is very easy to come out and automatically drive on the left – especially if there's no other traffic around.

The minimum age for driving in France is 18; foreigners are not permitted to drive on a provisional licence.

Full or dipped headlights must be used in poor visibility and at night; sidelights are not sufficient unless the car is stationary. Beams must be adjusted for right-hand drive vehicles, but yellow tints are not compulsory.

The use of seat belts (front and rear if fitted) and crash helmets for motorcyclists is compulsory. Children under 10 are not permitted to ride in the front seat unless fitted with a rear-facing safety seat, or if the car has no rear seat.

Priorité à la Droite: An important rule to remember is that priority on French roads is always given to vehicles approaching from the right, except where otherwise indicated. In practice, on main roads the major road will normally have priority, with traffic being halted on minor approach roads with one of the following signs:

Stop

Cedez le passage – give way

Vous n'avez pas la priorité – you do not have right of way

Passage protégé – no right of way

Particular care should be taken in towns, where you may wrongly assume you are on the major road, and in rural areas where there may not be any road markings (watch out for farm vehicles). Note that if a driver flashes the headlights it is to indicate that *he* has priority, not the other way round. Priority is always given to emergency services and also public utility vehicles e.g. gas, electricity and water companies.

The French recently changed the rules concerning roundabouts – in theory drivers already on the roundabout now have priority over those entering it, but beware; some drivers still insist that priority belongs to the drivers entering a roundabout.

Speed Limits

Speed limits are as follows, unless otherwise indicated: 80 mph (130 kph) on toll motorways; 68 mph (110 kph) on other motorways and dual carriageways; 56 mph (90 kph) on other roads except in towns where the limit is 30 mph (50 kph). There is also a *minimum* speed limit of 50 mph (80 kph) on the outside lane of motorways during daylight with good visibility and

on level ground. Speed limits are reduced in wet weather as follows: toll motorways: 68 mph (110 kph), dual carriageways: 62 mph 100 kph, other roads: 50 mph (80 kph).

On-the-spot fines can be levied for speeding; on toll roads, the time is printed on the ticket you take at your entry point and can thus be checked and a fine imposed on exit. Nearly all *autoroutes* (motorways) are toll roads. *Autoroutes* are designated "A" roads and national highways "N" roads. "D" roads are usually well maintained, while "C" or local roads, may not always be so.

Carry a red warning triangle to place 55 yards (50 metres) behind the car in case of a breakdown or accident (strongly advised, and compulsory if towing a caravan). In an accident or emergency, call the police (dial 17) or use the free emergency telephones (every 1 mile/2 km) on motorways. If another driver is involved, lock your car and go together to call the police. It is useful to carry an European Accident Statement Form (obtainable from your insurance company) which will simplify matters in the case of an accident.

Unleaded petrol (*essence sans plomb*) is now widely available in France. If in doubt, a map showing the location of filling stations is available from main tourist offices.

For information about current road conditions, telephone the Inter Service Route line on (1) 48 94 33 33 (this is a recorded anouncement in French and not always terribly clear).

Motorcycles & Mopeds

Rules of the road are largely the same as for car drivers. The minimum age for driving machines over 80cc is 18. GB plates must be shown and crash helmets are compulsory. Dipped headlights must be used at all times. Children under 14 years are not permitted to be carried as passengers.

Car Hire

As previously mentioned, hiring a car is an expensive business in France, partly because of the high VAT (TVA) rate – 33 percent on luxury items. Some fly/drive deals work out reasonably well if you're only going for a short visit – Air France for instance do a weekend fly/drive trip to Nantes. It can be

cheaper to arrange hire in the UK or USA before leaving for France. Offices of the major car hire companies are listed below:

Avis, central reservations office. Tel: (1) 46.09.92.12; fax: (1) 47.78.98.98. Avis has agencies in Blois, Bourges, Châteauroux, Orléans, Tours, Vendôme, Vierzon.

Budget, central reservations office. Tel: (1) 46.68.55.55. or toll-free: 05.10.00.01; fax: (1) 46.86.22.17. Budget has agencies in Bourges, Châteauroux, Montargis, Orléans, Tours, Vierzon.

Citer, central reservations office. Tel: (1) 44.38.61.61, or toll-free: 05.05.10.11. Citer has agencies in Blois, Bourges, Gien, Loches, Orléans, Tours, Vendôme.

Europcar, central reservations office. Tel: (1) 46.09.92.21; fax: (1) 49.10.55.00. Europcar has agencies in Blois, Bourges, Chartres, Châteauroux, Gien, Montargis, Orléans, Tours, Vendôme, Vierzon.

Hertz, central reservations office. Tel: (1) 30.45.65.65, or toll-free: 05.05.33.11; fax: (1) 47.48.51.51. Hertz has agencies in Blois, Bourges, Chartres, Châteauroux, Montargis, Orléans, Tours.

Routes

The beauty of touring the Loire by car is that it can be taken in very short stretches. It is often a matter of a few kilometres from one château to the next, and what is more, the French tourist authorities are very good at suggested tourist itineraries and provide maps and leaflets to help you. In the Loire Valley for instance you may choose to follow the route of the Valley of the Kings, which takes in all the major châteaux. Alternatively, you could try the Route des Plantagenêts whose influence on the region was considerable, or explore the Berry region, following the Jacques Coeur route. A more comprehensive list is given below; information is generally available from local tourist offices or from the other addresses shown here:

Route des Parcs et Jardins: covers Beauce, the Loire Valley and the Berry area exploring gardens dating from the Renaissance to the present day. Information: La Demeure Historique, 57 Quai de la Tournelle, 75005 Paris. Tel: (1) 43.29.02.86.

Route des Dames de Touraine: covers Indre-et-Loire, Loir-et-Cher and Indre, discovering the mark made on history by famous women of the region.

La Vallée des Rois: Loiret, Loir-et-Cher, Indre-et-Loire and continuing into western Loire, this route covers most of the grandest châteaux. Information from Château des Réaux, le Port-Boulet, Chouzé-sur-Loire, 37140 Bourgueil. Tel: 47.95.14.40.

A La Recherche des Plantagenêts en Touraine: follows the fortunes of the Plantagenets, taking in the famous châteaux of Amboise, Azay-les-Rideaux and Villandry along the way.

Route de la Vallée du Cher: follows the Cher Valley from Indre-et-Loire on into Auvergne. Information: Expoval, Maison des Produits de la Vallée du Cher, Saint-Georges-sur-Cher, 41400 Montrichard. Tel: 54.32.33.77.

Route François 1er Sologne-Berry: châteaux and other notable sites in Loiret, Loir-et-Cher, Indre and Cher. Information: Syndicat d'Initiative, Place de la Paix, 41200 Romorantin-Lanthenay. Tel: 54.76.43.89.

Route Jacques Coeur: a tour through Loiret and Cher, including the châteaux of Gien and Blancafort.

PILGRIMAGE ROUTES TO SANTIAGO DE COMPOSTELLA

Chemin de Paris: Paris; Orléans; St-Mesmin; Clery; Les-Trois-Cheminées; St-Laurent; St-Dier; Montbualt; Blois (cross from left to right bank); Chouzy; Onzain; Veuve; Le Haut-Chantier; Amboise; Montlouis; Tours; Montbazon; St-Catherine de Fierbois; St-Maure; Chatellerault: Poitou.

Chartres Route: Chartres; Pezou; Lisle; St-Ouen; Vendôme; Villiers-sur-Loir; Roches-l'Eveque; Montoire; Troo; St-Jacques des Guerets; Grange de Meslay; Abbaye de Marmoutier; St Cyr-sur-Loire; Plessis-les-Tours; Tours; Chambray-les-Tours.

Norman Route: Le Mans; Savigny; Fretay; d'Artins; Troo; St Jacques des Guerets; Montoire; Les Hermites; Tours (then as Chemin de Paris.)

Useful Addresses

Confraternity of St James (London): Chair Pat Quaile, 57 Leopold Road, London N2 8BG. (Advice and information on routes and different types of accommodation available).

La Société des Amis de St Jacques de Compostelle: 4 Sq. du Pont-de-Sèvres, 92100 Boulogne-sur-Seine, France.
Sankt Jakobsbusbruderschaft de Dusseldorf: West Germany.
Tours Tourist Office: leaflet entitled *Pelerinages Tourangeaux*.

Ramblers

The Loire Valley offers excellent opportunities for walkers, whether for a complete walking holiday, or just for a day's outing. There is a network of long-distance footpaths (*Sentiers de Grandes Randonnées* or GR) covering the whole of France; given enough time, you could follow the Loire from its source to the sea, along the GR3 or just the stretch from Orléans to Saumur which takes in most of the major châteaux over a distance of 155 miles (250 km).

The French Ramblers' Association, Fédération Française de la Randonnée Pédestre (FFRP), publishes Topoguides (guide books incorporating IGN 1:50,000 scale maps) to all France's footpaths but they are all in French. For information, contact the Centre d'Information Sentiers et Randonnées, 64 Rue Gergovie, 75014 Paris. Tel: (1) 45.45.31.02; fax: (1) 43.95.68.07. information is available in English.

However, there is a new publication from Robertston-McCarta's "Footpaths of Europe series": *Walks in the Loire Valley: Paris to Saumur*. This guide is a compilation of Topoguides of the region, translated into English, and includes information about accommodation along the way. All the above are available in the UK from McCarta (see Maps), or, in France, *Topoguides* are available from most good bookshops.

The Comité Region Centre pour la Randonnée Pédestre organises a variety of activities throughout the year: walks taking a day, a weekend or more, as well as special events, such as marathons. For more information write to them at BP 6002, 45060 Orléans, or contact the *départemental* tourist offices.

Walking holidays with accommodation either in hotels or under canvas can be booked through some of the Loisirs Accueil organisations run by the *départemental* tourist offices (see *Useful Addresses*).

Hitchhiking

With sensible precautions, hitch-hiking can be an interesting and inexpensive way to get around France. Would-be hitch-hikers may be discouraged by the difficulty of getting a lift out of the Channel ports, so it may be worth taking a bus or train for the first leg of your journey. Hitching is forbidden on motorways, but you can wait on slip roads or at toll booths.

Allostop Provoyah is a nationwide organisation which aims to connect hikers with drivers (you pay a registration fee and a contribution towards the petrol). Telephone numbers are: Paris. Tel: (1) 42.46.00.66; Nantes. Tel: 40.89.04.85.

Inland Waterways

There can be few more relaxing ways of exploring rural France than cruising at a snail's pace along its inland waterways. Despite its length, the Loire itself is notoriously difficult to navigate and many of its stretches are termed "Loire sauvage". Other rivers and canals are, however, very popular with amateur boaters and holidaymakers, in particular the Canal Latéral à la Loire, the Nivernais and Briare canals, the Maine, Sarthe and Loir.

Devotees of canal architecture will wish to incorporate the canal bridge at Briare into their trip. This remarkable edifice, whose foundations were laid by the engineer Eiffel's company, was built in 1896 to connect the Briare with the Loire lateral canal. A masterpiece of engineering, 664 metres long and now mainly used by pleasure boats, it was built to enable freight to be carried from the Channel to the Mediterranean.

Many companies hire fully equipped craft from early spring to late autumn. Some holidays can be booked through the local French tourist authorities; for the Berry region contact the Cher Loisirs Accueil office, for Anjou, the tourist office in Angers (see Useful Addresses). Some UK companies offer "package" holidays on inland waterways, a selection is listed below:
Blakes Holidays: Wroxham, Norwich, Norfolk NR12 8DH. Tel: (01603) 784131.
Crown Blue Line: 8 Ber Street, Norwich NR1 3EJ. Tel: (01603) 630513.

French Country Cruises: 54 High Street, Uppingham, Rutland LE15 9PZ. Tel: (01572) 821330.

Brittany Ferries: The Brittany Centre, Wharf Road, Portsmouth, Hants PO2 8RU. Tel: (01705) 827701.

Hoseasons Holidays Abroad: Sunway House, Lowestoft, Suffolk NR32 3LT. Tel: (01502) 50l50l.

Waterway Guides

These and other information are available from the Syndicat Interdépartementale du Bassin de la Maine, BP 2207, 49022 Angers, Tel. 41.88.99.38. There is also an excellent guide published in French/English by ECM, called *Navicarte de la Loire* (£11.95), which gives technical and navigation information, as well as mooring points, where to buy food, and tourist attractions on or near the waterway. The guide is available in the UK from Stanfords and other stockists (*see Maps*).

There now exists in France a national organisation whose sole aim is to develop and promote river tourism. The head office is the Maison de la France in Paris (see Useful Addresses), contact M Nicolas Lefevre-Zolotoff for information.

An alternative to a canal cruising holiday, but one less suited to families with young children, is to hire a canoe and either camp or stay in hotels. Holidays such as these are offered by the Loisirs Accueil services of the tourist authorities (see *Useful Addresses*). The regional tourist office in Orléans has produced a useful brochure for canoeists with details of routes, clubs and other information.

Where to Stay

Accommodation

Hotels are plentiful in the main towns of the region and along the main highways, but those tucked away in the smaller country villages can be the best. All hotels in France conform to national standards and carry star-ratings, set down by the Ministry of Tour-

ism, according to their degree of comfort and amenities. Prices (which are charged per room, rather than per person) range from as little as FF90 for a double room in an unclassified hotel (i.e. its standards are not sufficient to warrant a single star, but is likely to be clean, cheap and cheerful), to around FF400 for the cheapest double room in a 4-star luxury hotel.

Hotels are required to display their menus outside, and details of room prices should be visible either outside or in reception, as well as on the back of bedroom doors. It is possible for a hotel to have a 1-star rating, with a 2-star restaurant. This is ideal if you are on a budget and more interested in food than wallpaper or plumbing.

When booking a room you should normally be shown it before agreeing to take it; if it doesn't suit you, ask to be shown another (this may sound odd advice, but rooms can vary enormously within the same building). Prices are charged per room; supplements may be charged for an additional bed or a cot (*lit bébé*). You may be asked when booking if you wish to dine, particularly if the hotel is busy – though you are not obliged to take a meal along with the room, preference may in fact be given to hungry customers as there is not a lot of profit in letting rooms alone. Also the simple request, "*On peut dîner ici ce soir*?" will confirm that the hotel's restaurant is open (many are closed out of season on Sunday or Monday evenings).

Lists of hotels can be obtained from the French Government Tourist office in your country or from regional or local tourist offices in France. It is also worth buying from the Tourist Office in London the *Logis et Auberges de France* guide. This is an invaluable guide to an excellent and reasonably priced network of family-run hotels who aim to offer a friendly welcome and good local cuisine. The guide can be bought in bookshops in France but it is more expensive. It can be used to book hotels before travelling (for the central reservation office in Paris, tel: (1) 45 84 83 84); they also offer a "*Logis en Liberté*" or "Go as you please" service, whereby you can book several different hotels, participating in the scheme, for a flat rate. Some tourist offices will make hotel bookings for you, for a small fee.

Several other hotel chains and associations offer central booking facilities. These range from the very cheap and simple groups such as the Balladins chain of modest but very modern 1-star hotels, to the Concorde group of 4-star and de-luxe hotels.

A list of central booking offices follows, with UK and US contacts mentioned where available.

Altéa/Mercure, 7 Allée du Brévent, 91021 Evry Cedex Résinter. Tel: (1) 60 77 27 27, fax: (1) 60 77 21 08. UK office: Tel: 0181-741 4655, fax: 0181-748 3542. The Altéa group are also linked with Hotels Pullman, and between them they have several smart hotels in Normandy, including the Grand Hotel in Cabourg.

Balladins, 20 Rue du Pont-des-Halles, 94656 Rungis Cedex. Tel: (1) 46.87.51.93, fax: (1) 46 87.68.60. Budget-priced hotels.

Campanile, 31 Avenue Jean-Moulin, 77200 Torcy. Tel: (1) 64.62.46.46, fax: (1) 64 62 46 61. UK office: Red Lion Court, Alexandra Road, Hounslow TW3 1JS. Tel: 0181-569 6969, fax: 081-569 4888. Chain of mostly modern purpose built hotels.

Climat de France, 5 Avenue du Cap-Horn, ZAC de Courtaboeuf, BP 93, 91943 Les Ulis. Tel: (1) 64 46 01 23 or 05 11 22 11 (toll-free in France), fax: (1) 69 28 24 02. UK office: Voyages Vacances Int.; 34 Savile Row, London W1X 1AG. Tel: 0171-287 3181. Moderate to 4-star hotels.

Ibis/Arcade, 6–8 Rue du Bois-Griard, 91021 Evry cedex. Tel: (1) 60.77.27.27; fax: (1) 60 77 22 83. **UK office:** Resinter, 1 Shortlands, London W6 8DR. Tel: 0171-724 1000; fax: 0181-748 9116.

Minotels France Accueil, 163 avenue d'Italie, 75013 Paris. Tel: (1) 45 83 04 22; fax: (1) 45 86 49 82. **UK offices:** France Accueil Hotels, Westfield House, Bratton Road, Westbury, Wilts. BA13 3EP. Tel: 01373-824490; fax: 01373-825674. **Minotels Great Britain Ltd.,** 37 Springfield Road, Blackpool, FY1 1PZ. Tel: 01253-292000; fax: 01253-291111. **Canadian office:** Tours Chanteclerc, 65 Rue de Brésoles, Montréal, Québec H2Y 1V7. Tel: (514) 845 1236, fax: (514) 845 5794.

The following are hotel groups which do not have central booking facilities. Most of these groups offer something other than the average hotel. Each group produces its own brochure or list of hotels, available from the addresses below, but bookings have to be made with the individual establishments.

Formule 1, Immeuble le Descartes, 29 Promenade Michel-Simon, 93163 Noisy-le-Grand. Tel: (1) 48.15.12.13, fax: (1) 43 05 31 51. Budget-priced hotels, offering a booking service from one hotel to another in the chain.

Châteaux-Demeures de Tradition et Grandes Etapes de Vignobles, BP 40, 13360 Roquevaire. Tel: 42 04 41 97, fax: 42 72 83 81. Elegant hotels.

Relais et Châteaux, 9 Avenue Marceau, 75116 Paris. Tel: 47 23 41 42, fax: (1) 47 23 38 99. Independently-owned hotels and restaurants in former castles and many other historic buildings (guide available from French Government Tourist Offices abroad). UK information office: 7 Cork Street, London W1X 1PB. Tel: 0171-491 2516.

Les Relais du Silence, 2 Passage Duguesclin, 75015 Paris. Tel: (1) 45 66 77 77, fax: (1) 40 65 90 09. Two to 4-star hotels in particularly tranquil settings.

It is not possible to offer a comprehensive list of hotels for the whole region, for which we recommend the Michelin Red Guide. The following is just a small selection to suit all budgets. Star ratings are given thus P; CC means credit cards. Double room prices are given but should be taken as a rough guide only.

Hotels and restaurants are both included in the following listing: often one establishment combines both functions. Listing is according to region; regional châteaux with accommodation are listed first, followed by individual towns.

Chateaux d'Accueil: these are private homes with rooms for paying guests. The quality of the rooms, decor and comfort varies from château to château (as does the warmth of the hosts). But they can be a nice change from hotels, and in some the welcome is so warm that you really will feel like a house guest. They can be especially good for people travelling alone, as meals are usually taken around a big table with the other guests. However, if a romantic trip and a table for two is for you, you might opt for a hotel.

Hotel and restaurant closing days: double check on vacation closing times. Most of the hotels in the Loire tend to close for a while around Christmas, but the actual dates may change from year to year.

Le Loir

CHATEAUX D'ACCUEIL

• DISSAY-SOUS-COURCILLON
(39 km NW Tours)

Château de Courcillon. 72500 Château du Loir (5 km SE Dissay-Sous-Courcillon). Tel: 43.44.10.00. Credit cards: Visa. M et Mme Jaclard. Closing days: Sunday and Monday out of season, 1–20 February. One of the oldest châteaux in the Loire Valley; luxurious linen, spacious and comfortable. 9 rooms, some in tower wing, some in 19th-century wing: FF250–350, demi-pension FF330, breakfast FF40. Restaurant open to the public: menus FF75–165.

HOTELS & RESTAURANTS

• CHATEAU DU LOIR
(41 km La Flèche, 42 km Tours, 59 km Vendôme)

Hotel/Restaurants, Moderate/Good Value
Hôtel de la Gare. 170 Avenue J. Jaurès. Tel: 43.44.00.14; fax: 43.44.11.79. Credit Cards: Mastercard, Visa. Rooms: FF90–200, demi-pension FF125 –155. Restaurant: FF50–150. Closed Sundays, 20 August–4 September, 17 December–2 January.

BED & BREAKFAST

Dianne Legoff. 24 Place de l'Hotel de Ville. Tel: 43.44. 03.38. Clean and comfortable. Rooms: double FF130, family room FF160, breakfast FF20.

• LA FLECHE
(52 km NW Angers)

Hotel/Restaurants, Moderate/Good Value
Le Vert Galant. 70 Grande Rue. Tel: 43.94.00.51; fax: 43.45.11.24. Credit Cards: Mastercard, Visa. Rooms: FF140–190, demi-pension FF200 –270. Closed 20 December–9 January, restaurant closed Thursday. Restaurant: FF63–185.

Hotel, Moderate/Expensive
Le Relais Cicero. 18 Boulevard Alger. Tel: 43.94.14.14; fax: 43.45.98.96. Credit Cards: Mastercard, Visa. Quiet 17th-century house set back in private garden. Comfortable. No restaurant. Rooms: FF380–675. Closed 15 December–10 January and 10–25 February.

• MONTOIRE-SUR-LE-LOIRE
(19 km Vendôme, 83 km La Flèche)

Hotel/Restaurants, Moderate
Le Cheval Rouge. 1 Place Foche. Tel: 54.85.07.05; fax: 54.85.17.42. Credit Cards: Amex, Mastercard, Visa. Closed Tuesday night, Wednesday, 28 January–2 March. Rooms: FF52–180. Restaurant: Classic French cuisine, carte FF300, menus FF99 (weekdays only, FF140, FF173, FF240).

• TROO
(48 km NE Tours, 25 km Vendôme)

Restaurant, Moderate
Cheval Blanc. Rue A. Arnault. Tel: 54.72.58.22; fax: 54.72.55.44. Credit Cards: Mastercard, Visa. FF100–250. Closed Monday night, Tuesday, 15–31 October, 15–28 February.

North Anjou & Angers

CHATEAUX D'ACCUEIL

Château de Briottières. (25 km N Angers), 49330 Champigné. Tel: 41.42.00.02. Fax: 41.42.01.55. Credit cards: Amex, Mastercard, Visa. M. et Mme François de Valbray. Very warm welcome at a beautiful château; huge rooms with private baths, 18th-century furniture, 40 hectares of grounds. On the route from Normandy; convenient for travellers taking ferries to Normandy. Double rooms from FF500, breakfast FF40, table d'hôte FF250, by reservation.

Château du Plessis. (N of Angers off N162), La Jaille–Yvon, 49220 Le Lion d'Angers. Tel: 41.95.12.75. Fax: 41.95.14.41. Credit Cards: Mastercard, Visa. Closed 31 October–1 April. M. et Mme Paul Benoist. Rooms: FF620–770, table d'hôte FF190, breakfast FF35. Homely 16th-century family château with very warm welcome and English-speaking host.

HOTELS & RESTAURANTS

• ANGERS

(109 km W Tours, 45 km W Saumur)

Hotel/Restaurants, Moderate/Expensive

Hôtel Anjou. Restaurant Salamandre, 1 Boulevard Mar. Foch. Tel: 41.88.24.82; fax: 41.87.22.21. Credit Cards: Amex, Diners, Mastercard, Visa. Old hotel, recently restored and modernised. Large, well-equipped rooms. Rooms: FF265–420, demi-pension FF272–482. Closed (restaurant) Sunday. Restaurant: FF170–280.

Concorde. 18 Boulevard Mar. Foch. Tel: 41.87.37.20; fax: 41.87.49.54. Credit Cards: Amex, Diners, Mastercard, Visa. Large, modern hotel. Quiet and centrally located. Rooms: FF490–600, apartments FF650. Open all year round. Restaurant: Brasserie, carte FF110–185.

Hôtel Mercure. Place Mendès-France (Centre de Congrès), 49100 Angers. Tel: 41.60.34.81; fax: 41.60.57.84. Credit Cards: Amex, Diners, Mastercard, Visa. Modern building on the edge of a pretty garden. Bright, functional rooms. Rooms: FF500–600, apartments FF415. Restaurant: FF100–200.

Hôtel de France et Restaurant Plantagenêts. 8 Place Gare, 49100 Angers. Tel: 41.88.49.42; fax: 41.86.76.70. Credit cards: Amex, Diners, Mastercard, Visa. Efficient, comfortable with very helpful service; close to rail station and convenient for major sights. Rooms: FF340–600, demi-pension FF285. Restaurant: FF80–140. Closed (restaurant only) 21 December–6 January.

Altea Lac de Maine. (2 km W towards Nantes at Autoroute de Nantes exit). Tel: 41.48.02.12; fax: 41.48.57.51. Credit Cards: Amex, Diners, Mastercard, Visa. Rooms: FF400–500. Closed 25 December–7 January. Restaurant closed Sunday. Restaurant: FF80–140.

Hotel/Restaurants, Moderate/Good Value

Motel Ibis. Rue Poissonnérie, 49100 Angers. Tel: 41.86.15.15; fax: 41.87.10.41. Credit Cards: Mastercard, Visa. Rooms: FF310–350. Restaurant: FF80–150.

Fimotel. 23 bis Rue Bert, 49100 Angers. Tel: 41.88.10.10; fax: 41.88.85.46. Credit Cards: Amex, Diners, Mastercard, Visa. Rooms: FF280–300, demi-pension FF230 –250. Restaurant: FF65–100.

St Jacques. 83 Rue St-Jacques. Tel: 41.48.51.05. Credit Cards: Amex, Ec, Visa. Rooms: FF95–240, demi-pension FF115 –175. Restaurant: FF60–180. Closed (restaurant only) 16 August–12 September, Monday lunch, Sunday.

St Raphael. 13 Rue d'Esvière, 49100 Angers.Tel: 41.87. 55.58. Credit Cards: Amex, Diners, Visa. In a calm, quiet location with garden. Rooms: FF140–180. Restaurant: hotel guests only, dinner only: FF60. Closed Weekends and holidays.

Hotels, Moderate

Le Progrès. 26 Rue D. Papin. Tel: 41.88.10.14; fax: 41.8782.93. Credit Cards: Amex, Diners, Mastercard, Visa. Near rail station. Small bright rooms; those in back quiet. Rooms: FF280–350. Closed 20 December–5 January.

Saint-Julien. 9 Place du Ralliement. Tel: 41.88.41.62; fax: 41.20.95.19. Credit Cards: Mastercard, Visa. Large, sound-proofed rooms. Rooms: FF240–330.

Champagne. 34 Rue Papin. Tel: 41.88.78.06; fax: 41.87.03.94. Credit Cards: Amex, Diners, Mastercard, Visa. Rooms: FF170–280.

Europe. 3 Rue Château Gontier, 49100 Angers. Tel: 41.88.67.45; fax: 41.88.67.45. Credit Cards: Amex, Diners, Mastercard, Visa. Rooms: FF190–240.

Univers. 2 Place de la Gare. Tel: 41.88.43.58. Credit Cards: Amex, Diners, Mastercard, Visa. Rooms: FF145–240.

Hôtel du Mail. 8 Rue des Ursules. Tel: 41.88.56.22. Credit Cards: Diners, Mastercard, Visa. Small old grey house set in garden. Calm. Good value. Rooms: FF135–270.

Hôtel Royal. 8 bis Place Visitation, 49100 Angers. Tel: 41.88.30.25; fax: 41.81.05.75. Credit Cards: Diners, Mastercard, Visa. Rooms: FF95–180. Closed 22 December–2 January.

Roi René.16 Rue Marceau, 49100 Angers. Tel: 41.88. 88.62. Credit Cards: none. Rooms: FF145–245. Closed August.

Restaurants, Moderate/Expensive

Le Logis. 9 Place du Ralliement. Tel: 41.87.44.15. Credit Cards: Amex, Diners, Mastercard, Visa. Closed Saturday night and Sunday, 15 July –15 August. Michelin star, very good fish. Carte FF300, menus FF100, FF150, FF270.

Le Toussaint. 7 Place Kennedy, 49100 Angers. Tel: 41.87.46.20; fax: 41.87.96.64. Credit Cards: Amex, Dc, Mastercard, Visa. Closed Sunday night and Monday. Michelin star, good river fish from Loire, excellent wine list, Carte FF380–420, menus FF155, FF220.

Restaurants, Moderate/Good Value

L'Entrecôte. Avenue Joxe, 41900 Angers. Tel: 41.43. 71.77. Credit Cards: Visa. Closed Saturday and Sunday, 25 July–25 August. FF60–100.

• ST-SYLVAIN-D'ANJOU

(6 km NE Angers by Avenue Pasteur)

Hotel/Restaurants, Moderate/Expensive

Auberge d'Eventard. Route de Paris, N23, 49480 St-Sylvain-d'Anjou. Tel: 41.43.74.25. Credit Cards: Amex, Diners, Mastercard, Visa. Old rural auberge, with elegant restaurant. Rooms: FF110–270, apartments FF430, demi-pension FF275–350. Closed Sunday night and Monday, 2–23 January. Restaurant: carte FF300, menus FF150, FF220, FF275.

Hotel/Restaurants, Moderate

La Fauvelaie. Route du Parc-Expo. Tel: 41.43.80.10. Credit Cards: Visa. Formerly a farm on 3 hectares of pretty land. Calm. Rooms: FF110–220, demi-pension FF175–257.

Restaurant, Moderate/Good Value

Le Clafoutis. N23 La Lieue, 49480 St-Sylvain-d'Anjou. Tel: 41.43.84.71. Credit Cards: Amex, Mastercard, Visa. Closed Tuesday night, Sunday night and Wednesday, August and February school vacation. Good regional cuisine, nice atmosphere. Carte FF200–230, menus FF70 (weekdays only), FF110.

South Anjou & Saumur

CHATEAUX D'ACCUEIL

Château de Beaulieu. Route de Montsoreau, Saumur. Tel: 41.67.69.51. Comfortable manor house in Saumur, with very nice rooms. Rooms: FF500–700.

Château de Brissac. (18 km SE Angers), 49320 Brissac-Quince. Tel: 41.91.23.43/41.91.22.21. Very luxurious, enormous 16th-century château in beautiful grounds. Huge rooms, with Gobelin and Aubusson tapestries. Suites by arrangement: FF2,760, including candlelit dinner, breakfast, cocktails.

Château de la Jumellière. (30 km S Angers), 49120 La Jumellière. Tel: 41.64.33.01 or (1) 45.48.45.02. Prince et Princesse A.L. de Polignac. Closed 1 October–1 June. 5 rooms, 1 apartment, *table d'hôte* by reservation. House dates from 12th-century, renovated in 19th-century In beautiful grounds.

Le Domaine de Mestré. (12 km SE Saumur off D147), Mestré, 49590 Fontevraud. Tel: 41.51.75.87; fax: 41.51.71.90. M. et Mme Dauge. Farmhouse of the Abbaye de Fontevraud of the 13th and 18th centuries. 9 rooms, 1 suite. FF220 singles, FF365 doubles, FF470 triple, breakfast FF25, table d'hôte FF95. Demi-pension available.

HOTELS & RESTAURANTS

• CHENEHUTTE-LES-TUFFEAUX
(8 km NW Saumur by 161 and D751)

Hotel/Restaurants, Expensive
La Prieuré. Chenehutte-les-Tuffeaux, 49350 Gennes. Tel: 41.67.90.14; fax: 41.67.92.24. Credit Cards: Visa. Very pretty Relais et Châteaux, high above river with panoramic views and huge rooms. Simpler bungalows without views in the grounds; pool. Rooms: FF650–1500, apartments FF1,050 – 1,750, demi-pension FF625–1,150. Closed 5 December–3 January. Restaurant: high Gault & Millau rating; good fish. Carte FF350, menus FF200 (lunch only), FF275, FF340, FF390.

• CHOLET
(61 km SW Angers)

Hotel/Restaurants, Moderate
Fimotel. Avenue Sables-d'Olonne. Tel: 41.62.45.45; fax: 41.58.23.45. Credit Cards: Amex, Diners, Mastercard, Visa. Rooms: FF270–290. Restaurant: FF65–90. Open all year round.

Hôtel de l'Europe. 8 Place de la Gare. Tel: 41.62.00.97; fax: 41.71.86.31. Credit Cards: Amex, Diners, Mastercard, Visa. Rooms: FF230–280, demi-pension FF240. Restaurant: **James Barron**, 15 Place de la Gare. High Michelin rating, recent change in ownership. Carte FF300–350, menus FF95–360. Closed (restaurant) Saturday lunch and Friday.

Le Belvédère. (5 km SE by D20), lac de Ribou, 49300 Cholet. Tel: 41.62.14.02; Fax: 41.62.16.54. Credit Cards: Amex, Diners, Mastercard, Visa. In the country, nice views. Rooms: FF300–350. Closed Sunday, February school vacations, 23 July–22 August. Excellent restaurant with Michelin star. Restaurant: original modern French cooking; Japanese chef. Carte FF300, menus FF105 and FF185 (weekdays only), FF165 and FF215 (weekends and holidays only).

Campanile. Square de la Nouvelle-France, Parc de Carteron. Tel: 41.62.86.79; fax: 41.71.29.23. Credit Cards: Visa. Rooms: FF270, demi-pension FF322–344. Restaurant: FF70–100.

• FONTEVRAUD-L'ABBAYE
(16 km SE Saumur, 21 km W Chinon)

Hotel/Restaurants, Moderate
Hôtel Croix Blanche. 7 Place Plantaganêts. Tel: 41.51.71.11; fax: 41.38.15.38. Credit Cards: Mastercard, Visa. Small, family-run Logis. Rooms: FF285 for rooms overlooking garden. Closed 13–19 November, 8 January–7 February. Restaurant: FF51–142.

Restaurant, Expensive
La Licorne. Allée St Catherine. Tel: 41.51.72.49; fax: 41.51.70.40. Credit Cards: Amex, Mastercard, Visa. Excellent food: Michelin star. Closed Sunday night and Monday (except holidays), 28 August–3 September, end-January through February school vacations. Carte FF300, menu FF160.

Restaurant, Simple/Good Value
Auberge de l'Abbaye. 8 Avenue des Roches. Tel: 41.51.71.04. Credit Cards: Visa. Closed Tuesday night, Wednesday, 29 January–29 February, 2–27 October. Carte FF130, menus FF57 (weekdays only), FF63, FF103, FF110.

• GENNES
(15 km NW Saumur)

Hotel/Restaurants, Moderate
Aux Naulets d'Anjou. 18, Rue Crois-de-Mission. Tel: 41.51.81.88. Credit Cards: Mastercard, Visa. Modern friendly hotel. Rooms: FF200–260, demi-pension FF240–280. Closed 15 November–15 March; Restaurant closed Monday. Restaurant serves good French family cooking; menus FF80, FF120, FF160, FF210.

Hostellerie de la Loire. Avenue des Cadets du Saumur. Tel: 41.50.81.03; fax: 41.38.05.22. Credit Cards: none. Older hotel near river. Best rooms overlook garden. Rooms: FF150–320, demi-pension FF180–270. Restaurant: good family cooking; menus FF105, FF130, FF190. Closed Monday night and Tuesday except holidays, 28 December–10 February.

• MONTREUIL-BELLAY
(16 km S Saumur)

Hotel/Restaurants, Moderate
Hôtel Splendid. 139 Rue du Dr. Gaudrez. Tel: 41.53.10.00; fax: 41.52.45.17. Credit Cards: Mastercard, Visa. Good sized, comfortable rooms. Rooms: FF200–400, demi-pension FF190 –280, obligatory in season. Restaurant: FF65–200. Closed 15–30 January, Sunday night from 15 September–Easter. Le Relais de Bellay: annexe to Hôtel Splendid, 5-minute walk from the hotel; nicer rooms at FF230, pool, pretty views.

Restaurant, Moderate
Hostellerie Porte-St-Jean. 432 Rue Nationale. Tel: 41.52.30.41. Credit Cards: Visa. Closed Monday night, Tuesday, 23–30 June, 15–30 October, 2 weeks in January. Good, original cuisine using local ingredients. Carte FF250–280, menus FF85 (lunch weekdays only), FF108, FF160, FF195 (except holidays).

• **MONTSOREAU**
(11 km SE Saumur)

Hotel/Restaurants, Moderate/Good value
Hôtel Le Bussy and Restaurant Diane de Meridor. Tel: 41.51.70.18; fax: 41.38.15.93. Credit Cards: Mastercard, Visa. Rustically decorated rooms, some with fireplaces, views of château. Rooms: FF150–350, demi-pension FF250–325. Closed 15 December–31 January, Tuesday october–May. Restaurant: speciality Loire river fish; beautiful setting. FF90–270.
Loire. Tel: 41.51.70.06. Credit Cards: Mastercard, Visa. Rooms: FF160–270. Closed 15 January–1 March, Thursday and Friday out of season. Restaurant: FF80–150.

Restaurant, Simple/Good value
Café le Chapitre. Quai A. Dumas. Tel: 41.51.75.33. Credit Cards: none. Built into cave. Grills: FF40–90.

• **LES PONTS-DE-CLE**
(5 km S Angers)

Hotel/Restaurants, Moderate
Hôtel Campanile. Château du Mulin-Marcille. Tel: 41.44.92.44. Credit Cards: Visa. Rooms: FF230.
Le Bosquet. 2 Rue Maurice Berne. Tel: 41.57.72.42. Closed Sunday night, Monday, 20 August–6 September. Rooms: FF105–150. Restaurant: menus FF78, FF115, FF190. Good Value.

• **ROCHEFORT-SUR-LOIRE**
(20 km SW Angers)

Hotel/Restaurants, Simple/Good value
Le Grand Hôtel. Rue Gasmier. Tel: 41.78.70.06. Closed Sunday night, Monday out of season, 15 January–15 February. Friendly family-run hotel. Rooms: FF140–160. Restaurant: menus from FF70.

• **LES ROSIERS-SUR-LOIRE**
(30 km SE Angers, 14 km NW Saumur)

Hotel/Restaurants, Expensive
Auberge/Hôtel Jeanne de Laval. 54 Rue National. Tel: 41.51.80.17; fax: 41.38.04.18. Credit Cards: Amex, Diners, Mastercard, Visa. Rooms: Comfortable, opening on to garden or Loire, FF380–680. Excellent restaurant with Michelin star and high Gault & Millau rating. Good local river fish and *beurre blanc.* Carte FF300–500, menus FF170 (weekdays only), FF270, FF320. Closed Monday, 8 January–18 February.

• **ST. FLORENT-LE-VIEIL**
(42 km SW Angers)

Hotel/Restaurants, Moderate/Good Value
Hostellerie de la Gabelle. Tel: 41.72.50.19; fax: 41.72.54.38. Small, clean Logis by the river. Rooms: FF180–280, demi-pension FF240. Restaurant: FF60–200. Closed Friday night, Sunday night out of season, 23 December–3 January, 13–23 February.

• **SAUMUR**
(65 km W Tours, 53 km E Angers)

Hotel/Restaurants, Moderate
Anne d'Anjou. 32 Quai Mayaud (hotel). Tel: 41.67.30.30; fax: 41.67.51.00. Credit Cards: Amex, Diners, Mastercard, Visa. One of the best hotels in Anjou, with large pretty rooms and three apartments. Rooms: FF220–350, apartments FF410 –540. Closed 23 December–4 January. Restaurant Les Menestrels: (see restaurant listings).
Le Clos des Bénédictins. St-Hilaire-St-Florent (3 km NW on D751). Tel: 41.67.28.48; fax: 41.67.13.71. Credit Cards: Visa. New hotel in quiet location outside Saumur; beautiful view of valley and château; swimming pool. Rooms: FF190 320, apartment FF400–500, demi-pension FF260–300. Excellent restaurant, modern French cooking and superb local wine list. Carte FF250–300, menu FF150. Closed Sunday and Monday out of season, 2 January–1 March.
Hôtel du Roi René, Restaurant La Serre. 94 Avenue Gen.-de-Gaulle. Tel: 41.67.45.30; fax: 41.67.74.59. Credit Cards: Amex, Mastercard, Visa. Big modern hotel on Ile de Saumur; renovated sound-proofed rooms; view of château and of Loire. Rooms: FF250–350, demi-pension FF250–280. Restaurant La Serre: carte FF200, menus FF70, FF85, FF105, FF180. Closed Sunday night and Monday out of season.

Hotels, Moderate/Good Value
Central Hôtel. 23 Rue Daillé. Tel: 41.51.05.78; fax: 41.67.82.35. Credit Cards: Mastercard, Visa. Rooms: FF130–250.
Londres. 48 Rue Orléans. Tel: 41.51.23.98; fax: 41.51.12.63. Credit Cards: Amex, Diners, Mastercard, Visa. Rooms: FF200–270. Closed mid-December to mid-January.
Campanile. At Bagneux, Côte de Bournan. Tel: 41.50.14.40; fax: 41.38.35.36. Credit Cards: Visa. Rooms: large; in peaceful setting FF270.

Restaurants, Moderate to expensive
Les Menestrels. 11 Rue Raspail (in Hotel Anne d'Anjou gardens). Tel: 41.67.71.10. Credit Cards: Amex, Diners, Mastercard, Visa. Closed Sunday out of season, Monday lunch. Elegant modern French cooking. Carte FF280, menus FF170–350.
Les Délices du Château. Les Feuquières. Tel: 41.67.65.60; fax: 41.67.74.60. Credit Cards: Amex, Diners, Mastercard, Visa. Closed Monday 1 October–30 April and Sunday night. Carte FF300–350, menus FF150, FF250.

Restaurants, Moderate/Good value
Gambetta. 12 Rue Gambetta. Tel: 41.67.66.66. Credit Cards: Amex, Diners, Mastercard, Visa. Closed Sunday night and Monday 10 September–10 June.
L'Escargot. 30 Rue Mar. Leclerc. Tel: 41.51.20.88. Credit Cards: Mastercard, Visa. Closed 2–25 November, 20 February 10 March, Tuesday night and Wednesday, 1 October–30 April. FF75–120.

Tours & East Touraine

CHATEAUX D'ACCUEIL

• **LA NAZALLE**
(7 km NW of Amboise, 25 km E of Tours)

Château de la Huberdière. 37530 Nazelles. Tel 47.57.39.32. Mme Sandrier. Rooms: 5 rooms from FF210–380, 1 apartment accommodating 5–8 persons. Beautiful 17th-century hunting lodge in woods. Good food. Dinner FF95, breakfast included in room price. Open all year round.

- **VALLIERES**
(5 km W of Tours)

Manoir du Grand Martigny. 37230 Fondettes. Tel: 47.42.29.87; fax: 47.42.24.44. M. and Mme Desmarais. Rooms: 3 double rooms, 2 suites for 3–4 persons (good for families) FF450–950. No restaurant. 16th to 19th-century manor house in 16-acre park. Convenient for Tours. Friendly. Open 1 March–1 November, and in winter on request.

- **VILLELOUIN-COULANGE**
(2.5 km SE Montrésor, 36 km S Mintrichard)

Château des Genêts. 37460 Montrésor (between Montrésor and Nouans). Tel: 47.92.61.01. Simple guest house owned by English couple. Rooms: FF160 for double and breakfast, FF650 for 5 nights. Table d'hôte FF75. The owners offer tours of the countryside. Good for families with children.

HOTELS & RESTAURANTS

Hotel/Restaurants, Expensive
Hôtel Jean Bardet. 57 Rue Groison, 37100 Tours. Tel: 47.41.41.11; fax: 47.51.68.72. Credit Cards: Amex, Diners, Visa, Mastercard. Small, elegant hotel, 19th-century villa set in a tranquil park. Rooms: FF700–1300, apartments FF950 –1500; Heated pool. Restaurant: outstanding; has 2 Michelin stars and very high rating in Gault & Millau. Carte FF500–750, menus FF230, FF420, FF550. Closed Sunday night and Monday out of season, except holidays.
Hôtel Alliance. 292 Avenue Grammont, 37200 Tours. Tel: 47.28.00.80; fax: 47.27.77.61. Credit Cards: Amex, Diners, Mastercard, Visa. Large, comfortable hotel in a pretty setting. Rooms: FF450–520, apartments FF625 – 1,350; Heated pool, Tennis. Restaurant: (moderately priced), about FF140. Open all year round.
Hôtel Univers, Restaurant La Touraine. 5 Boulevard Heurteloup. Tel: 47.05.37.12; fax: 47.61.51.80. Credit Cards: Amex, Diners, Mastercard, Visa. Rooms: FF650–760, apartments FF670. Restaurant La Touraine: (moderately priced and very good), carte FF180–230, menus

FF140, FF170. Closed (restaurant only) Saturday.
Hôtel Bordeaux. 3 Place Maréchal Leclerc. Tel: 47.05.40.32; fax: 47.64.05.72. Credit Cards: Amex, Diners, Mastercard, Visa. Rooms: FF320–500, demi-pension FF413 –473. Restaurant: (moderately priced), FF115 menu on Sundays. Open all year round.
Hôtel du Groison. 10 Rue Groison. Tel: 47.41.94.40; fax: 47.51.50.28. Credit Cards: Amex, Diners, Visa. Small, charming hotel with guesthouse atmosphere. Rooms: FF500–920. Open all year round. Restaurant Le Jardin du Castel: excellent cuisine, good fish and other local dishes. Carte FF330–380, menus FF240–450. Closed Saturday lunch, Wednesday.

Hotel, Moderate
Hôtel Akilene. 22 Rue du Grand Marché, 17 Rue de la Rotisserie. Tel: 47.61.46.04. Credit Cards: Mastercard, Visa. Rooms: FF150–250 (good value). Comfortable old hotel spanning two streets in old Tours. Restaurant: FF70–140. Open all year round.

Hotels (without restaurants), Moderate
Hôtel Mirabeau. 89 bis Boulevard Herteloup. Tel: 47.05.24.60; fax: 47.05.31.09. Credit Cards: Amex, Diners, Mastercard, Visa. Rooms: FF250–320. Very good value for a centrally located hotel. Rooms on the street are sound-proofed. Closed Christmas holidays.
Hôtel du Musée. 2 Place François Sicard. Tel: 47.66.63.81; fax: 47.20.10.42. Credit Cards: none. Very good value, simple old-fashioned hotel near cathedral on quiet square. Rooms: FF120–2500. Open all year round.
Hôtel Balzac. 47 Rue Scellerie. Tel: 47.05.40.87. Credit Cards: Mastercard, Visa. Simple hotel, located in quiet old street near cathedral. Good value. Rooms: FF90–270. Open all year round.
Hôtel Le Royal. 65 Avenue de Grammont. Tel: 47.64.71.78; fax: 47.05.84.62. Credit Cards: Visa, Amex, Diners. Modern hotel, centrally located. Rooms: FF300–400. Open all year round.
Hôtel Central. 21 Rue Berthelot. Tel: 47.05.46.44; fax: 47.66.10.26.

Credit Cards: Amex, Diners, Mastercard, Visa. Rooms: FF300–400. Open all year round.
Hôtel Colbert. 78 Rue Colbert. Tel: 47.66.61.56. Credit Cards: Amex, Diners, Mastercard, Visa. Small, simple. Rooms: FF150–320. Open all year round.

Restaurants, Expensive
Barrier. 101 Avenue Tranchée, 37100 Tours. Tel: 47.54.20.39; fax: 47.41.80.95. Credit cards: Mastercard, Visa. Two Michelin stars and high rating in Gault & Millau. Carte FF400–500, menus FF230–560. Closed Sunday night.
Jean Bardet. 57 Rue Groison. (See hotel listings above).
Le Jardin du Castel. 10, Rue Groison. (See hotel listings above).
La Roche Le Roy. 55 Route de St-Avertin, 37200 Tours. Tel: 47.27.22.00; fax: 47.28.08.39. Credit Cards: Amex, Visa. Located in the suburb of St-Avertin, charming setting, Michelin star. Excellent food. Carte FF300, menus FF148 FF240 (good value). Closed 1–22 August, Saturday lunch and Sunday.

Restaurants, Moderate/Expensive
Le Lys. 63 Rue B. Pascal. Tel: 47.05.27.92. Credit Cards: Mastercard, Visa. High rating in Gault & Millau. Carte 300F, menus FF110–280 (good value). Closed Sunday night and Monday.
Les Tuffeaux. 19 Rue Lavoisier. Tel: 47.47.19.89. Credit Cards: Mastercard, Visa. Pretty restaurant, classic cuisine. Excellent selection of Vouvrays. Carte FF250, menus FF110 (weekdays, lunch only), FF150, FF200. Closed Monday lunch and Sunday.

Restaurants, Moderate
La Gourmandine. 49 Boulevard Palissy. Tel: 47.05.13.75. Credit Cards: Amex, Mastercard, Visa. Carte FF150, menus FF95 (weekdays only), FF145. Closed Monday lunch, Sunday and holidays, 14 July–16 August, 24 December–3 January.
L'Odéon. 10 Place de la Gare. Tel: 47.20.12.65. Credit Cards: Amex, Diners, Mastercard, Visa. Excellent brasserie offering traditional French cuisine, good fish. Carte FF250, menus FF88, FF135. Closed Sunday night.

Le Buffet de la Gare. Place du Mal-Leclerc. Tel: 47.05.46.12 or 47.05.46.17. Credit Cards: Mastercard, Visa. Surprisingly good restaurant attached to the rail station. Modern French cuisine by an ex-chef from Barrier. Carte FF250, menus FF68 (weekdays only), FF95 (weekends and holidays only), FF150. Closed Friday night and Saturday out of season.

Restaurant La Touraine. 5 Boulevard Heurteloup. (See hotel listings above)

Brasserie Buré (Relais Buré). 1 Place de la Résistance. Tel: 47.05.67.74. Credit Cards: Amex, Diners, Mastercard, Visa. Popular, moderately priced brasserie in Vieux Tours. Shellfish, grilled meats, choucrôute. FF100–140. Closed Monday.

L'Ecuelle. 5 Rue du Grand Marché. Tel: 47.66.49.10. Credit Cards: none. Old style French cooking, good value, menus from FF50. Closed Monday.

• AMBOISE
(25 km NE of Tours)

Hotel/Restaurants, Expensive
Le Choiseul. 36 Quai Charles Guinot. Tel: 47.30.45.45; fax: 47.30.46.10. Credit Cards: Mastercard, Visa. Beautiful refurbished 18th-century mansion, part of Relais et Châteaux chain. Facing river, with garden and pool. Rooms: FF530–920, apartments FF980, demi-pension FF480–630. Restaurant: high rating in Gault & Millau. Carte FF300, menus FF240–340. Closed 5 January–15 March.

Château de Pray. (3 km E by D751). Tel: 47.57.23.67; fax: 47.57.32.50. Credit Cards: Amex, Diners, Mastercard, Visa. Lovely small Louis XIII château in countryside. Rooms: FF580–820, demi-pension FF520–590, obligatory in season. Restaurant: FF200–260. Closed 1 January–10 February.

Novotel. (2 km S on Route de Chenonceaux), 17 Rue des Sablonnières. Tel: 47.57.42.07; fax: 47.30.40.76. Credit Cards: Amex, Diners, Mastercard, Visa. Comfortable big hotel in calm setting with nice views of the Loire; pool. Rooms: FF520–560. Restaurant: Grill, carte around FF150. Open all year round.

Hotel/Restaurants, Moderate
Le Lion d'Or. 17 Quai Ch. Ginot. Tel: 47.57.00.23. Credit Cards: Master-card, Visa. Small hotel overlooking the river at the foot of the château. Rooms: FF190–320. Restaurant: FF130–240. Closed 30 November–1 April.

Auberge du Mail. 32 Quai Gen. de Gaulle (by D751). Tel: 47.57.60.39. Credit Cards: Amex, Diners, Mastercard, Visa. Rooms: FF130–290. Closed Friday out of season. Restaurant: FF80–190.

Hotels, Moderate
La Bellevue. 12 Quai Ch. Guinot. Tel: 47.57.02.26; fax: 47.30.51.23. Credit Cards: Mastercard, Visa. Modern, comfortable; at the foot of the château, overlooking the river. Rooms: FF270–320, breakfast included. Good value. Closed 1 January–15 March.

Parc. 8 Rue L. da Vinci. Tel: 47.57.06.93; fax: 47.30.52.06. Credit Cards: Mastercard, Visa. Rooms: FF210–380. Closed 1 November–1 March.

Restaurants, Expensive
Le Manoir Saint Thomas. Place Richelieu. Tel: 47.57.22.52; fax: 47.30.44.71. Credit Cards: Amex, Diners, Mastercard, Visa. Closed week of 1 November, 15 January–15 February, Monday. Michelin star. Impressive Renaissance manor-house in a beautiful garden. Imaginative modern French cuisine. Excellent Touraine cellar. Carte FF300, menus FF200–320.

Le Choiseul. 36 Quai Charles Ginot. (See hotel listing above).

Restaurants, Moderate
La Bonne Etape. (2.5 km NE on D751). Tel: 47.57.08.09. Credit Cards: Amex, Diners, Mastercard, Visa. FF90–260. Closed 1 October–31 March, Tuesday night 1 April–30 September.

• CHENONCEAUX
(35 km SE Tours, 12 km S Amboise)

Hotel/Restaurants, Moderate
Le Bon Laboureur et Château. 6 Rue du Dr. Bretonneau. Tel: 47.23.90.02; fax: 47.23.82.01. Credit Cards: Amex, Diners, Mastercard, Visa. Very popular hotel, fills quickly. Bedrooms on courtyard. Rooms: FF300–600, demi-pension FF440–600, obligatory in season. Closed 30 November–15 March. Restaurant: FF165–280.

Ottoni. Rue Dr. Bretonneau. Tel: 47.23.90.09; fax: 47.23.91.59. Credit Cards: Amex, Diners, Mastercard, Visa. Rooms: FF330–490, demi-pension FF380–570. Closed 5 November–18 March. Restaurant: FF100–300.

La Renaudière. 24 Rue du Dr. Brettonneau. Tel: 47.23.90.04; fax: 47.23.90.51. Located on outskirts of town in peaceful setting. Credit Cards: Mastercard, Visa. Rooms: FF190–290, demi-pension FF200–350. Closed Sunday night, Monday lunch. Restaurant: FF85–180.

• GENILLE
(11 km NE Loches)

Hotel/Restaurants, Moderate/Simple
Auberge Agnès Sorel. Tel: 47.59.50.17. Credit Cards: Mastercard, Visa. Closed February, Sunday night and Monday except during July and August.
Rooms: FF170–230, 1 apartment FF350, demi-pension FF250. Restaurant: carte FF250, menus FF100–230.

• JOUE-LES-TOURS
(6 km SW Tours)

Hotel/Restaurants, Expensive
Château de Beaulieu. 1 Route Villandry. Tel: 47.53.20.26; fax: 47.53.84.20. Credit Cards: Diners, Mastercard, Visa. Beautiful rooms, quiet surroundings. Rooms: FF380–750, demi-pension FF350–470. Open all year round. Restaurant: menus FF160–270.

Hotel/Restaurants, Moderate
Campanile. Avenue du Lac. Tel: 47.67.24.89; fax: 47.53.80.02. Credit Cards: Mastercard, Visa. Rooms: FF280.

• LOCHES
(41 km SE Tours)

Hotel/Restaurants, Moderate
Georges Sand. 39 Rue Quintefol. Tel: 47.59.39.72; fax: 47.91.55.75. Credit Cards: Mastercard, Visa. Rooms: FF250–460, demi-pension FF280–320, obligatory in season. Closed 22–28 December. Restaurant: FF70–180.

Hôtel France. 6 Rue Picois. Tel: 47.59.00.32; fax: 47.59.28.66.

Credit Cards: Mastercard, Diners, Visa. Rooms: FF220–330. Closed Sunday night, Monday lunch except May–Sept, 2 January–8 February, 2–8 May. Restaurant: FF80–250.

Hôtel Luccotel, Restaurant Le Colvert. Rue des Lézards (on D760). Tel: 47.91.50.50; fax: 47.94.01.18. Credit Cards: Mastercard, Visa. Quiet setting; pool. Rooms: FF310–330, demi-pension FF330. Closed 18 December–10 January. Restaurant: closed Saturday lunch and 20 December–10 January. Carte FF230–250, menus FF130–200.

• **MONTLOUIS-SUR-LOIRE**
(12 km E Tours by D751)

Hotel/Restaurants, Moderate
Hôtel de la Ville. Place Mairie Tel: 47.50.84.84; fax: 47.45.08.43. Credit Cards: Mastercard, Visa. Rooms: FF160–230, demi-pension FF230. Closed 15 December–15 January. Restaurant: FF80–140.

Restaurant, Expensive
Roc-en-Val. 4 Quai Loire. Tel: 47.50.81.96. Credit Cards: Amex, Diners, Mastercard, Visa. Closed 13 February–7 March, Sunday night and Monday (except dinner in season). Beautiful manor house on the Loire with garden. Exquisite setting and service. Great wines, very good food, Michelin star. Carte FF350, menus FF165 (weekdays only), FF220 (lunch weekdays only), FF245, FF295.

Restaurants, Moderate
Tourangelle. Quai A. Baillet. Tel: 47.50.81.15. Credit Cards: Mastercard, Visa. Closed Sunday night, Tuesday night, Wednesday, 28 June–12 July, 20 December–3 January. FF68–170.

Relais de Belle Roche. (3 km S at Belle Roche), 14 Rue de la Vallée. Tel: 47.50.82.43. Credit Cards: Amex, Diners, Visa. Closed Tuesday night, Wednesday and March. Restaurant in a cave. Good value. Carte FF250, menus FF86–150.

• **MONTRESOR**
(34 km S Montrichard)

Hotel/Restaurants, Moderate/Simple
Hôtel de France. Tel: 42.94.20.03. Sweet village hotel with good, inexpensive restaurant. Rooms: FF100–180.

• **ROCHECORBON**
(3 km E Tours on N152)

Hotel/Restaurants, Expensive
Les Hautes Roches. 86 Quai de la Loire. Tel: 47.52.88.88; fax: 47.52.81.30. Credit Cards: Visa. New, pretty and small, right on the river. Rooms: FF580–1,100, apartments FF1,100–1,350. Hotel closed Sunday and Monday out of season. Restaurant: carte FF400, menus FF250–350. Closed Sunday night and Monday, except holidays.

Hotel, Moderate
Les Fontaines. St Georges, 6 Quai de la Loire. Tel: 47.52.52.86; fax: 47.52.85.05. Credit Cards: Amex, Diners, Mastercard, Visa. Rooms: FF190–320. Closed Sunday night in winter.

Restaurants, Moderate
L'Oubliette. 34 Rue des Clouettes. Tel: 47.52.50.49. Credit Cards: Mastercard, Visa. Closed Sunday night, Monday, 12–30 November. Good restaurant, carved into the rock. Carte about FF200, menu FF120–260.

La Lanterne. Tel: 47.52.50.02; fax: 47.52.54.46. Credit Cards: Mastercard, Visa. Closed Sunday out of season, Monday except holidays. FF130–250.

• **ST-MARTIN-LE-BEAU**
(22 km Tours, near Chenonceaux)

Hotel/Restaurants, Simple
Auberge de la Treille. 2 Rue d'Amboise. Tel: 47.50.67.17. Credit Cards: Visa. Rooms: FF140–270, demi-pension FF270, obligatory in season. Restaurant: carte FF250, menus FF80–150. Closed Sundaypm, Monday, 15 September–8 October.

• **VERNOU-SUR-BRENNE**
(15 km E Tours)

Hotel/Restaurants, Moderate
Hostellerie Les Perce-Neige. 13 Rue Anatole France. Tel: 47.52.10.04. Credit Cards: Amex, Mastercard, Visa. Rooms: FF170–280. Closed Sunday night, Mondays out of season, 2 January–2 February. Restaurant: menus FF110–220.

• **VOUVRAY**
(10 km Tours, 49 km Blois)

Hotel/Restaurants, Moderate/Simple
Auberge Grand Vatel. Avenue Brûlé. Tel: 47.52.70.32; fax: 47.52.74.52. Credit Cards: Mastercard, Visa. Rooms: FF210–270, demi-pension FF270. Closed Sunday night 1 October–31 March; Mondays. Carte FF250, menu FF130–250.

Restaurants, Moderate
Au Virage Gastronomique. 25 Avenue Brûlé. Tel: 47.52.70.02. Credit Cards: Mastercard, Visa. Closed 26 June–7 July, Wednesdays. FF120–270.

Auberge de Moncontour. 71 Rue du Petit-Coteau. Tel: 47.52.63.40. Credit Cards: Mastercard, Visa. Closed Sunday night, Monday. Carte FF220, menus FF90 (weekdays), FF120, FF150.

West Touraine

CHATEAUX D'ACCUEIL

Château Danzay. (On RD 749 between Chinon and Bourgueil, 4 km from Chinon), 37420 Chinon. Tel: 47.58.46.86; fax: 47.58.84.35. Jacques and Josiane Sarfati. 15th-century château with restaurant, warm atmosphere. Rooms: 7 guest rooms and 1 apartment, FF600–1400.

Château du Gerfaut. (24 km SW of Tours, right off D751 3 km from Azay-le-Rideau, 37190 Azay-le-Rideau. Tel: 47.45.40.16; fax: 47.45.20.15. Marquis and Marquise de Chenerilles. Large château in wooded grounds. Tennis and ballooning. Rooms: guest rooms (FF395–570, including breakfast). Table d'hôte by reservation. Open 1 April–1 November.

Château Montour. Beaumont-en-Veron, 37420 Avoine. Tel: 47.58.43.76. Mme Krebs. 17th to 18th-century manor house. Was once a working silk farm. Rooms: 3 guest rooms and 1 apartment. Open Easter–11 November.

Château des Réaux. (south of Bourgueil, just north of the river, Le Port-Boulet) 37140 Bourgueil. Tel: 47.95.14.40; fax: 47.95.18.34. 17th-century château built by the family who built Chenonceau and Azay-le-Rideau. Rooms: 7 guest rooms, 3 apartments, table d'hôte by reservation.

• AZAY-LE-RIDEAU

Hotel/Restaurants, Moderate/Expensive
Le Grand Monarque. 3 Place de la République. Tel: 47.45.40.08; fax: 47.45.46.25. Credit Cards: Amex, Diners, Mastercard, Visa. Recently refurbished, with nice rooms on to the garden. Rooms: FF330–550, apartments FF475 –600, demi-pension FF320–450, obligatory in season. Closed 10 December–4 January, and February school vacation. Restaurant: carte FF250–300, menus FF160–400. Restaurant closed 6 November–15 March.

Hotels, Moderate
Hôtel Val de Loire. 40 Route Nationale. Tel: 47.45.23.67. Credit Cards: Mastercard, Visa. Newly decorated, modern hotel. Rooms: FF200–320. Closed 12 November–20 March.
Hôtel de Biencourt. 7 Rue Balzac. Tel: 47.45.20.75. Credit Cards: Visa. Small Logis on a quiet street near the château. Rooms: FF220–370.

Restaurants, Moderate
Le Commerce. 50 Route Nationale. Tel: 47.45.40.22. Credit Cards: Mastercard, Visa. Restaurant connected to the Hôtel Val de Loire. Menus FF95–190. Closed 15 November–15 March.
L'Automate Gourmand. 11 Rue du Park, Chapelle-St-Blaise. Tel: 47.45.39.07. Credit Cards: Visa. Popular, lively bistro decorated with old toys. Simple French cooking. Closed Sunday night, Wednesday, 20 December–20 January. FF120–260.

• SACHE
(7 km SE Azay-le-Rideau on D17)

Restaurant, Moderate
Auberge du XIIe Siècle. Saché, 37190 Azay-le-Rideau. Tel: 47.26.88.77. Credit Cards: Amex, Diners, Visa. Pretty setting, medieval decor, very good classic French food, Michelin star. Closed February and Tuesday. Good value, menu FF180–360.

• BREHEMONT
(12 km from Azay-le-Rideau, 6 km from Langeais)

Hotel/Restaurants, Moderate/Expensive
Le Castel de Bray et Monts. 37130 Bréhémont. Tel: 47.96.70.47; fax: 47.96.57.36. Credit Cards: Amex, Diners, Mastercard, Visa. Pretty, small hotel in the country, beautiful garden, very nice rooms, good food. Rooms: FF270–600, demi-pension FF400–500. Closed Wednesday out of season (1 October–1 April), 21 December–10 January. Restaurant: carte FF300, menus FF120–250.

• CHINON

Hotel/Restaurants, Moderate/Expensive
Hostellerie Gargantua. 73 Rue Voltaire. Tel: 47.93.04.71. Credit Cards: Amex, Diners, Visa. In a pretty old palace in the centre of town. Nice rooms and the dining room has lovely a view of the river. Mixed ratings in the guides because it is a tourist trap. Rooms: FF250–600. Closed Wednesday out of season, end-November to 15 March. Restaurant: carte FF280, menus FF150–230.

Hotel/Restaurants, Moderate
La Boule d'Or. 66 Quai Jeanne d'Arc. Tel: 47.93.03.13; fax: 47.93.24.25. Credit Cards: none. A Logis de France, on the *quai*, with restaurant. Rooms: FF160–340. Closing days: Monday out of season, 15 December–1 February. Restaurant: menus FF100–200.

Hotels, Moderate
Chris Hôtel. 66 Quai Jeanne d'Arc. Tel: 47.93.03.13; fax: 47.93.24.25. Credit Cards: Amex, Diners, Mastercard, Visa. Pretty hotel with views of château and river. Rooms: FF250–350. Open all year round.
Hôtel Diderot. 4 Rue Buffon. Tel: 47.93.18.87; fax: 47.93.37.10. Credit Cards: Amex, Diners, Mastercard, Visa. Pretty 18th-century house on quiet street. Rooms: FF230–400. Closed 20 December–10 January.

Restaurant, Moderate/Expensive
Au Plaisir Gourmand. 2 Rue Parmentier. Tel: 47.93.20.48; fax: 47.93.05.66. Credit Cards: Visa, Mastercard. Closed Sunday dinner, Monday, 8–28 February and 12–30 November. The best in Chinon and one of the best in the region. Serving modern French cuisine. Carte FF300, menus FF180–330.

Restaurant, Moderate
L'Océanic. 13 Rue Rabelais. Tel: 47.93.44.55. Closed Sunday dinner, Monday. Unpretentious fish restaurant. FF100 and up.

• MARCAY
(6 km S Chinon by D749 and D116)

Hotel/Restaurants, Expensive
Château de Marcay. Marcay, 37500 Chinon. Tel: 47.93.03.47; fax: 47.93.45.33. Credit Cards: Amex, Visa. An elegant 15th-century château in a vineyard. Pool, tennis. Restaurant has Michelin star and very high rating in Gault & Millau. Thirty-eight rooms: FF495–1,500, six apartments FF1,155–1,415, demi-pension FF750–1,200, obligatory in season. Closed mid-January to mid-March. Restaurant: carte FF400, menus FF320–440.

• BEAUMONT-EN-VERON
(5 km N Chinon on D749)

Hotel, Moderate/Expensive
La Giraudière. 37420 Avoine. Tel: 47.58.40.36; fax: 47.58.46.06. Credit Cards: Amex, Diners, Mastercard, Visa. 17th-century manor house in park. Rooms: FF200–350. Closed January–13 March, Sunday/Monday out of season.

• DESCARTES
(52 km SE Chinon, 56 km S Tours)

Hotel/Restaurants, Moderate
Le Moderne. 15 Rue Descartes. Tel: 47.59.72.11; fax: 47.92.44.90. Credit Cards: Diners, Mastercard, Visa. Nice small hotel, recently restored. Rooms: FF230–270, demi-pension FF230. Closed Sunday and school vacation in February. Restaurant: FF80–190.

• L'ILE-BOUCHARD
(18 km E Chinon, 40 km S Tours)

Restaurant, Moderate/Expensive
Auberge de l'Ile. 3 Place Bouchard. Tel: 47.58.51.07. Credit Cards: Amex,

Mastercard, Visa. Closed Sunday night and Monday, 7 January–4 February. Good regional fare in a pretty setting. Carte FF250, menus FF170–270.

• **LANGEAIS**
(25 km W Tours)

Hotel/Restaurants, Expensive
Hôtel Hosten, Restaurant Le Langeais. 2 Rue Gambetta. Tel: 47.96.70.63; fax: 47.96.56.72. Credit Cards: Amex, Diners, Mastercard, Visa. Rooms: FF330–600. Closed Monday dinner, Tuesday, 10 January–10 February, 20 June–10 July. Restaurant: Michelin star and high Gault & Millau rating. Classical cuisine with some modern twists. Carte FF300.

Restaurant, Inexpensive
Crêperie du Château. 2 Rue Ann de Bretagne. Tel: 47.96.59.56. Credit Cards: none. Simple crêperie near the château. Closed Monday.

• **LIGUEIL**
(57 km S Tours, 53 km SE Chinon)

Hotel/Restaurants, Moderate
Le Colombier. 4 Place du General-Leclerc. Tel: 47.59. 60.83. Credit Cards: Visa. Closed January, 1–15 September. Rooms: FF150–220. Modest restaurant/hotel with family atmosphere. Simple rooms, good local fare. Restaurant: carte FF150, menus FF45 (weekdays only), FF60–155.

• **MONTBAZON**
(12 km S Tours)

Hotel/Restaurants, Expensive
Château d'Artigny. Route d'Azay-le-Rideau. Tel: 47.26.24.24; fax: 47.65.92.79. Credit Cards: Mastercard, Visa. Closed 26 November–6 January. One of the most elegant châteaux/hotels in the Loire. Michelin star and very high Gault & Millau rating. Grand house at the end of a tree-lined drive; large, refined dining room. Fantastic cave and excellent food. Rooms: FF600–1,575. Restaurant: carte FF460, menus FF290–450. **Domaine de la Tortinière.** (2 km by N10 and D287), Gués de Veigné, 37250 Montbazon. Tel: 47.26.00.19; fax: 47.65.95.70. Credit Cards: Mastercard, Visa. Closed 10 Decem-

ber–1 March, Wednesday lunch and Tuesday 15 October–31 March. Renaissance château in a beautiful park. Very good restaurant with excellent wines. Rooms: FF455–1,040. Restaurant: carte FF300–350, menus FF270–360.

Restaurant, Expensive
La Chancelière. 1 Place des Marronniers. Tel: 47.26.00.67; fax: 47.73.14.82. Credit Cards: Visa. Closed Sunday night and Monday (except holidays), 4 February–6 March, 2–11 September. 2 Michelin stars, very high Gault & Millau rating. Carte FF400–450, menus FF350.

• **SAINT-EPAIN**
(16 km S Azay-le-Rideau)

Hotel/Restaurant, Expensive
Château de Montgoger. 37800 St-Epain. Tel: 47.65.54.22. Credit Cards: Amex, Diners, Mastercard, Visa. A beautiful château in the country, surrounded by trees. Rooms: FF1,000–1,300, demi-pension obligatory. Open all year round. Restaurant: High rating in Gault & Millau, modern French cooking using excellent local ingredients. Carte FF350.

• **SAINT-PATRICE**
(9 km SW Langeais, 34 km SW Tours)

Restaurant/Hotel, Expensive
Château de Rochecotte. Saint-Patrice, 37130 Langeais. Tel: 47.96.91.28; fax: 47.96.90.59. Credit Cards: Mastercard, Visa. Elegant, grand château in a beautiful setting; very good restaurant, classic French with modern touches. Rooms: FF350–750. Closed 15–28 February. Restaurant: carte FF300–400, menu FF200.

• **SAVONNIERES**
(7 km SW Tours on D7)

Hotel/Restaurant, Moderate
Hôtel des Cèdres: Route du Château de Villandry. Tel: 47.53.00.28. Credit Cards: Mastercard, Visa. Set in a quiet park; pool. Rooms: FF300–400. Restaurant des Cèdres. Tel: 47.453.37.58. Credit cards: Visa. Closed 2–31 January, Sunday night and Monday October–Easter. FF100–280.

• **VILLANDRY**

(20 km W Tours, 10 km NE Azay-le-Rideau)

Hotel/Restaurant, Moderate
Cheval Rouge. Villandry, 37510 Joué-les-Tours. Tel: 47.50.02.07; fax: 47.50.08.77. Credit Cards: Mastercard, Visa. Rooms: FF280–300, demi-pension FF380. Closed 5 November–15 March, Mondays March–April and September–October. Restaurant: carte FF330–350, menus FF100–200.

Blésois

CHATEAUX D'ACCUEIL

Château de Colliers. (16 km NE of Blois), 41500 Muides-sur-Loire. Tel: 54.87.50.75; fax: 54.87.03.64. Christian et Marie-France de Gélis. 17th to 18th-century château, 5 km from Chambord. The house has been in the same family since 1779. Set on the south bank of the Loire. Rooms: 5 rooms. Table d'hôte by reservation. Open March–December, winter on request.

HOTELS & RESTAURANTS

• **BEAUGENCY**
(31 km NE Blois, 25 km SW Orleans)

Hotel/Restaurant, Expensive
Hôtel de l'Abbaye. Quai Abbaye. Tel: 38.44.67.35; fax: 38.44.87.92. Credit Cards: Amex, Diners, Mastercard, Visa. Rooms: FF430–570, apartments FF510. Restaurant: carte FF320–350, menus FF150 (lunch only), FF185.

Hotel/Restaurant, Moderate
Ecu de Bretagne. Place du Matroi. Tel: 38.44.67.60; fax: 38.44.68.09. Credit Cards: Amex, Diners, Mastercard, Visa. Pretty rooms on a garden: FF300–400. Restaurant: carte FF280, menus FF130–200.

Hotel, Moderate
Hôtel de la Sologne. Place St-Firmin. Tel: 38.44.50.27; fax: 38.44.90.19. Credit Cards: Mastercard, Visa. Very nice old stone house on a pretty garden. Good value. Centrally located but calm. Rooms: FF180–300. Closed 20 December–2 January.

Restaurant, Moderate/Good Value
Le Petit Bateau, "Chez Yvette", 54 Rue du Pont. Tel: 38.44. 56.38; fax: 38.46.44.37. Menus FF60–180.

• BLOIS
(60 km NE Tours; 56 km SW Orleans)

Hotel/Restaurant, Moderate/expensive
L'Horset La Vallière. 26 Avenue Maunoury. Tel: 54.74.19.00; fax: 54.74.57.97. Credit Cards: Amex, Diners, Mastercard, Visa. New hotel, centrally located, facing Palais de Congres. Rooms: FF480, demi-pension FF400. Restaurant: FF120–180. Open all year round.

Hotel/Restaurants, Moderate
Monarque. 61 Rue Porte Chartraine. Tel: 54.78.02.35; fax: 54.74.82.76. Credit Cards: Mastercard, Visa. Rooms: FF200 360, demi-pension FF300. Closed 17 December–2 January, Sunday (restaurant). Restaurant: FF75–185.
Hôtel Viennois. 5 Quai A. Contant. Tel: 54.74.12.80. Credit Cards: none. Rooms: FF80–140. Closed (restaurant only) Sunday night and Monday lunch, out of season. Restaurant: menus from FF60. Good value.

Hotels, Moderate
Ibis. 3 Rue Porte-Côte. Tel: 54.74.01.17; fax: 54.74.85.69. Credit Cards: Visa, Mastercard. Near the château, beneath the church clock tower. Nice bar. Rooms: FF190–280. Open every day.
Savoie. 6 Rue Ducoux. Tel: 54.74.32.21; fax: 54.74.29.58. Credit Cards: Amex, Mastercard, Visa. Rooms: FF135–250. Open all year round.

Restaurants, Expensive
La Bocca d'Or. 15 Rue Haute. Tel: 54.78.04.74. Credit Cards: Visa, Amex. Very high rating in Gault & Millau. Closed Monday lunch, Sunday (except holidays), 28 January–5 March. Carte from FF300, menus FF140.

Restaurants, Moderate
Au Rendez-Vous des Pêcheurs. 27 Rue de Foix. Tel: 54.74.67.48; fax: 54.74.47.67. Credit Cards: Visa. Open every day. Very good bistro serv-

ing regional cuisine (not only fish). Carte FF250, menu FF160.

• BRACIEUX
(18 km S Blois)

Hotel, Moderate
Ma Bonheure. 9 Rue René Masson. Tel: 54.46.41.57. Credit Cards: Mastercard, Visa. Rooms: FF280–360.

Restaurant, Expensive
Bernard Robin. 1 Avenue de Chambord. Tel: 54.46.41.22; fax: 54.46.03.69. Credit Cards: Visa. Closed Tuesday night, Wednesday, 20 December–31 January. Excellent cuisine, elegant restaurant with 2 Michelin stars and high Gault & Millau rating. Carte FF400–500, menus FF270–540.

• CANDE-SUR-BEUVRON
(15 km SW Blois, 50 km E Tours)

Hotel/Restaurant, Moderate
La Caillère. 36 Route des Montils. Tel: 54.44.03.08; fax: 54.44.00.95. Credit Cards: Amex, Diners, Mastercard, Visa. Rooms: (simple) FF280–350. Closed Wednesday and 15 January–1 March. Restaurant: Excellent food, innovative modern French cooking. Carte FF250–280, menus FF98 (weekdays), FF148, FF198, FF245.

• CHITENAY
(12 km Blois)

Hotel/Restaurants, Moderate
La Clé des Champs. 60 Grande Rue. Tel: 54. 70.42.03. Credit Cards: Mastercard, Visa. Rooms: pretty and clean, overlooking farmland and rose garden. FF120–220. Restaurant: Excellent French food using very fresh ingredients. Carte FF180, menus FF120, FF180. Closed Monday lunch, Tuesday, 2 January–2 February.
Auberge du Centre. Tel: 54.70.42.11; fax: 54.70.35.03. Credit Cards: Mastercard, Visa. Rooms: FF290–400. Restaurant: FF100–270. Closed February and Monday out of season.

• MONT-PRES-CHAMBORD
(7 km W Bracieux by D923)

Hotel, Moderate
St Florent. 14 Rue de la Cabardière. Tel: 54.70.81.00. Credit Cards: Mastercard, Visa. New hotel with agreeable rooms near forest. Rooms: FF170–250.

• MONTRICHARD
(43 km E Tours, 33 km S Blois)

Hotel/Restaurants, Expensive
Château de la Menaudière (3 km outside Montrichard on Route d'Amboise). Tel: 54.32.02.44 54.71.34.58. Credit Cards: Amex, Diners, Mastercard, Visa. In peaceful grounds, very comfortable retreat. Restaurant has good, elegant, modern cuisine. Rooms: FF400–700, demi-pension FF520–720, obligatory in season. Closed 30 November–1 March, Sunday night and Monday except holidays. Restaurant: FF200–300.

• CHISSAY-EN-TOURAINE
(4 km W Montrichard on D115)

Château de Chissay. Tel: 54.32.32.01; fax: 54.32.43.80. Credit Cards: Amex, Diners, Mastercard, Visa. Very comfortable Renaissance château in beautiful grounds; Pool. Relais et Châteaux. Rooms: FF490–1,500. Restaurant: FF180–300.

Hotel/Restaurants, Moderate
Bellevue. Quai du Cher. Tel: 54.32.06.17; fax: 54.32.48.06. Credit Cards: Amex, Diners, Mastercard, Visa. Modern hotel overlooking river; panoramic views from restaurant. Rooms: FF280–380, demi-pension FF280–340. Closed Monday/Tuesday out of season, 15 November–21 December. Restaurant: FF80–250.
Tête Noire. 24 Rue de Tours. Tel: 54.32.05.55; fax: 54.32.78.37. Credit Cards: Mastercard, Visa. Rooms: FF190–320, demi-pension FF280–360. Closed 4 January–8 February and Friday 15 October–15 March except holidays. Restaurant: carte FF210, menus FF100–250.

Restaurants, Moderate/Good value
Le Bistrot de la Tour. 6 Rue du Pont.

Tel: 54.32.07.34. Small simple bistro on the market place.

Le Grill du Passeur. 2 Rue du Pont. Tel: 54.32.06.80. Meat and fish grilled over open hearth. Closed 5 December–15 March. Carte FF160–180.

• **ONZAIN**
(16 km SW Blois)

Hotel/Restaurant, Expensive
Domaine des Hauts de Loire. Route d'Herbault. Tel: 54.20.72.57; fax: 54.20.77.32. Credit Cards: Amex, Mastercard, Visa. Elegant Relais et Châteaux hotel with Michelin star. Rooms: FF650–2,000. Restaurant: Good modern French cooking. Carte FF500. Closed Tuesday lunch and Monday except holidays.

• **CHOUZY-SUR-CISSE**
(6 km NE Onzain on D58)

La Carte. 2 Rue J. Perrin, 41150 Chouzy-sur-Cisse. Tel: 54.20.49.00; fax: 54.20.43.78. Credit Cards: Amex, Mastercard, Visa. 17th-century farmhouse in the countryside; pool. Rooms: FF500–650. Closed 30 November–10 March. Restaurant: carte FF320, menus FF170–220.

• **SEILLAC**
(7 km N Onzain)

Domaine de Seillac. 41150 Seillac. Tel: 54.20.72.11; fax: 54.20.82.88. Credit Cards: Amex, Diners, Visa. Château in pretty grounds, with simpler bungalows in the woods. Good for families. Rooms: FF390–630. Closed 20 December–5 January. Restaurant: FF150. Good value.

Hotel, Moderate
Château des Tertres. (1.5 km W Onzain on D58, Route de Monteaux). Tel: 54.20.83.88; fax: 54.20.89.21. Credit Cards: Amex, Mastercard, Visa. Pleasant manor house. Rooms: FF370–480. Closed 12 November–18 March.

Hotel/Restaurant, Simple/Moderate
Pont d'Ouchet. 50 Grande Rue. Tel: 54.20.70.33. Rooms: FF85–120, demi-pension obligatory in season. Closed Sunday night, Monday, 1 December–1 March.

• **TAVERS**
(3 km S Beaugency, 28 km SW Orleans)

Hotel/Restaurant, Expensive
La Tonnellerie. 12 Rue des Eaux-Bleues. Tel: 38.44.68.15; fax: 38.44.10.01. Credit Cards: Diners, Mastercard, Visa. Not very nice from the outside but lovely interior around a courtyard; pool. Rooms: FF720–900. Restaurant: carte FF350, menus FF320–450. Closed Tuesday/Wednesday, April–October.

• **TALCY**
(30 km Blois, 34 km Orleans)

Restaurant, Moderate
Auberge du Château. Tel: 54.81.03.14. Credit Cards: Visa. Carte FF180–200, menus FF60 (lunch only), FF90 (weekends and holidays), FF110, FF135.

• **VENDOME**
(32 km NW Blois, 56 km NE Tours)

Hotel/Restaurant, Moderate/Expensive
Le Vendôme. 15 Faubourg Chartrain. Tel: 54.77.02.88; fax: 54.73.90.71. Credit Cards: Mastercard, Visa. Rooms: FF280–460, demi-pension FF360 –420, obligatory in season. Closed 20 December–3 January. Restaurant La Cloche Rouge: carte FF300, menus FF100–300.

Hotel/Restaurants, Moderate
Capricorne. Facing rail station. Tel: 54.80.27.00; fax: 54.77.30.63. Credit Cards: Mastercard, Visa. Rooms: FF190–290, demi-pension FF240–290. Restaurant: FF60–200.
Grand Hôtel St Georges. 14 Rue Poterie. Tel: 54.77.25.42; fax: 54.80.22.57. Credit Cards: Amex, Mastercard. Rooms: FF130–280, demi-pension FF300–350. Restaurant: FF100–240. Closed Saturday lunch.

Restaurants, Moderate
Petit Bilboquet. (Route N10 towards Tours). Tel: 54.77.16.60. Credit Cards: Mastercard, Visa. Closed 6–27 August, Sunday night and Monday. FF120–180.

Sologne

CHATEAUX D'ACCUEIL

Château de la Beuvrière. (7 km SW Vierzon by N20, between Route Jacques-Coeur and Châteaux de la Loire), St-Hilaire-de-Court, 18100 Vierzon. Tel: 48.75.14.63; fax: 48.75.47.62. Credit Cards: Amex, Diners, Visa. Comte et Comtesse de Brach. 11th-century château, rebuilt in the Renaissance and recently restored. Set in a 1,000-hectare estate. Rooms: 11 guest rooms and 3 suites FF340–580. Closed 10 January–1 March, 15–22 August. Lunches and dinners by request.

• **CHAUMONT-SUR-THARONNE**
(35 km S Orleans).

Hotel/Restaurant, Expensive
La Croix Blanche. 5 Place Mottu. Tel: 54.88.55.12; fax: 54.88.60.40. Credit Cards: Amex, Diners, Mastercard, Visa. Rooms: FF250–500, demi-pension FF500. Closed Wednesday except July/August, 15 January–28 February. Restaurant: classic cuisines of Touraine and Southwest. Carte FF300, menus FF150–360.

Restaurant, Moderate/Expensive
La Grenouillère. Chaumont-sur-Tharonne 41600. Tel: 54.88.50.71. Credit Cards: Visa. Open every day. Good classic French cuisine. Carte FF250, menus FF100–200.

• **LA FERTE-ST-AUBIN**
(21 km S Orléans)

Hotel/Restaurant, Moderate
Hotel du Perron. 9 Rue du General Leclerc. Tel: 38.76.53.36; fax: 38.64.80.11. Credit Cards: Amex, Diners, Mastercard, Visa. Rooms: FF240–340. Closed 15–30 January. Restaurant: Good fish and game; sample Tarte Tatin; carte FF230–270, menus FF140–230.

Restaurant, Moderate/Expensive
Ferme de la Lande. (2.5 km NE on Route du Marcilly-en-Villette). Tel: 38.76.64.37. Credit Cards: Visa, Mastercard. Closed Wednesday except July/August. Carte from FF300, menus FF140–240.

• MENESTREAU
(10 km E La Ferté-St-Aubin by D17 and D108)

Hotel/Restaurant, Expensive
Château de Villiers. Route Vouzon, 45240 La Ferté-St-Aubin. Tel: 38.76.90.12. Credit Cards: Amex, Diners, Mastercard, Visa. Quiet, in pretty grounds. Rooms: FF400–980, demi-pension FF350 –600. Closed 18–26 December, 15 January–15 February. Restaurant: FF120–200.

• LA FERTE-ST-CYR
(13 km S Beaugency)

Hotel/Restaurant, Moderate
Hôtel St Cyr. 15 Faubourg Bretagne. Tel: 54.87.90.51. Credit Cards: Diners, Mastercard, Visa. Modern Logis. Rooms: FF190–280. Closed 16 January–15 March, Monday (except evenings 15 June–15 September), Sunday night out of season. Restaurant: FF80–210.

• LAMOTTE-BEUVRON
(36 km S Orléans, 40 km NE Romorantin)

Hotel/Restaurants, Moderate
Monarque. Avenue Hôtel de Ville. Tel: 54.88.04.47. Credit Cards: Amex, Diners, Mastercard, Visa. Rooms: FF120–250, demi-pension FF185–230. Closed 16–26 August, 1 February–1 March, Tuesday night and Wednesday. Restaurant: FF90–250.
Hôtel Tatin. 5 Avenue de Vierzon. Tel: 54.88.00.03. Credit Cards: Visa. Rooms: FF290–470. Closed Sunday dinner, Monday, last three weeks in January through the third week in February. Restaurant: simple French fare, good game and Loire fish. Home of the famous Tarte Tatin, which is available all day long in the restaurant.

• NOUAN-LE-FUZELIER
(44 km S. Blois, 8 km S Lamotte-Beuvron)

Hotel/Restaurants, Moderate
Moulin de Villiers. (3 km NE by D44 on Route de Chaon). Tel: 54.88.73.55. Credit Cards: Mastercard, Visa. In beautiful forest setting with private pond; calm; simple rooms. Rooms: FF170–290. Closed Tuesday night and Wednesday in November/December,

1–15 September, 2 January–18 March. Restaurant: FF85–200.

• ST-VIATRE
(8 km W by D93)

Hotel/Restaurant, Moderate
Auberge de Chichonne. P. de l'Eglise. Tel: 54.88.91.33; fax: 54.96.18.06. Credit Cards: Amex, Mastercard, Visa. In the peaceful countryside, the old house has been thoroughly modernised. Rooms: FF320, demi-pension FF350. Closed Tuesday night, Wednesday, 24–26 December, March. Restaurant: FF100–200.

Hotel, Moderate
Les Charmilles. Route de Pierrefitte-sur-Sauldre (D122). Tel: 54.88.73.55. Credit Cards: Mastercard, Visa. Outside the village; peaceful setting. Rooms: FF270–400. Closed 15 December–15 March, Monday October–December.

Restaurant, Moderate
Le Dahu. 14 Rue H.-Chapron. Tel: 54.88.72.88. Credit Cards: Amex, Mastercard, Visa. Closed Tuesday night and Wednesday (except 1 July–10 September). Inventive regional cuisine. Good fish. Carte FF300, menus FF130–250.

• ROMORANTIN (ROMORANTIN-LANTHENAY)
(68 km S Orléans, 41 km SE Blois)

Hotel/Restaurant, Expensive
Grand Hôtel du Lion d'Or. 69 Rue G. Clémenceau. Tel: 54.76.00.28; fax: 54.88.24.87. Credit Cards: Amex, Diners, Mastercard, Visa. Luxurious Relais et Châteaux right in the middle of Romorantin. Recently refurbished, with pretty garden and beautiful restaurant. Rooms: FF650–1,850. Closed early-January to mid-February. Restaurant: two Michelin stars and one of the highest Gault & Millau ratings. Carte FF400–700, menus FF400–650.

Hotel/Restaurants, Moderate
Le Colombier. 10 Place du Vieux-Marché. Tel: 54.76.12.76. Credit Cards: Mastercard, Visa. Rooms: FF240–300. Closed 15–22 September, 15 January–15 February. Restaurant: FF180–230, menus FF90 (weekdays only), FF155. Good value.

Le Lanthenay. (2.5 km N Romorantin), Place de l'Eglise, Lanthenay. Tel: 54.76.09.19; fax: 54.76.72.91. Credit Cards: Mastercard, Visa. Quiet hotel in peaceful setting. Good value. Rooms: FF250–280, demi-pension FF300. Closed 25–30 September, mid-February to mid-March, restaurant closed Monday and Sunday night. Restaurant: FF100–270.

• VIERZON
(85 km S Orléans, 74 km SE Blois)

Hotel/Restaurants, Moderate
La Sologne. (2 km S on Route Châteauroux by D918). Tel: 48.75.15.20. Credit Cards: Mastercard, Visa. In a pleasant, quiet setting; nicely furnished rooms. Rooms: FF230–350. Closed (restaurant only) Christmas and February school vacations, Saturday lunch and Sunday except holidays. Restaurant La Grillade: FF130–220.

Restaurant, Moderate
La Grange des Epinettes. 40 Rue Epinettes. Tel: 48.71.68.81; fax: 48.71.69.06. Credit Cards: Amex, Diners, Mastercard, Visa. Open every day. Carte FF200–250, menus FF80–220.

Berry

HOTELS & RESTAURANTS

• ISSOUDUN
(129 km Tours, 34 km Vierzon)

Hotel/Restaurant, Expensive
La Cognette. 2 Boulevard Stalingrad (restaurant) and Rue Minimes (hotel). Tel: 54.21.21.83; fax: 54.03.13.03. Credit Cards: Amex, Diners, Mastercard, Visa. Very comfortable hotel and elegant restaurant with Michelin star and high Gault & Millau rating. Rooms: FF350–600, demi-pension FF380–650. Closed Sunday night, Monday (except holidays), 2–26 January. Restaurant: carte FF450, menus FF200 (weekdays only), FF300, FF380, FF480.

Hotel/Restaurant, Moderate
Hôtel France, Restaurant Les Trois Rois. 3 Rue P. Brosslette. Tel: 54.21.00.65; fax: 54.21.50.61.

Credit Cards: Amex, Diners, Mastercard, Visa. Rooms: FF180–260, demi-pension FF250 –350. Restaurant: FF90–280.

• DIOU
(12 km N Issoudun on D918)

Restaurant, Moderate/Good Value
Restaurant L'Aubergeade. Tel: 54.49.22.28. Credit Cards: Mastercard, Visa. Closed Wednesday and Sunday nights, 20 December–4 January. Good wines from region of Reuilly. Carte FF180–200, menus FF80 (weekdays only), FF110 (weekends and holidays only), FF120 (weekdays only).

• ST-AIGNAN-SUR-CHER
(39 km S Blois, 61 km E Tours)

Hotel/Restaurant, Moderate/Good Value
Grand Hôtel St Aignan. 7 Quai Jean-Jacques Delormes. Tel: 54.75.18.04. Credit Cards: Mastercard, Visa. Rooms: FF95–300, demi-pension FF180–300. Closed Sunday night, Monday out of season, 15 December–1 February, Friday night and Saturday lunch 1 November–1 March. Restaurant: menus FF68–190.

• NOYERS-SUR-CHER
(1 km N St-Aignan-sur-Cher)

Restaurant, Moderate
Relais Touraine et Sologne. Le Boeuf Couronné. Tel: 54.75.15.23. Credit Cards: Diners, Mastercard, Visa. Closed Tuesday night and Wednesday except school holidays, 4 January–20 February. FF120–280.

• VALENCAY
(55 km S Blois)

Hotel/Restaurant, Expensive
Hôtel d'Espagne. 9 Rue du Château. Tel: 54.00.00.02; fax: 54.00.12.63. Credit Cards: Amex, Mastercard, Visa. Rooms: FF470–670, apartments FF900–1,000, demi-pension FF560–760. Closed Sunday/Monday 15 October–15 March. Restaurant: carte FF400, menus FF200 –320.

Restaurant, Inexpensive
Chêne Vert. Tel: 54.00.06.54. Credit Cards: Mastercard. Closed Sunday

night and Saturday except 25 June–16 September, last week in May, 4 December–16 January. FF70–150.

• VEUIL
(6 km Valençay)

Restaurant, Inexpensive/Good Value
St-Fiacre. Tel: 54.40.32.78. Credit Cards: Mastercard, Visa. Closing days: Tuesday night and Wednesday. FF180.

Orléans & Orléanais

HOTELS & RESTAURANTS

• ORLÉANS
(130 km SW Paris, 112 km NE Tours)

Hotel/Restaurant, Expensive
Sofitel. 44 Quai Barentin. Tel: 38.62.17.39. Credit Cards: Amex, Diners, Mastercard, Visa. Rooms: FF495. Restaurant La Venerie: carte FF300, menu FF120.

Hotels, Moderate
Orléans. 6 Rue A. Crespin. Tel: 38.53.35.34; fax: 38.53.68.20. Credit Cards: Amex, Mastercard, Visa. Rooms: FF280–390.
Jackhotel. 18 Cloître St-Aignan. Tel: 38.54.48.48; fax: 38.77.17.59. Credit Cards: Visa, Diners. Small and central, with garden. Rooms: FF230–300.
Terminus. 40 Rue de la République. Tel: 38.53.24.64. Credit Cards: Amex, Mastercard, Visa. Rooms: FF200–280. Closed 24 December–7 January.
Les Cèdres. 17 Rue Mar. Foch. Tel: 38.62.22.92; fax: 38.81.76.46. Credit Cards: Amex, Diners, Mastercard, Visa. Rooms: FF200–390.
Marguerite. 14 Place Vieux Marché. Tel: 38.53.74.32. Credit Cards: Visa, Mastercard. Rooms: FF140–200.

Restaurants, Expensive
La Crémaillère. 34 Rue N.-D.-de-Recouvrance. Tel: 38.53.49.17. Credit Cards: Amex, Diners, Visa. Closed Sunday night, Monday. The best in Orléans with two Michelin stars and a very high Gault & Millau rating. Carte FF380–470, menus FF220–320.
Les Antiquaires. 2–4 Rue au Lin. Tel: 38.53.52.35; fax: 38.62.06.95. Credit Cards: Amex, Diners, Visa. Closed Sunday, Monday, 25 December–1 January, 23–30 April, 30 July–

20 August. Michelin star and high Gault & Millau rating, very good local fish and game. Carte FF280–400, menus FF200–300.
La Poutrière. 8 Rue Brèche, 45100 Orléans. Tel: 38.66.02. 30. Credit Cards: Amex, Diners, Mastercard, Visa. Closed Sunday night, Monday. Michelin star, high Gault & Millau rating. Classical French. Carte FF300, menus FF160–260.

Restaurants, Moderate
Lautrec. 26 Place Châtelet. Tel: 38.54.09.54. Credit Cards: Amex, Diners, Mastercard, Visa. Closed 15–31 July, 15–31 December, Sunday. Belle époque restaurant near old market, modern French cooking with Southwestern French influence. Carte FF300, menus FF110, FF140, FF200.
Loire. 6 Rue J. Hupeau. Tel: 38.62.76.48. Credit Cards: Amex, Mastercard, Visa. Closed Saturday lunch, Sunday, 1–7 May, 14–27 August, 8–15 January. Carte FF130–300.
Chez Jean. 64 Rue Ste. Catherine. Tel: 38.53.08.15. Credit Cards: Amex, Mastercard, Visa. Closed Friday night, Sunday except holidays, 15 August–6 September. Good value, FF65–180

• OLIVET
(5 km S Orléans by D15)

Hotel/Restaurant, Moderate
Le Rivage. 635 Rue Reine Blanche, 45160 Olivet. Tel: 38.66.02.93; fax: 38.56.31.11. Credit Cards: Amex, Diners, Mastercard, Visa. In a pretty, calm setting on the Loiret. Rooms: FF370–470, demi-pension FF500, obligatory in season. Restaurant: carte FF300–350, menus FF170–300. Closed 25 December–15 January. Restaurant closed Sunday nights 1 November–19 March.

• CLERY-ST-ANDRE
(15 km SW Orléans)

Hotel/Restaurant, Moderate
Les Bordes. 9 Rue des Bordes. Tel: 38.45.71.25. Credit Cards: Visa. Large red-brick and stone house, with large rooms. Pretty grounds. Rooms: FF100–350. Restaurant: carte FF200, menus FF70–150.

• GIEN
(64 km SE Orléans)

Hotel/Restaurant, Moderate to Expensive
Le Rivage. 1 Quai de Nice. Tel: 38.37.79.00; fax: 38.38.10.21. Credit Cards: Amex, Diners, Mastercard, Visa. Great service, pretty location. Rooms: FF300–500, apartments FF400 –600, demi-pension FF335, obligatory in season. Closed 4 February–9 March. Restaurant: Michelin star, good Loire river fish and game, carte from FF300, menus FF160–350.

Hotel/Restaurant, Moderate
Hôtel Beau Site, Restaurant La Poularde. 13 Quai de Nice. Tel: 38.67.36.05. Credit Cards: Amex, Diners, Visa. Rooms: FF320–370. Restaurant: Good value, FF90–300. Closed Sunday night, 27 August–3 September, 1–15 January.

• ST-THIBAULT
(5 km NE Sancerre by D955 and D4)

Hotel/Restaurant, Moderate
L'Etoile. 2 Quai de Loire. Tel: 48.54.12.15. Credit Cards: none. Rooms: FF105–350. Closed Wednesday out of season, 15 November–1 March. Wonderful restaurant overlooking the Loire, specialising in grilled fish and meat. Good cheese tray and Sancerre. Carte FF250, menus FF120–350.

• SANCERRE
(201 km S Paris, 71 km E Vierzon)

Hotel/Restaurant, Moderate
Hotel Panoramic. Rempart des Augustins. Tel: 48.54.22.44; fax: 48.54.39.55. Credit Cards: Amex, Mastercard, Visa. New hotel without much charm, but beautiful views. Rooms: FF300–350, demi-pension FF280–380. Restaurant Tasse d'Argent, 18 Rempart des Augustins. Tel: 48.54.01.44. Credit Cards: Amex, Diners, Mastercard, Visa. FF100–280.

Restaurant, Moderate/Expensive
La Tour. 31 Place de la Halle. Tel: 48.54.00.81; fax: 48.78.01.54. Credit Cards: Amex, Mastercard, Visa. Closed Monday night and Tuesday except July/August, 18 December–5

January, 2 weeks in March. Carte from FF300, menus FF120–200.

Bed & Breakfast

Bed and breakfast accommodation is fairly widely available in private houses, often on working farms, whose owners are members of the Fédération Nationale des Gîtes Ruraux de France. All such accommodation is inspected by a local representative of the Fédération to ensure that standards are maintained in accordance with its "star" rating (which in fact is shown by ears of corn on a scale of one to four). Bookings can be made for an overnight stop or a longer stay. Breakfast is included in the price (from around FF140 for one person, FF180 for a couple) and evening meals – usually made with local produce and extremely good value – are often available.

Staying with a family in this way provides an ideal opportunity really to get to know the local area and its people. Brochures of all recognised Gîtes-Chambres d'hôtes are available from Gîtes de France organisation in each *département*. Some 14,000 chambres d'hôtes (guest rooms) are listed in *French Country Welcome*, available from the Gîtes de France office in London (*see Self Catering*), price £11.50 (£12.85 by post).

B&B Abroad offer a straightforward bed and breakfast service which can include ferry bookings if desired. They will book accommodation at either a single destination or various stops around the region. Contact: 5 Worlds End Lane, Green St Green, Orpington, Kent BR6 6AA. Tel. 01689-855538.

Café-Couette is a Paris-based organisation offering B&B, or as they call it, *Hébergement chez l'habitant*. Contact them at 8 Rue de l'Isly, 75008 Paris. Tel: (1) 42 94 92 00, fax: (1) 4294 93 12. The Café-Couette brochure is also available from the French Government Tourist Office in London, price £8.50 (£9.50 by post).

For B&B on a slightly grander scale, try Château Welcome, PO Box 66, 94 Bell Street, Henley-on-Thames RG9 1XS. Tel: 01491-578803. They organise stays in privately-owned châteaux where an evening meal is often also available. In Canada: book through Tours Chanteclerc, 65 Rue de

Brésoles, Montréal, Québec H2Y 1V7. Tel: 514-845 1236; and at 100 Adelaide Street West, Toronto, Ontario M11 1S3. Tel: 416-867 1595.

If you do not wish to book anything in advance, just look out for signs along the road (usually in the country) offering *chambres d'hôtes*. You will be taking pot luck, but you may be delighted by the simple farm food and accommodation on offer.

Self Catering

France probably has the best network of self-catering holiday cottages anywhere in Europe. The Fédération Nationale des Gîtes Ruraux de France was set up over 30 years ago with the aim of restoring rural properties (by means of offering grants to owners) on condition that these properties would then be let as cheap holiday homes for the less well-off town and city dwellers. These *gîtes* (literally – a place to lay one's head) have now become extremely popular with the British as an inexpensive way of enjoying a rural holiday in France. There is a terrific selection of *gîtes* in the Loire Valley, ranging from very simple farm cottages to grand manor houses and even the odd château.

The properties are all inspected by the Relais Départemental des Gîtes de France (the county office of the national federation) and given an *épi* (ear of corn) classification. The *gîtes* are completely self-catering (in many cases expect to supply your own bed linen), but most have owners living nearby who will tell you where to buy local produce (and, if the *gîte* is on a farm, they will often provide it). One salutary note: many of these cottages are on farms, and as such, are surrounded by wildlife – so if you are squeamish about the odd mouse in the kitchen, stay in a hotel! Having said that, the properties should be, and generally are, kept clean and in good order.

Most of the properties are rather off the beaten track and a car, or at least a bicycle, is usually essential. Bicycles can often be hired locally or even from *gîte* owners. Car hire is expensive, but some fly/drive packages still make this a relatively inexpensive way to visit the region, as *gîtes* can cost as little as F1,200 week for the whole house.

Many companies now offer "package tours" to *gîtes* and other self-catering properties, which include ferry travel and other services. A few are listed below; see also the small ads in the Sunday press. *Gîtes* do get very heavily booked in high season, so start the process in the New Year. If you prefer to deal directly with France, the Service Loisirs Accueil (*see Useful Addresses*) will send you a list of all the *gîtes* in their *département*.

Alternatively, you can book through the London booking office: Gîtes de France, 178 Piccadilly, WIV 9DB. Tel: (0171) 493 3480 – for a £3 membership you have the choice of over 100 gîtes in the region; or buy the *French Farm and Village Holiday* (Farm Holiday Guides, Seedhill, Paisley PA1 1JN). This book lists around 100 gîtes in the Loire Valley with full details for the independent traveller of how to book (sample letters in French are given).

The main ferry companies also offer gîte holidays in association with the Gîtes de France office in London – apply to the ferry companies for their brochures. The following companies also offer self-catering packages:

AA Motoring Holidays, PO Box 128, Fanum House, Basingstoke RG21 2EA. Tel: 01256-493878.

Air France Holidays, Gable House, 18-24 Turnham Green Terrace, London W4 1RF. Tel: 0181-742 3377.

Allez France, 27-29 West Street, Storrington RH20 4DZ. Tel: 01903-742345.

Hoseasons Holidays Abroad, Sunway House, Lowestoft NR32 3LT. Tel: 01502-500555, fax: 0502-500532.

Kingsland Holidays, Brunswick House, Exeter Street, Plymouth PL4 0AR. Tel: 01752-251688.

Vacances en Campagne, Bignor, Pulborough, West Sussex RH20 1QD. Tel: 01798-869433. The company has overseas agents in the US, and Canada (contact Sussex office for addresses).

VFB Holidays, Normandy House, High Street, Cheltenham GL50 3HW. Tel: 01242-526338.

Camping

There is a good choice of campsites right along the Loire Valley. The Comité Régional du Tourisme (see Useful Addresses) produces a list of all recognised sites in the region, along with a list of those that have facilities for handicapped visitors. As with other types of holiday accommodation, the sites get heavily booked in high season, so advance booking is well worth considering. The Camping Service at 69 Westbourne Grove, London W2 4UJ. Tel: (0171) 792 1944, can book sites and arrange ferry travel.

Campsites, like hotels, have official classifications – from one-star (minimal comfort, water points, showers and sinks) to four-star luxury sites which allow more space to each pitch and offer above-average facilities, which often include a restaurant or takeway food, games areas and even swimming pools. The majority of sites are two-star. Average prices are around FF25 per person per night at a one-star site, to around FF50 at a four star.

If you really like to get back to nature, and are unimpressed by the modern trappings of hot water and electric power, look out for camp-sites designated "*Aire naturelle de camping*" where facilities will be absolutely minimal and prices to match. These have a maximum of 25 pitches and so offer the opportunity to stay away from some of the more commercial sites (which can be huge).

Some farms offer "official" sites also under the auspices of the Fédération Nationale des Gîtes Ruraux (see self-catering, above); these are designated "*Camping à la ferme*". Again, facilities are usually limited but farmers are only allowed to have six pitches and, if you are lucky, you will get to know and enjoy the farm life and some of its produce.

Package camping holidays: these are now very popular with British holidaymakers and ideal for other overseas visitors too, as all the camping paraphernalia is provided on the site – you only have to take your normal luggage. Many companies now offer this type of holiday, mostly with ferry travel included in the all-in price. Like other package tours, the companies have couriers on the sites to help with any problems. It is interesting to note that, where such companies have taken over sections of existing sites, facilities have improved to meet the demands of their customers and to the benefit of all the campers. Be warned, though, that some of the sites are very large, so might not suit those who wish to get away from it all.

A selection of package operators is listed below; for others, check the Sunday press.

Canvas Holidays, 12 Abbey Park Place, Dunfermline KY12 7PD. Tel: 01383-621000. Pioneers in the field; offer a nanny service.

Eurocamp Travel, Canute Court, Toft Road, Knutsford, Cheshire WA16 0NL. Tel: 01565-626262.

French Country Camping, 126 Hempstead Road, Kings Langley, Herts WD4 8AL. Tel: 01923-261316.

French Life Holidays, 26 Church Road, Horsforth, Leeds LS18 5LG. Tel: 0113-2390077, fax: 0113-2584211. Offer a "multicentre" deal.

Keycamp Holidays, Ellerman House, 92-96 Lind Road, Sutton SM1 4PL. Tel: 0181-395 4000.

Solaire International Holidays, 1158 Stratford Road, Hall Green, Birmingham B28 8AF. Tel: 0121-778 5061.

Sunsites, Canute Court, Toft Road, Knutsford, Cheshire WA16 0NL. Tel: 01565-652222.

USEFUL ADDRESSES & PUBLICATIONS

The *French Federation of Camping and Caravanning Guide* (FFCC), lists 11,300 sites nationwide, and also shows which have facilities for disabled campers. Available in the UK from Springdene, Shepherd's Way, Fairlight, East Sussex TN35 4BB.

Michelin *Green Guide – Camping/Caravanning France*. Very informative and also lists sites with facilities for the disabled. Published annually in March. Camping and Caravanning Club, 11 Lower Grosvenor Place, London SW1.

Caravan Club, East Grinstead House, East Grinstead, Sussex RH19 1UA.

Youth Hostels

Holders of accredited Youth Hostel Association cards may stay in any French hostels. These are run by two separate organisations: Fédération Unie des Auberges de Jeunesse (FUAJ), 27 Rue Pajol, 75018 Paris. Tel: (1) 44.89.87.27; fax: 44.89.87.10, which is affiliated to the International Youth Hostel Federation, and the Ligue Française pour les Auberges de

Jeunesse (LFAJ), 38 Boulevard Raspail, 75007 Paris. Tel: (1) 45.48.69.84; fax: 45.44.57.47. There are about 20 accredited hostels in the region available by post from the YHA, 8 St. Stephen's Hill, St Albans, Herts. Tel: (01727) 845047, or in person from:.

14 Southampton Street, London WC2E 7H7. Tel: (0171) 836 8541. They will also handle membership queries. Tel: (0171) 836 1036.

In the USA apply to American Youth Hostels Inc., PO Box 37613, Washington DC 20013/7613. Tel: (202) 783 6161.

Gîtes d'Etapes offer hostel accommodation and are popular with ramblers and horse riders (some offer stabling). All official *gîtes d'étapes* come under the auspices of the Relais Départementaux des Gîtes Ruraux (for addresses contact the Service Loisirs Accueil, *see Useful Addresses*). Prices are similar to youth hostels – around FF50 per night for basic accommodation, but up to FF110 or more in the more luxurious establishments which may be on farms offering riding facilities and/or stabling. You do not have to be a member of any organisation to use them.

Attractions

Special Attractions

For most people, the culture of the Loire Valley is inextricably linked with its fabulous châteaux whose history goes right back to the time when the earliest castles and fortresses were built purely for defensive purposes. Gradually, over the centuries, the châteaux began to be built more for leisure and pleasure than anything else – summer residences and hunting lodges for the incumbent royalty. This led to wealthy merchants putting up flamboyant residences all along the Loire to vie with each other for royal attention.

In the battle to attract tourists today, many châteaux offer more than simply the historic buildings them-

selves. Some have superb gardens or wildlife parks, many incorporate museums and an increasing number put on *son-et-lumière* performances (see *Live Arts*).

However, there are many other reasons for visiting the Loire. Many of the venues listed in the Attractions section are quite particular to the region and well worth seeking out. For instance The Loire landscape is dotted with windmills; some have fallen into disrepair, but quite a few have been saved – notably by a group of volunteers called "Les Amis des Moulins", and are open to the public. Le Moulin de la Herpinière near Turquant is perhaps the most famous, and is incidentally, surrounded by troglodyte dwellings.

Perhaps one of the most fascinating aspects of the region, these caves or troglodyte dwellings are to be found in the chalk cliffs along the Loire, particularly in the west of the region. Few are now inhabited, but many are still used – either for storage or for the cultivation of mushrooms. Some are used as private homes, and some can be visited.

Not all the homes were humble peasant dwellings either; a few were established in quite a grand style. Most of the dwellings that remain date from the 15th century, although there are a few earlier examples. The white stone (*tuffeau*) that was excavated to make the dwellings was used for other buildings above ground – from châteaux to ordinary urban houses – providing the characteristic white and grey slate architecture.

The following places all have a large number of troglodyte dwellings: Chinon, Langeais, Montoire, Mauvières, Rochcorbon, Saumur, Vouvray and Veretz. In Touraine it is not done to visit inhabited caves, but in Anjou the locals are more receptive to surprise visits. On the whole, it is best to restrict yourself to commercial wine cellars or dwellings open to the public. Incidentally, the word "troglodyte" is not appreciated by many locals, who prefer the less colourful term caves demeurantes (inhabited caves). Even so, caves troglodytes remains the term in popular use, with all its barbaric associations.

The prestigious National Riding School, just outside Saumur, is open to the public and its famous Cadre

Noir presents frequent riding displays during the tourist season.

The region is famous for its production of flowers for the commercial market and Doué-la-Fontaine in Maine-et-Loire is known as the City of Roses. It celebrates this fact with a rose festival at the beginning of July and "rose days" throughout the month at the Parc des Ecuries Foulon where the rose garden has around 500 varieties.

The sparkling wine produced in the region, now competes creditably (at least in the UK) with the real thing and is made by the champagne method. Some viticulteurs are happy to open their cellars to the public.

Places of Interest

The biggest attraction of the Loire Valley is undoubtedly the châteaux, but even the most eager seekers after culture do need some variety, so this section gives a broad selection of alternative places to go.

The following listing covers a variety of different activities: technical visits, parks and gardens, caves (wine cellars) open to the public, steam railways and so forth. Some of the suggested venues are quite particular to the region and are well worth seeking out.

All places listed below are open daily, morning and afternoon (not including public holidays), except where otherwise specified. Most close for a long lunch break – 12 noon or 12.30 until 2pm or 2.30. A list of *son-et-lumière* performances and details of museums and châteaux are given under the heading of Live Arts.

Many of the major towns in the region offer guided tours of the town – enquire at the Office de Tourisme or Syndicat d'Initiative.

ANGERS: Maine-et-Loire.
Arboretum Gaston Allard, Rue Château d'Orgemont. Tel: 41.86.10.10. Also well worth a visit are the Jardin des Plantes and the Jardin du Mail.

APREMONT: Cher.
Floral park in the grounds of the château in an attractive medieval village. Restaurant. Park open Easter to 30 September. Tel: 48.80.41.41..

ARTENAY: Loiret.
Le Moulin de Pierre d'Artenay, on RN 20. Built in 1848, one of hundreds of windmills in the wheat-growing area of Beauce, this mill ceased production in 1902. As it was made of stone, not wood like most of the others, the building survived and has been restored to working order. Open the third Sunday in the month, April–October. Tel: 38.80.40.17.

AUTRECHE: Indre-et-Loire.
Domaine de Beaumarchais. Breeding park for wild boar. Tourist train and slide shows. Open April–30 September. Tel: 47.56.22.30.

BAUGÉ: Maine-et-Loire.
Château and Museum. Open 15 June–15 September, 11am–12pm and 3 – 6pm.
Croix d'Anjou in the Chapelle de la Girouardière (13th-century relic from the Crusades). Open every day except Thursday, 3 –4.30pm (Sundays until 4pm). Ring bell at 8 Rue de la Girouardière.
Pharmacy 17th-century, in the Hôpital St Joseph. Open 10am (10.30 Sundays and holidays) to 12 noon and 3–5.30pm (4.30pm, October–May).
Church in Le Vieil Baugé (3miles/5 km SE of Baugé). Leaning, twisted steeple and 11th–13th-century choir.

LA BORNE: Cher.
Atelier Bindel, La Borne, 18250 Henrichemont. Tel: 48.26.93.38. Pottery open to the public. See too the Pottery Museum, open afternoons Easter–1 November. Tel: 48.26.73.76.
BOURGEUIL: Indre-et-Loire, on N749, 25 miles (45 km) west of Tours.
The **wines** of Bourgeuil and St-Nicolas-de-Bourgeuil are produced virtually from a single type of grape, Cabernet Franc, and the results are delicious. There is a **Cave Touristique** in the town open to the public (check for availablity, BP 68, 37130 Bourgeuil. Tel: 47.97.72.01) and information is also available from the Tourist office.

BREIL: Maine-et-Loire.
Moulin au Jau, watermill, open mid-June to mid-September. The park of the Château de Lathan is also open all year.

CHALONNES-SUR-LOIRE: Maine-et-Loire.
A narrow-gauge **tourist train** runs along the granite Corniche Angevine giving good views of the river and this attractive town. Tel: 41.78.25.62.

CHAMBORD: Loir-et-Cher.
A coach shuttle (*navette*) links Chambord with Cheverny and Blois.
Walks: The national long-distance footpath, the Grande Randonnée 3, runs from St Dye sur Loire to the Château de Beauregard, cutting across the Domaine de Chambord.

CHÂTELAIS: Maine-et-Loire.
Domaine de la Petite Couère. Opening in 1990 is a new venture comprising an animal park, reconstructed village square with old shops and exhibitions, and a collection of vintage vehicles. A tourist train will run round the park. For information. Tel: 41.92.22.51.

CHÂTEAUNEUF-SUR-CHER: Cher.
Animal park in the grounds of the château, featuring wild and exotic species. Closed November–April except for Sunday afternoons. Tel: 48.60.64.21.

CHAVANNES: Maine-et-Loire.
La Magnanerie silk farm is situated in a former troglodyte dwelling, and visitors can follow all the processes of silk production there. Open Saturday and Sunday afternoons, June–October (Tuesday–Sunday afternoons in June and July). La Magnanerie, Chavannes, 49200 Le Puy Notre Dame. Tel: 41.52.29.16.

CHEMILLE: Maine-et-Loire.
Jardin des Plantes Médicinales. Collection of medicinal herbs and plants. Best seen mid-May to mid-October, but open all year. Tel: 41.30.35.17.

CHINON: Indre-et-Loire.
Centrale Nucléaire de Chinon, on the D7, 25 miles (45 km) west of Tours. Type "A" and "B" reactors on the left bank of the Loire, one of which was the first nuclear power station in France. It was decommissioned in 1973 and now serves as a museum. For more information and details of group visits, contact CPN de Chinon, Services Relations Publiques, BP 80, 37420 Avoine. Tel: 47.98.77.77.
A narrow-gauge **steam train** operates

from Chinon station for a round trip to **Richelieu** and back (120 minutes). It runs on Saturday and Sunday afternoons from mid-May to mid-September with extra daily trips 25 July–12 August. Tel: 47.58.12.97.
There is also a Railway Museum at Richelieu.

COUTURE-SUR-LOIR: Loir-et-Cher.
Manoir de La Possonnière (birthplace of poet Pierre de Ronsard). Open Saturday and Sunday afternoons, April–1 November, plus Wednesday, Thursday and Friday afternoons, 16 June–31 August. Tel: 54.72.40.05.

DÉNEZÉ-SOUS-DOUÉ: Maine-et-Loire.
Caverne Sculpté, carved cave discovered recently which dates back to the 16th century, showing several hundred carved figures in a remarkable underground site. Open every afternoon, Easter to mid-November (all day July and August); Saturday and Sunday out of season. Information: DAP, 49700 Dénezé-sous-Doué. Tel: 41.59.15. 40.

DOUÉ-LA-FONTAINE: Maine-et-Loire, 10 miles (17 km) from Saumur.
Parc des Ecuries Foulon, former park of the ruined château, now maintained by the council with a magnificent rose garden (5,000 plants covering 500 varieties). Best seen June–October, but open all year. Tel: 41.59.93.85
Parc Zoologique des Troglodytes, Les Minières, Route de Cholet, specialises in exotic domestic animals, e.g. Vietnamese pigs, dwarf goats. Tel: 41.59.18.58. See too the former quarry which was transformed into an amphitheatre in the 15th century. It conceals a network of deep galleries. At nearby **La Fosse** inhabited caves are open to visitors.
Le Moulin Cartier, the last windmill (1910) to be built in Anjou and now restored by Les Amis des Moulins; also wine tasting. Open July–15 September. Information from Percher Frères, Viticulteurs, 49700 Les Verchers-sur-Layon. Tel: 41.59.20.49.

EPINEUIL-LE-FLEURIEL: Cher.
Ecole de **Grand Meaulnes**. The school which provided the setting for Alain Fournier's novel is open to the public 1 April–15 November (closed Tuesday). Tel: 48.63.04.82.

LA FLÈCHE: Sarthe.
Military school (Prytanée), especially the Chapelle St-Louis (17th century).
Chapelle Notre-Dame-des-Vertus (remarkable painted ceilings and 16th-century wood carvings).
Zoological Park (at Tertre Rouge to southwest of La Flèche). Open 9am–7pm (closes at nightfall from October –end-March); closed January. Tel: 43.94.04.55.

GENNES: Maine-et-Loire.
The countryside around Gennes is notable for is **megalithic monuments**: dolmens and menhirs (both types of standing stones) along with an amphitheatre constitute an "open-air museum", which comes under the auspices of the town's Archaeological Museum. Winter opening restricted to Saturday afternoon and Sunday. Tel: 41.51.83.33.
Also nearby is the **Moulin de Sarré**, watermill. Open daily 1 May–30 September. Tel: 41.38.07.10.

GIEN: Loiret.
Faïncerie de Gien, pay a visit to the famous earthenware factory. Tel: 38.67.00.05; also the Museum (*see* listings).

INGRANNES: Loiret.
Arboretum des Grandes Bruyères, gardens at the heart of the Orléans forest. Open by appointment. Tel: 38.57.12.61.

LE LION D'ANGERS: Maine-et-Loire.
Haras National, Domaine de l'Isle Briant, national stud open to the public. Also a regular venue for race meetings. Tel: 41.95.82.46.

LE MANS: Sarthe.
Cathédrale St-Julien (11th–15th century). Spectacular flying buttresses, 16th-century organ, 12th–13th-century stained-glass windows.
Le Vieux Mans, especially Rue de la Reine Bérangère. 15th–16th-century houses.
Musée d'Histoire et d'Ethnographie (numbers 7–11) with interesting ceramic and pewter collections. Open 10am–12 noon and 2–6pm. Closed Monday and Tuesday. Musée de Tessé: Art museum. Enamel champlevé portrait of Geffroi V Plantagenêt (12th-century), Italian and

Loire Valley Primitives and objects from Ancient Egypt, Italy and Greece. Open 9am to 12pm and 2pm to 6pm. Free entrance.
Eglise Notre-Dame-de-la-Couture. 17th-century tapestries, 16th-century marble Virgin and Child. 9am–4pm (3pm on Saturday).

LOURESSE-ROCHEMEINER: Maine-et-Loire.
Situated on a plain, 3 miles/6km north of Doué-la-Fontaine, this troglodyte village features two underground farms. Open daily April–1 November. Tel: 41.59.18.15

LUCHÉ-PRINGÉ: Sarthe.
Church (13th–16th century) with remarkable 16th-century wooden *pietà*.

LUSSAULT-SUR-LOIRE: Indre-et-Loire.
Aquarium de Touraine. Opened in 1994. Tel: 47.23.44.44.

MALICORNE: Sarthe.
Tessier art workshop and potteries. Guided tours daily of workshops and museum. Closed Sunday mid-September to Easter.

MAULEVRIER: Maine et Loire.
Parc Oriental, is an exotic park in the Japanese style, complete with pagoda and 200 species of trees, beautifully created by architect Alexandre Marçel at the turn of the century. Exhibition and sale of bonsai. The garden is a place of pilgrimage for Buddhists. Open every afternoon and Tuesday–Friday mornings in summer. Tel: 41.55.50.14.

MEHUN-SUR-YEVRE: Cher.
Centre Régional des Métiers d'Art, Les Grands Moulins. Studios of 200 artists and craftsmen (sculpture, engraving, tapestry, jewellery), and shop. Open afternoons Thursday to Sunday, March to December (also Wednesday May to September). Tel: 48.57.36.84.

MONTBOUY: Loiret.
Amphithéâtre de Chenevières – Gallo-Roman ruins. For information, Tel. 38.97.53.03.

MONTRICHARD: Loir-et-Cher.
Caves Monmousseau, 75 Route de Vierzon. Wine tasting in old cellars. Tel: 54.32.07.04. See too the nearby

Champi-Jandon mushroom farm at Bourré. Tel: 54.32.56.20.

NOGENT-SUR-VERNISSON: Loiret.
Arboretum National de Barres, created in 1873 with 10,000 trees of 2,800 different species. Closed weekends mid-March to mid-November. Tel: 38.97.62.21.

NANCAY: Cher.
One of the largest **radio telescopes** in the world can be seen here (visits organised for groups only, by prior arrangement).

NOYANT-LA-GRAVOYÈRE: Maine-et-Loire.
La Mine Bleue, underground caves of former slate mine. Slate was a very important factor in the local economy until as recently as the 1930s when this mine was closed. Here the mine has just been reopened as a tourist site. Donning hard hats, visitors are taken underground and shown round the galleries by means of a miners' train. *Son-et-lumière* displays help set the scene. Also at the site is the St-Blaise leisure park with various amusements for adults and children. Closed November–May (mine also closed Tuesday in summer). Tel: 41.61.55.60.

MONTREUIL-BELLAY: Maine-et-Loire.
L'Aquarium des Poissons de Loire, most of the 40 species of fish found locally are on view; also a diorama of 200 animals in their natural habitats and a small country museum. Closed Monday and winter. Tel: 41.52.35.90.

OBTERRE: Indre.
Haute-Touche safari park. Closed November to end-March. Route d'Azay, Obterre, 36290 Mézières-en-Brenne. Tel: 54.39.20.82.

ORLÉANS: Loiret.
Park Floral Orléans-la-Source, floral park with roaming wildlife. There is a restaurant within the park (Tel: 38.63.20.51), and a little train which runs afternoons in season (except Friday). The park itself is closed in the morning from mid-November to 1 April. Tel: 38.63.33.17.

OUZOUER-SUR-TREZÉE: Loiret.
There are Gallo-Roman ruins in the

outbuildings of the Château de Pont-Chevron. Tel: 38.31.92.02.

PITHIVIERS: Loiret.
A tourist steam train runs from the SNCF station in Rue Carnot. See too the Transport Museum. Open Sunday afternoons May–9 October. Tel: 38.30.50.02.

POILLY-LEZ-GIEN: Loiret.
Chevrerie du Grand Bardelet, farm producing goats cheese, also exhibition of old farming equipment, video. Tel: 38.67.29.24.

PONCÉ-SUR-LOIR: Sarthe.
Poncé Arts and Craft Centre, Paillard Mill on the bank of the river. Watch the artists at work pursuing their various crafts: pottery, glass-blowing, wrought ironwork, woodwork, weaving, making lampshades. Closed on Sunday. Workshops may be visited: 8am–noon and 2–6.30pm. Tel: 43.44.45.31.
Château (16th century). Remarkable Renaissance staircase and interesting folklore museum. Open 10am–12 noon and 2–6pm. Closed mornings on Sunday and holidays).

LA POSSONNIÈRE: Maine-et-Loire.
Moulin de la Roche, is a completely restored windmill and can be seen in action every Sunday and public holiday between 15 March and 15 November at 2.30pm and 7pm It lies 12 miles (20 km) west of Angers on the road between La Possonnière and St-Georges-sur-Loire, near l'Arche leisure park. Tel: 41.39.14.40.

RILLE: Indre-et-Loire.
Lac du Rillé, take a trip on the tourist train around the lake. Open Sunday afternoons May–13 July; Wednesday afternoon mid-July to mid-August. Tel: 47.24.60.19.

ST-AIGNAN-SUR-CHER: Loir-et-Cher.
Beauval Bird Park. Tel: 54.75.05.56.

ST GEORGES-DES-SEPT-VOIES: Maine-et-Loire.
L'Hélice Terrestre, fascinating displays of modes of troglodyte dwellings. Tel: 41.57.95.92.

ST-LAURENT-DE-LA-PLAINE: Maine-et-Loire.
Musée des Vieux Métiers, 7 Place Abbé Joseph Moreau. Important collection of old tools, machines and implements, including wine-presses and looms, as well as reconstructed workshops. Open April–October inclusive. Tel: 41.78.24.08.

SAUMUR: Maine-et-Loire.
Ecole Nationale d'Equitation, St-Hilaire-St-Florent – just outside the town, the famous riding school is open to the public. Guided visits to the stables, outdoor arenas and saddleries. Entry prices vary according to what is included in the visit (afternoon visits are cheaper). The Cadre Noir cavalry also puts on over 20 displays throughout the summer. For information contact the tourist office or the school at BP 207, 49400 Saumur. Tel: 41.53.50.50.
Gratien & Meyer, Route de Montsoreau – free visit and tasting at the company's wine cellars; open daily July and August, or by reservation. BP 22, 49400 Saumur. Tel: 41.51.01.54.
Hôpital de la Providence, at Ardilliers, these caves were used as temporary refuges.

SAVONNIÈRES: Indre-et-Loire.
Petrifying caves (grottes pétrifiantes). Privately-owned caves where objects have literally been "turned to stone". Also on site are displays of prehistoric fauna, collections of fossils and a Gallo-Roman cemetery. Situated 8 miles (14 km) west of Tours.

SEUILLY: Indre-et-Loire.
Maison Natale de Rabelais, La Devinière, 37500 Chinon. Museum in the writer's birthplace, situated across the River Vienne from Chinon. Closed Wednesday, 1 February to mid-March and October until November. Tel: 47.95.91.18.

THORE-LA-ROCHETTE: Loir-et-cher.
The Valley du Loir tourist train runs from here, weekend afternoons 1 June to 31 August. Tel: 54.72.80.82..

TOURS: Indre-et-Loire.
Tropical Aquarium at the Château Royal, Quai d'Orléans. Tel: 47.64.29.52. Opendaily April to mid-November, afternoons only in winter.

TRÔO: Loir-et-Cher.
Troglodyte house – Grotte pétrifiante.
Open April through September, 8am–8pm.
Eglise St-Jacques-des-Guérets. 12th-century wall paintings.

TURQUANT: Maine-et-Loire.
Moulin de la Herpinière – completely restored windmill. Open daily 1 May–31 October, weekend afternoons in winter. Tel: 41.51.75.22.

LE-VAL-HULIN: Maine-et-Loire.
Troglo Tap. Situated in the cliffs, this cave was famous in the last century for production of pommes tapées, a savoury delicacy made from dried apples, rehydrated with wine, which was popular with the British Navy. Museum visits and tastings, April–September (daily July–August, otherwise weekends). Troglo Tap, Le Val Hulin, 49730 Turquant. Tel: 41.51.48.30.

VENDÔME: Loir-et-Cher.
For visitors wishing to experience village life at first hand, the Vendôme tourist office organises home-stays or visits to local farms. Called A la rencontre de paysans en Vendômois, the programme lets you watch the running of small bakeries, farms or troglodyte wine cellars. If you are suffering from boundless energy, remember that the Grandes Randonées national footpath links Vendôme and Montoire.

VILLANDRY: Indre-et-Loire, on D7, 10 miles (17 km) west of Tours.
The formal **Renaissance gardens** of the Château of Villandry are well worth a mention in their own right; a supplementary entrance fee is payable if you wish to visit the château. Gardens open all year; the chateau is closed from mid-November to mid-March. Tel: 47.50.02.90.

VILLAINES-LES-ROCHERS: Indre-et-Loire.
Société Coopérative Agricole de Vannerie. The town is noted for its basketwork, examples of which are exhibited and for sale at the co-operative (founded 1849). Tel: 47.45.43.03.

VOUVRAY: Indre-et-Loire, on N152, 6 miles (10 km) east of Tours.
The vineyards of Vouvray are spread over 8 communes and the **Cave des Grands Vins de Vouvray**, Rue de la Vallé Coquette, is open to the public

for visits and tastings. Tel: 47.52.75.03.

Visit too, Espace de la Vigne et du Vin, Rue Victor Hérault. Open all year. Tel: 47.52.76.00.

An Aerial View

The Loire Valley is a popular region for ballooning and trips are offered to the general public by various companies. This makes an exhilarating and novel way of seeing the châteaux. Tourist flights are also offered by helicopters and light aircraft – not nearly so romantic, of course! These trips, naturally, are quite pricey.

The Loir-et-cher Loisirs Accueil organises trips (*see Useful Addresses*), or try the following companies:
France Montgolfières, La Roulière, 41400 Monthou-sur-Cher. Tel: 54.71.75.40; fax: 54.71.75.78.
Air Espace, Le Château, 37310 Cigognè. Tel: 47.23.57.64; fax: 47.30.37.41.
La Compagnie des Montgolfières, BP 1442, 45004 Orléans cedex. Tel: 38.54.51.07.

Balloon Vacations are offered by Buddy Bombard's Great French Balloon Adventures, operating from two bases near Amboise and Tours. Trips of 3 or 7 nights include meals and château accommodation. Bombard describes the flights as "aerial naturewalks where we can pick leaves from the tops of trees if we wish"; most flights last about 2 hours and pass over farms, vineyards, villages and châteaux often hidden from view. For one-day flights. Tel: 80.26.63.30. Information on tours: The Bombard Society, 6727 Curran Street, McLean Virginia, 22101 USA. Tel: (800) 862-8537, or (703) 448-9407. Fax (703) 883-0958.

Museums & Art Galleries

Most museums charge an entrance fee; for those that are state-owned, expect to pay between FF25 and FF40 (half price on Sunday). Reductions are usually given for children, senior citizens and students – on production of a valid card. Those listed here are open every day, morning and afternoons (except public holidays) except where otherwise specified. Most close for lunch from noon or 12.30 to around 2.30pm.

Municipal museums generally have local exhibits and show the history of the area. Collections that are particular to the region and worth visiting are those dedicated to the horse (Saumur), the cultivation of mushrooms (also Saumur), Joan of Arc (Orléans), and pottery (Gien).

Museums housed in châteaux are mentioned here, but details of châteaux themselves are listed in the Architecture section.

ANGERS: Maine-et-Loire.
Apart from the château, Angers has several good museums. The **Musée Jean Lurçat et Tapisserie Contemporaine**, 4 Boulevard Arago, exhibits tapestries, ancient and modern. Tel: 41.87.17.50. Fine arts can be enjoyed at the **Musée des Beaux-Arts**, 10 Rue du Musée. Tel: 41.88.64.65. The **Galerie David d'Angers**, 33 bis Rue Toussaint, offers the works of the sculptor. Tel: 41.87.21.03. All these museums are closed Monday, mid-September to mid-June. There is also a **Natural History Museum** at 43 Rue Jules Guitton (Tel: 41.88.63.20) and a **Museum of Palaeontology** at 41 Place Imbach (Tel: 41.86.05.84); both of these are open Wednesday/Thursday and Saturday/ Sunday afternoons only.

Just outside the town, the company which produces the famous Cointreau liqueur has its own museum: **Espace Cointreau**, Carrefour Molière, St-Barthélemy. Closed Sunday. Tel: 41.43.25.21. Also at St-Barthélemy is the **Musée Européen de la Communication** at the Château de Pignerolles; closed November to April. Tel: 41.93.38.38.

AMBOISE: Indre-et-Loire.
Musée de la Poste, Hôtel de Joyeuse, 6 Rue de Joyeuse. Early history of the postal service in France, from its inception by Louis XI as a relay of horses to its later development as a letter delivery service. Closed Monday and all of January. Tel: 47.23.19.80.
Manoir de Clos-Lucé. Recently made working models of 40 of Leonardo da Vinci's inventions in the house where he spent his final years. He is buried in the castle chapel. See the film of his life. Closed January. Tel: 47.57.62.88.

BAGNEUX: Maine-et-Loire.
Small village outside Saumur, with enormous dolmen hidden away in local café garden. **Le Dolmen de Bagneux**, 56 Rue du Dolmen, Bagneux. Tel: 41.50.23.02.

BRAINE-SUR-ALLONNES: Maine-et-Loire.
Musée Historique et Archéologique. Closed Monday. Tel: 41.52.87.40. There is also a museum in a 13th-century fortified house and a painted cave. Open afternoons April–October. Tel: 41.52.87.40.–

BLOIS: Loir-et-Cher.
Musée d'Histoire Naturelle, Les Jacobins, Rue Anne de Bretagne, covers the natural history of the region. Open all day in July and August, otherwise afternoons only. Closed Monday. Nearby is the **Museum of Religious Art**, open Monday to Friday afternoon. Tel: 54.78.17.14.

BOURGES: Loiret.
Musée du Berry, Hôtel Cujas, 4 Rue des Arènes. Closed Monday and Sunday afternoon. Tel: 48.57.81.15.

BRIARE: Loiret.
Musée de l'Automobile, Rue Mal de Lattre de Tassigny (on N7). Vehicles from 1895 to 1960. Closed mornings mid-September to 1 May.
See also the **Musée de la Mosaïque et des Emaiux**, devoted to mosaics and enamelling, 1 Boulevard Loreau. Closed Monday except June to September. Tel: 38.31.20.51.

LA BUSSIÈRE: Loiret.
Château des Pêcheurs, 45230 Châtillon-Coligny – aquariums and museum of freshwater fishing. Open every day, except Monday, mid-March to mid-November.
Tel: 38.35.93.35.

CHÂTEAUNEUF-SUR-LOIRE: Loiret.
Musée de la Marine de Loire et du Vieux Châteauneuf – history of navigation on the river and of the people who worked on or alongside it. Open all week July and August (except Monday). Rest of year open weekends. Tel: 38.58.41.18, ext. 335.

CHÂTEAU-RENAULT: Indre-et-Loire.
Musééc du Cuir, on the RN 10, 18 miles (30 km) north of Tours. History

of the leather industry in a former tannery. Open afternoon on Wednesday, Saturday and Sunday, mid-May to mid-September. Tel: 47.56.03.59.

CHINON: Indre-et-Loire.
Musée Animée du Vin et de la Tonnellerie, 12 Rue Voltaire. All you need to know about local wine and barrel production. Tel: 47.93.25.63.

CHOLET: Maine-et-Loire.
The Musée des Guerres de Vendée, Rue Travot, recounts the history of the Vendée wars. Closed Tuesday. Tel: 41.62.20.78. *See* also the **Musée des Arts**, 50 Avenue Gambetta. Closed Tuesday. Tel: 41.62.29. 78. and the **Maison Paysanne de la Goubaudière**, Lac de Ribou. Closed Tuesday and every morning. Tel: 41.62.21.46.

DESCARTES: Indre-et-Loire.
Musée René Descartes et René Boylesve, 29 Rue Descartes. Dedicated to the philosopher who gave his name to the town, and the novelist Boylesve. Closed mornings and all day Tuesday. Tel: 47.59.70.61.

DOVE-LA-FONTAINE: Maine-et-Loire.
Musée des Commerces Anciens, Ecuries du Baron Foullon, Jardin des Roses. Features 20 old-style shops covering a century from 1850–1950. Closed monday. Tel: 41.59.28.23.

GIEN: Loiret.
Musée de la Faïençerie, Manufacture de Gien, Place de la Victoire. Fine pottery in the place where it is produced. Tel: 38.67.00.05. The château also houses an **International Museum of Hunting**. Tel: 38.67.00.05

ISSOUDUN: Indre.
Musée de Pharmacie, St-Roch et Apothicaire, 23 Rue de l'Hospice St-Roch. For those interested in the history of medical science. Closed all day Tuesday and Monday –Thursday morning, plus all of January. Tel: 54.21.01.76.

MONTJEAN: Maine-et-Loire.
Ecomusée de la Marine et des Industries de Loire – history of the development of the river and its connected industries: coal, lime and hemp. Open every afternoon except Monday, May–mid-September. Tel: 41.39.08.48.

MONTSOREAU: Maine-et-Loire.
Musée du Champignon – mushroom museum. Tel: 41.51.70.30.

ORLÉANS: Loiret.
Musée Historique et Archéologique de l'Orléanais, Hôtel Cabu, Place de l'Abbé Desnoyers. Housed in an elegant Renaissance building, the collection includes the Gallo-Roman bronzes found at Neuvy-en-Sullias in 1861 – said to be the finest such collection ever discovered. Closed Tuesday. Tel: 38.53.39.22.
Maison de Jeanne d'Arc, Place du Général de Gaulle. Dedicated to Saint Joan, with dioramas. Closed Monday, otherwise open mornings, except May–October when open all day. Tel: 38.79.25.45.
Musée des Beaux-Arts, 1 Rue Fernand Rabier – fine arts. Closed Tuesday. Tel: 38.42.07.83.

PONTLEVOY: Loir-et-Cher.
Musée du Poids Lourd – heavy goods vehicles. Musée municipal collection includes fascinating early photographs of the town and its inhabitants, and publicity material from the Poulain chocolate works. Closed Monday except during July and August. Tel: 54.32.60.80.

PREUILLY-SUR-CLAISE: Indre-et-Loire.
Musée de la Poterne, on the N752, 26 miles (42 km) south of Loches – old tools, crafts and local folklore. Open afternoons during school holidays. Tel: 47.94.50.04

RICHELIEU: Indre-et-Loire.
Museum in the **Hôtel de Ville** in the town founded by the Cardinal. Closed Saturday/Sunday (except July and August) and Tuesday. Tel: 47.58.10.13.

ROCHECORBON: Indre-et-Loire.
Musée de la Coiffe et Broideries de Touraine, 68 Quai de la Loire. Museum of embroidery, including traditional lace caps. Closed Tuesday and all of January, plus mornings in winter. Tel: 47.52.80.16.

ROMORANTIN: Loir-et-Cher.
Musée Municipal de la Course Automobile, 29–31 Faubourg d'Orléans. Racing cars. Open mid-March to mid-November; closed all day Tuesday and Monday and Sunday mornings. Tel:

54.76.07.06. The Town Hall (Hôtel de Ville) also houses the **Musée de Sologne**. Refurbished, check for opening hours. Tel: 54.76.07.06.

SACHÉ: Indre-et-Loire.
Museum dedicated to the writer Balzac, located in the château, where, thanks to the hospitality of friends that owned it, Balzac spent the best part of 10 years. Closed December and January. Tel: 47.26.86.50.

ST-LAURENT-DE-LA-PLAINE: Maine-et-Loire.
Musée des Vieux Métiers – traditional trades and crafts of the area; the largest museum of its kind in France. Tel: 41.78.24.08.

SAUMUR: Maine-et-Loire.
The château houses three museums: decorative arts; horses and toys. The first two are closed on Tuesday, the toy museum is closed October to March except on Sunday afternoon. Tel: 41.50.30.46. For the toy museum. Tel: 41.67.39.23.
Maison du Vin de Saumur, 25 Rue Beaurepaire – history of local wine production. Closed Monday, October–April and Sunday all year. Tel: 41.51.16.40.
Musée des Blindés – collection of armoured vehicles. Tel: 41.67.20.96.
Musée du Champignon, Route de Gennes, 49400 St-Hilaire-St-Florent – history of the cultivation of mushrooms, an important product for the area. Closed 15 November–15 January Tel: 41.50.25.01.

TOURS: Indre-et-Loire.
Several notable museums. The **Musée des Beaux Arts** in the former Archbishop's Palace at 18 Place François Sicard, is recognised as being one of the country's best provincial fine arts museums. Closed Tuesday. Tel: 47.05.68.73. The **Musée Grévin**, situated in the Royal Château brings history to life with over 30 waxwork tableaux animated by sound and light. Closed mornings mid-November–end of March. Tel: 47.61.02. 95.
The Hôtel Gouin is another worthy setting for the **Musée Archéologique**, 25 Rue du Commerce. Closed Friday, October through to mid-March. Tel: 47.66.22.32
Musée des Vins de Touraine, Celliers St-Julien, 16 Rue Nationale, traces the

development of wine production in the region. Closed on Tuesday. Tel: 47.61.07.93.

Slightly more esoteric is the **Musée des Equipages Militaires et du Train**, Rue du Plat d'Etain, which deals with the history of military baggage trains. Closed weekends. Tel: 47.77.20.35.

Another little specialist museum worth a look is the Petit Musée du Costume, 54 Boulevard Béranger. Open Tuesday to Sunday afternoons, except January. Tel: 47.61.59.17.

TRÉLAZE: Maine-et-Loire.
Musée de l'Ardoise, 32 Rue de la Maraîchère. Traces the history of slate mining in the region. Open Tuesday to Friday July to 15 September; Sunday afternoons in winter. Closed December to 15 February. Tel: 41.69.04.71.

VALENÇAY: Indre.
Car museum located in the château. Closed weekdays mid-November to mid-March.
Tel: 54.00.10.66.

VILLESAVIN: Loir-et-Cher.
This **château** at Tour-en-Sologne, 41250 Bracieux houses a collection of cars and horse-drawn carriages. Tel: 54.46.42.88.

Chateaux

"Valley of the Kings" is an apt title for a region whose wealth of châteaux and other fine buildings is quite awe-inspiring. A single trip is by no means enough to take in all the treasures of the region and it is easy to be tempted to try to see too much. Take it slowly – you may only go 6 miles (10 km) from one château to the next in a day, but you will be amply rewarded.

The delights of the Loire do not lie simply in the beautiful architecture and fine gardens. Some of the châteaux have the most splendid collections of tapestry, fine pottery and paintings. Others try to recreate history in spectacular tableaux and son-et-lumière displays – in fact that "art" was invented in the region. For opening times see Museums. Expect to pay an entrance fee.

AMBOISE: Indre-et-Loire.
Former royal château, now managed by the St Louis Foundation. Sumptu-

ous decoration and fine internal gardens. Tel: 47.57.00.98.

ANGERS: Maine-et-Loire.
A good example of sturdy military architecture, the largest existing fortress in France now houses several museums, the tapestries of the Apocalypse are of note. Tel: 41.86.81.94.

APREMONT-SUR-ALLIER: Cher.
A completely furnished castle which has been occupied by the same family since 1722, overlooking a medieval village. Also contains a carriage museum. Open every afternoon (except Tuesday); closed 25 December–Easter. Tel: 48.80.41.41.

AZAY-LE-RIDEAU: Indre-et-Loire.
Moated château built between two arms of the River Indre. Splendid example of the early Renaissance. Tel: 47.45.42.04.

BEAUREGARD: Loir-et-Cher.
Houses the "Gallery of the Famous", one of the few remaining such panelled galleries, illustrating the history of France from Philip VI to Louis XIII by means of over 300 portraits. Closed January to April and on Wednesday (except October). Château Royal de Beauregard, Cellettes, 41120 Les Montils. Tel: 54.70.40.05.

BLANCAFORT: Cher.
Dates back to the 15th century. Open April to November. Tel: 48.58.60.56.

BLOIS: Loir-et-Cher.
Royal château with Renaissance wing and famous staircase; also museum. Tel: 54.74.06.02.

BRISSAC: Maine-et-Loire.
At 7 storeys, Brissac is one of the tallest castles in France and it has some 150 rooms. Decorations include ancient tapestries. Open April to mid-October. Closed Tuesday, except in July and August. Tel: 41.91.22.21.

LA BUSSIÈRE: Loiret.
Known as the fisherman's castle, with aquaria and angling museum, plus park laid out by Le Nôtre. Open Easter to mid-October (not Tuesday, except July/August). Château La Bussière, 45230 Châtillon-Coligny. Tel: 38.35.93.35.

CHAMBORD: Loir-et-Cher.
One of the great royal châteaux, started by François I and built to a plan ascribed to Leonardo da Vinci. Also a game reserve with observation posts. Tel: 54.50.40.18.

LA CHAPELLE-D'ANGILLON: Cher.
The oldest château in the département, with monumental terrace overlooking an extensive man-made lake. Also houses museum dedicated to novelist Alain-Fournier. Closed Sunday morning. Tel: 48.73.41.10.

CHÂTEAUNEUF-SUR-CHER: Cher.
Dates back to the 11th century; has an exhibition of automata in settings from Perrault's fairy tales, also wildlife park. Open April to beginning November; Sunday afternoons only out of season. Tel: 48.60.64.21.

CHAUMONT-SUR-LOIRE: Loir-et-Cher.
Fine white stone edifice, with the appearance of a traditional medieval castle. Also park and stables. Tel: 54.20.98.03.

CHENONCEAU: Indre-et-Loire.
Spectacular castle built on six arches across a tributary of the Loire. Fine Renaissance decoration; also wax museum. Restaurant and child-minding available. Tel: 47.23.90.07.

CHEVERNY: Loir-et-Cher.
Still a private home, and also an important centre for hunting (see the trophy hall). Built by the team responsible for Blois and Chambord – the architect Boyer and painter de Mosnier. Also visit the orangery. Tel: 54.79.25.38.

CHINON: Indre-et-Loire.
Early château, much of which is now in ruins. However, good collections of tapestries, a waxworks museum and an audio-visual presentation of Joan of Arc's arrival at Chinon. Closed Wednesday December to January. Tel: 47.93.13.45.

CINQ-MARS: Indre-et-Loire.
Substantial remains of a 12th-century keep, birthplace of Cinq-Mars who conspired against Cardinal Richelieu. Cinq-Mars-la-Pile, 37130 Langeais. Closed Monday. Tel: 47.96.40.49.

DUNOIS: Loiret.
Fifteenth-century fortress built for the early Lords of Beaugency, houses Orléans regional folk museum. Closed Tuesday. Château Dunois, 45190 Beaugency. Tel: 38.44.55.23.

DURTAL: Maine-et-Cher.
Château (15th–16th century). Open July and August every day except Tuesday and Sunday morning, 10am–12 noon and 3–6pm. Entrance at top of the hill, at rear of château.

GIEN: Loiret.
Early Renaissance château with fine 15th-century timbered hall. Also international hunting museum. Closed Monday, except May to November. Tel: 38.67.69.69.

LE GRAND-PRESSIGNY: Indre-et-Loire.
Dates back to 12th century. Also prehistory museum. Closed Wednesday October to mid-March. Tel: 47.94.90.20.

LANGEAIS: Indre-et-Loire.
Royal castle where Charles VIII married Anne of Brittany, now immortalised in the waxworks museum. Fifteenth and 16th-century decor, faithfully refurbished at the turn of this century. Fine collection of Flemish and Aubusson tapestries. Tel: 47.96.72.60.

LOCHES: Indre-et-Loire.
Fifteenth-century royal residence where Charles VII kept his mistress, Agnès Sorel. She was poisoned and her tomb can be visited. Closed Wednesday October to mid-March. Tel: 47.59.01.32.

LE LUDE: Sarthe.
Moated fortress: built around a central courtyard in the 13th century, later embellished under the influence of the Italian Renaissance. Terrace overlooks the gardens which stretch for 600 ft (200 metres) along the Loire. Guided tours: April–September 3–6pm (30 minutes). Gardens: 10am–12 noon and 2–6 p.m; 10 FF. *Son et lumière* show: Friday and Saturday evenings (between 9.30pm and 10.30pm depending on month) from 2nd weekend in June to 1st weekend in September. Tel: 43.94.60.09.

MAUPAS: Cher.
Built in the 15th century for the governor of Berry. Privately owned, but many furnished rooms open to the public including a state bedroom, drawing rooms, games room and kitchen. Open daily July to mid-September, then afternoons and Sunday until mid-October and Easter to July. Château de Maupas, Morogues, Cher. Tel: 48.64.41.71.

MEUNG-SUR-LOIRE: Loiret.
Twelfth-century castle, much altered in the 17th century and greatly embellished internally during the 18th. Closed mid-November to March (except weekends). Tel: 38.44.36.47.

MONTGEOFFROY: Maine-et-Loire.
This château is unusual in that it has been occupied by the Contades family since it was built in 1722, and, even more remarkable, they have kept it exactly as it was then, internally and externally. Open April–November. Tel: 41.80.60.02.

MONTPOUPON: Indre-et-Loire.
Has a hunting theme, plus a restaurant. Open March to end-October, but weekends only until mid-June and during October. Château Montpoupon, Céré-la-Ronde, 337460 Montrésor. Tel: 47.94.23.62.

MONTRÉSOR: Indre-et-Loire.
Early (11th century) castle; exhibits include Italian Primitives. Open April to end-October. Tel: 47.92.60.04.

MONTREUIL-BELLAY: Maine-et-Loire.
An 11th-century fortress which later developed, like so many others, into a country retreat. Open 1 April to end-October. Closed Tuesday (except July and August). Tel: 41.52.33.06.

LE PLESSIS-BOURRÉ: Maine-et-Loire.
Inhabited château surrounded by a wide moat, and richly furnished. Guards room has unusual ceiling painted with humorous scenes and allegorical figures. Closed mornings, December to March, and Wednesday and Thursday mornings, except July and August. Tel: 41.32.06.01.

PLESSIS-LÈS-TOURS: Indre-et-Loire.
Louis XI's residence near Tours, showing his reconstructed bedchamber.

Closed Tuesday. Château de Plessis-lès-Tours, 37520 La Riche. Tel: 47.37.22.80.

SAUMUR: Maine-et-Loire.
Referred to as the "Castle of Love" by the poet-king René of Anjou, the château has indeed a very romantic situation overlooking the Loire. It houses three museums. Closed Tuesday, November to April. Tel: 41.51.30.46.

SULLY-SUR-LOIRE: Loiret.
Fine moated castle, noted for being the home of Henri IV's famous finance minister. The keep has a fine timbered roof. Tel: 38.36.25.60.

TALCY: Loir-et-Cher.
Sixteenth century château. Features an exhibition on the poet Ronsard. Closed Tuesday in winter. Tel: 54.81.03.01.

TOURS: Indre-et-Loire.
Royal château and museum which relates the history of the Touraine. Closed mornings November to mid-March. Quai d'Orléans. Tel: 47.61.02.95.

USSÉ: Indre-et-Loir.
Fairytale château in sumptuous Renaissance style, set against a backdrop of the Chinon forest, where, appropriately, waxwork scenes from Sleeping Beauty provide an added dimension. Also royal apartments. Open mid-March to mid-November. Château d'Ussé, Rigny-Ussé, 37420 Avoine. Tel: 47.95.54.05.

VALENÇAY: Indre.
Château, park, zoo and car museum. Open mid-March to mid-November (park open all year). Tel: 54.00.10.66.

LA VERRERIE: Cher.
Renaissance château with English connections as it was the home of the Duchess of Portsmouth, King Charles II's mistress, for over 60 years. Still inhabited, but many rooms on show. Open March to end-November. Situated on the D89 at Oizon. Tel: 48.58.21.25.

VILLANDRY: Indre-et-Loire.
The beautiful gardens are its most famous feature, but this, the last of the

great Renaissance châteaux, warrants a visit in itself. Gardens open all year. Château closed mid-November to mid-February. Tel: 47.50.02.09.

VILLESAVIN: Loir-et-Cher.
Sixteenth-century château and carriage museum. Open mid-March to end-September, then afternoons only to 20 December. Château Villesavin, Tour-en-Sologne, 41250 Bracieux. Tel: 54.46.42.88.

Notable Buildings

Angers: Maine-et-Loire.
Twelfth-century former hospital, L'hôpital St-Jean is now a museum housing Lurçat's tapestries of the Song of the World. The 13th-century Abbaye Toussaint has a glass roof, the better to show off the sculptures of David d'Angers. The St-Maurice Cathedral bears witness to the Plantagenet presence in the region. Tel: 41.87.41.06.

ARDILLIERS: Maine-et-Loire.
Hôpital de la Providence, caves near Saumur which were used as temporary refuges.

ASNIÈRES: Maine-et-Loire.
Abbey, damaged during the Revolution, but retains superb Gothic choir. Open July and August (not Tuesday).

BLOIS: Loir-et-Cher.
Apart from the château itself, Blois has some fine buildings, not least the 18th-century Bishop's Palace which is now the Town Hall. See also the Maison des Acrobates, Rue des 3 Clefs, the best medieval half-timbered house to have survived the wars; the 12th-century keep tower, Tour Beauvoir; and the Fontaine Louis XII, the Flamboyant Gothic fountain that supplied the town's water in the 15th century. The Jacobins Monastery, Rue Anne de Bretagne, now houses the museums of Natural History and Religious Art.

BOURGES: Loiret.
Palais Jacques Coeur, Rue Jacques Coeur, dates back to the 15th century. See too the cathedral.

BOURGEUIL: Indre-et-Loire.
Former Benedictine abbey. Open weekend afternoons April to October. Tel: 47.97.72.04.

CLÉRY-ST-ANDRÉ: Loiret.
Fifteenth-century *basilica* which houses Louis XI's tomb. Tel: 38.45.70.05.

CUNAULT: Maine-et-Loire.
Fine example of a Romanesque priory with a remarkable 223 carved capitals. Tel: 41.67.92.44.

FONTEVRAUD-L'ABBAYE: Maine-et-Loire.
Founded in 1101, Fontevraud was one of the most important monasteries in western Christendom and certainly the largest. Both nuns and monks were ruled by an abbess and the community comprised five priories. This former royal abbey is now a regional cultural centre. Tel: 41.51.71.41.

GERMINY-DES-PRÉS: Loiret.
Early 9th-century Carolingian oratory with superb mosaic of the same date depicting the Ark of the Covenant. Near Châteauneuf-sur-Loire. Tel: 38.58.27.97.

ST-BENOÎT-SUR-LOIRE: Loiret.
St Benedict's basilica was established by monks from Monte Cassino in the 7th century, but the present Romanesque buildings date from the 11th. It was the most important centre for monastic scholarship in France until the 12th century. Closed Sunday mornings. Tel: 38.35.72.43.

ST-COSME: Indre-et-Loire.
Priory, made famous for being the home of the 16th-century poet Ronsard, now equally popular for its beautiful gardens. St-Cosme Priory, 37520 La Riche. Closed Monday in winter. Tel: 47.37.32.70

ST-SATUR: Cher.
Remarkable viaduct and unfinished church.

SANCERRE: Cher.
The 12th-century Tour des Fiefs dominates this pretty town which also boasts a 15th-century belfry and many other buildings from that date.

SOLESMES: Sarthe.
Abbaye St-Pierre (only the 11th–15th century abbey church at the back of the courtyard is open to the public). 16th-century sculpture, Les Saints de Solesmes, in the transept. Services in Gregorian Chant open to the public: mass 9.45am; sext 1pm; vespers 5pm; compline 8.30pm. The church is open 9am–6pm and for the compline service.

TOURS: Indre-et-Loire.
St-Gatien Cathedral, Gothic and Renaissance architecture, fine stained-glass windows. Also worth a visit is the St-Martin Basilica, Rue Baleschoux whose crypt houses St Martin's tomb.

VENDÔME: Loir-et-Cher.
Former Abbaye de la Trinité dating back to the 11th century and its flamboyant Gothic church should not be missed.

Live Arts

A wealth of theatrical and musical events can be enjoyed in the region. Most of the main towns, e.g. Tours, Blois and Orléans, have their own centres for performances, while Angers is home not only to the Orchestre Philharmonique des Pays-de-la-Loire, but is also the national centre for both contemporary dance and dramatic art. The region is well known for its *son-et-lumière* presentations, which were first produced here – although purists may quibble at these being called "arts" events. They are very enjoyable, however, and most succeed in their aim of bringing history to life by their performances.

The first listing here gives details of places where arts events are staged. Apart from those shown below, many of the châteaux are used for performances on an intermittent basis. Details of all local arts events can be obtained from the nearest tourist office. The second is a diary of events (this is very wide ranging, and not all those listed are strictly cultural happenings). Finally, the major venues for *son-et-lumière* presentations are given.

Venues

ANGERS: Maine-et-Loire.
Théâtre Municipal. Enquire at tourist office for programme.

BLOIS: Loir-et-Cher.
A full programme of events, from rock concerts to light opera and Shakespeare, is presented at **La Halle Aux Grains**, Place de la République, 41000 Blois. Tel: 54.56.19.79; fax: 54.56.12.56.

FONTEVRAUD L'ABBAYE: Maine-et-Loire. Major cultural centre for western France, offering a year-round programme of events (mostly musical). **Centre Culturel de l'Ouest,** Abbaye Royale de Fontevraud, 49590 Fontevraud. Tel: 41.51.73.52; fax: 41.38.15.44.

MESLAY: Indre-et-Loire.
La Grange de Meslay – here an audiovisual display of the history of the Touraine, using *dioramas* and backprojected images, is shown on a giant screen. Performances: Saturday, Sunday and public holidays in the afternoons. Apart from that, the Grange is often used for concerts and other events, in particular the **Fêtes Musicales en Touraine** in June. Grange de Meslay, 37210 Parçay-Meslay. Tel: 47.29.19.29.

Diary of Events

JANUARY
ANGERS: Maine-et-Loire. Film festival.

FEBRUARY
ANGERS: Maine-et-Loire. Honey fair.
CHALONNES-SUR-LOIRE: Maine-et-Loire. Wine festival, last weekend.
SAUMUR: Maine-et-Loire. Wine festival, second weekend.

MARCH
ANGERS AND AVRILLE: Maine-et-Loire. Festival de Théatre Masqué.

APRIL
BOURGES: Cher. *Printemps de Bourges*, international song festival.

MAY
CHAMBORD: Loir-et-Cher. Festival de Chambord, regional festival of theatre, music and dance which continues throughout June.
ORLÉANS: Loiret. Fêtes de Jeanne d'Arc, historical pageant in full costume. (Sometimes in April.)
SAUMUR: Maine-et-Loire. International Horse Show, first weekend.

JUNE
BLOIS: Loir-et-Cher. Fêtes Louis XII, spectacle in period costume in the château, continues on certain days of the month to early September.
CHARTRES: Eure-et-Loire. Organ Festival held.
CHINON: Indre-et-Loire. Series of lectures by the brotherhood of "Entonneurs Rabelaisians" (Rabelaisian imbibers). Also in September and October.
SAUMUR: Maine-et-Loire. International Festival of Military Music (odd-numbered years) or Flower festival (even-numbered years). Last Sunday.
SULLY-SUR-LOIRE: Loiret. International Festival of Sully, Orléans and Loiret, continues throughout July.
TOURS: Indre-et-Loire (and other venues, including the Grange de Meslay). Fêtes Musicales de Touraine, concerts and other performances, continuing into July.

Also at Tours in June (sometimes in May), the Florilège Vocal de Tours is held – national and international competition for choral singers.

JULY
AMBOISE: Indre-et-Loire. Festival Estival, summer festival of music and drama which continues throughout August.
ANGERS: Maine-et-Loire (and other venues). Festival d'Anjou, theatre, music, etc. around the region.
BOURGES: Cher. Summer festival of music and theatre, continues into August.
CHAMPIGNE: Maine-et-Loire. Fête du Moyen Age, medieval festival.
DOUE-LA-FONTAINE: Maine-et-Loire. Rose festival, mid-July.
LOCHES: Indre-et-Loire. Festival de Théatre Musicale.
LE NOYER: Cher. Festival of religious and chamber music at Château de Boucard.
LE PUY-NOTRE-DAME: near Montreuil-Bellay, Maine-et-Loire. Festival of wine and mushrooms, first Saturday.
ST-CALAIS: Sarthe. Fête du Lac, mid-July.
ST-EPAIN: Indre-et-Loire. Music festival, end July, beginning of August.
TOURS: Indre-et-Loire. Garlic and basil fair.

AUGUST
BLANCAFORT: Cher. Music festival.
BREIL: Maine-et-Loire. Fête de la Chasse et de la Vénerie, hunting festival, last Sunday.
BUÉ-EN-SANCERRE: Cher. Foire aux Sorciers, folk festival.
CHINON: Indre-et-Loire. Two special markets, one in medieval style, one *fin-de-siècle.*
MONTAILLE: near St-Calais, Sarthe. Festival Retro, agricultural show, end of the month.
MONTOIRE-SUR-LOIRE: Loir-et-Cher. International folk festival, second week.
ROCHEFORT-SUR-LOIRE: Maine-et-Loire. Anjou folk festival, mid-August.
VOUVRAY AND MONTLOUIS: Wine fairs, 15 August.

SEPTEMBER
ANGERS: International folk festival.
CHÂTEAU-DU-LOIR: Sarthe. Comice Agricole, agricultural show.
Fontevraud-l'Abbaye and at Saumur, Maine-et-Loire. International festival "Art et Lumière", end of the month.
ST-CALAIS: Sarthe. Fête du Chausson aux Pommes, literally the apple-turnover festival, first three days of the month.

OCTOBER
ANGERS: Maine-et-Loire. Festival of 20th-century music.
AZAY-LE-RIDEAU: Indre-et-Loire. Apple fair.
BOURGEUIL: Indre-et-Loire. Chestnut fair.
MOULIHERNE: Maine-et-Loire. Apple fair.
PREUILLY: Indre-et-loire. Foire aux prunes, plum fair.

NOVEMBER
MONTLOUIS-SUR-LOIRE: Indre-et-Loire. Festival de Jazz Touraine.

Son-et-Lumiere

Several of the major châteaux along the river now offer *son-et-lumière* performances during the summer season. Generally, they show scenes of local or regional historical interest – some with very large casts of local amateurs. Tickets are from around FF35, and can be quite pricey – up to FF80 or FF100. There are usually reductions for children (although most performances do not start until around 10pm), and there may be an additional charge for firework displays.

Performances normally last at least an hour and are, of course, out of doors. The titles listed here were correct at the time of going to press, but may be changed from one year to the next. Further information can be obtained from the châteaux themselves or from the local tourist office. A few son-et-lumières are performed at venues other than châteaux, but this is made clear in the listing.

AMBOISE: Indre-et-Loire.
A la cour du Roy François, Renaissance piece, Wednesday and Saturday July to October, plus Sunday, mid-July to mid-August. Tel: 47.57.14.47 (tourist office).

AZAY-LE-RIDEAU: Indre-et-Loire.
Puisque de vous n'avons autre visage, period costume at this Renaissance château. Performances every evening, mid-May to end-November. Tel: 47.45.44.40. (tourist office).

BLOIS: Loir-et-Cher.
Ainsi Blois vous est conté at the château, with 24 participants; mid-May through to mid-November. Tel: 54.78.72.76.

CHAMBORD: Loir-et-Cher.
The first-ever son-et-lumière performances are said to have taken place here; now showing April to November. Further details: Château de Chambord, 41250 Bracieux. Tel: 54.20.31.32.

CHENONCEAU: Indre-et-Loire.
Au temps des dames de Chenonceau, mid-June to mid-September. Tel: 47.23.90.07.

CHEVERNY: Loir-et-Cher.
Rêves en Sologne in July and August. Tel: 54.74.06.49.

LE LUDE: Sarthe.
The people of Le Lude have been performing at the château for over 30 years now. The current spectacle is presented by 350 costumed local "actors". Performances: Friday and Saturday mid-June to 31 August, with fireworks at every performance. Tel: 43.94.60.09.

LE MEIGNANNE-ANGERS: Maine-et-Loire. A new spectacle at the Château de St-Venant, mid-June. Tel: 41.32.60.97.

MEUNG-SUR-LOIRE: Loiret.
Alice au Pays des Merveilles. Interpretation of Lewis Carroll's work at the château in July. Tel: 38.44.32.28.

SAUMUR: (St-Hilaire-St-Florent), Maine-et-Loire.
Les Féeries Florentaises, performed in July and August – not at the château itself, but just outside the town. Tel: 41.51.03.06.

Nightlife

For evening entertainment (particularly late at night), you need to be in the major towns of the region – Tours, Angers, Blois, etc. – where you will find plenty going on. Rural France, as in country areas anywhere, generally limits its entertainment to a local level – small bars, cafés and restaurants, village hops and other gatherings. Do not be put off, though, if staying in a gîte or other country accommodation; you are likely to be warmly encouraged to join in the festivities. Some of the châteaux around the region also offer cultural events – concerts, theatre and so forth (see Culture Plus).

Information about nightclubs, cinemas and other entertainment is available from the tourist offices in all big towns, or at your hotel. Tours in particular has a growing number of café-concert and café-theatre venues, offering a variety of events from rock music to new plays.

In Anjou, much of the evening entertainment, in summer at least, is organised by the Anjou Festival, with various events at venues throughout the county (see Diary of Events).

Shopping

Shopping Areas

Over the past couple of decades most major towns in the region have made the sensible decision to keep the town centre for small boutiques and individual shops. Many of these areas are pedestrianised and so rather attractive (although beware – some cars ignore the voie piétonnée signs). The large supermarkets, hypermarkets, furniture stores and do-it-yourself outlets are grouped on the outskirts of the town, usually designated as a Centre Commercial. This laudable intent is somewhat marred by the horrendous design of some of these centres – groups of garish functional buildings which make the town's outskirts very unattractive. This is the case at Tours, where the suburbs are an endless sprawl of great blocks of flats and vast shopping complexes.

These centres are fine for bulk shopping for self-catering or for finding a selection of wine to take home at reasonable prices, but otherwise the town centres are far more interesting. It is here that you will find the individual souvenirs that give a taste of the region, alongside the beautifully dressed windows of delicatessens and pâtisseries.

Food shops, especially bakers, tend to open early; boutiques and department stores open from 9am, but sometimes not until 10am In town centres, just about everything closes from 12 noon until 2pm or later, although out-of-town hypermarkets are often open all day. Most shops stay open until at least 6.30 or 7pm. Most are closed Monday mornings and large stores generally all day. If you want to buy a picnic lunch, remember to buy everything you need before midday. Good delicatessens (charcuterie) have a selection of delicious ready-prepared dishes, which make picnicking a delight.

Just about every town has a weekly market. Even if you do not wish to buy produce, they are irresistible. Most start early in the morning and may close at midday. In any case, the French usually visit early to get the best of the produce. Children are invariably fascinated by the sale of live animals – rabbits, poultry and so forth – only to be horrified to learn that, often as not, they are for the pot and not the back garden.

In a region that is famous for its flower production, the markets of the Loire are particularly colourful. Other local produce, such as wine and mushrooms, are also prominent. Your nearest tourist office will be able to tell you the market days of local towns, or ask your *gîte* owner or hotel receptionist.

Buying Direct

You may be tempted by all the signs you see along the road for *dégustations* – tastings. Many wine producers and farmers will invite you to try their wines and other produce with an eye to selling you a case, or, for instance, a few jars of pâté. This is a good way to try before you buy and can sometimes include a visit to a wine cellar. Farm produce is often more expensive to buy this way than from supermarkets – but do not forget that it is freshly produced, and not factory processed. This may not be true of wine and it can be more reliable, as well as cheaper to buy something you have already tried and know you like.

Clothing

Most shops will let you try on clothes (*essayer*) before buying. Children's sizes, in particular, tend to be small compared with UK and US age ranges. Hypermarkets have good-value children's clothes.

Export Procedures

On most purchases, the price includes TVA (VAT or Valued Added Tax). The base rate is currently l8.6 percent, but can

be as high as 33 percent on luxury items. Foreign visitors can claim back TVA; worth doing if you spend more than FF4,200 (FF2,000 for non-EU residents) in one place. Ask the store for a *bordereau* (export sales invoice). This must be completed to show (with the goods purchased) to customs officers on leaving the country (pack the items separately for ease of access). Then mail the form back to the retailer who will refund the TVA in a month or two. Certain items purchased (e.g. antiques) may need special customs clearance.

If you have a complaint about any purchase, return it in the first place to the shop as soon as possible. In the case of any serious dispute, contact the local Direction Départementale de la Concurrence et de la Consommation et de la Répression des Fraudes (see telephone directory for number).

Sports & Leisure

Participant Sports

Whatever sport you wish to pursue, you are likely to find opportunities to do so in the region. Most medium-sized towns have swimming-pools and even small villages often have a tennis court, but you may have to become a temporary member to use it – enquire at the local tourist office or *mairie* (town hall) which will also provide details of all other sporting activities in the locality. General information is given below.

Water Sports

Although land-locked, the region offers many opportunities for water sports, often based around man-made or natural lakes or sometimes on safe stretches of river, called a Base de Loisirs. These bases or leisure centres generally offer facilities for all kinds of sporting activities, not just those on the water itself. They usually also have a café, bar and/or restaurant as well

as a picnic area, so they make an ideal venue for families.

Many also offer tuition in the various sports available – canoeing, windsurfing etc; fees are usually charged at an hourly or 30-minute rate. Where boating and windsurfing is permitted, equipment is often available for hire; or you may also take your own equipment, usually without a supplementary charge.

Main bases in the region and facilities:

ANGERS: Maine-et-Loire.
Parc de Loisirs du Lac de Maine: Centre Nautique, Route de Pruniers. Bathing, boating, pedalo boats, golf, games, restaurant and picnic area. Also on the site, nature reserve and campsite. Open all year round. Tel: 41.22.32.10.

ARGENT-SUR-SAULDRE: Cher.
Etang du Puits: bathing, waterskiing, sailing, minigolf, children's games.

CHAUMONT-D'ANJOU: Maine-et-Loire.
Etang de Malagué: bathing, pedalos, punts, games, picnic area. Open all year round.

CHEFFES-SUR-SARTHE: Maine-et-Loire.
Aloa, Parc de Loisirs, La Grande Maison: supervised bathing, sailing, windsurfing, pedalos, motorboats, water toboggans, crazy golf, and more. Crêperie, bar, picnic area. Open Easter–October at weekends and daily in July and August.

CHEMILLE-SUR-INDROIS: Indre-et-Loire.
Man-made lake with beach, fishing, sailing, pedalos, punts, tennis, volley ball, children's games, picnic area and caravan hire. Open mid-June to 19 September.

CHOLET: Maine-et-Loire.
Parc de Ribou: sailing, windsurfing, canoes, pedalos, walks, ponies, climbing, archery, games, restaurant, bar, picnic area. Open Monday to friday all year round.

COUTURE-SUR-LOIR: Loir-et-Cher.
Etang de Ronsard: private lake and water-skiing school; children's amusements, bar and campsite.

LE FUILET: Maine-et-Loire.
Base de Loisirs du Village Potier: punts, games, restaurant, bar, picnic area. Open all year.

GESTE: Maine-et-Loire.
Base de Loisirs de la Thévinière: sailing, windsurfing, pedalos, canoes, walks, riding, games, bar, picnic area. Open mid-June to mid-September.

LUNAY: Loir-et-Cher.
Plan d'Eau de la Montellière: bathing, pedalos, children's games, tennis nearby, picnic area.

MANSIGNE: Sarthe.
Base de Plein Air et de Loisirs: sailing, windsurfing, bathing, tennis, fishing, minigolf. Open April–September.

MARCE: Maine-et-Loire.
Parc de Détente, Les Tilleuls, Route de Beauvau: supervised bathing, games, ponies, bar, crêperie. Open Sunday, April to mid-September; daily July and August. Tel: 41.95.43.43.

MARCON: Sarthe.
Lac des Varennes, and some activities also on the Loir river: sailing, windsurfing, canoes, bathing, pedalos, fishing, tennis. Also a campsite. Open March–November.

NOYANT-LA-GRAVOYÈRE: Maine-et-Loire.
Parc de Loisirs St-Blaise: bathing, tennis, riding, footpaths, canoes, pedalos, games, restaurant. Open April to 31 August (closed Wednesday, Saturday and Sunday afternoon except July and August).

LE PLESSIS-DORIN: Loir-et-Cher.
Ferme de Beaulieu: bathing, windsurfing, pedalos, canoes, tennis, table tennis, bicycle hire.
Tel: 54.80.85.35.

LA POISSONNIÈRE: Maine-et-Loire.
L'Arche leisure park: pedalos, minigolf, ponies, games, narrow-gauge railway, restaurant, bar, picnic area. Open Sunday April–September and daily June to August. Tel: 41.72. 21.09.

RILLE: Indre-et-Loire.
Base de Loisirs de Pincemaille: 37340 Savigné-sur-Lathan. Popular not only for sporting facilities, but also for nature observation and bird watching.

LA TESSOUALLE: Maine-et-Loire.
Base de Loisirs du Verdon: windsurfing, volleyball, minigolf, restaurant.

VINEUIL: Loir-et-Cher.
Lac de Loire: (on left bank, on D951 from Blois to Orléans). Sailing, motor boats, water skiing, canoes, pedalos. Tel: 54.78.82.05.

Water sports holidays: (particularly canoeing) can be arranged through the départemental Loisirs Accueil services (see Useful Addresses). Stretches of the region's rivers are suitable for canoeing or motorboats. Details from local tourist offices and from the following national organisations: Canoë-Kayak Club de France, 47 Quai Ferber, 94360 Bry-sur-Marne. Tel: 48.81. 54.26; Fédération Française de Canoë-Kayak, 17 Quai de la Marne, BP 58, 94390 Joinville-le-Pont. Tel: 45.11.08.50. A booklet, *Randonnés en Canoë-Kayak* is available from the regional tourist office (see Useful Addresses), giving details of trips organised by local clubs.

The Loire Valley is the ideal region for a cycling holiday. With so many of the châteaux just a few kilometres apart, it does not have to be at all strenuous. To take your own *vélo* is easy since cycles are carried free on most ferries and trains – or you can rent cycles for a reasonable cost; main railway stations usually have them for hire and you can often arrange to pick up a bike at one station and leave it at another one. Alternatively, try bicycle retailers/repairers or ask at the local tourist office.

Some youth hostels rent cycles and also arrange tours with accommodation in hostels or under canvas. Cycling holidays are arranged by the Loisirs Accueil services in the individual départements (*see Useful Addresses*).

Holidays called Vélo Bleu Vélo Vert are offered in the west of the region by the Comité Régional de Tourisme, 2 Rue de la Loire, 44200 Nantes. Tel: 40.48.24.20; fax: 40.08.07.10. While many people view cycling holidays as perhaps rather spartan, Susi Madron's Cycling for Softies offers a more luxurious option, following easy routes and staying at very comfortable hotels along the way. For details of these all-in tours, contact the company at 2–4 Birch Polygon, Rusholme, Manchester M14 5HX. Tel: (0161) 248 8282.

French Routes, 1 Mill Green Cottages, Newbridge, Yarmouth, Isle of Wight. Tel: (01983) 78392, offers a route planning service for individual tourists and will also arrange bicycle hire and accommodation.

It is advisable to take out insurance before you go. Obviously the normal rules of the road apply to cyclists (see Getting Around). Advice and information can be obtained from The Touring Department, Cyclists Touring Club, Cotterell House, 68 Meadrow, Godalming, Surrey GU7 3HS. Tel: (01483) 417217. Their service to members includes competitive insurance, free detailed touring itineraries and general information sheets about France whilst their tours brochure often lists trips to the Loire Valley, organised by members. The club's French counterpart, Fédération Française de Cyclotourisme offers a similar service, including holidays. Contact them at 8 Rue Jean-Marie-Jego, 75013 Paris. Tel: (1) 44.16.88.88; fax: (1) 44.16.88.99. Rob Hunter's book *Cycle Touring in France* is also useful as a handbook. Also the IGN Cyclist's Map, No. 906, *France Vélo* carries much essential information.

Such is the French passion for cycling that local clubs organise many trips lasting a day or more and visitors are often more than welcome to join in. In the Touraine, for example, a network of almost 70 routes has been devised. Weekend, or longer tours, starting from St-Patrice, near Langeais, are organised by the national Bicyclub, 8 Place Porte de Champerret, 75017 Paris. Tel: (1) 42.27.28.82.

Details of cycle tours organised in Sarthe can be obtained from M. Alex Poyer, Comité Départemental du Cyclotourisme, 15 Rue Alfred de Vigny, 72000 Le Mans. Tel: 47.66.55.92.

Horse Riding

Saumur, home of the national riding school, is considered the capital of the horse in France, and so it is hardly surprising that the region has good facilities for all equine sports, for both participants and spectators (see Spectator Sports section). Some 220 centres across France offer riding holidays, under a charter guaranteeing quality set up by the Syndicat National du Tourisme Equestre. Contact: A.P.T.E. France, 60 Grande Rue, 60510 La Neuville-en-Hez, tel: 44.78.01.50; fax: 44.78.00.86. This organisation can also provide information about marked bridleways, riding centres and insurance.

Holidays on horseback or with a horse-drawn caravan can be booked through the Loisirs Accueil services in Cher and Loir-et-Cher (see Useful Addresses), who also organise treks for a single day's outing. The local tourist office will provide details of stables (of which there are plenty in the region) if you simply wish to hire a horse by the hour or day.

Golf

In recent years, golf has caught on in a big way in France and the Regional Tourist Boards have joined forces with the French Golf Federation in an effort to promote it better and set standards. General information can be obtained from the Comité Régional au Tourisme (*see Useful Addresses*). For the serious golfer, who can expect to pay around FF180 for green fees (this is for the whole day), the following courses, mostly 18-hole, all offer good facilities (those marked * are members of the Golf Federation):

AMBOISE: Indre-et-Loire.
Swin-Golf: L'Arbrelle, Route des Ormeaux. (10 holes).

ANGERS: Maine-et-Loire.
Moulin Pistrait: 49320 St-Jean-des-Mauvrets. (18 holes).

ARDON: Loiret.
Golf Club de Sologne: 45240 La Ferté-St-Aubin.

AVRILLE: Maine-et-Loire.
Golf de la Perrière: St-Jean des Mauvrets, 49240 Avrillé. (18 holes, plus 9). *

BALLAN-MIRÉ: Indre-et-Loire.
Château de la Touche: Ballan-Miré,

37510 Joué-lès-Tours. (18 holes). The Loisirs Accueil Service of Indre-et-Loire (see Useful Addresses) can arrange golfing holidays with accommodation nearby.

CHEVERNY: Loir-et-Cher.
Golf du Château Cheverney, 41700 Contres.

CHOLET: Maine-et-Loire.
11 Allée Chêne Landry, 49300 Cholet. (18 holes, plus 3).

MARCILLY: Loiret.
Golf de Marcilly: Domaine de la Plaine, 45240 Marcilly. * The Loiret Loisirs Accueil service offers golfing holidays here with accommodation nearby. (See Useful Addresses).

OUCQUES: Loir-et-Cher.
Golf de la Bosse: La Guignardière, 41290 Oucques.

ST-LAURENT-NOUAN: Loir-et-Cher.
Golf Les Bords: 41220 St-Laurent-Nouan.*

ST-SATUR: Cher.
Golf Club du Sancerrois: St-Satur, 18300 Sancerre.

TOURS: Indre-et-Loire.
Golf d'Ardrée: BP No. 1, St-Antoine-du-Rocher, 37360 Tours. (18 holes). *

VIGLAIN: Loiret.
Golf Club de Sully-sur-Loire: 45600 Sully-sur-Loire. The Loisirs Accueil service in Loiret (see Useful Addresses) can book holidays with accommodation at this course.

Apart from the holidays shown here, Loiret Loisirs Accueil offers a three-day golf pass; three days' reserved games, plus accommodation.

Other companies offering golfing holidays in the area are as follows:
French Expressions, 4 Belsize Court, London NW3 5QU. Tel: (0171) 794 1480.
Golf en France, Model Farm, Rattlesden, Bury St. edmunds, IP30 OSY. Tel: (01449) 737678.
French Life Holidays, 26 Church Road, Horsforth, Leeds LS18 5LG. Tel: (0113) 2390077.

Apart from the famous 24 *Heures du Mans* motor race, which falls just outside our region, the Loire, with its horsey connections, is perhaps most notable for its equestrian events. They may not be as prestigious internationally as, say, Longchamp, but the courses at Saumur, Le Lion d'Angers, Angers itself and Cholet offer between them a variety of events throughout the year. Information: tourist office in Angers or the Fédération Régionale des Sociétés de Courses Anjou-Maine-Centre-Ouest, 25 Rue des Arènes, 49021 Angers. Tel: 41.88.07.80.

A sort of vintage version of the 24-hour race is held in Blois towards the end of June – the 4 Heures de Blois – also known as the Grand Prix des Grands-Mères Automobiles.

Details of other local sporting events can be obtained from the nearest tourist office.

Language

Getting By

It is said that you will hear the purest spoken French in Anjou, so this is the place to go if you wish to perfect your knowledge of the language. Certainly, visitors who are less than happy with their fluency will at least not have to battle with impenetrable accents and dialects that can be encountered in other areas of the country. Even visitors with a good knowledge of the language, however, would probably benefit from touring the châteaux and other grand buildings with some kind of glossary of architectural terms to hand.

Words & Phrases
GENERAL

hello, *bonjour/bonsoir*
thank you, *merci*
you're welcome, *de rien*

please, *s'il vous plaît*
good-bye, *au revoir*

the airport, *l'aéroport*
the bank, *la banque*
customs, la douane
the police station, *la gendarmerie*
the bathroom, *la salle de bains/les toilettes*
the train station, *la gare*
the metro stop, *la station de métro*
the post office, *le bureau de poste*
the embassy, *l' ambassade*

Help!, *Au secours!*
Where is, are...?, *Où est, sont...?*
What is it?, *Qu'est-ce que c'est?*
When?, *Quand?*
How much is it?, *C'est combien?*
Do you have?, *Avez-vous..?*
What time is it?, *Quelle heure est-il?*

the hospital, *l'hôpital*
the doctor, *le médecin*
the nurse, *l'infirmière*
I am sick, *Je suis malade*
medicine, *les médicaments*

to dial a number, *composer un numéro*
to call collect, *téléphoner en P.C.V.*
to make a person-to-person call, *téléphoner avec préavis*

Eating Out

breakfast, *le petit déjeuner*
lunch, *le déjeuner*
dinner, *le dîner*
a cup, *une tasse*
a glass, *un verre*
a plate, *une assiette*
a napkin, *une serviette*
a fork, *une fourchette*
a knife, *un couteau*
a spoon, *une cuillère*
the bill, *l'addition*
the waiter, *Monsieur* (never *garçon*)
the waitress, *Mademoiselle* or *Madame* according to age

DRINKS

drinks, *les boissons*
coffee, *du café*
coffee with milk, *du café au lait*
tea, *du thé*
beer, *une bière*
wine, *du vin*
mineral water, *de l'eau minérale*
juice, *du jus*

FRUIT & NUTS

fruit and nuts, *les fruits et les noix*
pineapple, *ananas*
cherries, *cerises*
strawberries, *fraises*
raspberries, *framboises*
chestnuts, *marrons*
hazel nuts, *noisettes*
grapefruit, *pamplemousse*
grapes, *raisins*

MEAT

meat, *viande*
beef, *boeuf*
lamb, *agneau*
mutton, *mouton*
pork, *porc*
ham, *jambon*
bacon, *lard*
veal, *veau*

steak, *bifteck*
rump steak, *châteaubriand*
chop, *côte*
rib steak, *entrecôte*
roast beef, *rosbif*
leg of lamb, *gigot d'agneau*
pork cold cuts, *charcuterie*
sausages, *saucisse*

chicken, *coq*
young cock, *poulet*
goose, *oie*
duck, *canard*
duckling, *caneton*

brains, *cervelles*
liver, *foie*
tongue, *langue*
kidney, *rognon*

wild game, *gibier*
rabbit, *lapin*
guinea hen, *pintade*
pheasant, *faisan*

snails, *escargots*
frogs' legs, *grenouilles*

SEAFOOD

eel, *anguille*
mackerel, *maquereau*
cod, *morue*
bass, *perche*
salmon, *saumon*
trout, *truite*

shrimp, *crevettes*
crawfish, *écrevisses*
mixed shellfish, *fruits de mer*
lobster, *homard*

oysters, *huîtres*
spiny rock lobster, *langouste*
mussels, *moules*
clams, *palourdes*

VEGETABLES

vegetables, *légumes*
mushrooms, *champignons*
cabbage, *chou*
cauliflower, *chou-fleur*
green beans, *haricots verts*
turnip, *navet*
potato, *pomme de terre*

DAIRY PRODUCTS & DESSERTS

dairy products, *produits laitiers*
butter, *beurre*
cheese, *fromage*
egg, *oeuf*
fritters, *beignets*
cake, *gâteau*
ice cream, *glace*
pie, *tarte*

Glossary of Architectural Terms

chancel – altar, sanctuary and choir
narthex – porch
nave – central space of church, often flanked by aisles
transept – wings of the cruciform at right-angles to the nave
apse – half-domed or vaulted semi-circular recess at east end
apsidal chapels – chapels radiating from the apse
chevet – semi-circular east end often with attached apses
ambulatory – aisle running round east end behind the sanctuary
tympanum – recessed space above a doorway, triangular or semi-circular and ornamented
lintel – horizontal beam over door or window
pilaster – rectangular column attached to the face of a wall
capitals – top of a column, often elaborately carved
clerestory – row of windows above the aisle roof lighting the nave
triforium – arcade of windows above the arches of the nave
retable – ornamental screen behind the altar
corbel – supporting bracket

Further Reading

Other Insight Guides

The 190-title *Insight Guides* series includes more than 20 books on France, including *Insight Guides*: France, Normandy, Brittany, Burgundy, Paris and Provence.

Insight Pocket Guides

Insight Pocket Guides are specifically written for the short-stay visitor, providing a series of carefully timed itineraries designed to help you get the most out of a short trip. Titles in this series include: Paris, Brittany, Alsace, Provence, Corsica and Côte d'Azur.

Insight Compact Guides

Apa Publications' third series is *Insight Compact Guides*. Titles include Provence, Burgundy, Paris and Normandy. The books are portable, handy mini-encyclopedias packed full of facts and photographs.

Index

A
B
C
D
E
F
H
I
J
a
b
c
d
e
f
h
i
j
k
l